# A Widening Sphere

## CHANGING ROLES OF VICTORIAN WOMEN

# A Widening Sphere

CHANGING ROLES OF VICTORIAN WOMEN

## Edited by Martha Vicinus

INDIANA UNIVERSITY PRESS
Bloomington & London

First Midland Book Edition 1980

Copyright © 1977 by Indiana University Press

Manufactured in the United States of America

**Library of Congress Cataloging in Publication Data**
Main entry under title:
A Widening sphere.

    Includes index.
    1. Women—Great Britain—History—Addresses, essays, lectures.   2. Women—Great Britain—Social conditions—Addresses, essays, lectures.   3. Feminism—Great Britain—Addresses, essays, lectures.
4. Great Britain—Social conditions—19th century—Addresses, essays, lectures.   I. Vicinus, Martha, 1939-
HQ1596.W44   301.41'2'0941   76-26433
ISBN 0-253-36540-6   2 3 4 5 81 80
ISBN 0-253-20245-0 pbk.

# Contents

# Acknowledgments

The editor would like to thank MaryJo Wagner, Editorial Assistant of *Victorian Studies* (1974–75), who assisted in the early stages of preparing the anthology, and Gail Malmgreen, who read through the introduction with a scrupulous eye for unexamined assumptions and awkward phrasing. Our discussions of the nineteenth century over many years has been a major influence on my understanding of Victorian women.

"Sexuality in Britain, 1800–1900: Some Suggested Revisions," by F. Barry Smith, is a revised version of a paper first published in *The University of Newcastle Historical Journal,* II (1974), 19–31.

Judith Walkowitz is grateful to the Rutgers Research Council for grants which facilitated research for this essay. In particular she would like to thank Daniel J. Walkowitz for much of the material on Southampton women and Portsea Hospital, and Susan Tracy, who helped to compile statistical data from the manuscript census. Thanks also to Mary Hartman and Rudolph Bell for their critical comments on the essay.

Rita McWilliams-Tullberg would like to thank the authorities of Girton and Newnham Colleges, Cambridge, for permission to use their archives and Trinity College, Cambridge, for permission to examine material in the Wren Library. Research for this article was financed by the British Academy Thank-Offering to Britain Fund Fellowship. This chapter is based in part on material gathered for a history of women at Cambridge University. The full story can be found in Rita McWilliams-Tullberg, *Women at Cambridge—A Men's University, though of a Mixed Type* (London: Victor Gollancz, 1975).

Barbara Kanner expresses her appreciation to the interlibrary loan staff of the UCLA Research Library, especially to Edith Fuller. Thanks are due also to Kanner's library assistant, Steven Halasey.

# Introduction

## New Trends in the Study of the Victorian Woman

IN 1869 JOHN STUART MILL DESCRIBED IN *The Subjection of Women* THE rigid slavelike stereotype of the nineteenth-century wife and mother. But he also spoke of the enormous potential of women, which he saw being realized in the period when he wrote. His sense of their widening sphere of moral and social activities was not wholly a product of his own idealism. By the 1860's the woman question had become one of the most important topics of the day. Job opportunities, marriage laws, female emigration, and education were only some of the issues debated at the time. Women themselves—and particularly middle-class women—were increasingly concerned with what their roles were, and what they should be. Spokeswomen of every political persuasion felt called upon to write about the woman question. The stereotypes we formerly thought characterized the "typical" Victorian woman upon closer examination prove to be less rigid—though no less pervasive. The constant debate in support of or attacking these stereotypes, thoroughly documented by Barbara Kanner's two bibliographies,* is some indication of the Victorians' concern with the imperfect enforcement of social values and ideals in a rapidly changing world.

It is difficult now to evaluate how satisfied Victorian women were with their lot. A woman who was discontented would most likely seek an individual rather than a group solution to her predicament. Clearly the limited choice of employment and low pay for all classes of women meant that marriage was the most attractive option. But the

* The first bibliography appeared in *Suffer and Be Still* (Bloomington: Indiana University Press, 1972).

very fluidity of the larger world of Victorian England, with the constant challenges of industrialization and urbanization, meant that women could not remain within a static role of domesticity.[1] Even the most contented could not help but be affected by the intense debate on the position of women that swirled around them. By the 1860's middle-class women in particular were taking on an increasingly large number of tasks that might require public agitation. A small band of activists hoped to widen the definition of women's "proper sphere." They argued that just as women had an obligation to educate their children in morality, so too did they have the wider responsibility to educate society on moral issues. As far back as 1845 the conservative author of widely sold books on female deportment, Sarah Stickney Ellis, urged young women to form some opinion on the evil of slavery. Pioneers of the women's movement did not argue so much for the similarity of women to men as for the existence of women's special skills in regard to children, health care, education, and domestic morality. Such talents, when appropriately applied, not only would give the family a happier and better life, but also would help to eliminate the most grievous wrongs of society. Philanthropy had traditionally been women's particular concern, and its definition during the nineteenth century was broadened to include virtually every major social problem. It is from the narrow base of woman's special duties and obligations that women in the nineteenth century came to expand their fields of action and their personal horizons.

This expansion proceeded unevenly and was based on assumptions that could not always be reconciled. Respectability, that watchword of the Victorians, was the goal of outsiders, from actresses to shopkeepers, and its possession the prized attribute of even the most militant. Demands for increased economic opportunities and freedom of action were subordinated to family responsibilities and personal respectability. Many single women who had been active in various women's organizations dropped out after marriage until their children were grown. Despite the admiration they might have felt for her in private, few women cared to emulate George Sand and risk public condemnation alone. Whatever the discrepancies between the ideal of the perfect lady and the humdrum reality of daily life, large numbers of middle-class women felt the pressures of this narrowly defined ideal. The judgment of society on the private and public behavior of women was often severe for unconventional fictional characters, from Maggie Tulliver in *The Mill on the Floss* (1860) to Sue Bridehead in

*Jude the Obscure* (1896). Yet even within the confines of Victorian life, all classes of women were being changed and were changing society.

All of the essays published in this anthology discuss women's widening sphere, though sometimes they describe the narrow limits of this struggle, or the enormous length of time it took to achieve even the most minimal gains. The essays are, in some measure, a development from the earlier volume, *Suffer and Be Still*. They are also a reconsideration of certain generalizations made then, when serious study of the Victorian woman was just beginning anew. It is now possible to write about areas previously unexplored. Scholars of the Victorian period are expressing considerable discomfort with the old clichés about women. Earlier notions about female sexuality and prostitution have been substantially altered with increasing research and debate. The passivity, frigidity, and uselessness of the female model idealized during the Victorian era in etiquette books and some fiction has come under attack for its extreme simplicity. Indeed, research is now frequently concerned with the relationship, whether close, distant, or confused, between the prescribed ideal of womanhood and the actual reality. We no longer generalize so readily about the Victorian woman.

This increase in academic caution, however, has fortunately not prevented an increase in the variety and methods of studying the Victorian woman. Although much time has been spent examining the lives of the eminent or rehearsing once again the more colorful aspects of the militant suffrage movement during the Edwardian period, women's studies has benefited enormously from the growing mass of published material and the debates and discussions of less familiar issues. Family history, folklore, anthropology, structuralist criticism, the sociology of literature, demography, and psychoanalysis have been brought to bear upon the study of women. While some studies seem to have been written solely to capitalize on the growing book market, and other efforts have often been rather tentative and inconclusive, most of the debates themselves have been provocative. Those who predicted that women's studies was a passing fad have been faced with an increasingly rich and sophisticated body of scholarship demonstrating the importance of women's studies in altering an imbalance in the study of the past and changing present.

The analysis of women in Victorian literature has just begun to move away from close image and character studies or the examination of a single female writer. The relationship of women writers to each other, to their audiences, and to the publishing trade is currently under scrutiny. The particular forms used by women writers, such as gothic, domestic realism, and children's tales, are also being analyzed. It is difficult, nevertheless, to know how best to approach the study of women in literature. Most of the specific issues that were hotly debated in the public affairs sections of Victorian periodicals made virtually no impact upon their fiction and poetry columns. Although much poetry—particularly that of Tennyson—was concerned with public issues, only the most conservative domestic verse was well received by readers and critics. So often concerned with love, courtship, and marriage, fiction rarely dealt directly with the growing complexity of women's sphere. Despite these seeming limitations, Victorian literature functioned as both an expression of and a shaper of the culture and its conflicts. For many men and women, reading the works of the best known and loved writers was a means of managing the emotional ambivalences they felt in regard to their changing roles. Art gave order to and understanding of the conflicting demands placed upon individuals by personal needs, families, and society. Its interpretation of events, feelings, and beliefs was the more penetrating because it was oblique. Although Anthony Trollope's heroines seldom if ever contemplate a career, they must frequently face a conflict between their personal desires and public propriety. Alice Vavasor loves and is sexually attracted to John Grey in *Can You Forgive Her?* (1864–65), but her ambition to influence political events—to have power indirectly—leads her to break off the engagement. The desire for a life of one's own, even within one's own home, has seldom been better delineated. The classic works of Victorian literature cannot tell us much specifically about female suffrage, the rising number of single women, or job opportunities, but they can illuminate the emotional conflicts and resolutions of men and women concerned with woman's proper place. Fortunately the interdisciplinary nature of women's studies encourages us to place literature in a broader context; the next decade should see the expansion of the study of cultural and social forces that brought women writers and a female literary sensibility to the fore during the Victorian period.

A great deal more work has been done in the social history of women than in literature, but a number of areas are still relatively unknown. Many women were active leaders in their churches, and some founded minor sects.[2] The educational opportunities for the average girl and the priorities of such education should be considered more thoroughly. The biases of the developing social sciences have only been touched on since Jill Conway's article appeared in *Victorian Studies* in 1970.[3] Although women and medicine has received much attention, women and science has led to little more than biographical studies of Mary Somerville and a few other women. The activities of various working-class political movements, as well as the development of women's trade unions, should not be underestimated. Fortunately the differences between single and married women in relation to their families, economic position, and social status are being systematically explored by family historians. But much work still needs to be done, and sources are often scarce, fragmentary, or simply unavailable. This lack of evidence, however, has fostered a closer look at conventional sources and a seeking out of the previously unconsidered or suspect.

When *Suffer and Be Still* was published women's studies was just beginning to establish its own respectability in academia. At that time Barbara Kanner pointed out the paucity of scholarly studies relating the Victorian woman's status and role to the larger socioeconomic changes of the time. For the most part her comment still holds true, but we now have an increasing number of shorter studies that have furthered our understanding of sex as a variable in the study of art, literature, and history. The essays that follow contribute both to our understanding of the position of women in Victorian society and to an analysis of how and why the female population was affected by larger trends in that society. Part two of Kanner's annotated bibliography provides documentation of other areas of importance. The very wealth of subject matter, and its potential for further exploration, is evidence of the importance of reconsidering our traditional ways of studying women. How women effected change from within male-proscribed roles, how they redefined their status in some areas (such as education), and lost it in others (such as social production), are all important aspects of how we should place the Victorian woman in her proper—but changing—sphere.

The area which has most fascinated our generation looking back at the Victorians is sexuality. This interest probably tells us more about ourselves than about our forebears, but despite the large number of popular books many questions remain unanswered. Our conventional notions of Victorian sexual mores have been altered by recent investigations of the birth control movement, female sexuality, and demographic patterns. F. Barry Smith cogently argues for a reassessment of

Victorian prudery, as embodied in the works of Dr. William Acton and "Walter's" *My Secret Life*. He briefly outlines the connection between repression and late Victorian attitudes toward children and sexuality, and also indicates how severe and capricious enforcement of the laws against male homosexuality contributed to the repressive atmosphere of the time. He suggests a variety of sources that should be reexamined and points the direction in which future studies might proceed. Both he and Judith Walkowitz discuss the intricate and shifting relationship between sexual mores and social pressures. The Contagious Diseases Acts and the agitation against them forced a division between the working-class prostitute and her community. Both compulsory registration under the Acts and middle-class reformers' attempts to publicize their plight set these women apart from others and made it more difficult for them to find either employment or simple anonymity. Private and public behavior—and beliefs—were never static, and our understanding of them for different classes and periods is still fragmentary.

A great deal has been published about Victorian sexuality, but much of it is of dubious value. In contrast, the legal position of women has been rarely studied, although most scholars have recognized the importance of the legal disabilities under which Victorian women lived. At the beginning of the Victorian period, according to common law, a married woman had no separate identity from her husband. Many women felt keenly the discrepancy between their legal position and their actual earning power. By law whatever a wife earned belonged to her husband, no matter how he treated her or what he earned himself. Lee Holcombe documents one of the few examples of a woman's pressure group operating as part of a larger successful reform movement. Reform of the married women's property laws was an uphill battle, but it was in tune with the century's slow yet nearly complete overhaul of the British legal system. While the legal impact of redefining a married woman's relationship with her husband was diffused over many years, the various reforms ultimately gave wives a separate legal identity and enabled them to retain their own earnings. The long-term results of these changes were enormous. Not least of them was the close link between the leadership agitating for property reforms and those seeking female suffrage. The experience gained in fighting for more equitable laws for women in regard to divorce and personal property led naturally to the fight for suffrage.

If at times the battles fought by Lady Caroline Norton and the Married Women's Property Committee seem remote from the concerns of the average Victorian, problems of employment were not. While suffrage remained the most important symbolic and political issue of the nineteenth-century women's movement, the most crucial economic demand was wider employment opportunities. Large numbers of women from every class could not afford to stay at home, tending their own children or those of their brothers and sisters. Work of some sort was a necessity. For the working class there was domestic service, the single largest form of employment and one that was growing rapidly throughout the Victorian period.[4] Alternatively there were agricultural labor and a variety of jobs related to sewing and cleaning, such as laundry work, charring, seamstressing, tailoring, glovemaking and lacemaking. Virtually all of these jobs were pitifully paid piecework. Perhaps even more serious than the very low wages most women received was the seasonal nature of their employment. In a family economy, periods of hard times could sometimes be tided over, but as increasing numbers of young people moved into the cities they were without ready recourse to family support. Judith Walkowitz discusses the difficulties of the very poor in the seaport towns of Plymouth and Southampton. For the young farm women who came to these towns their isolation, low pay, and vulnerability to unemployment easily led to prostitution. It was a strategy for survival until other work could be found or specific financial difficulties overcome.

Poor housing and sanitation in the new towns affected both men and women. Women were especially subject to tuberculosis. Contrary to common assumptions during the nineteenth century and the twentieth, TB, rather than occupational diseases or childbearing, was the primary killer of women. Indeed, women showed a comparative increase in life expectancy during their childbearing years in contrast with men during the nineteenth century, according to Sheila Johansson. As she documents, women in general more than men benefited from the long-term changes brought about by industrialization and urbanization. Until more detailed studies are done of specific counties and towns, however, it is difficult to account for occasional discrepancies in this trend. For the present her demographic study demonstrates not only the long-term rise in life expectancy for women, but also the short-term liabilities. The enormously high death rate from tuberculosis and other malnutrition- and sanitation-related diseases before the age of menarche provides a grim reminder of the double standard in feeding and clothing young girls.

Turning to the middle class, we find even fewer job opportunities than for working-class women. Life expectancy at this social level, of course, was generally higher; indeed, it was among the middle class that the concern for "redundant women" expressed itself so frequently and poignantly. The number of single women between the ages of fifteen and forty-five rose from 2,765,000 in 1851 to 3,228,700 in 1871, with a rise in the surplus of single women to single men of 72,500 to 125,200 (a 72.7 percent rise in twenty years).[5] Male emigration and women's improved demographic position were the most obvious causes for this shift. Rather like the downtrodden governess and the starving seamstress, the "redundant" middle-class woman caught the attention of journalists, who often ignored more pressing problems facing women as a whole. Yet the concern with unmarried women who statistically could never find a mate had an important effect: the limited employment available for respectable women and the necessity of expanding opportunities became matters of public debate. Middle-class commentators were faced with the dilemma of recognizing the need for a greater variety of socially acceptable jobs, or of advocating in the face of irrefutable statistics the supremacy of a domestic life.

As a partial answer to this dilemma early feminists, such as Maria Rye and Emily Faithfull, made it their life's work to improve job opportunities and pay for middle-class women. Their organizations are better documented than those of working-class women, so we are better able to measure the degree of progress they made. It is within the context of middle-class feminism that we can best understand the limitations a class-ordered society imposed upon women. Respectability demanded a certain level of outward and inward gentility, and it defined certain jobs as demeaning. A. James Hammerton shows how a feminist emigration society was caught between irreconcilable definitions of its proper task. Since antifeminists advocated wholesale emigration for single women, feminists were reluctant to embark upon sending unqualified but marriageable women to the colonies. They came to find themselves in the predicament of sending highly trained —and genteel—women who probably could have found equally satisfactory employment in England.

The paradox faced by the Female Middle Class Emigration Society can also be found in middle-class efforts to improve female education. Many single women who desperately needed work could not find it because of their limited training. Next to legal reforms, educational reforms during the second half of the nineteenth century were probably the most effective sphere of agitation by middle-class women.

Educational standards for training teachers, male and female, were rising, and as more emphasis was placed on the necessity of education, both sexes benefited. The results for women, however, were somewhat mixed. Improved educational standards, combined with new opportunities made possible by the telephone, telegraph, and typewriter, meant that the more venturesome members of the middle class could find jobs that were both respectable and clean. But for the tiny elite who sought, and gained, higher education the results were less clear. As McWilliams-Tullberg points out, degree-less Cambridge women could have the personal satisfaction of knowing that they had completed one of the most demanding curricula in the country, but their knowledge did not open new doors in science, law, or other traditional male fields. While Vivie Warren is last seen in *Mrs. Warren's Profession* as a partner in a thriving female law firm, in actuality neither she nor her friend Honoria Fraser could do conveyancing or other work that required a law degree. For most Cambridge women teaching was the only career available—in positions of more prestige and remuneration, but otherwise little different from those of their less-privileged sisters, who for years had crowded into the only respectable profession for middle-class women.

Better education meant, in theory, financial independence and wider career choice, but as with similar legal reforms, women found that the end results of their agitation were often less than the promise. The range of employment available for women was a result of societal changes brought about by industrialization; for example, the growing bureaucracies of the late nineteenth century were an important new area offering low-paying but respectable jobs. Nevertheless, without pressure from feminist individuals and organizations, educational standards and the climate of opinion would never have been modified to meet the challenge of these new positions. Holcombe, Walkowitz, Hammerton, and McWilliams-Tullberg all demonstrate in different ways the impact of larger social changes upon a particular group of women. Each chapter shows how the struggles of women were most successful when they chimed with larger social and economic needs, and least successful when they clashed with a specific power base or with dominant attitudes.

The constrained definition of respectable behavior by which upper-class women lived was under constant pressure throughout the century, and inevitably changed. It is difficult now for us to understand its attractions, but as Carol Christ shows, the appeal of the "angel in the house" went beyond a simple definition of feminine excellence. Many men, and particularly artists, found the Victorian definition of active male virility confining. Coventry Patmore and Alfred Lord Tennyson compared the strident and disordered strivings of men unfavorably with the calm and ordered world of the ideal woman. Their ambivalence about male sexuality and aggression was resolved by idealizing feminine passivity. In their poetry they frequently presented not only pure "angels," but also heroes who were tested, and in the process gained the more feminine virtues of kindness, gentleness, and receptivity to the needs of others. Ironically, the very women who were attempting to throw off the limiting stereotypes Tennyson and Patmore revered at the same time were anxious to retain and expand the characteristics of purity and moral leadership that these poets praised. A close analysis of why men of their stature so admired feminine passivity can tell us much about the emotional conflicts felt by a society undergoing rapid change.

We can see how idealized conduct meshed with social realities in the popular fiction discussed by Sally Mitchell. In the *Family Herald* and the *London Magazine* of the 1840's and 50's, stereotyped female characters were sufficiently similar to the average reader to enable her to identify with the heroine's plight. Despite the melodramatic trappings of the complicated plots, young women faced real sexual, and sometimes economic, problems that could not always be resolved by marriage happily ever after. In mass circulation magazines we can see more clearly the commonly shared attitudes and emotions among large sections of literate working people. The priorities—and opportunities— of young women are dramatized in the fiction. This world is always respectable, particularly in regard to the maintenance of physical virginity. Little effort was made to show job alternatives to a readership that already knew the limitations of women's work from experience and who generally entered marriage thankfully. Magazines created and furthered a shared background and outlook, while providing material for the private fantasies of their readers. These mass-readership magazines are, therefore, an important means of understanding better the dissemination of specific ideals among large numbers of women.

The confines and attractions of the stereotyped respectable woman, so strongly a part of women's magazines, are discussed by Christopher Kent in his examination of the reputation of actresses throughout the century. Acting was the highest paid profession a woman could enter—if she were successful—and it gave her more freedom than any other occupation. Moreover, it was one of the few spheres in which women could be involved in the creation of a persona rather than wait passively to be acted upon. Whereas in virtually every other occupation they held ancillary roles to men, women were at the center of the theater. The fact that the field was so overcrowded is some evidence of its popularity for women seeking independence, fame, and perhaps financial reward. Yet the very freedom and power of women stars on stage and off contributed to the disrepute of the profession. While feminists in the second half of the century were struggling to expand the horizons of women, actresses were gaining entrée into reputable circles and a form of social equality they had never experienced before. But, like so many breakthroughs for women in political and economic areas, the social acceptance of actresses was part of a larger change in attitudes. The victories won by the entire acting profession during this time brought an increased recognition of acting as an appropriate career for middle-class women, though only in particular roles and at particular theatres. It was a very limited triumph, circumscribed by the desire for respectability.

Nineteenth-century women were not always the passive, submissive and pure creatures of popular idealizations, but neither were they ever completely free from this stereotype. Its most pervasive and effective form of control was through the social and individual demand for respectability. While we can now judge Victorian women to have been more varied, active and complex than previously considered, we must not create a new stereotype that ignores the limits within which Victorians lived and changed. Rather, we should recognize the struggle to achieve independence—economic and personal—within the framework of traditional social values as being a hallmark of the times. Those of us brought up in the shadow of this tradition can perhaps well appreciate its strength in molding women, generation after generation. Undoubtedly many middle-class women were happy in their proper sphere. But those who wished for more—for an active participation in social questions of the day, for an economically viable livelihood, for legal justice—it was essential to widen that sphere. The strength and endurance of so many against formidable odds is the best evidence of the Victorian women's willingness to suffer, but also to speak out again and again. Their unshakable conviction that women had peculiar and special characteristics which could and should influence society sustained them through years of struggle. It is a model that has much to offer the present generation of feminists.

# A Widening Sphere

## CHANGING ROLES OF VICTORIAN WOMEN

# 1. Victorian Wives and Property

### Reform of the Married Women's Property Law, 1857–1882

### Lee Holcombe

IN 1869 SUSANNAH PALMER APPEARED IN THE RECORDER'S COURT IN London, charged with stabbing her husband. He had treated her so brutally for many years that at last she left him in order to support herself and her children and establish a new home. Then her husband appeared and seized and sold all her possessions—as he had every legal right to do.[1] A few years later Millicent Garrett Fawcett had her purse snatched by a young thief in London. When she appeared in court to testify against him, she heard the youth charged with "stealing from the person of Millicent Fawcett a purse containing £1 18s. 6d., the property of Henry Fawcett," and she recalled, "I felt as if I had been charged with theft myself."[2] Such were two women's experiences of the common law relating to married women's property. One was a poor working woman who would have gone unnoticed in her time but for her tragic story. The other, happily married to a distinguished Cambridge professor and Liberal member of Parliament, was for years the outstanding leader of the women's suffrage cause in England.

The stories of women so different as these two illuminate the arguments used by Victorian feminists in their demands for reform of the married women's property law and for other legal reforms as well. On the one hand, the law often inflicted grievous practical hardships upon women. On the other, the law, regarding a woman as only a part, even a chattel, of her husband, destroyed her independence, her identity, and her self-respect. Reform of the common law affecting women stands out, therefore, as a major achievement of nineteenth-century feminism.[3]

Reform of the law and feminism itself were responses to the

changing economic and social position of women in a time of rapid transition. They reflected the passing of a traditional society, dominated by a landed aristocracy and patriarchal in its attitudes toward women, and the advent of a modern industrialized society, increasingly rationalistic, secular, and democratic, unsure of what position women should have in the new order of things, but well aware, amidst all the vagaries of politics and personalities, that old laws must be brought up to date to meet the needs of the times.

## I

Among the great achievements of the Victorian age were the remolding of English law and the complete overhaul of an antiquated and chaotic system of courts. The criminal law was rendered more humane, the law of real property was simplified, and the foundations of modern company law were laid, to cite but a few examples of reform. In the early nineteenth century there existed a variety of superior courts—three common-law courts, four courts of equity, the ecclesiastical courts, and courts of admiralty and of bankruptcy—which administered separate bodies of law, afforded different remedies to suitors, and used different procedures and even different vocabularies. The conflict between the substance and the administration of the common law and of equity was especially glaring. Reform of the courts began in the 1830's and culminated in passage of the great Judicature Act of 1873 (36 & 37 Vict., c. 66). This Act, with later amendments, consolidated all existing superior courts into one Supreme Court of Judicature, which was competent to deal with all cases and whose judges were to be guided by the general principle that in "any conflict or variance" between the rules of equity and of the common law, "the rules of equity shall prevail."[4] It was in this climate of legal reform that the law relating to married women's property came under attack and was at last amended. There is no better example than this reform to show the conflict between the common law and equity and the eventual superseding of the common law by equity through legislative action.[5]

In the eyes of the common law, married women had no identity apart from their husbands. As the saying went, in law "husband and wife are one person, and the husband is that person." Where property was concerned, this meant in practice that a husband assumed legal possession or control of all property that belonged to his wife upon marriage and any property that might come to her during marriage. The extent of his possession and control depended on the nature of the property, for the common-law rules distinguished clearly between real and personal property. (Briefly, real property may be defined as property in freehold land, personal property as that in leasehold land and in chattels, that is, property other than land.)

Under the common law a husband enjoyed control over his wife's real property and the income from it during marriage, but he could not dispose of any of this property without her consent, which had to be duly recorded in court. If a husband died before his wife, her real property reverted to her possession and control absolutely. In addition, by the ancient practice of dower a widow was entitled to a life interest in one-third of the lands to which her husband had ever been entitled. However, under the provisions of a statute of 1833 a husband could set aside his wife's dower rights if he chose. The object of the statute was to make simpler the disposition of land, but its effect was to infringe upon the common-law protection of widows. A married woman could not make a will devising her real property. If she predeceased her husband, this property went not to him but to her children or other legal heirs, subject to the so-called "curtesy of England," which was analogous to a widow's dower rights and by which her husband enjoyed a life interest in all her lands provided a child had been born of the marriage.

On the other hand, a woman's personal property passed into the absolute possession of her husband. He could use and dispose of it during his lifetime in any way he chose. He could also make a will disposing as he pleased of his personal property, including that which had come to him from his wife. His wife and children might receive absolutely nothing under his will, for the medieval doctrine of "reasonable parts," under which a widow must receive at least one-third of her husband's personal property and children also a share, had long since dropped out of the common law. If a husband died intestate, his personal property was divided according to statutory provisions under which his widow never received more than half, the remainder going to his children or other near relatives or, if he had none, to the Crown. A wife, in contrast, could make a will bequeathing her personal property only with her husband's consent, and this consent he could withdraw at any time before probate. If she died intestate, all her personal property became, or rather remained, her husband's absolutely.

In these rules the common law clearly showed its origins in

medieval times, when land was the chief form of property and wealth. At that time the common law gave considerable protection to married women, for they retained ownership of their real property and had a life interest in their husbands' lands as well. When personal property, compared to land, was relatively small in amount and value, it did not matter so much that wives lost ownership of theirs and also had no claim upon their husbands'. But medieval times were long past, and the common law did not serve well a society no longer feudal in structure nor chiefly agricultural in its pursuits. Now, more often than not, a woman's property consisted not of land but of personal property— money from her earnings and from investments, household furnishings, stock in trade—and these, when she married, were no longer hers but her husband's.

The common-law rules relating to married women's property might be justified by the fact that the husband as head of the family had to support his wife and children and should have his wife's property to help him do so. But what if he shirked this responsibility? A woman had the right, acting as her husband's agent with his express or implied consent, to pledge his credit for the purchase of necessary supplies, but he could withdraw his consent to that at any time. In any event, obtaining supplies on credit was clearly a practice of the more prosperous classes and not one generally suitable or available to the poorer classes. A wife could not sue her husband, since legally they were the same person, and she had no effective means of enforcing her claim to support. The law merely provided that a husband must not allow his wife and children to become charges on the parish. A woman could apply for relief only to the Poor Law guardians, who in turn could recover from the husband the amount of any relief granted. But the guardians might refuse to act, and cases were reported of poor women actually starving to death in these circumstances.[6]

The common-law provisions might also be justified by the fact that the husband was the legal representative of his wife. Having no legal identity apart from her husband and no property under her control during marriage, a wife could not enter into contracts or incur debts except as her husband's agent, and therefore could not sue or be sued. Instead, her husband was responsible for her debts and contracts and also for her torts committed both before and during marriage. In the case of a tort committed against her, the husband sued in her stead and the damages he collected were his property and not hers. Here, reformers maintained, the state of the law was unfair to husbands and wives alike. Whether or not they had acquired property from their wives upon marriage, husbands had to pay the bills and answer in court for the misdeeds of their wives, who were freed of all accountability. The injury to women lay not only in the fact that rights were denied them but also in the fact that obligations were not placed upon them. Under the law married women were classed together with criminals, lunatics, and minors—legally incompetent and irresponsible.[7]

Diametrically opposed to these common-law views and rules were the principles and practices of equity, which had developed over the centuries to correct the injustices and omissions of the common law and which by the nineteenth century had come to recognize a wife's existence and right to property separate from her husband. Extending and developing the device of trusts, which were unknown to the common law, equity proceeded upon the principle that although a person could not hold property, it could be held for his or her benefit by a trustee. This meant that by prenuptial agreements, "marriage settlements" as they were called, a woman's family or friends or the woman herself could designate certain property, whether real or personal, as being her "separate property" or "separate estate," free from her husband's common-law rights of possession or control. The trustee of property under a marriage settlement was obligated to carry out the terms of the settlement or, in the absence of specific terms, to deal with the property according to the instructions of the married woman. If no trustee was specially appointed, the courts of equity named the husband as such, since under the common law the property would have been his, but as such he likewise must deal with the property according to the terms of the settlement or his wife's wishes.

A married woman with a separate estate in equity enjoyed virtually the same property rights as an unmarried woman. She could receive the income from her settled property and spend it as she pleased. She could make her separate property liable for debts that she incurred, and she could sue and be sued with respect to her separate property in the courts of equity. She could give away or sell this property freely. Finally, she could leave her separate property to anyone she wished by a will that her husband did not have to approve and that the courts of equity would uphold.

The relief from the common law that equity afforded was, however, far from being fair and satisfactory. For one thing, equity gave married women the rights without the responsibilities of property. A wife with separate property had no obligation to help support her family, and her husband was not freed from his common-law responsibility for her debts and torts. Much more serious was the fact that the protection of equity was beyond the reach of all but women of the wealthiest classes. Only they could afford the expensive proceedings of the courts of equity, and only they had property sufficient in amount and suitable in nature to be tied up in marriage settlements. It was not feasible for women who were not wealthy to settle upon themselves, through expensive equitable proceedings, small sums of money or even small fortunes of a few hundred pounds. Only one married woman in ten, it was estimated, had separate property in equity secured to her. In short, as reformers liked to put it, what in fact existed was one law for the rich and another for the poor.

The life of Caroline Norton vividly illustrated the hardships that the common law imposed upon married women with respect to property and other matters as well.[8] A celebrated society beauty in her younger days and a popular hostess in high Whig circles, the Honorable Mrs. Norton had separated from her uncongenial husband in 1836, but under the law she could not obtain a divorce. Much of the property that came to her from her parents passed, under the operation of the common law, into the possession of her husband, who refused to pay her an adequate allowance after their separation. Forced to make her own way in the world, she turned to writing and won considerable acclaim for her poetry, novels, and stories. But under the common law her earnings belonged to her husband, who periodically tried to gain possession of them. In 1836 Norton unsuccessfully sued Lord Melbourne, then Prime Minister, for damages, charging him with adultery with his wife, who as a legal nonperson could not appear in her own defense. Also, exercising his rights under the common law, which gave the father all rights of custody of children and the mother none, Norton abducted their three small sons and thereafter refused to let his wife see them. The first of Mrs. Norton's polemical pamphlets to be published helped to win passage of the Act of 1839 that gave mothers certain limited rights to their children. In 1853, not for the first time, one of Mrs. Norton's creditors sued her husband for debts she had incurred in his name, since legally they could not sue her. Subpoenaed as a witness, she made a dramatic appearance in court, and the following year she issued a pamphlet entitled *English Laws for Women in the Nineteenth Century*, telling of how she "had learned the English law piecemeal by suffering under it." With reform of the divorce law before Parliament, Mrs. Norton next published in 1855 *A Letter to the Queen on Lord Cranworth's Marriage and Divorce Bill*, again recounting her sufferings, and ending: "Meanwhile my husband has a legal lien on the copyright of my works. Let him claim the copyright of this!"

The case of Mrs. Norton inspired the first public activities of a young woman who was just beginning a long and distinguished career in the women's movement, and to whom also much credit is due for winning the first installment of reform of the married women's property law.[9] Barbara Leigh Smith (1827–91) was the eldest child of a wealthy member of Parliament, Unitarian in religion and Radical in politics, whose London house was a meeting place for many noted reformers. He believed strongly in equal rights for women, giving his three daughters an education as good as that of his two sons and bestowing upon them equally handsome annual allowances when they came of age. Bred in such an atmosphere, Miss Leigh Smith early turned her abundant energies and wide sympathies to women's causes, and in 1854 published her first work, a little pamphlet entitled *A Brief Summary, in Plain Language, of the Most Important Laws concerning Women.*

The publication of Miss Leigh Smith's pamphlet aroused considerable public interest and made her name known to others who were interested in legal reform.[10] It attracted the attention of the Law Amendment Society, which was presided over by Lord Brougham, the brilliant if erratic former Lord Chancellor, and which included many other distinguished men who were likewise friends of the Leigh Smith family. The Society referred the matter of property law reform to a committee chaired by Sir Thomas Erskine Perry, who had served as Chief Justice of the Supreme Court of Bombay and was best known as an advocate of constitutional reforms in India, and who had now returned to the English political scene as Liberal M. P. for Devonport. The committee's report denounced the existing law and called for its amendment.[11]

To promote the cause of reform the country's first real feminist committee was now organized, including personal friends and sympathizers of Barbara Leigh Smith such as Bessie Rayner Parkes and Maria Susan Rye, who would later make their mark in other fields of feminist activity. In 1855 the little group began a country-wide campaign to gather proof of hardships caused by the law and to collect signatures on a petition to Parliament requesting reform. Mrs. Norton's case was famous, but now a mass of evidence was accumulated showing that sufferings such as hers occurred every day and in all ranks of society. Also, as Bessie Parkes later wrote, "In the effort to obtain signatures people interested in the question were brought into communication in all parts of the kingdom, and the germs of an effective [women's] movement were scattered far and wide." There were more than 26,000 signers of the petition. In London alone 3,000 signatures were obtained, including those of such literary celebrities as Elizabeth Barrett Browning, Mary Howitt, Anna Jameson, Harriet Martineau, Elizabeth Gaskell, and Geraldine Jewsbury.[12]

In March 1856 the women's petition was presented in Parliament, by Lord Brougham in the upper House and by Perry in the Commons, and contrary to expectations it was "received very respectfully . . . without a sneer or a smile."[13] The petition pointed out that "the law expresses the necessity of an age, when the man was the only money-getting agent, but . . . since modern civilisation, in indefinitely extending the sphere of occupation for women, has in some measure broken down their pecuniary dependence upon men, it is time that legal protection be thrown over the produce of their labour." Among the "middle and upper ranks" of society "married women of education are entering . . . the fields of literature and art, in order to increase the family income," while women of the lower classes were widely employed in factory work and in "other multifarious occupations." Official statistics supported this claim that the common law, embodying as it did the ideals of a society in which men protected and supported their womenfolk at home, no longer fit the realities of the time. The census of 1861 revealed that there were 3,436,749 working women in the country, more than one-third of the labor force, and of these women 838,856, or nearly one-fourth, were married (3 Hansard, CXCI, 1020, CXCII, 1360). All working women, the petition declared, needed protection for their earnings, but the need was especially great among women of the lower classes, who were not protected "by the forethought of their relatives [by marriage settlements in equity], the social training of their husbands, and the refined customs of the rank to which they belong." Such a woman, the petition continued, "may work from morning till night to see the produce of her labour wrested from her [by her husband], and wasted in a gin-palace."

Two months after presentation of the petition Perry moved in the Commons a resolution declaring that the rules of the common law relating to married women's property were "unjust in principle and injurious in their operation," that the principles of equity were "in accordance with the requirements of the age and in conformity with the opinions and usages of the wealthier and better classes of society," and that "the conflict between law and equity on the subject ought to be terminated by a general law based on the principles of equity which should apply to all classes." This resolution had already been carried unanimously a few days earlier at a large public meeting in London sponsored by the Law Amendment Society to arouse interest in the question. Some members of the House heartily agreed that reform was needed, while others denounced the "vicious principle" of Perry's resolution. The Solicitor General, Sir Richard Bethell, was not enthusiastic, but the Attorney General, Sir Alexander Cockburn, a brilliant advocate who was soon to be appointed Chief Justice of the Court of Common Pleas, cordially approved the resolution. Still, Cockburn urged Perry not to press the House to vote on an abstract question but to introduce legislation instead, and accordingly Perry withdrew his resolution.[14]

In 1857 Perry introduced a Married Women's Property Bill that was based on the recommendations of the committee of the Law Amendment Society over which he had presided. Simple and clear in its provisions, the bill would have made married women as capable as unmarried women of acquiring, holding, and disposing of property both real and personal. They would be capable of making contracts and of suing and being sued; they and not their husbands would be liable for all debts they incurred and torts they committed before and after marriage; they would be able to dispose of their property freely by will or, if they died intestate, the same principles of distribution would apply to their property as applied to their husbands' property. Sir Richard Bethell, now the Attorney General, was not encouraging, declaring that the bill "must involve a material change in the social and political institutions of a nation" and would tend to place women "in a 'strong-minded and independent position,'" a position that "the most amiable women" did not desire (3 Hansard, cxlv, 276). Nevertheless, the bill easily passed its second reading by a vote of 120 to 65, but then it was dropped (3 Hansard, cxlvi, 1515–23).

Perry recalled years later that the Divorce Bill "took the wind out of our sails."[15] This bill came down from the House of Lords in the same month that Perry's bill had its second reading, and was accepted by the Commons after long and rancorous debate.[16] The Divorce Act of 1857 (20 & 21 Vict., c. 85) transferred jurisdiction in all matters relating to the dissolution of marriages from the ecclesiastical courts to a new secular Court of Divorce and Matrimonial Causes. This court was empowered to grant both judicial separations, which were previously obtained through the ecclesiastical courts, and absolute divorces, which before this were available only by private act of Parliament. The Act also contained important provisions concerning the property of married women. A woman who obtained either a judicial separation or a divorce was to have all the rights of an unmarried woman with respect to property. A woman deserted by her husband without cause could apply to a court for an order protecting against her husband and his creditors all property she acquired after her desertion, and she would then have all the rights of an unmarried woman over this property. Interestingly, these provisions had been inserted in the Divorce Bill as originally introduced at the instance of Lord St. Leonards, the distinguished and respected former Lord Chancellor, who hoped thereby to "prevent a greater evil," namely, passage of Perry's "most mischievous" bill, which would "place the whole marriage law . . . on a different footing and give a wife all the distinct rights of citizenship" (3 Hansard, cxlv, 800). Perry, on the other hand, had hoped that passage of his measure would prevent that of the Divorce Bill, which he thought would lead to the "corruption of morals" (3 Hansard, cxlv, 268).

The Divorce Act was significant as the first recognition by Parliament that in certain cases married women should have control over their property. But the protection order system which it created was very far from being an adequate measure of reform. It did not protect wives whose husbands squandered their property before leaving or stole it when they deserted. It allowed a husband to live apart from his wife, not deserting her within the letter of the law, and to swoop down upon her periodically to take property she had acquired during his absence. It did not apply in the case of a wife who left her husband as it did in the case of a man who left his wife—no protection order could have been granted to Susannah Palmer. For these reasons, and also because women were too shy or proud to publicize their wrongs by appearing in court, few protection orders were issued—only one hundred in the first three years of the operation of the system.[17]

The cause of property law reform languished for a decade after passage of the Divorce Act. Now it could be argued that "if injured wives were protected, what did uninjured wives want with their property?" Barbara Leigh Smith's little committee pledged itself to continue work in the cause, but in fact it soon melted away. Miss Leigh Smith herself was married in 1857 to a Frenchman, Dr. Eugène Bodichon, and thereafter made her new home in Algeria, while her friends in England turned to other good causes, notably the founding in 1858, under the editorship of Bessie Parkes, of the *English Woman's Journal* as an official organ of the women's movement, and the promotion by Maria Rye and many others of wider opportunities for women's employment.[18]

## II

It was with the revival of general reform activity and the beginning of an organized feminist movement in the later 1860's that reform of the married women's property law again came to the fore. Much of the credit for this belongs to the towering figure of John Stuart Mill and, again, to Barbara Leigh Smith Bodichon. Universally respected as a thinker and writer, Mill was elected to Parliament in 1865 in spite of—hardly because of—his advanced views about equal rights for women. Madame Bodichon was now spending more of her time in England and resuming an active role in the women's movement. Together with friends she took up the question of women's suffrage, and at her request Mill presented in Parliament in 1866 a petition asking for women the right to vote. Women's suffrage committees were formed in London, Manchester, and several other cities, and were soon united in a national organization. In 1867, during the debates on the great Reform Bill, Mill introduced an amendment that would have extended the franchise to women on the same terms as men. Mill argued that women needed the vote to protect their interests and remedy their grievances, and he cited as an example the law affecting married women's property, concluding that "grievances of less magnitude . . . when suffered by parties less inured to passive submission, have provoked revolutions" (3 Hansard, CLXXXVII, 817–29). Mill's amendment was defeated, but his speech made a great impression.

Now a Married Women's Property Committee was organized to work for reform under the leadership of Ursula Mellor Bright and Elizabeth Wolstenholme, later Mrs. Elmy. The former, one of the outstanding women in the Society of Friends, was the wife of Jacob Bright, Radical M. P. for Manchester for a quarter century and a vigorous champion of women's rights.[19] Miss Wolstenholme, head of a small boarding school for girls near Manchester, was active with Emily Davies and others in efforts to improve the education of women, was a supporter of Josephine Butler's campaign to repeal the Contagious Diseases Acts, and was closely associated with Lydia Becker in the work of the Manchester women's suffrage committee.[20]

Late in 1867 the Married Women's Property Committee presented a petition to the executive council of the Social Science Association requesting help in obtaining reform. This association, organized ten years earlier under the leadership of Lord Brougham, included among its members many of the most eminent men and women of the time, and long served as a remarkable forum for the discussion of social problems and as a powerful lobbying group.[21] Early the next year the committee of the Association to which the matter had been referred presented its report. This committee, like that of the Law Amendment Society a decade earlier, urged reform of the married women's property law and submitted a draft bill that was almost identical with Perry's bill of 1857, embodying the principle that a married woman should have the same legal rights over property as an unmarried woman.[22] Two months later the bill was introduced in Parliament.

Now, in the sessions of 1868–70, reform of the married women's property law obtained the full-dress debate in Parliament that it had not received in 1857, and attracted widespread comment in the press as well. The discussions are especially interesting as one of the earliest public airings of the whole question of "women's rights." Preeminent among the supporters of reform was Mill, whose *Subjection of Women* was published in 1869, while the debates were in progress. (In the same year a third edition of Madame Bodichon's *A Brief Summary . . . of the Most Important Laws concerning Women* appeared.) With Mill in favor of reform were some of the most distinguished men in the Commons. Among them were George John Shaw Lefevre, afterward Baron Eversley, who was being spoken of as a possible future Prime Minister although he was actually never to achieve the first rank in political life; Robert Lowe, who was to be Gladstone's first Chancellor of the Exchequer and later Home Secretary; Sir George Jessel, whose legal talents earned him the post of Solicitor General in 1871 and, two years later, that of Master of the Rolls, where he proved one of the ablest men ever to hold that high office in the courts of equity; and Russell Gurney, the respected and popular Recorder of London (he presided at Susannah Palmer's trial) and Conservative M.P. for

Southampton. Few outstanding members spoke against reform. The most prominent were Henry Charles Lopes, a successful lawyer who was later appointed a justice of the Supreme Court and raised to the peerage as Baron Ludlow, and Henry Cecil Raikes, who quickly won a place in Conservative counsels after his election to Parliament in 1868, becoming chairman of committees in 1874 and serving later as Postmaster General.[23]

In arguing their case, opponents of reform appealed to patriotic and religious sentiment, masculine egotism, and conservative feeling generally. They extolled the long and honorable history of the common law, which could be traced back to the Conquest. They dwelt upon the fact that the law recognized the sacramental nature of marriage. As in the eyes of the Church husband and wife became one flesh, so in the eyes of the law they became one person, and it "was written in nature and in Scripture that the husband was and ought to be lord of his household" (3 Hansard, cxcv, 786). The law, Lopes argued, recognized also the practical facts of life, that "the wife was the weaker vessel . . . and that the husband was . . . better fitted to bear the brunt of the outer world" (3 Hansard, cxcv, 775). To change the law, Raikes asserted, "would disturb the peace of every family, and destroy for ever that identity of interests at present existing between husband and wife . . . the basis of the Christian family and the peculiar characteristic of English society" (3 Hansard, cci, 889). It would lead to independence of attitude and action on the part of women and to "a great deal of immorality," because in any quarrel with her husband a wife could say, "I have my own property, and if you don't like me, I can go and live with somebody who does" (3 Hansard, cxcii, 1360). Finally, Raikes declared, reform would give recognition to the "novel principle of civil equality between the sexes" and would "create a factitious, an artificial, and an unnatural equality between man and woman" (3 Hansard, cci, 888).

All of these arguments the reformers ably countered. The question, said Robert Lowe, was not whether the law could be traced through "a long succession of ages in the most barbarous times" but whether it was just, and it was not (3 Hansard, cxcii, 1364). It was, Jessel argued, a relic of the days of slavery, and the legal position of married women was exactly that of slaves, dependent upon masters and deprived of property rights (3 Hansard, cxcv, 770–71). Women, said Jacob Bright, were hardly "mentally incapacitated" for managing property, for unmarried women and widows enjoyed the same property rights as men (3 Hansard, CXCII, 1361). Mill regretted that his opponents seemed to think it "impossible for society to exist on a harmonious footing between two persons unless one of them has absolute power over the other" (3 Hansard, CXCII, 1371), while Gurney could not understand how "any one who really knew what domestic harmony was" could suppose that "the glory and the joy of married life depended on the husband having possession of his wife's property, and the power to stop the supplies" (3 Hansard, CXCV, 768). Independence for women would surely result from reform, Bright agreed, but this would be a great gain, for it would lead to "an increase of respect for women and of real respect," so much more valuable than the conventional politeness that was so easy to pay (3 Hansard, CXCII, 1363). With an independent status a woman of the better classes would be able to exercise her wisdom and judgment as she could not do now against the "arbitrary authority" of her husband, and a woman of the humbler classes would no longer be considered a "mere drudge" without any rights (Select Committee on Married Women's Property Bill, 360, 369, 416). As for independence leading to immorality, Jessel asked whether opponents of reform would be willing to deprive husbands of their property "because it sometimes was applied to support a mistress" (3 Hansard, CXCV, 773). On the question of equality of the sexes Shaw Lefevre summed up well: "Let them have as far as possible fair play, remove unequal legislation, and women would then speedily find their true level, whatever that might be, for which by nature they were intended" (3 Hansard, CXCI, 1024).

More telling than these rather theoretical arguments, however, was the practical proof offered by reformers that the common law could be abrogated without dire results. They pointed first to equity. Every marriage settlement drawn up, Lowe declared, was a tacit condemnation of the common law. No member of Parliament would allow his own daughter to marry without a settlement, and Parliament should stand *in loco parentis* for all women, granting them that protection of their property now available only to women of the wealthier classes (3 Hansard, CXCII, 1365). The measure he supported, said Jessel, "was emphatically a poor woman's Bill" (3 Hansard, CXCV, 770). In addition, the reformers pointed out that Canada and many states of the United States had amended the common law they inherited from England to allow married women control over their property, and that there was general satisfaction with the change and no demand for a return to the old system.[24] While Raikes and others denounced the proposed "Americanization" of English institutions (3 Hansard, CXCII, 1353, CXCV, 778, 784–86, CCI, 888–89), Gurney assured them that this was no "leap in the dark"—a reference to passage of the Reform Bill of 1867—but a reform of tried and proven value (3 Hansard, CXCV, 768–69).

Finally, there was obviously widespread popular feeling in favor of reform, for as Gurney said, the law "was the cause of daily misery and almost daily crime" (3 Hansard, CCI, 879). Many cases of hardship for women in all ranks of society were reported, of which that of Susannah Palmer was only one of the most notorious. Petitions with thousands of women's signatures were coming in to Parliament, and one member who was a large-scale manufacturer reported that he never passed his factory gates without his women workers asking him when Parliament would pass a reform measure. Great weight was attached to the fact that the famous Pioneer Co-operative Society of Rochdale, representing the best class of working men, allowed married women workers to invest money in the Society in their own names and refused to pay out this money to husbands without their wives' consent, although the practice was of doubtful legality. Even "the wilder men," it was reported, "say the protection of their wives' earnings is a safeguard for their families."[25]

Opponents of the bill admitted that cases of hardship existed, but argued that these were exceptional and that the whole principle of the law applying to all women should not be subverted for the benefit of the small minority of women who suffered under it. They recommended instead a narrower measure of reform: extension of the protection order system of 1857 to cover wives who were mistreated by their husbands as well as wives who were deserted (3 Hansard, CXCII, 1355, 1357, 1369, 1373, CXCV, 779, CXCVIII, 402–3). Supporters of the bill countered by saying that the protection order system had not worked well in the past, and that wives living with husbands who mistreated them would hardly risk further mistreatment by applying to a court for protection. In any case, they argued, was it just for men to have their property as a matter of course while women could have theirs only if they proved to a court's satisfaction that their husbands were cruel (Select Committee on Married Women's Property Bill, 365, 376, 415, 419, 421, 424, 426, 429)? The debates in the Commons showed, in short, that all agreed on the necessity for some amendment of the law, and the only question was what form it should take.

The Married Women's Property Bill which Shaw Lefevre introduced in 1868 was opposed by the Conservative Attorney General, Sir John Karslake, but was read a second time when the Speaker cast his vote in favor in order to break the tie. It was then referred to a select committee, which could not complete its work before the end of the session but which approved the principle of the bill, all the witnesses heard having testified vigorously in its favor, and suggested that details of the measure be worked out by another select committee during the next session.[26]

The Parliament that met in 1869 was a new one, the first to be chosen by the enlarged electorate created by the Reform Bill of 1867, and the Liberals under Gladstone were now in office, having won a resounding victory at the polls over Disraeli's Conservatives. Now, when Russell Gurney introduced the same Married Women's Property Bill that Shaw Lefevre had brought in the year before, government approval was voiced by the Solicitor General, John Duke Coleridge, later Lord Coleridge, Chief Justice of the Court of Common Pleas and afterward Lord Chief Justice of England, head of the new Supreme Court of Judicature. The bill was read a second time, was considered by another select committee which reported it with minor amendments, and easily passed its third reading by a vote of 131 to 33. It was then introduced and given a second reading in the Lords, but clearly only as a matter of courtesy to the government and because it was too late in the session for the bill to be passed.[27]

In 1870 Gurney introduced the bill as amended by the select committee the year before. Now, in an attempt to prevent its passage, Raikes introduced his own bill to amend the law, a complicated measure embodying the suggestions made earlier that the protection order system be extended. Remarking on a "great example of a Raikes' progress," Coleridge urged approval of Gurney's much broader measure instead. Raikes's bill was repudiated by a vote of 208 to 46, and Gurney's was accepted and sent on to meet its fate in the Lords.[28]

In the upper House the bill met with universal disapproval. The opposition was led by Lord Penzance, whose views of marriage might be explained by the fact that he was judge of the Divorce Court, and by the former Lord Chancellor Lord Westbury, the same brilliant, arrogant, and irascible Sir Richard Bethell who had opposed Perry and "strong-minded women" in 1857. Penzance warned the advocates of women's rights that marriages were "less frequent than they used to be or possibly ought to be" and wondered what inducement men would have to marry if in taking a wife they took "a

*Punch's Fancy Portraits. The Right Honorable Osborne Morgan (October 7, 1882, Punch, vol. 83), shows Morgan, sponsor of the Married Women's Property bill of 1882, being thanked by two women, one of whom is kneeling on a locked trunk labeled "Married Women's Property."*

partner with separate interests" free to spend her money as she chose. Westbury suggested, among much else, that if women could freely dispose of their property they would squander it on diamonds, race-horses, and lovers. Even Lord Shaftesbury joined in this, although he did dwell movingly on the suffering of poor women under the law and declared that some measure of reform must be passed. Clearly the opinion of the House, like that of the bill's opponents in the Commons, was that the measure went much farther than was necessary to correct existing evils, and at the suggestion of Lord Cairns it was referred to a select committee to be revised (3 Hansard, ccii, 600–622). Cairns, who had served as a judge in equity and then briefly as Lord Chancellor under Disraeli, was universally respected and his recommendations carried great weight.

The select committee of the Lords, led by Lord Cairns, tore the Commons' bill to shreds. Of its twenty clauses, fourteen were struck out and replaced by new provisions, and four others were substantially amended. It was, in fact, an entirely different bill that the Lords passed and sent down to the Commons. Again it was late in the session, too late for substantial amendments to be made by the lower House, and at Gurney's urging the bill was passed.[29]

So the Married Women's Property Act of 1870 (33 & 34 Vict., c. 93) became law. In rewriting the Commons' measure the Lords had thrown out the phrase "her own property" referring to the property of a married woman and substituted for it the words "property held and settled to her separate use" or, simply, her "separate property." Here the Lords were applying the principles and the exact language of equity to the property of all married women, doubtless in a conscious effort to move with the current of legal reform around them, namely, in the direction of the fusion of law and equity and the superseding of the law by equity in case of conflict between the two. By the provisions of the Act, married women were to have as their "separate property," with the equitable rights attaching thereto, property that fell into roughly three categories: the earnings and property they acquired by their own work after passage of the Act; money invested in several specified ways—in annuities, in savings banks, in the public stocks and funds, in incorporated or joint stock companies, in the shares of provident, friendly, building, loan, and other such societies, and in insurance policies on their own or their husbands' lives; and, with qualifications, property coming to them from the estates of persons deceased.

*A Widening Sphere*

Comment on the Act, then and later, in the Commons and outside of Parliament was scathing. In the first place, this was a clear case of obstruction of the popular will, as expressed in the elected House of Parliament, by the hereditary and appointed upper House. Here one sees the beginnings, or rather the revival, of that conflict between Lords and Commons which would grow in intensity over the years as Liberal governments found themselves thwarted by the Conservative Lords, and would culminate long after in passage of the Parliament Act of 1911. As for the Act itself, as Gurney pointed out, the Lords had rejected the general principle approved by the Commons, that an unjust law should be repealed, and merely applied specific remedies to the worst cases (3 Hansard CCIII, 1488). Their Lordships, said another member, apparently wrote the measure "by contributing each a section, without any of them taking care that the different sections should be consistent one with another" (3 Hansard, CCXVIII, 611). As a result it "bristled with anomalies and absurdities" (3 Hansard, CCXIV, 669).

Some of these defects were obvious in the wording of the Act, while others became obvious only as the Act was interpreted by judicial decisions. For example, under the Act a husband was freed from liability for his wife's premarital debts even though he might have acquired all of her property upon marriage, and a married woman could hold as her separate property all property that came to her as next of kin of an intestate but no legacy larger than £200 left to her by will (3 Hansard, CCXIV, 669). A Supreme Court ruling in 1878 held that a woman could be sued with respect to her separate property only for debts she contracted before marriage, not for debts she contracted after marriage.[30] In the same year a stipendiary magistrate in Manchester, in the case of a certain Mrs. M'Carthy, ruled that a woman could not sue her husband to recover her separate property that he had stolen—this despite the specific provision in the Act of 1870 that a married woman was to have all civil and criminal remedies "against all persons whomsoever." Presumably the magistrate was operating under the old common-law rule that since husband and wife were one person, they could not steal from each other or sue each other.[31]

Still, the Act of 1870 had value. Speaking for the Married Women's Property Committee, Elizabeth Wolstenholme and Lydia Becker called it "a real and great gain," providing as it did an immediate remedy for glaring evils and affecting large numbers of women

(*The Times,* 25 August 1870). It was also, as the *Annual Register* noted rather wistfully, "a first recognition of a new principle, another small sign of the times . . . that the old creeds were passing away, and, whether for good or evil, all things becoming new."[32]


## III


In the years that followed, agitation for further reform of the law continued. Refusing to accept the Act of 1870 as "even a temporary settlement of the question," the Married Women's Property Committee pledged to continue their organization "intact and in working order . . . to press the subject upon public attention" (*The Times,* 25 August 1870). Speeches were made, especially before the sympathetic Social Science Association.[33] Articles were published and then reprinted. Petitions were circulated for signature and presented to Parliament. Dinner parties were given to interest influential friends in the cause. Every year the Committee held a general meeting in London to review the progress to date and plan for future action.[34]

Yet all this activity long availed nothing. In 1873 the women's friends in Parliament introduced a bill substantially the same as that passed by the Commons in 1869 and 1870. Supported by the government, it easily passed its second reading in the Commons but had to be dropped because of the lateness and difficulties of the session.[35] The chief business of the session was passage of the all-important Judicature Bill. Thereafter, it was said, the government front bench resembled a row of extinct volcanoes, their reforming energies spent, and the general election early the next year swept the Conservatives under Disraeli back into office.

The cause of reform fared ill under the Conservative government. To be sure, two reform measures were passed with government support. The Act of 1874 (37 & 38 Vict., c. 50) amended the Act of 1870 by restoring a husband's liability for his wife's premarital debts and torts, but specified that in future he would be responsible for these only to the extent of property which he had acquired from his wife upon marriage. Its sponsor, John Morley, freely admitted that it was designed to protect not married women but their creditors.[36] The second measure, passed in 1877 (40 & 41 Vict., c. 29), amended the married women's property law in Scotland. At government insistence the bill was shorn of many of its original provisions during its passage

*A Widening Sphere*

through Parliament, and as enacted it merely went a short way toward assimilating Scots law to English law by granting a married woman control over her earnings and defining a husband's liability for his wife's premarital debts.[37]

Beyond these limited measures the Conservatives adamantly refused to go (3 Hansard, CCXXXV, 71–81, CCXLIV, 257–64). It was not because they rejected all domestic reform, nor because the government's time and energies were increasingly absorbed by affairs in Europe and by Irish problems. Rather, the explanation seems to rest with Lord Cairns, now again Lord Chancellor, who had been the chief architect of the Act of 1870. Irately responding to Lord Coleridge, who in 1877 introduced a broad measure of reform, Cairns declared, "It was settled seven years ago that married women were not to be unmarried so far as their property was concerned. . . . The Act of 1870 had worked admirably, and, moreover, it remedied every grievance upon which any person could put his finger" (3 Hansard, CCXXXV, 77–80). The reformers could only await the Liberals' return to power.

This came in 1880, after an election campaign unprecedented in English history. Gladstone personally stumped the country, as no Prime Minister had ever done before, taking his case directly to the people. Feminists were heartened especially by the fact that he appealed to women for aid in his campaign, and few constituencies were without women canvassers and many had women speakers for the Liberals' cause. At the election many old opponents of women's suffrage and of women's rights in general were defeated, and many supporters of women's causes came in.[38] Now a group of younger men in Parliament took up the cause of property law reform. Among these were Hinde Palmer, a distinguished lawyer and Queen's Counsel who sponsored a number of bills to reform the law of property, and George Osborne Morgan (later Sir George), Judge Advocate General in the new government, who was best known for his opposition to religious disabilities.

At first, however, the Liberal government was slow to move in the matter of reform. Two bills introduced in the Commons in 1880, one to amend the married women's property law in England and the other to amend the law in Scotland, were approved by the government only with qualifications and they dropped from sight after their second reading.[39] Irish problems dominated domestic politics, while attention abroad was focused on the British occupation of Egypt. Also, Lord

Selborne, the Lord Chancellor, was thought to be as much opposed to reform as his Conservative predecessor, Lord Cairns. The former Sir Roundell Palmer, one of the greatest equity lawyers of the century and a devout Churchman, Selborne was a conservative in all but name, and during the campaign of 1868–70 he had publicly denounced the proposed reform of the married women's property law as likely to destroy domestic peace and harmony and to make women "unfeminine" (*The Times*, 27 January 1870).

Yet it was Selborne's influence that carried the women's cause to victory at last. This was especially fitting, for he had been the moving spirit on the distinguished royal commission whose recommendations were embodied in the Judicature Act of 1873, passed during his first tenure as Lord Chancellor. Doubtless Selborne now viewed reform of the married women's property law as merely drawing the logical conclusions from the principles of the Judicature Act. Early in 1881 Hinde Palmer led a deputation to wait upon Selborne, and reported him to be now favorable to reform (*The Times*, 8 and 24 January 1881). Soon a bill amending the married women's property law in Scotland was passed with government support (44 & 45 Vict., c. 21), Selborne himself sponsoring it in the House of Lords.[40] The same year a bill to amend the law in England received a second reading, was considered and amended by a select committee chaired by the Attorney General, Sir Henry James, but had to be withdrawn late in the session.[41] Early in 1882 Selborne introduced the amended bill in the Lords, where it easily passed. It was then piloted through the Commons almost as easily by Osborne Morgan.[42]

So the Married Women's Property Act of 1882 (45 & 46 Vict., c. 75) became law, quietly and almost without debate.[43] It proceeded upon the general principle that married women should have the same property rights as unmarried women but, following the precedent set by the Act of 1870, it referred not to a married woman's "own property" but to her "separate property." (This change in the measure as originally introduced was made by the select committee of 1881.) In effect, the Act of 1882 bestowed upon every married woman an equitable marriage settlement, thereby carrying out the principles of the Judicature Act that the common law and equity must be fused and that in the event of conflict between them equity must prevail.[44]

Despite the conservatism of its language, the Act of 1882 revolutionized the law. A woman married after the Act came into effect on 1 January 1883 was to have as her separate property all property from whatever source which she owned at the time of marriage and which she acquired after marriage. Women married before 1883 were to have as their separate property all property they acquired after the Act went into effect. Women could enter into contracts and sue and be sued with respect to their separate property, and could dispose of this property freely by sale or gift or otherwise during their lifetime and by will after their death.

While spelling out the rights of married women, the Act also spelled out their responsibilities. A married woman with separate property was as liable for the support of her husband as he was for hers, and liable for the support of her children and grandchildren in like manner. (This provision had also been included in the Act of 1870, which was now repealed.) A wife's separate property was primarily liable for her debts, contracts, and torts, her husband's liability being limited to the amount of any property which he had acquired from her upon marriage, and a married woman was now made subject to the bankruptcy laws. (This was a reenactment, with additions, of the Act of 1874, which was now also repealed.)

To insure to married women protection of their separate property, the Act provided that they should have the same civil and criminal remedies as unmarried women "against all persons whomsoever." However, this reenactment of a section of the Act of 1870 was now qualified by the provision, designed to safeguard domestic harmony, that husbands and wives could not begin criminal proceedings against each other while they were still living together. Interestingly, the first case to arise under the Act was that of a husband who charged his wife with stealing some of his property and running off with another man (*The Times*, 16 February 1883).

A few months after passage of the Act the Married Women's Property Committee held its last meeting. The Act was hailed as "a great measure of justice" that would "raise the dignity and stability" of marriage. Osborne Morgan paid tribute to "the devoted band of earnest-minded women, who, with very slender resources at their back and in the face of determined opposition, were resolved to secure for the poor women of this country that control over their own property which their richer sisters enjoyed." Special thanks were tendered to Mrs. Bright and Mrs. Elmy. Then the Committee disbanded, its work done (*The Times*, 21 November 1882).

Two more Married Women's Property Acts were added to the statute book in the Victorian period. That of 1884 (47 & 48 Vict., c. 14) amended two apparently contradictory provisions of the Act of 1882 relating to criminal proceedings between husband and wife. Providing that married persons were competent and admissible witnesses against each other, it was another blow to the old common-law rule of the identity of husband and wife.[45] The Act of 1893 (56 & 57 Vict., c. 63) was made necessary by judicial decisions in cases arising under the Act of 1882. It provided that a contract entered into by a married woman with respect to her separate property was valid even if she had no separate property at the time the contract was made but acquired it afterward. Also, a married woman's will disposing of her separate property was valid even if she had no separate property at the time the will was made, and her will did not require reexecution after her husband's death.[46] With these clarifying amendments, the Act of 1882 stood as the basic law on the subject for more than fifty years.

In demanding reform of the married women's property law, feminists were fortunately not swimming against the currents of the time but were moving with the currents charted by some of the finest legal minds of the age. The Victorians swept away the clutter of courts inherited from earlier times and replaced them by one Supreme Court, which was to fuse the different bodies of law previously administered in the separate courts and, in particular, to see that in case of conflict the rules of equity should prevail. When reform of the married women's property law came, therefore, it was by the application to all classes of women of the equitable provisions and remedies once confined to women of the wealthier classes. Reflecting the humanitarian and increasingly democratic temper of the Victorian age, the reform was "simply one more application of the principle insisted upon by the historians of English law, that in England the law for the great men has a tendency to become the law for all men" (Dicey, p. 395).

Why, then, in such an age of legal reform did it take twenty-five years to pass an effective Married Women's Property Act? Echoing Mill's comments in Parliament in 1867, feminists argued that here was proof that women needed the franchise in order to protect their interests. If women had had votes and could have brought pressure to bear directly upon Parliament and successive governments, the desired reform might have come much earlier than it actually did. As it was, women had to depend upon the feminist sympathies and the efforts of individual members. Between 1857 and 1882, eighteen Married Women's Property bills were introduced in Parliament. All were private members' bills, and as such their fate depended upon the attitude of the government and the state of Parliamentary business. A majority in the Commons favored reform, as shown by the fact that all the bills that came on for a second reading there passed easily, with the single exception of the Bill of 1868. But only five bills were enacted into law, all with government support.[47]

Sentiment in Parliament in favor of reform was aroused chiefly by the obvious fact that in practice the common law caused widespread hardship and suffering among women, especially those of the lower classes. What, then, were the practical effects of the Married Women's Property Acts? They were sweeping measures, for they affected every married person in the country and, it might be said, touched them in a very sensitive spot, namely, their pocketbooks. An interesting speculation in this connection is suggested by a comment made during the debates of 1870 by Lord Shaftesbury. He estimated that if roughly 800,000 wives were employed at wages of, say, £20 a year, then it was a matter of £16 million annually that needed to be protected from these women's husbands (3 Hansard, cciii, 397). If we could know and add to this £16 million the value of property other than their earnings which belonged to women of the middle and upper classes and which also would have passed to their husbands but for the Married Women's Property Acts, we should come up with a very large sum indeed. Is it too much to suggest that these Acts carried through one of the greatest expropriations and reallocations of property in English history? At the same time, we cannot know the number of women in England who but for passage of the Acts would have been abused and despoiled of their property by their husbands. Perhaps it is enough to know that cases such as that of Susannah Palmer could no longer occur.

Important as the practical effects of the Married Women's Property Acts were, it was, rather, their psychological effect that contemporaries emphasized. Speaking of the "novel sense of independence" that married women would now feel, one writer declared, "The difference caused by mental change is much greater than the difference caused by material change, and the mental change will be very great. . . . This increase of individuality is about to accrue, moreover . . . when women are seeking individuality with a sort of passion, when they are crying for 'rights' which are all rights to be separate and unmerged in their husbands" ("Moneyed Wives," p. 10). In short, as feminists always claimed, emancipation was not only a matter of fact but also, and perhaps above all, a state of mind.

"Until married women's property is protected by the same laws that protect the property of the rest of her Majesty's subjects, it is idle to talk of the emancipation of women" ("Married Women's Property," ATYR, XXIV, 89). So, clearly and concisely, did one contemporary sum up the issue involved in property law reform. The Married Women's Property Acts gave to wives this equal protection under the law, and their passage was clearly a landmark on Victorian women's road to liberation.

# 2. The Forgotten Woman of the Period

## Penny Weekly Family Magazines of the 1840's and 1850's

~

### Sally Mitchell

THE VICTORIAN NOVEL AS WE KNOW IT WAS WRITTEN BY, FOR, AND LARGELY about the 60,000 or so families who could afford a guinea for a year's library subscription[1] or a shilling a month to buy a new book as it came out in parts or in a magazine. The customs and values of the established middle class are preserved in these novels and in memoirs, diaries, letters, history, and laws. The lives of the poor are recorded—if largely through middle-class eyes—in parliamentary blue books, sanitary investigations, and the works of sociologists, muckrakers, and novelists-with-a-purpose. By the beginning of the Victorian period the industrial working class existed as a distinct group with mores and traditions largely established, and available to us through the work of recent historians. But there still remains a segment of the population which is largely forgotten. They were people too busy earning and cooking their daily bread to write about themselves, and successful enough at it that no one mounted investigations to find out how they survived or if they were likely to make a revolution. They did not lead public lives; their women in particular were, in this era, more and more withdrawn from any direct contact with national economic life into an increasingly private sphere.

One place that we can gain some understanding of them is in their own reading matter. The people between the two nations—the shopkeepers, tradesmen and artisans, the clerks and accountants demanded by the expansion and consolidation of business and government, the engineers and technicians of the new trades, the dressmakers and tradeswomen and superior servants and innkeepers—supplied the audience for mass literature. The most widely read publications in

England in the 1840's and 1850's were the *London Journal* (1845–1912) and the *Family Herald* (1842–1939).[2] They were, significantly, neither cheap reading of the crime-and-passion variety nor women's magazines, but family magazines. In their overwhelming popularity we discover the existence of a group in the process of developing characteristics that we define as Victorian. The mass readership was made up of people with aspirations for respectability, and the mass magazine both directed and reflected woman's role in a period when the pattern of femininity was taking on a new character.

The mass audience was drawn from the most rapidly expanding segment of the population. Economic growth increased the opportunity for mobility. Urbanization—with the 1851 census, more than half of the population of England was, for the first time, living in cities—altered the pattern of social relationships. Family structure had been changed by the removal of production from the home consequent to the industrial revolution: women lost their primary economic function and men took on the role of provider. And, if one were neither so poor as to need to send children to the factory at seven nor so well-to-do as to make nursery-maids, governesses, and boarding schools inevitable, the woman in the home took on responsibility for the supervision of a much longer childhood. The woman who had a little leisure for reading was, to an extent, socialized through what she read; the woman isolated at home with her children socialized in turn the next generation. And so the best-selling magazines are of interest to us because they provided the common background and shared experiences of the silent, respectable, aspiring, forgotten women of the period.

This chapter is an examination of the *London Journal* and the *Family Herald* during the 1840's and 1850's. The first part discusses the circulation, staff, finances, audience, and function of the magazines. The second part examines the values expressed in the fiction they printed. And finally, a discussion of the differences between the specifically sexual stories in the two magazines brings out some of the contradictions and paradoxes in the mass image of woman. The study is limited to the first two decades of the Victorian era; first, because it is the period of greatest change and second, because during that period the *London Journal* and the *Family Herald* dominated the mass market. By the 1870's the audience had fragmented. The elimination of the stamp tax made newspapers competitive; there were public libraries and inexpensive reprints of new novels; and there were special interest magazines for those of various ages and sexes.[3]

Mass literature became a commercial possibility at about the time Queen Victoria ascended the throne. High-speed presses and cheaper paper lowered the cost of printing; stereotyping permitted the production of large quantities with only one setting of type; railways allowed the cultivation of a national audience. A number of publishers recognized that the same profit could be made by selling a magazine to thirty thousand people at a penny each instead of to three thousand at sixpence[4] and that a lot more people could afford to spend a penny than could part with a larger sum. In 1840 seventy-eight magazines costing twopence or less were issued in one week.[5] By the mid-fifties the *Family Herald* and the *London Journal* dominated the market; their combined sale was at least three quarters of a million copies per week. If most of these issues were read aloud in the family or passed along to friends, one of the two magazines must have reached nearly one person in three among the literate population.[6] (By way of comparison, the Dickens novel with the greatest immediate sale was *The Old Curiosity Shop* (1840–41) at 100,000 per part.)[7]

The successful formula for mass sales was to provide something for everyone. An issue of the *London Journal* or the *Family Herald* contained sixteen quarto-sized pages jammed with fine print. There would be an installment of an adventurous serial—in the early years both magazines relied heavily on the works of Alexandre Dumas and Eugene Sue—a piece of short fiction or a true-life adventure, and a page of answers to correspondents on personal, legal, and medical problems. There was usually some improving article—an essay on history or biography or antiquity—and often a piece on a contemporary social or economic problem. And there were odds and ends of filler material: household hints, recipes, puzzles or riddles, and reports of factual oddities.

On the surface the chief difference between the two leading magazines is that the *London Journal's* front page usually carried a dramatic woodcut illustrating the serial and the *Family Herald's* did not. The superficial difference provides a clue to the tone of the two magazines. The *Family Herald*, established in 1842, was not only the first true mass publication in England (that is, it was the first to be composed and printed entirely by machine),[8] it was also the earliest cheap magazine to use "family" in its title. The title and the lack of

*Cover illustration, 5 September 1846.*

illustrations gave it a respectable aura. Three out of four letters printed in the correspondence column came from women. The week's leading short story was often about children who go to the aid of long-estranged sisters or keep the household together during mother's illness or father's business failure. The social problem articles were more likely to be about adulterated food than unhealthy working conditions. One regular feature was a page of "parlour magic and pastimes."

The *London Journal,* founded in 1845, was by reputation more "trashy" than the *Family Herald;*[9] it was also more serious. The reputation is probably based on the front-page woodcuts illustrating the often-violent serials, and it is perhaps because the magazine was more extreme—more sensational—that it was less timid about social questions. It ran a long series entitled "The Influence of Employments on Health" and, in 1848, another filled with practical advice on emigration. Its authors wrote about history and science in full-length articles rather than snippets; it ran a basic French course for several years. The letters column reveals a preponderance of male inquiries, at least in the early years.

The audience for these magazines was drawn primarily from those who clustered around the boundary line between working and middle classes. They included the petty bourgeoisie and the labor aristocracy, but the rapid expansion in their ranks during the 1840's and 1850's came with the creation of clerical, technical, and supervisory jobs that had hardly existed a generation earlier. To build rail lines by the hundreds in the late 1840's required thousands of navvies, but it also called for surveyors, instrument-makers, bookkeepers, paymasters, deputy supervisors, draftsmen, station masters. When the *London Journal* carried matrimonial advertisements for a time in the early fifties, the "unhappy bachelors" included a merchant's clerk with £130 a year, a surveyor with £295, a junior in an engineer's office at £100, one in a government office at £350, a merchant with £200, and a clerk who earned only £70 but, at age thirty, was willing to take a wife up to forty. One "gentlemanly" man with twenty-four shillings a week (the average wage for, say, a cotton spinner or a miner) was told by the editor that it was too little to marry on.

The audience for the penny family magazines was an audience of changing aspirations, expectations, and opportunities. New jobs and new social relationships were open to individuals whose literacy gave them the necessary qualifications. The people who wrote letters to the *London Journal* and the *Family Herald* wanted to know how to get into the customs office, the post office, the police force, technical apprenticeships, art schools, and journalism; how to get a passport, a song published, an invention patented; how to learn grammar, optics, languages. The readership crossed class lines defined either economically or socially: the common denominator was the aspiration for respectability. Clerks might be paid less than £1 a week—Bob Cratchit earned only sixteen shillings—but a clerk would not think of himself as working class. A lot of men whose work was manual and more or less dirty earned at least twice Cratchit's income: railway engine drivers, shipwrights, instrument makers, compositors, cabinet-makers, and others. The price of many basic commodities fell after 1848. It became possible for a skilled worker to choose whether to drink or to spend his money for possessions. He crossed a social line when he bought a carpet and a piano and started to worry about crime in the streets and schools for his children.[10]

The mass magazines provided, both intentionally and unintentionally, the commonly shared information, attitudes, and emotional reactions that delineate respectability. The readers of the *London Journal* and the *Family Herald* actively sought information about the values, standards, and mechanical details of living in a milieu which was new to them. Their letters to the correspondence column reveal their conscious mobility. They want to eradicate the traces of their origin that linger in their grammar and pronunciation. They ask the kind of questions about etiquette and general knowledge that would be impossible for anyone with a polite background and more than a rudimentary education. The advertisers urge them to buy textbooks, life assurance, and fashion magazines, to learn elocution, French, Italian, and music.

The *London Journal's* matrimonial advertisements can be seen as an attempt to fill a second role which is ordinarily the function of a social group, though there was, apparently, no machinery for actually putting the correspondents in touch with one another. Changing social position isolated individuals. Ambitious men moved educationally and often physically away from their local roots. And if they became, in the process, too respectable to pick up girls in pubs and dance halls, their female counterparts had even fewer resources. Small farmers' daughters, no longer essential to the work of house and dairy, were sent to boarding school; they returned with tastes and culture that could not be satisfied by village boys. In urban areas one of the first impulses of the newly prosperous was to keep the girls at home and educate them

*A Widening Sphere*

in polite accomplishments at an age when their brothers had already begun apprenticeships or business life.[11] Women of this sort were becoming culture-bearers; they looked down on the men they knew. Both men and women were changing their aspirations. The press provided information and social contacts—if only imaginative social contacts—which would ordinarily be found in a stable social group.

The third role which the penny magazines played in the consolidation of a mass audience was that of creating a shared background and outlook. Because they had read the same fiction, literally millions of people were supplied with emotional experiences that they held in common. The effect must have been particularly important for women. Their educations were narrow. They were relatively housebound; they were not freed from their chores by a staff of servants, nor did they pay month-long visits, nor did they live in the streets and the gin-shop like the nonrespectable poor. Such women read in part for escape; the most blatantly romantic and aristocratic serials often supplied a personal vehicle for the escapist by featuring a character with whom the reader could identify—a poor relative, a foundling, or humble governess. Because such fiction included characters whose moral standards and habits of mind the reader was willing to take for her own, she found a confirmation of her own values as well as an escape from what was unsatisfactory in her surroundings. The vast circulation of the magazines assisted in the formation of a pool of common material for private fantasy.

Can we assume that popular literature, by virtue of its popularity, reflects what the readers want to hear and expresses their own mores? Or do the values purveyed in the penny magazines derive rather from the attempt of editors, authors, and publishers to impose their own values on the mass audience?

Both papers were business ventures. The *Family Herald,* in fact, was started primarily to give employment to the newly developed compositing machine in which its publisher had a financial interest. The publisher of each paper hired at the outset an editor with some following in the working class. James Elimalet ("Shepherd") Smith of the *Family Herald* had in 1833 edited Robert Owen's journal *The Crisis,* though he soon left Owen to promulgate his own "universal religion."[12] The first editor of the *London Journal* was G. W. M. Reynolds, known as a Chartist and as the author of best-selling penny dreadfuls.[13] There is little direct reflection of Reynolds' radicalism in the *London Journal*—the penny magazines were barred by the Stamp

Act from comment on news or politics—and when he left the paper at the end of 1846 he was succeeded by John Wilson Ross, a university-educated dabbler in classical scholarship and esthetics whose qualification as editor of a popular magazine lay chiefly in his ability to translate Feval. Nevertheless, both G. W. M. Reynolds and "Shepherd" Smith were men of distinctive political and moral views; they wrote the answers to the correspondents and they formed the general tone of the two magazines.

They did not, however, read all of the stories that they printed, and it is more difficult to discover what part authors' inbred biases or overt purposes may have played in the moral content of the fiction. Most of the short stories are either anonymous or printed under a pseudonym or a name that is impossible to trace. A few of the serialists can be discovered in biographical references. One, Thomas Miller, came from the class he wrote for: he was a basket-maker by trade. The others were for the most part professional journalists inhabiting a faintly Bohemian world. J. F. Smith was the son of a theatrical manager, did some acting in his youth, and wrote melodrama as well as fiction. Mrs. Grey worked as an editor for Lloyd of Salisbury Square; she wrote penny dreadfuls for him and also turned out three-volume novels suitable for the middle-class lending libraries. Bracebridge Hemyng (whose father was a civil administrator in India) did the interviews with prostitutes for Henry Mayhew and later became an immensely prolific writer of adventure stories for boys' magazines.

Even professionals, however, could not automatically produce what the mass reader demanded. Charles Reade was the only reputable writer of the period to make an acknowledged contribution to one of these two papers. His serial, we are told, "nearly wrecked" the *London Journal*.[14] Reade was adept at supplying plot and incident, but he failed to create characters with whom the reader could empathize. The successful authors must have been those who had, perhaps instinctively, a sympathy with the popular mind.

For whatever the editors or authors may have tried in an attempt to shape the values of penny magazine readers, the final argument is essentially a financial one. Despite the technological advances mentioned earlier, publishers had to attract a lot of buyers in order to cut the price of sixteen large pages weekly down to a penny and still make a profit. A middlebrow magazine like *Blackwoods*, which sold for half a crown, was doing well when it reached a circulation of six or eight thousand; a penny weekly needed to sell in the neighborhood of thirty thousand copies to meet the fixed expenses (i.e., typesetting, payments to contributors, distribution, etc.)[15] A number of earnest periodicals conducted by reformers like William and Mary Howitt and Mrs. S. C. Hall or by church and pure literature societies imitated the popular format in an attempt to fill the demand for cheap reading with something which was scrupulously wholesome and which had a religious, moral, or economic product to sell. Few of them reached enough buyers to be self-sustaining.[16] The *London Journal* and the *Family Herald* were run not by societies but by publishers whose object was to make money. They were astonishingly successful at it; the *London Journal* at one point is said to have had an annual profit exceeding £10,000 and the proprietor of the *Family Herald* left legacies of nearly £50,000 when he died in 1859.[17]

It is instructive to look briefly at a periodical that tried for three years to compete with the leaders, changing its tone and emphasis several times in the process. The first issue of *The Penny Satirist and London Pioneer* carried the motto "The Greatest Happiness of the Greatest Number." It was successor to *The Penny Satirist* (1837–46), a broadsheet of the sort which had, earlier in the century, featured crudely satiric and often sexual jokes about the aristocracy and royal family. *The Penny Satirist* itself was only moderately scurrilous; both its publisher and its editor, B. D. Cousins and "Shepherd" Smith, were former associates of Robert Owen. Their motive may have been to disseminate among broadsheet readers their own brand of equalitarian iconoclasm, though Smith later said that "the principal use of such papers is for opening the trade" among an audience not much in the habit of buying literature.[18]

By 1845 *The Penny Satirist* had lost most of its circulation to the new magazine-style periodicals. The name and format were changed in order to compete. Nevertheless, the word "Pioneer" in the title, linked as it is with the cooperative movement, still carried radical overtones, and the first issue began with an ironic, gently antiroyalist "Court Circular." The broadsheet tradition persisted further to the extent that there was nearly always a story about illicit sex, usually involving the upper classes. The prurience has an air of smugness; the reader is constantly assured that it is evil for aristocrats to be so wicked. The advice in the letters column is more sternly moralistic than in either of the other two papers.

Before long "The Penny Satirist" was dropped from the title;

the magazine became simply the *London Pioneer* and moved more directly onto the *London Journal*'s territory; the two papers ran simultaneously the same serial by Eugene Sue, and the *Pioneer* followed it with one entitled "The Outcasts of London; or Pauline the Victim of Crime."[19] Both title and content reveal the influence of G. W. M. Reynolds's penny-issue novel *The Mysteries of London,* which was then in the midst of its highly successful career. The heroine of "The Outcasts of London" is the ward of the president of a "Council of Crime" which plans most of the robberies and burglaries in the city. Minute detail about the criminal world and equally flamboyant exposés of the morals of the aristocracy and clergy provide the action. When a fashionable minister tries to rape Pauline the images and clichés are straight out of contemporary pornography: "despite her violent struggles and her piercing screams, he placed her beside him on a soft, crimson velvet couch, which stood opposite to a splendid mirror. . . ."[20] The seed of envy inside this sort of story is only too obvious; despite the repeated diatribes against the upper classes Pauline is ultimately discovered to be the legitimate heiress of a baronet.

"The Outcasts of London" is a fine example of serial construction, with the heroine in peril at the end of virtually every installment, yet even while it was running the paper underwent a change in tone. The subtitle became "A Journal of Progression in Science, Literature, and all that tends to Instruct and Amuse the Human Race." Correspondents' criticism forced the editor on to the defensive; it was necessary to write about vice, he insisted, to show how unattractive and unrewarding it was. The tale was not mere sensational invention; it was based on "the confessions of a police officer."[21]

It is hard to see why the proprietors would have given up the "Pauline" sort of tale if it were selling well. They may have discovered that the audience massive enough to support a penny magazine simply didn't have sufficiently broad tastes. At any rate, the *Pioneer* began actively to cultivate its readership among women. It printed quieter, more domestic short fiction. The correspondence column came to be dominated by women asking questions about manners, proprieties, and personal problems. With the beginning of volume three the title became *The London Literary Pioneer* and the subtitle "Family Journal of Amusement and Utility." Two years earlier the paper had regularly run antiroyalist satire; the first issue of the third volume had a large pictorial fold-out of "The Royal Family at Home."

But did women want only to read about the home? In July 1848 the *Pioneer* featured a series of tales about heroic women from history. The concluding installment argues that the good life for women "does *not* consist in treating them as idols to be worshipped, or as trinkets to be worn for display. . . . The days of chivalry are gone; but it is our misfortune . . . to retain many of its false rules and objectionable customs." The secret of emancipation for women is to recognize that the creator "in his wisdom, never placed a flower, or a rock, much less a human being, in a position in which it lacked the power to sustain itself."[22]

In context even this appeal to feminine economic and intellectual independence is startling. The year was 1848, the subject was in the air, and the *Family Herald* contribution was a poem beginning "'The rights of women'—what are they?/ The right to labour and to pray . . ." and concluding with an espousal of "The path of patience under wrong;/ The path in which the weak grow strong."[23] Apparently the time was not yet ripe for the *Pioneer*'s alternative. In September the magazine added a fashion page as a last attempt to find out what its readers really wanted. The issue of October 21 carried complaints from subscribers in Cheltenham, Lancaster, Bristol, Barnet, and the Isle of Wight about their inability to get the paper from local news agents, and by the end of the year it was no more.

The *Pioneer* had tried the range in its search for enough readers to keep it alive. It is impossible to discover to what extent bad management and distribution may have hindered its prosperity, but apparently neither extreme—overt sexuality of incipient feminism—struck a chord with a mass audience. What the really large number of readers wanted to hear fell somewhere in between, in the territory occupied by the *London Journal* and the *Family Herald*.


## II


For a clearer view of the values purveyed in the two leading penny magazines we must turn to their fiction. The serials in this period were usually of foreign origin or featured aristocratic characters in a picturesque historical period. The shorter stories, on the other hand, sometimes had an urban English setting and characters who did some sort of work for a living; they were frequently subtitled "A Story From Real Life." Even so, we do not discover much direct information about the lives and habits of penny magazine readers; real life is sweetened and purified and (usually) given a happy ending. Perhaps it does not ultimately matter whether these stories were intended to supply models to imitate or whether they do reflect attitudes already held by the readers. What such fiction does provide is an experience of life held in common by the audience of the millions. The stories are not simply tracts; we perceive the values in the selection of character, subject, and resolution.

Upward mobility may explain why there was not sufficient interest in the world of Pauline—it was not only too close and too threatening but it was unrewarding. The "realistic" short stories usually feature characters of a slightly higher social class than the reader; the tradesman's daughter read about the merchant's daughter to learn how she behaved. Another extremely common heroine is the officer's orphan working as governess. She need not be a bridge into the social elite; her employer is sometimes a grocer instead of a lord. She is an attractive model, for she demonstrates to the woman of narrow means that ladyhood is not dependent on income, nor destroyed by the necessity of working, but lies in manners and bearing.

The values expressed are not wholly identical with those of middle-class light fiction. Marriage across class lines is one regular theme. The subsurface content is a variety of democratic individualism: people should be judged for their own worth and achievement, not by who their parents are. The issue frequently hinges on the perseverance and faithfulness of a woman who defies family and society and waits until her lover has earned his fortune and so removed the social bars. The class difference is often more apparent than real; when, for example, the squire's daughter marries the groom, he turns out to have a wealthy uncle and inherits enough money to retrieve the fortunes of his now bankrupt father-in-law.[24] But when the heroine succumbs to family pressure and makes a "correct" marriage, the result is nearly always misery; the socially suitable mate is a bounder and the outcast prospers.[25]

Another difference from middle-class fiction, and again one tending toward a stronger image for women, is that the stories in the penny magazines do not usually make a point of the stigma of work outside the home for an unmarried woman. Employed heroines may be oppressed by the dullness or difficulty of a job but seldom by its disgrace. Heroines frequently work for a while and then marry a man who is happy to have a useful woman around the house. Other differences between the aura of this fiction and its middle-class equivalent are more subtle. Penny magazine heroines do not demonstrate their virtue and social concern by visiting the poor or teaching in the schools. Religion, churchgoing, and curates do not figure much.

On the other hand, there are almost no direct criticisms of middle-class values except for those which are also commonly expressed in standard Victorian fiction; both library novel and penny magazine, for example, are against social pretense and conspicuous spending. And only seldom, in allusive undercurrents, do we find any reflection of working-class values. In one story laid in Ireland a peasant girl refuses the proposal of a self-made English M.P. whom she had loved when he was young and poor because she would not be at ease with the incongruity of rank and religion and because, more importantly, she despises the part he had taken in bringing an Irish rebel to justice.[26] Class solidarity may be expressed here under the coloration of national and religious differences.

The values expressed by the mass magazines are intended to be broadly acceptable. There is a vaguely Christian theism, but no theology of any sort; there is a promise made by the *London Journal* in the first issue never to "offend with political bias, or interfere with domestic tranquility."[27] The latter phrase can be taken in two ways, but the *London Journal* surely intended it in the narrower sense. The central image of Victorianism is the enclosed family; it provided an escape from the disorder and confusion of the world into the perfection of a miniature, individually-created social order.

Yet the very image of the family as a social order was based on a paradox. Women were inferior to men and were therefore to be submissive, protected, and supervised; women were superior to men—in moral and spiritual qualities—and were therefore to be deferred to. The tensions of this paradox were constantly delineated in the fiction. Should a wife conceal something from a husband for his own good? Should she ask for a separate household allowance so that she can plan her expenditures? Should she obey his requests if others will be harmed? The resolutions are mixed: sometimes the husband learns to love her for her moral superiority; sometimes she learns to love him by making sacrifice of her own independent personality.

Romantic love has always been the substance of popular literature. What is striking in this fiction is that the family looms so large as an image just at the moment in time and point in class at which it was no longer an imperative unit. So long as industry had remained in the cottage, the wife at her loom was an economic partner. In rural areas, for another generation, nearly everything that was consumed by a laborer's family was produced at home. Among the urban working poor the wife's income gave her an obvious share in the family's survival. Marriage and premarital chastity were less important since the household itself had a function.[28]

The idealization of family life in the penny weekly magazines helped to define and justify a new role for women who had lost their economic value. One aspect of the role was motherhood. Penny magazine fiction reveals less paternalism (in the strictest sense) than one might expect: fathers are often wrong; children defy them and women defy them for the children's sake and it sometimes turns out well. Both magazines printed stories about the effect of childhood experience on adult character. Motherhood provided woman with both a useful function and a sphere for her moral superiority.

The family mystique served another function: Victorian psychology found it possible to deal with woman's sexual longing most easily in terms of the maternal instinct. The men in these stories are curiously colorless, even considering the stereotyped nature of the characters in general. It was perhaps dangerous for the imagination to dwell on the qualities of men. The physical instinct was sublimated in fantasies of the family .

Finally, and cold-bloodedly, the family provided economic security. Single working women in this period were usually balanced, at best, on the fringes of poverty. Penny magazine fiction was escape literature, presenting life not as it was but as readers wanted it to be. Even though almost forty percent of the women between twenty and forty-four were unmarried and the female redundancy caused by male emigration probably hit hardest at the ambitious working class,[29] the family magazines did not depict alternatives for the woman who remained single: they fed, instead, the fantasy that love and marriage would eventually come, bringing in train emotional fulfillment, legal and economic protection, and a satisfactory place in the social system.

## III

The difference between the *Family Herald* and the *London Journal* is most clearly revealed by the manner in which the two magazines approach female sexuality. Because it was a dangerous ground, it is unlikely that readers' emotions remained uninvolved in such stories. More importantly, analyzed in some detail, they almost invariably carry implications about the role of woman in the social and moral system.

The *Family Herald* announced in the first volume that "great poets, such as Shakespeare, Pope, Dryden, Moore, and others, have written many things which we would not print. The public wink at the faults of great men. . . . A periodical for the public must be more discreet than a bound book."[30] In the assumption that the *Family Herald*'s readers would be insulted by any departure from propriety an implicit double standard is struck down. In novels and women's magazines of the preceding period, when it was safe to assume that only the middle and upper classes could read, loss of chastity was a disaster for a woman of the reader's own class but a servant or a shopkeeper's daughter might sometimes reform and marry happily. This dual morality is still evident in many library novels of the 1840's and in Dickens. But the *Family Herald* was written for the shopkeeper's daughter with the tacit assumption that her standards of personal chastity were the same as those of the higher classes. There is none of the preaching that we find in tracts or the *Servant's Magazine*; there are no stories about the horrible fate of women who fall.[31]

The *Family Herald* did not, however, completely ignore the sexual side of human existence. Its readers could not afford to depend on the ignorance of daughters as an assurance of innocence. There were dangers and opportunities unknown in classes where the mother had little to do except watch over her daughters and could spare servants to protect them when they went out. One probable reflection of reality in penny magazine fiction is the frequency with which a man approaches a woman alone on the street. She could not afford to be ignorant of his motives.[32] The *Family Herald* was fairly open in both verse and nonfiction. There is, for example, a chilling reminder of the hazards of job-hunting in an article about a woman who answered an advertisement for a position as lady's companion and received in reply an offer from a man of twenty-five that she "place herself under his protection" in return for "an annual allowance, sufficient to live respectably."[33] The correspondence column offers consoling advice to women who have partaken in carefully-worded activities such as to "anticipate the marriage day."[34]

The *Family Herald*, then, recognized sexual irregularity but didn't print stories about it. On the other hand, neither did it wholly ignore dangerous topics in the manner of religious papers such as the *Leisure Hour*. This fictional purity had a prurient side; recognizing the readers' awareness of sin, and yet refusing to write openly about sin even to punish it, the paper skittered endlessly around the edges of the subject with stories that are intentionally deceptive: the heroine, or her mother, appears to be unchaste, but the story fizzles out in misunderstood appearances, concealed marriages, changes of identity, amnesia, stolen parish registers, and so forth.[35] These stories are sometimes interesting for their portraiture of woman's strength under adversity, but their ultimate message is that form is all-important. It does not matter how the characters treat each other, or how society makes them miserable, if the precious paper is at last found and they are allowed to walk clutching it into the sunrise.

Another common story follows the archetype of the traditional seduction tale but leaves out the crucial event. A young woman loves a man (usually of a higher class); he promises marriage but later loses interest; she dies of poverty and a broken heart. The sin on which the consequences follow is not the sexual act but the confession of love or even the feeling of love before it has been permissibly released by marriage. Take "The Hospital.—A Sketch from Real Life."[36] Francesca Vitelli, the daughter of a Florentine official, falls in love with the English ambassador and, as she tells us, "concealed not my passion." He goes home promising to return quickly, but soon stops writing. She follows him to England, struggles with poverty as an assistant in an artificial flower shop, sees him with his fiancée, sickens, and dies in the hospital of which he is one of the governors. This makes possible an agonizing recognition scene at the end. Successful martyrdom provides a subversive triumph: women are morally and emotionally finer than men, and men's power can be attacked by bringing them to their knees with guilt and remorse and consciousness of their failings. But the overt purpose of the tale is, in the words of the narrator, to illustrate to young women "the fatal consequences which may accrue from the indulgence of that morbid enthusiasm, which many a young female thoughtlessly revels in. . . ."

A remarkable number of stories in the *Family Herald* follow a similar pattern. In "The Lost One"[37] Emily St. Vincent is courted by Henry Seymour, a captain of dragoons. He asks if she loves him. She responds ("trembling violently"), " 'Nay, nay, Seymour! do not press me to make a confession a maiden should not!' " He persists; she admits her love; he kisses her and proposes that they fly. She is, naturally, insulted; he threatens suicide; she reaffirms her love and then faints. "This," says the author, "was the point to which Seymour wished to bring her; his pride was flattered, and he deemed himself master of her soul." We hold our breaths. Nothing happens; he revives her and takes her home.

Emily subsequently marries another man. Her reputation (though explicitly not her virtue) is compromised while her husband is abroad, he demands a separation, she goes insane and dies in childbirth. This is all very rapidly sketched. Her chief indiscretion—certainly the chief incident of the story—is her premarital admission of love. Once Henry Seymour knows of her feelings he is sure that he can lead her to ruin. Even for the Victorians love had a physical as well as an idealistic sense; surely that is what underlies all the talk about love coming only after marriage. The popular magazines do not wholly confirm what we have taken as accepted mid-century medical opinion; i.e., that women probably did not have and certainly were not aware of sexual desire until after they had experienced intercourse.[38] We do have a sense that the characters in these stories felt, even if they didn't necessarily recognize, physical attraction. A woman who loves a man is likely to want to do something about it, and the reader of penny magazines had a degree of opportunity to realize her desires. There is a revealing letter in the *London Journal:* "ANN wishes to know whether she acts imprudently or not, in visiting a young man whom she loves at his lodgings? We answer, without hesitation, very imprudently . . . it is unwise to thrust temptation in the way."[39] We are startled, first of all, that a Victorian woman literate enough to write to a paper would ask the question, and second, that the answer is given not in terms of what the neighbors will think but on the basis of physical probabilities.

The advice columns, it is true, were more frank than the fiction, since they were supposedly free from the emotional overtones that might lead readers to emulation. But the same assumption underlies many stories. Penny magazine readers were not totally hedged about with protection and proprieties. And thus the numerous sentimental scenes at the beside of the technically virtuous young dying of unrequited love, though they may provide a useful outlet for the overwrought feelings of readers whose physical desires are not only frustrated but also unmentionable, have the moral intent of suppressing those feelings. The editor is constantly advising correspondents not to expect anything special in the way of emotional reaction to a suitor; he replies to an orphaned governess who has received a proposal from a man forty years her senior that "it is merely a question of expediency, as marriage in general is; it is 'Can I do better—would it be better to accept a home of this kind than to run the risk of having none at all?' Women all reason thus, and so do men. The ideal of love is never realised; the heart is never thoroughly satisfied; if it is, danger awaits it, for perfect satisfaction is of short duration on this planet."[40] This is a cold-blooded view for a magazine that depended almost entirely on love for the subject matter of its fiction, but it is consistent with the morality of the stories.

A high proportion of the tales in the *Family Herald* are romantic. Wedding bells provide the suitable ending. But despite the sentiment and the sentimentality there is a note—sometimes overt, more often an undercurrent—of antiromanticism and feminine individualism. Some of the most sentimental tales serve to counteract the ethos that woman is properly a creature of the emotions. Woman's goal is marriage, which provides her with station, role, duties, and economic security; anything—including emotion—that interferes with the goal is counterproductive; and it is woman's responsibility to provide for her own happiness.

The *London Journal,* as has been suggested, was less reticent and was more concerned about social questions than the *Family Herald.* The letters column does not mince words in helping readers to cope with the consequences of sexual misadventure. Correspondents regularly ask how to affiliate an illegitimate child, or if the East India Company will force an officer to support his bastard, or if it is legal to marry again if one's wife has disappeared with another man. The *London Journal* also printed stories about sexual irregularity. Nearly all had sordid endings, but the woman's grief and misery were intended as a demonstration of other evils rather than as a simple warning against unchaste behavior.

"A Mother's Sin,"[41] for example, is a lurid tale in the first-person narrative style of the last dying confession broadsheets which had long been sold at public executions. The mother's sin is pride; after the death of her husband, who had earned £300 a year, she will not consider sending her daughters out to work; she keeps the house and takes in lodgers. One of them promptly seduces the eldest daughter (who is called Beauty). Things go rapidly to the worst; Beauty is transported for theft, her sisters take to the streets, and the mother becomes addicted to gin. The final horror cannot quite be revealed: "I cannot tell you how I led on Beauty's daughter. . . . The child I had destroyed. Ah! murder, murder! there is a crime worse than murder." This would lose its point if we did not know of the demand for child prostitutes in Victorian London. William T. Stead opened the horrified and unbelieving eyes of the middle class to the trade later in the century,[42] but presumably the readers of the *London Journal* were expected to take in the implication.

The story reveals other tacit understandings important to the women who read penny magazines. It is quite apparent that a woman unprotected and unprovided for cannot expect to maintain the family's place in the middle class. The mother learned false values from her social aspiration; she raised her daughters "used to better things" and would not retreat by letting them go out to service. She had a choice, within the system, and she erred.

"The Slave of the Needle"[43] more directly condemns the system itself. Henry Mayhew's series on needlewomen, which had appeared in the *Morning Chronicle* a few months earlier (6-23 November 1849), had revealed that a woman with no means of support but needlework almost invariably found it necessary, at least on occasion, to add to her income by prostitution. "The Slave of the Needle" presents an attractive heroine, Annie Lee, who supports her mother by sewing shirts. The reader is intended to identify with Annie; she is quietly dressed, clean, gentle, naturally dainty. After her mother dies Annie falls into a state of depression: she is unable to make herself work, even to buy food. Watkins, the middleman who employs her, buys her a meal. Annie is neither so young nor so innocent as Mrs. Gaskell's Ruth; her mother's dying words had been a warning against men's evil intentions. Watkins is a coarse man; Annie has always been afraid of him. And yet, after food, wine, and above all, human sympathy, she finds herself almost overwhelmed by sexual feelings. The author makes it explicit that a woman may have such feelings quite independent of love and admiration for a man: in a person of essentially loving nature, he says, whose outlet for love has been denied, "appetites, like ravenous beasts of prey, break the laws imposed by religion and social morality. . . ." So far as I know this is, for the period, an unparalleled remark about a chaste and otherwise admirable woman. But the psychological exploration is dropped as quickly as it is raised. The author retreats into economic generalizations about the needle trade. Flattery and need account for Annie's fall. Watkins tires of her,

*The Forgotten Woman of the Period* [ 47

she falls ill and is driven to prostitution, drinks to drown her guilt, and dies. Her death is a release, not a punishment; the author uses woman's degradation to criticize the economic system.

These two stories and others like them portray the social and economic causes that lead to unchastity. More common is the story that deplores the social consequences. The latter type usually begins after the fall and often after the body is fished dripping out of the Thames; the woman is the victim of man's villainous passions, and her miserable end is due not to any flaw in her own character but to a society in which she loses her home and job and is shunned in public. More crudely sensational stories cast the blame not on society but on a single man; sometimes the villain is even a wronged husband. In "Kew Church," for example, the wife has had a child while her husband was away at war. He promptly kills the child "as an offering to the evil spirit of vengeance"; she follows grief-stricken "to that region 'where the wicked cease from troubling and the weary are at rest.' "[44] Here, as often in stories of this type, the plot is so slender that the tale seems only to exist as an exercise in sadness. The urge to weep, the desire to seek occasions and fictions that will bring tears, arises in many at an age or during periods when personal frustrations are, from the nature of things, insoluble. The evident popularity of such stories with the mass audience of the early Victorian period suggests the emotional tension of the woman who perceives wrongs—both socially and in her own situation—but is absolutely without power.

In all of these *London Journal* stories some outside force—the husband, the seducer, the economic system, conventional prudery—destroys the woman's life but not her soul. She has lost her capability for sin; as a victim she is guiltless before God. To treat woman's fall as a social problem rather than a religious one is an attitude which seems progressive, but it has sticky connotations. It depends on a view of woman as a weaker vessel who must be protected rather than as an individual who can be criticized for her errors. She is a victim; she has committed no crime but she must still be punished by death, barring rare instances in which a benevolent man rescues her. In the *London Journal* man may alter events; woman is simply acted upon.

Neither paper, obviously, approved of sex outside of marriage. The stories that even touch on the subject are few in number compared to the easy romances in which the man's worth and the woman's faith triumph in a filled cradle beside the hearth. But the ones that do appear reveal a fundamental division in the conception of woman's role.

THE

# LONDON JOURNAL;

### And Weekly Record of Literature, Science, and Art.

88. Vol. IV.]        FOR THE WEEK ENDING OCTOBER 31, 1846.        [PRICE ONE PENNY.

*Cover illustration, 31 October 1846.*

[ 49

The *London Journal* is moral in a broader sense than the specifically prudish; many of its stories demonstrate a social concern which is parallel to the development of the social problem novel in the same period. But the actual content of such stories is almost always pity for the victims of social injustice rather than an attack on its causes; even in "The Slave of the Needle" nothing is said about the foundation of the sweated labor system, nor does the author follow Mayhew to the extent of mentioning that the enormous government contracts for uniforms were almost entirely filled by this method. Furthermore, the image of woman in the sexual stories is one of utter helplessness. To treat her as a social problem excludes her from the doctrine of self-help that dominates the instructive departments of the *London Journal.*

A man, in *London Journal* fiction, faced with a crisis similar to Annie Lee's finds it possible to do something to improve his situation— he learns shorthand and gets a better job, saves the banker's daughter from a fire, takes the shilling and comes back a hero from the Crimea. But women are forbidden such individual effort: if they rise in the world it is only through marriage. The possibility of making broad changes in the social or economic condition of a larger group through organization does not play any significant role. The author of "The Slave of the Needle" raises the spectre of outcast power only to make it both horrid and futile—in the person of a toothless, haggard, gin-besodden crone who hovers about Mrs. Lee's deathbed hoping that she can be roused to "curse the monster" (man, and the male-created economic system) before she dies. "I do daily," she says, "but I want the curse of a good heart to blight them." The only potential solution offered is an appeal to the hearts of good women—but given the narrow household budgets of *London Journal* readers, it seems rather futile to hope that individuals will stop buying the cheap shirts produced by sweated labor.

This ambivalence illuminates the paradox that lay beneath the ideal of the pure, moral, family-centered woman. Man recognized sexuality in himself and felt guilty about it. Aggression, competitiveness, and hard-heartedness were necessary for worldly success—and yet they, too, were qualities in conflict with religion and social conscience. And so the ideal was expressed in the person of the woman enclosed within the family. There, fulfilling her duty to her husband, she could be free of the taint of sexual desire; there, because she lacked selfishness, she could create the peace in which moral virtues could rule. But it was only possible within the security of the family. Woman could not possess the aggressive qualities needed to compete in the world and still retain moral superiority. Without male protection she must be helpless.[45]

The *Family Herald,* which lacks even the social awareness of the *London Journal,* seems at first glance to crystallize the reactive prudery of readers fighting for respectability. Yet the stories that deal with the unchaste woman by analogy—the stories in which she sins by love rather than fornication—do suggest that women are responsible for their own destinies. Security and happiness are in the woman's hands; all men are not ideal and it is up to her to preserve her bargaining counters and her rational judgment untouched by emotional considerations in order to see quite clearly what she is getting into.

Neither magazine proposed any role for woman outside of marriage. The *London Journal's* correspondence editor could be insufferably paternalistic about it, as in his advice to a stage-struck girl: "Turn your attention to matrimony . . . Nothing rationalizes the mind quicker than marriage; and we recommend it as a certain cure for those little follies which, somehow or other, manage to creep into the wilful heads of our young women."[46] But when the *Family Herald* remarks that for women to meddle in politics would be as inappropriate as for husbands "to turn us out of our kitchens, and take upon themselves to lecture us on the most approved method of flavoring a hash or manufacturing an apple-dumpling"[47] the expression has an air of satisfied vigor: it deals with woman's sphere, in which she is competent, rather than woman's place. The penny magazines played a part in creating the wife-and-mother ideal for women whose mothers and grandmothers had filled a different role, but they did not do it unilaterally.[48] Popular magazines owed at least part of their popularity to repeating what the woman who read them wanted to hear. She knew about the harsh and unrewarding reality of the market for female labor; she wanted something else. The home did not yet give her enough leisure to feel restive; in its confines, and particularly in the nurture of children, she had useful work to do. The family magazine's vision of ideal life purified and ennobled set forth a system of values which convinced the forgotten woman that she was important. If there was some additional subliminal effect—if the *London Journal* taught social sympathy and the *Family Herald* encouraged individual self-interest—both contained possibilities for the future of women in the nineteenth century.

# 3. Feminism and Female Emigration, 1861-1886

A. James Hammerton

THE UNMARRIED MIDDLE-CLASS WOMAN IS BY NOW ONE OF THE BETTER-known figures of Victorian social history. Recognized by Victorians as a social and often moral problem, and frequently sensationalized in contemporary literature, the plight of the young, genteel spinster has rivaled the women's suffrage movement as a traditional focus for the study of women in history. The main features of the problem are fairly clear-cut. Middle-class female education was governed by expectations of marriage, yet the increasing percentage of women over men during the nineteenth century put marriage beyond the reach of thousands of women. For the middle-class victims of this process, particularly those whose families had suffered a serious decline in fortune, the need for another respectable source of support was frequently urgent but rarely fulfilled. The result was the "distressed gentlewoman," judged by her society to have "failed in business"[1] and forced to demean herself by seeking employment for which she had little or no training. One of the few ill-paid outlets available to her was teaching, and this remained so for many years after the feminists began their campaign for wider employment opportunities in the late fifties. Consequently we owe most of our knowledge of the distressed gentlewoman to discussion of the governess; apart from marriage and motherhood Victorian society offered little in the way of a realistic alternative.

Emigration was, however, one outlet Victorians regarded with increasing seriousness after the 1850's. For a variety of reasons the number of single, middle-class female emigrants was never large enough to affect the social and demographic problem in Britain significantly, but the promotion of female emigration and its results certainly warrant serious analysis.[2] Between 1862 and 1914 voluntary societies helped more than twenty thousand women of various classes to emigrate to the British colonies. The records of these societies provide a rich source for the study of both middle-class emigrants and middle-class promoters of emigration. The first of these societies, the Female Middle Class Emigration Society, operated from 1862 to 1886. Numerically its achievements were slight compared with those of its successors, for in twenty-four years it helped only 302 women to emigrate. But unlike the later societies, the F.M.C.E.S. was a feminist organization; its activities touched feminist principles at some sensitive points and brought to the surface some deeply held feminist opinions on class, employment, and marriage. This chapter will therefore examine the relationship at these points between feminism and middle-class female emigration, and it will attempt to determine the extent to which the feminists established emigration as a realistic outlet for Victorian distressed gentlewomen.

## I

The early activities of the middle-class feminist movement in the late fifties were the immediate cause of the first serious attempt to encourage middle-class women to emigrate. The founding of a feminist journal,[3] the participation of women and sympathetic men in the annual congresses of the National Association for the Promotion of Social Science, and the encouragement from prominent women such as Harriet Martineau[4] all stimulated the rapid development of a movement aimed particularly at ending the exclusion of women from serious education and middle-class occupations. From the beginning the middle-class feminists—or "Ladies of Langham Place"—faced some awkward questions of priorities. Feminist speakers at the early Social Science Congresses were preoccupied with the need to find wider employment opportunities outside the overcrowded trades of teaching and needlework.[5] But they agreed that they must give female education priority before they could "open a fair field to the powers and energies we have educed" (Martineau, p. 336). In the meantime thousands of ill-educated women needed immediate work. Bessie Parkes, the editor of the *English Woman's Journal*, asked whether "we are trying to tide the female population of this country over a time of difficulty, or are we seeking to develop a new state of social life?" (TNAPSS, 1862, pp. 808–809). Most feminists worked vigorously toward both ends, and a long-term campaign for higher education and professional qualifications coexisted with a search for short-term palliatives to alleviate the pressing employment problems.

The search for new forms of employment available to young ladies, however, was beset with difficulties. The feminist Society for Promoting the Employment of Women, founded in 1859, recognized that teaching was becoming a more precarious occupation for untrained distressed gentlewomen.[6] By the 1860's it was more difficult than ever for a woman with a superficial education to become a governess. The new secondary schools for women founded after 1848 had quickly become prestige institutions catering largely to the upper middle class.[7] Many of their graduates took up teaching as a serious profession, and very soon their superior qualifications did much "to raise the standard and improve the tone of education generally"; by the 1860's they had become the generally accepted standard for governesses.[8] Sarah Harland, a mathematics lecturer at Newnham College, observed later that "the usual opening for impecunious gentlewomen, that of teaching, had been taken up by others with higher qualifications for the work, who are without the impulse of poverty" (TNAPSS, 1884, pp. 417–18). The Employment Society's initial policy, therefore, was to give more suspect occupations a new air of respectability and thereby open them to women of a higher social class. They concentrated on manual occupations from which most Victorian young ladies would shrink. The earliest openings came in telegraph offices, printing, lithography, hair-dressing, and various semi-menial vocations.[9] But with the exception of law-copying and bookkeeping most of these new opportunities appealed primarily to socially mobile women from the lower middle class. Bessie Parkes estimated in 1860 that these "less refined" women constituted one third of the middle-class female work force. She added that most of the "semi-mechanical employments" so assiduously promoted by the feminist employment societies were only suitable for this class; the salary of a telegraph clerk, after all, hardly allowed her to look and live "like a lady."[10] The mass of untrained distressed gentlewomen were consequently helped little by the first ad hoc measures to relieve the pressure for employment, and they were invariably forced back into some form of underpaid teaching.

Office work provided one of the few new outlets that would not compromise a lady's gentility, and significantly it was the overwhelming demand for such employment among gentlewomen that led the feminists to promote emigration. Maria S. Rye had these women in mind when she opened a law-copying office in Lincoln's Inn Fields as a branch of the Employment Society. Recruiting women as copyists was a simple matter. Rye was inundated with applications and on one occasion 810 women applied for a single position paying only £15 a year. Faced with this situation, she quite independently advised and assisted the applicants to emigrate, and in 1861, without any formal organization, she helped twenty-two educated women to reach various colonies by providing loans and arranging for their protection and reception.[11] The emigration idea spread rapidly among the feminist circle at the Social Science Association and the employment societies, who initially saw it as a panacea for women of a "superior class" who were unemployable in Britain. At the Social Science Congress in 1860 Bessie Parkes argued that many women, unsuited to the "semi-mechanical arts," required

a wider field of intellectual and moral exertion than the compositor's case or the law copyist's desk can afford; and seeing, as I do daily, how great is the comparative delicacy both in brain and in the bodily frames of women of the middle and upper class of the bad effect on them of long hours of sedentary toil, and of the supreme difficulty of introducing them in great numbers into the fields of competitive employment, the more anxious I become to see the immense surplus of the sex in England lightened by judicious, well-conducted, and morally guarded emigration to our colonies, where the disproportion is equally enormous, and where they are wanted in every social capacity.

She hoped that large-scale emigration would allow the remaining gentlewomen in Britain to be trained "in all those functions of administrative benevolence, which are in fact but a development of household qualities" (TNAPSS, 1860, p. 818).

At the 1861 Social Science Congress Maria Rye described her work and appealed for help in establishing a formal society to promote the emigration of educated women. Like Bessie Parkes, she viewed emigration as the basic solution to the problem of distressed gentlewomen in Britain, and she expected that the colonies would benefit equally, "an elevation of morals being the inevitable result of the mere presence in the colony of a number of high class women." Unlike Parkes, however, she already had some experience of female emigration and had communicated with interested persons in Australia, New Zealand, and Natal who had impressed upon her their great need for domestic servants. To meet this need she suggested that a dual emigration system of gentlewomen and "superior servants" might be established. The various colonial immigration schemes strictly excluded all women above the working class. She therefore advocated a system of loans to a variety of middle-class women, with a network of representatives in each colony to receive the emigrants and arrange suitable employment.[12] At the same meeting the other speakers, including the General Secretary, G. W. Hastings, made enthusiastic reference to emigration as the "best and natural solution" and the "truest remedy" for educated women (TNAPSS, 1861, pp. xlii, 632, 686). Rye's efforts culminated in the formation of the Female Middle Class Emigration Society in May 1862, but in the meantime the rapid publication of her paper as a separate pamphlet and its appearance in the *English Woman's Journal* publicized the subject beyond feminist circles, and a popular debate ensued in *The Times* on the merits of female emigration.

Despite its general tone of approval,[13] the press debate soon revealed that female emigration was unlikely to proceed without encountering practical difficulties and public controversy. The first difficulty had bedeviled earlier efforts to send single gentlewomen to the colonies.[14] It arose from frequent assertions that there was insufficient colonial demand for working gentlewomen, especially for governesses. "J.K. A Returned Australian Governess" described to *The Times* how she was forced to do daily needlework in Melbourne because of the sparse demand for governesses, and finally returned to England on the proceeds of a subscription raised by her friends (24 April 1862). Other letters warned against sending governesses to Australia without prearranged employment, and 's.G.O.' (Lord Osborne) suggested that the women most in need of emigration would be least qualified to fill the position of really competent governesses. To send out women who were useless to the colonies would be worse folly than to send convicts (23, 28, and 30 April 1862). More ominously, Stephen Walcott, a member of the Land and Emigration Board, reported that the latest information from Australia indicated no demand whatever for such a "superior class" of women as governesses; a few might succeed if they had friends in the colony to care for them indefinitely, but any large-scale project would only end in disappointment and disaster (26 April 1862). These forebodings did not daunt Maria Rye, for the experience of her own emigrants, who had all obtained well-paying situations, was exactly to the contrary.

She insisted that there were openings "for many hundreds of women vastly superior to the hordes of wild Irish and fast young ladies who have hitherto started as emigrants" (29 April 1862).

A second difficulty raised some particularly awkward questions for a feminist society purporting to extend opportunities for women beyond marriage and motherhood. The Christian Socialist Charles Kingsley praised Rye's project on the ground that all attempts to open new occupations to women were mere substitutes "for that far nobler and more useful work which Nature intends her—to marry and bear children" (11 April 1862). His implication that the new Society would be little more than a colonial marriage bureau sparked an immediate controversy over the merits of "matrimonial colonization." Kingsley's brother-in-law, Lord Osborne, protested at the mere hint that emigration for work might be a masquerade for a degrading form of husband-hunting (28 April 1862). A *Times* leader answered by pointing out that the imbalance of the sexes in Britain and Australia rendered female emigration a necessity, whatever the pretext; and in any case a woman who emigrated under responsible and respectable protection "is guilty of no more indelicacy than a girl who goes to a ball or an archery meeting" (28 April 1862). Again Maria Rye disposed of the argument: if women were not so fastidious about whom they married at home they could easily find unworthy (i.e., lower-class) husbands immediately; there was no reason to think they would be less scrupulous in the colonies. Her society sought to find decent employment for women overseas, and marriage was a matter for individual decision (29 April 1862). The debate was a circular one but contained important implications for the future conduct of the Society.[15]

Unfortunately for the Society the controversy over its formation coincided with a heightened interest in the problem of the increasing disproportion between the sexes in Britain and the complementary shortage of women in the colonies.[16] The interlocking controversies over the "redundancy" of women and the panacea of emigration raised sensitive issues for feminists. Many of them opposed female emigration because it was a popular antifeminist solution. It appeared all too readily as a device to confine women to their "proper sphere" of the household and as an unjust safety valve to siphon off pressure for progressive reform. The most nettlesome provocation was William Rathbone Greg's frequently reprinted essay "Why are Women Redundant?"[17] For Greg, all the surplus women were "redundant" only in the sense that they lacked the opportunity to fulfill their "natural" role in relation to men. Domestic servants, for example, were not redundant because they "fulfill both essentials of a woman's being, *they are supported by and they minister to, men.* We could not possibly do without them." Greg blamed the heavier emigration of men for altering the balance, but female emigration could now create the "natural rectification" by providing wives for the surplus men in North America and Australia. Only a massive emigration of up to 40,000 women a year, in the spirit of Caroline Chisholm's work, would suffice to eliminate the redundancy of 405,000 adult women in Britain.[18] He estimated that the largest group of redundant women belonged to the class immediately above the laboring poor, "the daughters of unfortunate tradesmen, of poor clerks, or poorer curates." These women had all been disciplined in "the appropriate school of poverty and exertion," and their education and refinement would insure their adaptability to new conditions in the colonies. The one thing to avoid was the feminist solution of making single life as easy, attractive, and lucrative as it was for men, and thereby encouraging further "redundancy" of women (*National Review*, xxvii, pp. 434–60).

In 1862, as we have seen, the feminists were by no means opposed to female emigration, but Greg's blatant association of emigration with antifeminism, together with some discouraging reports from the colonies, caused many of them to change sides. Frances Power Cobbe thought Greg's remedy amounted to a sentence of transportation or starvation for all old maids. She favored emigration to give women a free choice between marriage and profitable employment—a choice most women were still unable to exercise in Britain—but estimated that the colonial demand for educated women was so low as to render the proposal irrelevant to women's problems.[19] By 1863 there was further confirmation from some colonies that the demand for governesses was limited, and Jessie Boucherett regretted that this seemingly obvious solution to the quest for women's work would provide little relief so long as women lacked specialized occupational training.[20] A writer in the *Victoria Magazine,* a new feminist journal, thought that the colonial news could only disappoint those who,

misled by the statistical accounts of the disparity of the sexes, which, of course, reveal nothing as to the *causes* of the disparity, took for granted that the whole question of the employment of educated women could be summarily disposed of by wholesale shipments to the colonies. It may be hoped that we shall now have

*A Widening Sphere*

no more suggestions about making homes for settlers, as the only and the very easy solution of this troublesome problem.[21]

The republication of Greg's essay in 1868 and 1869 brought a further round of comment. Mary Taylor, one of the more radical early feminists,[22] replied indignantly:

The men who emigrate without wives, do so because in their opinion, they cannot afford to marry. The curious idea that the women, whom they would not ask in England should run after them to persuade them would be laughable if it were not mischievous. Those who adopt it must dispense with that cultivated forethought that makes both sides wish for some provision for the future before entering into matrimony. It is true there is a certain number who have attained their object, and have the means to marry, but the greater number are intentionally single, as are the corresponding class in England.[23]

Most feminists continued to support the prudent and modest efforts of the Female Middle Class Emigration Society, but they were united in rejecting promotion of the idea for Greg's wrong reasons.

Regular publicity, both critical and favorable, did not prevent the Society from quietly pursuing its declared objective.[24] It could not, however, evade some of the basic questions raised in the continuing debate. In the face of colonial warnings against sending governesses, Maria Rye's insistence that her own emigrants all obtained decent employment, often with several alternative offers, did not always conform to facts reflected in early private letters from the emigrants to the Society. From Australia, New Zealand, and South Africa women frequently reported that governesses' positions were scarce or ill-paid, and many experienced difficulty at first in adjusting to a situation in which, materially at least, they were no better off than in Britain.[25] Furthermore, the insistence by the Society's critics that the women workers most needed by colonists were domestic servants, and that even the most refined and accomplished governess must be prepared to do some plain housework on occasion, demanded the Society's attention. An ex-Australian resident's paper at the 1862 Social Science Congress recommended that intending emigrants should "undergo a short training on the theory, at all events, of household work and duties, and needlework of the most useful kinds, and in medicine so far as to treat ordinary diseases" (TNAPSS, 1862, p. 812).

Together, the issues of inadequate colonial demand for governesses and the need for domestic training raised the question of exactly what kind of system the organizers intended. It could be a mere agency for placing governesses in the colonies or a more comprehensive project to enable a wide range of middle-class women to find varieties of employment, including domestic service, abroad. The different approaches of Maria Rye and her successor, Jane Lewin, on these issues epitomized two contrasting views on female emigration and employment. Maria Rye, in the tradition of Victorian philanthropy, was content to promote the emigration of women of all classes, whether for professional work, domestic service, or eventual marriage. Jane Lewin, in the newer feminist tradition, made a clear-cut distinction between the husband-hunting advocated by Greg and the professional career concept. Ultimately it was Lewin's approach that prevailed, with paradoxically limiting effects on the scope of the Society's activities.

## II

Rye's approach showed a keen awareness of the need for domestic preparation and adaptability on the part of educated female emigrants, and while she directed the Society the special requirements dictated by rougher colonial conditions remained the prime consideration.[26] She hoped to accommodate the colonies' particular needs by maintaining a two-tier emigration system. Two classes of women, both above the working-class but very different in social origins and training, would receive assistance. First, "a few really accomplished governesses, who command from £40 to £100 in England, and who could obtain situations in the colonies, equal in money value and superior in social position and comfort." Second,

a class beginning with the half-educated daughters of poor professional men, and including the children of subordinate government officers, petty shopkeepers, and artisans generally, who have been accustomed to domestic economy at home, and on whom the want of employment often pressed heavily.[27]

Besides well-trained governesses, Rye hoped to send out women from the lower middle class who would presumably be willing to enter domestic service. But she insisted that regardless of their origins all of them must be prepared to stoop to menial work, and she inserted a clause in the Society's rules to that effect: "Every applicant is examined as far as possible, with regard to her knowledge of cooking, baking, washing, needlework, and housework, and is required to assist

*A Widening Sphere*

in these departments of labour, should it be necessary" (F.M.C.E.S., *First Report*, 1861–62, p. 3). Given her understanding of the mutual social needs of female emigration, Rye's plans had the makings of a large-scale project.

Rye's management of the Society, together with her policy, however, was short-lived. Her intimate knowledge of colonial requirements led her progressively to an exclusive interest in working-class emigration. Almost immediately after the Society's formation in May 1862, and quite independently of her work with it, she began to foster the emigration of Manchester cotton operatives and other working-class women. News of a rising demand for servants—but emphatically not governesses—in British Columbia prompted her to help recruit working-class women in cooperation with the newly formed Columbian Emigration Society. At the same time the Queensland and New Zealand governments asked her to recruit female domestic servants for their assisted passages. Altogether in 1862 she independently helped four-hundred women to emigrate, of whom only forty were governesses, and she decided to accompany one-hundred of them to New Zealand.[28] Her basic reason for leaving was to investigate the demand for women workers in Australia and New Zealand and to complete the Society's arrangements for reception facilities. Her experience confirmed her view that there was ample room in the Antipodes for all classes of women, provided they were hard-working and adaptable. After her return in 1865, however, she left the Society's work to others in order to concentrate exclusively on working-class emigration.[29]

Rye's work as Honorary Secretary of the Society was taken over by her coworker, Jane Lewin, who occupied the position until her retirement in 1881 and conducted most of the routine administration and interviewing. Lewin shared Rye's conviction that the most refined women must be prepared, when required, to help with household work; the Society, as she put it, "requires education of the hands, as well as of the head." But she abandoned Rye's concept of a two-tier system of female emigration in which women without formal teaching qualifications would play a major role. Under her direction eligible emigrants ranged from the highly accomplished finishing governess to "a woman who can do little beyond teaching English correctly" (Lewin, TNAPSS, 1863, pp. 612–16). In short, she reduced the Society's function to that of a colonial placement agency for governesses. It was this factor, more than any lack of overseas demand for governesses, which constricted the Society's operation to token proportions during its twenty-three years and inhibited the growth of a larger project of female emigration from the middle-classes until the eighties.

The surviving records of the Society indicate that Jane Lewin pursued her objective consistently. From the Society's reports it is possible to determine the initial colonial occupations of 222 out of its 302 emigrants. Of these, 113 were either governesses or schoolteachers, 34 joined friends or relatives on arrival, 20 were married shortly after arrival, 16 were unemployed for reasons of health, age, or misconduct, 9 returned to England, and 8 were lady's companions. Only 22 took occupations that might identify them as lower middle class, such as milliners, dressmakers, cooks, nursery-governesses, and singers.[30] Furthermore, the emigrants' correspondence indicates that many women who failed to obtain immediate employment ultimately took up teaching. Out of 114 correspondents 98 eventually turned to some form of teaching or intended to do so, and only 5 entered menial or less respectable occupations.[31] Lewin was clearly insisting on teaching qualifications from most of her applicants, for a later report observed that the smaller numbers of actual emigrants had been out of all proportion to the large numbers who applied (*5th Report*, 1883, pp. 3–4). The Society's capacity to provide loans was undoubtedly limited, but had it encouraged a wider social range of women, its ability to attract further subscriptions should have increased accordingly.[32]

Some caution is necessary in interpreting the Society's records, for a woman's colonial occupation would be an unreliable guide to her social position in Britain. Since governessing was a popular means of achieving upward social advancement among women of the lower middle and working classes, and since moderate teaching ability was the sole qualification, the Society might easily have admitted women from all classes. The content of most of the letters, however, suggests that their writers came from middle- or even upper-middle-class origins. Many complained condescendingly of the breeding of their employers, like Annie Davis, who, when moving to a new position in Sydney, noted that "in my new home I shall make acquaintance with a new class of people—'*the nouveaux riches*', but I may consider myself now 'colonized' so it will be only viewing a new phase of life." She found them "very vulgar," however, and left them after only five months.[33] Similarly, Sarah Henderson "was certainly not remarkably comfortable in my first situation, as the husband of the person I was living with was an exceedingly vulgar low-minded man."[34] The women complained frequently of vulgar working-class emigrants during the voyage. Marion Hett found their presence unduly irksome.

Certainly if one could choose one would not select a ship which carried Government emigrants. The girls were always on the poop with us, and often annoyed us extremely by their levity of conduct. They ought never to come out in a ship with mixed passengers, but if possible emigrants should have a ship to themselves. . . .[35]

The tone of these letters suggests a level of gentility not common to the lower middle class. Emigrants like the station master's daughter who had been an impecunious dressmaker in England and went to Colorado as a nurse and helper were rare exceptions to the general rule (F.M.C.E.S., *5th Report*, No. 219). Many of the Society's emigrants may not have been distressed, but most of them were undoubtedly gentlewomen.

Þ The Society assisted some women for whom economic or psychological hardship had clearly played little or no part in their decision to emigrate. Caroline Haselton, who could afford to send regular donations back to the Society, was able to move about freely. She taught for high wages in South Africa and Australia, and her last letter from Melbourne contained inquiries about the possibility of teaching in India or South America.[36] Annie Davis was delighted with her new circumstances in Sydney but added that her English experience "was a singularly happy one."[37] Many of the Society's most enterprising women had sufficient capital and qualifications to be able to establish their own school after arrival. Its greatest success story in this respect was Miss S. A. Hall. She emigrated to South Africa in 1868 and nine years later made persistent requests to Lewin to send out teachers for her thriving school at Graaf Reinet. She obtained highly qualified teachers all of whom had commanded good salaries in Britain; three of them were honors students from prominent English educational institutions. The Society recruited at least seven women of this stamp for Hall, and each obtained a high salary in the range of £100 to £150.[38] No doubt they proved a valuable addition to Hall's school and to the English community in Graaf Reinet, but they were hardly from the class most in need of emigration. In bypassing less-qualified women who had been thrown out of employment by competition with the new generation of well-educated teachers, the Society was ignoring the class with the greatest social need.

Þ Under Jane Lewin's direction the Society clung to her policy of

YOUNG LADY ENGAGING HERSELF AS GOVERNESS TO A FAMILY OF
DISTINCTION IN THE BUSH.

64 ]

PARTIAL VIEW OF THE BUSH RESIDENCE, INTRODUCING A PORTION OF THE FAMILY REFERRED TO.

Melbourne Punch (*2 March 1861*). *Despite the enthusiastic reports of so many of the F.M.C.E.S. women,* the Melbourne Punch *did not think that utopian working conditions awaited all colonial governesses.*

governess emigration, despite consistent evidence from its own emigrants that the colonies offered relief to gentlewomen not because they earned higher wages as governesses but because they adapted to a social environment that exerted fewer social taboos on the kind of work middle-class women could perform. Some emigrants did complain about low salaries but invariably they felt compensated by close companionship in a more egalitarian social atmosphere. Mary Long took a governess' position in a clergyman's family in Canterbury at only £30 and did a great deal of needlework and housekeeping besides teaching four children; in spite of all this she was content because "kindly treated and quite one of the family," and she concluded that, regardless of salary, "I would rather be a governess here than in England."[39] Eleanor Blackith earned the same salary at Napier, New Zealand, but had no complaints, noting that she would "help Mrs. Simcox in anything and she treats me exactly like a sister"; in a subsequent letter, still thrilled at being treated "exactly as one of the family," she boasted that since arriving she had "become quite clever in the art of cooking."[40]

This tolerance toward household chores and delight at becoming "one of the family" pervades almost the entire correspondence of the Society's emigrants. Miss L. Geoghegan became a governess in the Australian bush and was soon impressed with the lack of social discrimination against governesses; bush life, "a strange mixture of roughing and refinement," could be dull, but "I can rake or hoe in the garden as I please and the freedom to please oneself more than compensates for the monotony." The position of the rural governess, she observed, could be an exalted one, despite the need to light the schoolroom fire:

It is a totally different life from what it is at home. In nearly every instance you are looked on as the Intellectual member of the Establishment; you are the constant companion and associate of the Lady, considered—I might say indulged in every way, and your only difficulty is to civilize the children.[41]

From Dunedin, New Zealand, Eliza Brook wrote that although the work was rougher than in England, "where everyone works there is no occasion for pride"; governesses were appreciated in Dunedin and could command from £30 to £60, "but to those who object to be on equality with the family and are afraid to render assistance when required I do not think there is such good promise."[42] In case Jane Lewin missed the point, Mrs. H. Herbert, the Society's representative in Hawke's Bay, New Zealand, spelled out colonial requirements yet again. To insure adaptability, she insisted, the accent must be on youth; ladies of forty were too old to be transplanted to the roughness of colonial life; household conditions for gentlewomen were different: "there are fewer servants—sometimes the family is left for weeks without any—and a governess who stood on her dignity and refused to help would do a foolish thing."[43]

From the insistence that governesses must be prepared to help with the household chores it was a short step to suggest that the less well-qualified adopt domestic service or other menial work as a full-time or at least initial colonial occupation. This step Jane Lewin refused to take, despite evidence that it could have been a feasible proposition. The Society's emigrants and colonial representatives repeatedly urged that only highly qualified intending governesses should be sent out; teaching standards were high, especially in the cities where government schools were beginning to supplant governesses, and the mediocre would fare much better as colonial servants.[44] Annie Davis, whose own qualifications gave her ample security as a governess, remarked

Were I in the position of the third or fourth rate Governess (I was about going to say second) in England, I would unhesitatingly become a domestic servant in Australia in preference . . . I have no doubt it would require some common sense and humility for such a Governess to become a Servant, and she would find herself infinitely better off (salary apart). Servants are more considered, there is more freedom and independence here than at home. If my words could reach some of my toiling sisters at home I would say "Be sensible, undergo a little domestic training and come out here to take your chance with others with a certainty of succeeding withal."[45]

The available evidence reveals few actual domestic servants among the Society's emigrants,[46] but the letters certainly suggest that many of the women soon came to share Annie Davis's strong views and were at least prepared to turn to other forms of menial work when teaching was unavailable. Annie Hunt, who had worked as a law-copyist in England, refused to mix with the freshly arrived dressmakers and needlewomen in Melbourne, but she was quite content to become a "milliner-dressmaker-machinist" with a family up-country.[47] In Brisbane, Agnes MacQueen knew of many instances where intending governesses were compelled "to take situations in shops at a better rate of pay."[48] Miss J. Merritt, who described her employers as "rather low," was nevertheless well-conditioned in colonial ways, and admitted candidly that she would rather become a servant than a governess at £25.[49] There was ample precedent for successfully implementing Annie Davis's suggestions, but they were unlikely to appeal to a feminist-run emigration society.

In view of the controversy that accompanied the origins of the F.M.C.E.S., it is hardly surprising that Jane Lewin shrank from the concept of genteel domestic service.[50] In some respects her policy was a triumph for middle-class feminism against those familiar notions of women's "proper sphere" so tenaciously upheld by moralizing anti-feminists like Greg and the *Saturday Review*. Indeed, given the terms of the original controversy, Lewin had little real alternative. While a more flexible policy might have helped more of those distressed gentle-women and lower-middle-class women genuinely in need of emigra-tion, the predictable charges of "matrimonial colonization" could easily have been seen as a threat to the entire venture. If feminists like Lewin were to promote emigration, therefore, both ideology and expediency required it to be a path to emancipation and independence rather than a mere supportive prelude and training period for the contingency of marriage. In these terms Lewin's policy was a clear success. At the opposite end of the spectrum Maria Rye had joined the feminists simply in order to further piecemeal efforts to improve the material conditions of unemployed women, and she saw no inconsistency in later helping whole families and abandoned children to emigrate. Characteristically, she withdrew from the Society for Promoting the Employment of Women when its members joined the women's suffrage movement (Kamm, p. 102; D.N.B. *Supplement, 1901–1911,* pp. 245–46).

Significantly the Society began slowly to change its policy back to Maria Rye's original scheme after Jane Lewin's retirement as Honorary Secretary in 1881. None of her successors were particularly prominent feminists, and one of them, Julia Blake, was attracted to the Society through her previous work with other emigration societies rather than through feminism.[51] The last report of the Society indicated a cautious return to Rye's policy:

Half-educated teachers must be warned to turn to any other means of living (such as 'Mother's Help') rather than face the just competition with the well-trained teachers, who, if holding a certificate from any of our Universities, can still com-mand a good salary.

(*6th Report,* 1883–85, pp. 3–6)

This attitude reflected the more ambitious policies being pursued by recently established emigration societies. But the depleted funds and modest facilities of the F.M.C.E.S. prevented the implementation of a new policy on any large scale. Other societies had assumed the major burden of promoting female emigration, and the old Society was eventually absorbed by them (Monk, pp. 10–13). The paradox of the first Society was that in twenty-three years it probably did more to inhibit than to encourage female emigration.


## III


The F.M.C.E.S. attitude toward domestic service was in many respects representative of the more general attitude of middle-class feminists. During the seventies a number of schemes were canvassed to promote "domestic service for gentlewomen" in Britain. One of these schemes, devised by Rose Mary Crawshay, established a London placement office, offered cookery lessons, and placed over a hundred gentlewomen as servants within eight months.[52] The success of these projects was, understandably, short-lived, but the impact and publicity was enough to draw a sharp response from the feminists. The *Victoria Magazine* considered the "new-fangled term 'lady-help'" a tribute to a vulgar spirit that degraded the meaning of the word "lady," and dismissed it as an attempt to glamorize "the unpalatable idea of domestic service." Domestic service was unfit for gentlewomen and in any case quite impracticable (April 1876, 510–12, 562–63; June 1876, 185–86). Louisa M. Hubbard, proprietor and editor of the women's magazine *Work and Leisure,* argued that gentlewomen should accept domestic service only if they were willing "to relinquish the social position accorded to persons belonging to the educated and cultivated classes." If faced with charity or starvation, gentlewomen should certainly turn to domestic service, and would probably be respected for their refinement by discriminating persons. But a problem remained:

The test of class seems to us to be very much one of education and culture. . . . We only suggest that a line should be drawn somewhere, and that while a lady should be ready to accept any respectable employment which will support her when she needs it, she should not expect to enjoy the privileges of education and culture while relinquishing the exercise of both in a class possessing neither.[53]

In the same book Hubbard applied a similar standard to emigration. The qualities necessary for successful emigration seemed to be precisely those which would make a woman independent of it and able to choose her own career. Capability and training were required as much in the colonies as at home.

The only hope, therefore, for those who do not possess them is to go where the mere fact of being a woman, and therefore able to cook or wash, or do other feminine work, in however blundering a way, may stand them in some stead.

Furthermore, conditions on emigrant ships "are still such as would be almost unendurable to a gentlewoman, and are trying enough, even to persons accustomed to roughing it" (Hubbard, p. 131).

The feminist attitude toward domestic service revealed a class-conscious preoccupation with the implied loss of gentility in outlets such as the "lady-help" or emigration. For most middle-class feminists this attitude constituted a conflict that could easily inhibit their effective contribution to the cause. Feminists were, indeed, beginning to scrutinize their notions of middle-class ladyhood, but they had not yet rejected the prevailing definition. Since the colonial demand for domestic servants clashed with the requirements of that definition, the feminists were naturally reluctant to interpret the colonies' need as their opportunity. Activities that might compromise a gentlewoman's social position conflicted at too many points with a middle-class feminism concerned primarily with a female elite. Colonial social conditions required a reordering of traditional British categories of class, status, and female employment, a difficult task for women whose class-consciousness overshadowed their feminism. Not surprisingly, then, it was of little consequence to the feminists that the emigrants themselves found warnings like those of Hubbard's irrelevant.

Jane Lewin's retirement in 1881 heralded the end of the connection between feminism and middle-class female emigration. By 1886, when the F.M.C.E.S. was absorbed into the recently formed Colonial Emigration Society, middle-class emigration had returned to the charge of philanthropists, where it had begun. From the 1880's to 1914 a variety of more ambitious female emigration societies, in the mainstream of voluntary work, helped over twenty-thousand women to emigrate.[54] Unlike the F.M.C.E.S., they freely used genteel domestic service and potential marriage as incentives to emigration. Their history is beyond the scope of this paper, but the numbers alone suggest the degree to which the uneasy relationship between feminism and female emigration had operated as an inhibiting factor. The greatest victim of that relationship was the distressed gentlewoman, the very misfit the "Ladies of Langham Place" had begun by trying to help. Piecemeal educational reform had worsened her competitive position in Britain, but middle-class feminism had little to offer a genteel lady without formal teaching qualifications. The distressed gentlewoman remained a casualty, not only of the Victorian social system, but of most attempts to reform it.

# 4. The Making of an Outcast Group

## Prostitutes and Working Women in Nineteenth-Century Plymouth and Southampton

∽

### Judith Walkowitz

THIS ESSAY IS AN EXPLORATORY VENTURE INTO THE SOCIAL HISTORY OF AN outcast group in Victorian England. It focuses on working-class prostitutes in the 1870's and 1880's, who were subjected to a police and medical registration system established under the Contagious Diseases Acts, and who, with middle-class reformist support, forcibly resisted the requirements of the Acts. These Acts[1] were ostensibly passed as sanitary measures to control the spread of venereal disease among the military stationed in garrison and dock towns; in actual practice, however, their administration extended well beyond the sanitary supervision of common prostitutes. As single women residing outside their families, registered women were perhaps the most vulnerable members of their community; consequently, official intervention into their lives offered police an easy opportunity for general surveillance of the poor neighborhoods in which they resided. These women were used as a leverage on the working-class community, not simply because of their marginal status within that community, but also in good part because they shared certain social characteristics with the mass of the urban poor. Their temporary move into prostitution reflected the fluid social identity among the casual laboring poor who so violated Victorian society's sense of order and place. In the districts where the Acts were enforced prostitution, petty theft, and the seasonal migration of the poor into the countryside to pick hops and strawberries were all means by which the chronically underemployed endured through hard times. The Contagious Diseases Acts were part of the institutional and legal efforts to contain this occupational and geographic mobility.[2] The Acts represented an attempt to clarify the relationship between the unrespectable and respectable poor. They were designed to force prostitutes to accept their status as public women by destroying their private identities and associations with the poor working-class community.

By first establishing the general social profile of prostitutes in two ports, Plymouth and Southampton, which were placed under the Contagious Diseases Acts[3] and which saw substantial resistance to the Acts, we may begin to assess the degree to which the lives of registered women were integrated into the conventional framework of working-class life. In particular the first section outlines the options open to women who moved into prostitution and the way in which prostitution represented a transitional stage in their adult lives. The second section discusses the impact of the Contagious Diseases Acts on registered women and their community as well as their articulated response to the Acts. It examines the extensive public resistance mounted against the Acts by the "unrespectable" poor, as well as the degree to which the poor ultimately acquiesced in the social isolation of prostitutes. Finally, we shall relate the experience of registered women to long-term changes in working-class prostitution and to the social economy of the laboring poor in the late Victorian and Edwardian periods.

I

No systematic survey of motives and social origins of registered prostitutes comparable to the work of A. J. B. Parent-Duchâtelet in Paris or William Sanger in New York was undertaken by C. D. Acts authorities in Plymouth or Southampton.[4] Still, it has been possible to construct a general profile of the women registered under the Contagious Diseases Acts from hospital and police records, from local newspaper reports of petty session trials of prostitutes, and from public testimonies of local authorities and repeal workers. In December 1871 there were 503 registered women in Greater Plymouth (pop. 132,792 and called the Three Towns, made up of Plymouth, Devonport, and East Stonehouse) and 160 women in Southampton (pop. 53,741).[5] From these sources a uniform picture emerges: they were young single women who resided in lodgings, who catered to a working-class clientele, and who were born in the immediate district or in the surrounding countryside.[6] Their migration patterns appear to be no different from those of the general population for the two districts or for young single women in particular.[7] In general, the registered women of both districts appear more indigenous to the two districts than suggested by the official testimonies of local police and magistrates, anxious to blame "social disorder" on nonresidents. Still, census and hospital records for Plymouth indicate that a significant number of women were recent arrivals from the local countryside—about five out of ten—although local authorities overstated their proportions.[8] One needs to ask whether such women came to Southampton or to Plymouth for different reasons than other rural migrants and whether the disruptive character of the transition to an urban setting was in part related to their move into prostitution.

Rural poverty, the declining employment opportunities for women in agricultural areas, and the closing of mines in Devon and Cornwall, where formerly women could obtain surface work, impelled young women as well as young men into nearby urban areas to find alternative employment. In thus migrating they were not necessarily breaking with traditional roles and values. As Louise Tilly and Joan Scott have noted, young women's entrance into the urban job market represented a continuation of long-held values which prescribed that women work to support themselves and contribute to the family income.[9] However, family conflict as well as family obligation may have motivated a young woman to leave her home to move to the city or to take another residence in town. The discomfort of poor, overcrowded homes and the problems of family life, beset by high birth rates, high mortality rates, and the emigration of men overseas, may have rendered domestic service in more prosperous households (initially at least) an attractive alternative. Some women clearly left their families simply to get away, with not much forethought about their future. Police and rescue workers cited substantial numbers of youthful runaways who found themselves in notorious brothels soon after their arrival in the city (*P.P.* 1875, XLI, *P.P.* 1876, XLI). Young women, restless with the subordination and fatalistic acquiescence expected of their class, may have been most likely to make this break. Thus the repeated negative description of young "fallen" women as "wild and impulsive" by their parents as well as rescue workers can be turned on its head—indicative, perhaps, that these young women were more inclined to self-assertion than most of their working-class contemporaries.[10]

Premarital sexuality among the urban poor was an adaptation

and continuation of customary rural practices, but this kind of cultural transition was not free from jolting dislocations. For instance, premarital sexuality and premarital pregnancy had traditionally culminated in marriage, thereby posing no serious threat to a stable rural community. However, pregnant single women enjoyed a more uncertain fate both in the mid-Victorian countryside and in urban settings, where parental authority was not always present or as effective a constraint on young men who could readily go elsewhere (Scott and Tilly, p. 57). Furthermore, the bastardy clauses of the 1834 Poor Law Act assigned women sole responsibility for supporting their illegitimate children, thereby diminishing legal pressure on men to marry.[11] On the other hand, increased geographic mobility and the relative anonymity of urban life also released women from the claustrophobic social pressures of the rural village.[12]

It is impossible to tell how many registered prostitutes were social casualties of this rocky transition. Illegitimacy rates in southeast and southwest England were lower than for England and Wales as a whole, although reporters for the *Morning Chronicle* in the 1840's noted the entrenched tradition of premarital sexuality among the "Methodist" fishermen, miners, and agricultural workers of the South.[13] In the 1870's registered women's testimonies frequently indicated that they had passed through various stages of sexual involvement with men before going on the streets—whether it be serial monogamy or more general promiscuity.[14]

Occupational dislocation seems to have been an important factor in women's move into prostitution as well. Plymouth and Southampton officials generally agreed that the previous work experience of registered women had been as maids of all work—the bottom rung of the ladder of domestic service—although their move into prostitution had been occasioned by a period of unemployment. As one doctor remarked, "They get out of place and they have nowhere to go and they adopt this as a last resort, as a means of livelihood; some go back to service and again return to the streets" (*P.P.*, 1871, xix, Q. 10677). However, the 1871 census listings for women previously identified as common prostitutes in Plymouth indicate a more diverse occupational background. Of thirty-one women between the ages of fifteen and twenty-nine who were traced to residences on three notorious streets in Plymouth, only two were actually listed as prostitutes, four as domestic servants, and the rest as dressmakers, tailoresses, seamstresses, bookbinders, or unemployed.[15] The listings were by no means an accurate reflection of their present occupational status—at their trials none of the women claimed to be holding down respectable jobs; rather the listings may have reflected what they might have done in the past and what they could expect to go back to when they finished their present career. The listings represent an attempt to blend into the neighborhood—to give occupations appropriate to the working-class community in which they resided. These *were* the employment opportunities for working women in Plymouth and Southampton. As milliners, dressmakers, tailoresses, domestic servants, and launderesses, young women would rarely earn more than six to eight shillings a week, working fourteen hours a day—barely half of what a male day-laborer would earn. And as "improvers," shopworkers, or general maids of all work, they earned considerably less. Much of this employment was highly casual, structured around the demands of the local season. When living outside their families these women were subject to periodic layoffs and were hard pressed to survive on their own without a "friend." Placed in a vulnerable economic and social position, some women who could not rely on family, relatives, or lovers may have found the shorter hours and better pay of prostitution a temporary and relatively attractive solution to their immediate difficulties.[16]

Indeed, the standard of living of prostitutes was perceptibly higher than other working women. A prostitute, even a sailor's woman, could earn the weekly wages of a respectable working woman in a day, at a shilling a "shot." Prostitutes had a room of their own; they dressed better; they had spending money and access to the pub, the principal facility in the working-class neighborhood that provided heat, light, cooked food, and convivality.[17] Contracting venereal disease was an occupational hazard for these women, but it is likely that their general standard of health was better than the dressmakers and launderesses who slaved away fourteen hours a day. Consumption, the disease generally associated with overwork and undernourishment, was the great killer of adult females, not syphilis.[18] But while the proceeds of prostitution raised the prostitutes' living standard to that of unskilled male workers, this by no means represented an economic way out of the lower strata of the working class. Furthermore, economic benefits have to be weighed against the exposure and physical danger of the occupation as well as the likelihood of its diminishing profitability as women aged. For practical and psychological reasons, most women were probably ill equipped to endure the rigors of the "profession" for more than a few years.

*A Widening Sphere*

While periodic unemployment influenced women's move into prostitution, other seasonal factors were at work as well. Local police from dock and garrison towns reported the enormous increase of street-walkers and disorderly behavior among prostitutes upon the arrival of ships or new regiments. Clearly the high profitability of prostitution at this time attracted women onto the streets and into the districts.[19]

For most "public" women prostitution represented only a temporary stage in their life that they would pass through. The age concentration of registered women in their early twenties strongly supports the likelihood that they had had prior work experience out-side the home as well as having engaged in noncommercial sexual activity. In addition, registered women appear to have stayed in prostitution for two or three years, leaving in their mid-twenties at a very critical point in their lives—when most working-class women were settling into some domestic situation with a man, whether it be formal or common-law marriage. The timing here is very important. For as long as prostitution represented a temporary stage in a woman's career, and as long as she could leave it at her discretion, she was not irre-vocably scarred or limited in her future choices.

Some information is available on the subsequent history of registered women. From all the public testimonies the likelihood of their returning to respectable employment without leaving the two districts was very small. Rather, women escaped registration two ways. Some left the district entirely—with more than seventy percent of Southampton women (who could migrate to nearby urban areas) and twenty percent of Plymouth women exercising this option during the period in which the Contagious Diseases Acts were enforced (*P.P.* 1882, LIII). Others, after a few years on the streets, tended to settle into a more permanent relationship with one or more sailors, living with them when they were in port and drawing their half-pay in their absence. They also sometimes supplemented that income with the proceeds of casual prostitution (*P.P.* 1871, XIX, Q. 7500, 10 292–95, 11 199). This pattern seems to have been widespread among sailors' prostitutes elsewhere; it was observed by Bracebridge Hemyng and police authorities among Stepney prostitutes, the police noting that these women readily integrated themselves into the social life of the neighborhood.[20] Again, this pattern suggests prostitution's ambiguous relationship to working-class sexual and social norms. As one observer noted, "concubinage" was "not only the door into prostitution, but also the door out of prostitution very often" (*P.P.* 1871, XIX, Q. 20209).

*The Making of an Outcast Group*

If prostitution represented a temporary stage in a woman's life, one would want to know whether she was rendered a social outcast during that transitional period. Prostitutes lived among the casual laboring poor, who were accustomed to hard times and who also had to make difficult, temporary accommodations to social necessity. Poor neighbors were nonetheless of different minds about prostitutes. Some saw prostitution as a threatening and illegitimate form of social behavior. Others came to understand and tolerate prostitution as one of a series of strategies adopted by women to survive, even though it was not an option officially sanctioned by the poor community.

Plymouth and Southampton prostitutes resided in narrowly defined areas that were readily subject to police surveillance. While these streets were notorious as "red light" districts, in reality a more diverse social and economic life was present there. Residence on these streets was largely determined by economic necessity, although the general neighborhood tolerance of certain illegal or unrespectable behavior, as well as the availability of accommodations for transients, may have also attracted the large number of single men and women living apart from their families.[21] While highly visible, these young people formed a distinct minority of the street population. Most people lived in families; even in brothels prostitutes were outnumbered by members of the brothelkeeper's family and by other lodgers living in families. The family operated as the main support system among people who existed just at or below subsistence level, where all adults and most children were required to contribute to the family income.

For most residents of these neighborhoods the conditions of casual employment not only enforced economic cohesion within the family but also required men and women to vacillate between casual work in large governmental and commercial establishments and odd forms of self-employment. Hence, fluctuations in income and occupation were experiences that neighbors shared in common with prostitutes. In addition, residents of these communities often found themselves on the wrong side of the law as well as physically constrained by institutions like the workhouse, prison, or in the case of prostitutes, the lock hospital, which were used interchangeably for the confinement of the socially deviant.[22]

Despite many shared experiences, prostitutes remained distinct from the social profile of their neighborhood in a number of ways. First, as mentioned earlier, their standard of living was perceptibly higher than other women. Second, their living arrangements also set them apart. Young women residing in lodgings appear strikingly cut off from the family system that was the organizing social and economic principle of these streets. Not only were they residing apart from their families, but they also were living independent of lovers and children as well. Prostitutes tended to form personal attachments with sailors who were not permanently in residence.[23] As a consequence, sailors could not exercise the same kind of control over their women's lives as men who habitually lived off the "wages of sin." In the case of children, various explanations for the small number of children residing among sexually active females are possible; some prostitutes were sterile, as a result of having contracted gonorrhea; some boarded their children out or left them in the workhouse; some used a combination of contraceptive techniques, abortion, and infanticide (J. Walkowitz, "We Are Not Beasts," diss. pp. 238–40).

While not residing with their families, their lovers, or their own children, prostitutes did have living companions. Single women tended to live together in clusters of three or four in a few residences on Southampton streets and scattered throughout the notorious Plymouth streets. As we shall see, these groups formed the basis of an important and supportive female subculture. In addition, prostitutes had substantial financial connections with other residents. The economy of prostitution hardly appears to have been highly formalized or rationalized: women were self-employed, paying only rent to brothelkeepers, who nonetheless made larger profits off prostitutes than other lodgers, charging them anywhere from 3s. 6d. a week for a room to 13s. for room and board. Still, it would be incorrect to characterize the older women in charge of "disreputable" lodgings as the exploitative professionals generally associated with the term "brothelkeeper." They were largely poor women with families left to shift for themselves. Taking in lodgers represented one of the few employments that enabled women to support their families. These women did not own the houses; they rented them from male landlords. And at least four Plymouth and Southampton women pleaded in court that they ran brothels to "keep the children off the parish" (J. and D. Walkowitz, "We Are Not Beasts," p. 205).

Prostitutes resided in special working-class districts, among a very poor population that stood to benefit substantially from their commerce. It may be that many residents tolerated prostitutes more out of financial need than out of any strong sympathy and understanding of the women's plight. Yet this toleration easily wore thin if official

*"Outside a Lodging House, Flower and Dean Streets, Spitalfields,"*
*from George R. Sims, ed.,* Living London *(London, 1902), II.*

pressure was brought to bear on neighbors and relatives who led very fragile social and economic lives.


## II

In their struggle for survival the very poor maintained a delicate balance between private interest and public responsibility, between the toleration and segregation of marginal social behavior. This fragile social equilibrium was upset by the enforcement of the Contagious Disease Acts. On the one hand, the Acts generated an extensive public resistance movement among the women and their community. On the other hand, by forcing prostitutes and their neighbors publicly to acknowledge what had been informally tolerated, they may well have forced a stricter redefinition of acceptable behavior, thereby facilitating the social isolation of prostitutes.

One may observe a shift in attitudes and self-perception among the prostitutes themselves, forced upon them by the public exposure of the police registration and examination procedures. This is most plainly seen in the women's reaction to the periodical examination. Their vehement hostility to the internal examination may have partially been a reaction to the coarse brutality of the doctors, as feminists alleged. No more than three minutes was spent on each examination; the instruments may have still been hot from immersion in boiling water (if they were sterilized at all) (*P.P.* 1871, xix, Q. 8429). And of course a tense resistant woman could find the examination by speculum painful. Annie Clark found the examination "painful" and "disgraceful" and declared, "I would rather spend fourteen years in prison than submit to it" (*Shield*, 17 December 1870). Elizabeth Hounson, who held the record for multiple jailings—five times—for refusing the examination, also maintained she preferred imprisonment to such "degradation": "She tore the summons up when it was served upon her and did not appear at her fifth trial" (*Shield*, 26 May 1874). Another woman who vowed to go to prison rather than to submit to examination told Josephine Butler, the feminist repeal leader, "We ought all to show the officers that we have some respect for our own persons" (Josephine Butler, "The Garrison Towns of Kent," *Shield*, 25 April 1870).

Like the middle-class feminists, registered women regarded the periodic examination as a peculiarly unnatural and degrading experience, a form of "instrumental" rape.[24] When a repeal agent asked two women the difference "between exposing themselves to any man who came to have connexion with them and showing themselves to the doctor," they turned upon him "fiercely" and replied:

I should have thought you'd have known better nor that. Ain't one in the way of natur,' and the other ain't natur' at all. Ain't it a different thing what a woman's obliged to do for a living because she has to keep body and soul together, and going up there to be pulled about by a man as if you was cattle and hadn't no feeling, and to have an instrument pushed up you, not to make you well (because you ain't ill) but just that men may come to you and use you to their sils [sic]. (P.P., 1871, XIX, Q. 20297)

Nonetheless, it would be misleading to dwell exclusively upon the brutal and sadistic character of the examination; more subtle means for humiliation were built into the whole procedure. In a society so profoundly classbound as English society, an examining doctor would have had to do or say very little to make a registered woman feel worthless and degraded. The examination was demeaning because of its public character. Streetwalking at night was one thing; being forced to attend examination during the day, often taunted on the way by young boys who loudly questioned subjected women whether they were going up to the "Bougie Fair" or the "meat market" was another (P.P. 1871, XIX, Q. 7206, 10548). One woman confided to a female missionary that "it was no use trying to reform now, she was registered as a prostitute and everybody would know what she had been doing, and what she was. Going up for examination, she said, was worse than going with 20 men . . ." (P.P. 1871, XIX, Q. 12631). The domiciliary visitation by the police and the central location of the examination house made it impossible for a subjected woman to keep her private and public worlds apart. This is what destroyed her self-respect.

In this way the Acts forced prostitutes to readjust their self-image. Repealers complained that the Acts hardened the women by forcing many "who may not have made up their mind to continue as prostitutes" to acknowledge their outcast status. While women appealing for legal aid to repealers made no attempt to hide the fact that they had been prostitutes, some certainly evidenced a strong ambivalence about their past and even expressed confusion as to what it meant to be a prostitute. Clearly the categories of acceptable social and sexual behavior were not that well defined. Harriet Hicks is a case in point.

At her trial in 1870 Hicks, a former prostitute who was then living out of wedlock with a butcher, had applied to be released from the lock hospital on the grounds that she was no longer a prostitute nor suffering from venereal disease. However, at her trial, when asked whether she still was a prostitute, she responded, "No, only to the one man." A sympathetic magistrate then intervened and explained to her, "You mean that you are not a prostitute, other than as living with one man without marriage?" to which Hicks meekly replied, "Yes, that's what I mean."[25] Hicks' confused response that she was a prostitute "only to the one man" suggests that she may not have understood the question—that the very word "prostitute" might have been foreign to her general usage. One must question whether a poor woman's testimony before a middle-class audience truly reflected her private self-estimation. It is unlikely that prostitutes fully internalized the notion of being "fallen" when they knew they could "rise" again. Moral reformers and rescue agencies appear to have failed to move these women from a "shame" to a "guilt" culture or to have forced any inner compulsion to be consistent in their public and private lives. Rather, the women seem to have effected a practical and psychological compartmentalization of their lives, except when subjected to concerted public stigmatization.

In fact, public shaming was one of the principal functions of police registration and surveillance. The "water police," as they were referred to by the poor, made daily visits to known brothels; there they obtained the names of new arrivals and endeavored to place these women on the register. In many ways they resembled both an occupying military force billeted on a subject population as well as a general morals police. Police inspector Anniss actually lived above the examination house on Flora Street in Plymouth, around the corner from the most notorious Plymouth streets. Over the years he was frequently called upon to testify at divorce cases, affiliation cases, and petty theft cases where a woman's character had to be ascertained.[26] Likewise, after the Acts were suspended in 1883, James Disberry, a former metropolitan police constable, was actually hired as a rescue agent because of his intimate knowledge of the women (*W.D.M.*, 6 April 1886).

Through their surveillance and harassment, the police made it impossible for a woman, once placed on the register, to have her name removed unless she left the district or married. Women complained bitterly of the "policemen a hunting you up . . . coming to your house, threatening you, and letting all the people around know what you are. If you wants to live quietly in your neighborhood, you can't do so.

I've shifted more than once, but they were soon after you ordering you up to that beastly place" (*P.P.*, 1871, xix, Q. 20297). A Devonport magistrate, generally sympathetic to the Acts but concerned about police intimidation, cited the case of Bessie Blewitt, who had abandoned prostitution and had gone to live with a man in a private house. In investigating the basis for her request to be removed from the register, the police went "several times to this house, where, in every probability . . . the persons she was lodging with would refuse to allow her to remain," forcing her back into a brothel (*P.P.*, 1871, xix, Q. 8303). Indeed, according to the magistrate, Mr. Ryder, numerous women testified in court that they were remaining in brothels because they could not get any other place. This locked them into public registration as a prostitute. In the case of Elizabeth Bond the justices said that "while she was lodging at a brothel the presumption was . . . that she was engaged in prostitution" (*P.P.*, 1871, xix, Q. 8303).

Numerous cases were reported to the Royal Commission of 1871 that demonstrated the obstacles women encountered in extricating themselves from prostitution under the Acts. These cases also underscored the difficulty faced by any member of the laboring poor community seeking to help the women in establishing bona fide respectable credentials before the law. Such was the dilemma of Eliza Kemp, who "took the line upwards from prostitution" by settling down with a sailor, but who was nonetheless interfered with by the police. "Her story was that, 12 months ago she was a prostitute but from that time had been living with a man named Martin, who had gone to sea, leaving her an allottment of 2£ a month, and that is strong evidence in her favour. That is looked upon as nearly as good as marriage among that class." Police charged her with going with another man and the repealers took up her case. Like Harriet Hicks, the woman appeared helpless before the complexity of legal entanglements, as well as reluctant to implicate her friends. "Now it is curious when we first asked this poor girl whether she had any witnesses, and what her defense was, and it is was only by suggesting and pressing her with questions that we dug out of her where she lived, and who her friends were, and at last we found they were most valuable witnesses." In fact, when observed by the police, Kemp had been in the company of Mr. and Mrs. Thornton, who themselves were repudiated as unrespectable, hence unreliable, witnesses by the prosecution. On cross-examination, Mrs. Thornton admitted she "was not married to Thornton, but she had lived with him for six years and had two children by him." Speaking of Mrs. Thornton's position, the repeal spokes-man noted, "that whole class is one in which marriage is an exception; but on the other hand, it is extremely important that any remnant of decency remaining should be taken hold of and respected . . ." (*P.P.*, 1871, xix, 19558).

The resistance of registered women and their community to the Acts must be seen in light of the economic and legal sanctions applied against those who tried to protect registered women. In the case of the Plymouth area perhaps the greatest weapon of the police was their power to inform against governmental employees and naval pensioners who let out rooms to prostitutes. If a pensioner proved uncooperative, his pension could be stopped, dock laborers and artisans could be dismissed, and pubs and beershops harboring diseased prostitutes could be placed "out of bounds" for the men in service (*P.P.*, 1882, ix, App.). Police also established a certain "discipline" among the unre-spectable poor; brothelkeepers brought to court on the complaints of moral reformers were sometimes exposed as spies, reporting any new woman who took a room to the police in order to buy protection.[27]

It is thus impressive that 420 cases of violation of the C.D. Acts were brought before the Southampton magistrates between 1870 and 1877, while the Three Towns, where government influence was far stronger, had 118 such cases, 75 of them occurring between 1870 and 1871 (*P.P.*, 1882, liii). These cases represent only a small portion of the women refusing to attend examination during the periods of in-tense political resistance; in Plymouth during the summer of 1870, for instance, the law courts were thoroughly swamped, and only a selected number of recalcitrant women were brought up (*P.P.*, 1871, xix, Q. 1322–24). In these early years the resistance of subjected women was stimulated by repeal agitation and offers of legal assistance, but the women also received substantial support from members of the laboring-poor community.

The collective and individual support accorded prostitutes by their friends and neighbors underscores the role of women in those neighborhoods. Women seem to have been the organizing force be-hind public demonstrations in the defense of registered women. In their response to the Contagious Diseases Acts, they appear motivated by personal sympathy for the plight of a neighbor, as well as by hostility toward the metropolitan police as interlopers in their com-munity. Nonetheless, the women of the community were clearly divided in their reaction toward registered women. Some bitterly opposed the

*The Making of an Outcast Group*

presence of prostitutes on the streets. And even respectable women who aided prostitutes appeared ambivalent toward registered women; in some cases only a deep resentment against the water police may have overpowered a certain repugnance and distance they felt toward prostitutes.

Many of the women who intervened on behalf of registered women were prostitutes or brothelkeepers themselves, but repeal workers also reported complaints by "poor but respectable neighbors" of the "heartless way in which the girls [brought under the Acts] were treated" (*Shield*, 4 July 1870). When the police tried to apprehend Mary Ann Ferris of Granby Street, two of her female friends struggled to release her from their custody, while sympathetic and curious crowds assembled which "became large and followed the policemen and the women through the most public streets to Devonport [where the lock hospital was located]" (*Shield*, 28 February 1871). In addition, popular support for the women and hostility to the police were manifested in the courtroom. For instance, the acquittal of Inspector Annis in 1876 from the charge of molesting a virtuous young shop girl was met with "a perfect storm of indignation and the Bench was literally hissed and howled at from all parts of the Court, and particularly from the crowded gallery." The newspaper account specifically noted the behavior of women in the mob: "Men and women—indeed, the *women seemed ten times more fierce than the men*—stamped their feet, shook their fists and fairly grinned at the magistrates, and the Court ultimately broke up in confusion" (emphasis added; *D.I.*, 7 and 14 October 1876).

Women brought under the Acts were often assisted by individual neighbors; they were hidden when police came, lent money, or permitted to pay their rent when they had the money. In 1883, at the trial of Mrs. Lang of 11 Central Street, Plymouth, for brothelkeeping, Ellen de Courcy was asked how much she paid for her room: "She took a room from Mrs. Lang and paid her what she could."[28] While this may have perpetuated a system of indebtedness to brothelkeepers,[29] it also reflects the tradition of mutual aid among the poor, who understood much better than most middle-class reformers and philanthropists the character of seasonal and irregular employment and the hazards of poverty.

Female neighbors not only protected women from the police; they were also instrumental in aiding young women's escape. Since 1870 there had existed in Plymouth a kind of underground railway that spirited women out of the district to rescue homes in London. The local rescue worker indicated that two-thirds of the young women who applied for help had been found or brought there by poor women (*Shield*, 10 February 1877). Lodging-house keepers often assisted in prostitutes' escape, although they may have been instrumental in bringing these young women into the trade. R. B. Williams, of the Rescue Society of London, reported one instance where a lodging-house keeper, "more merciful than the agents of the law" had hidden two new arrivals in a cupboard and

with a transient compunction of conscience or with a desire to compound for other misdoings, which I have not unfrequently seen amongst this class, took the two girls the same night to a benevolent person at Plymouth, who has frequently sent girls to the Rescue Society, remarking, "These poor things are very unhappy-minded about theirselves [*sic*] and, as they will soon be made as bad as others if they go up to Flora Lane [the examination house], I shall be glad if you will try to get them into a Refuge, or anywhere where they can get respectable again (*Shield*, 15 July 1871).

Prostitutes also maintained important relations with their families. Many of the young women had left home for financial reasons; on a day-to-day level they were expected to rely on their own resources. Nevertheless, the aid they could receive in times of crisis was a testimony to the enduring family support that persisted. Thus, while a number of young girls were apparently orphans, others were able to depend on their female relatives when faced with legal prosecution. At their trials aunts, mothers, and married sisters, who resided in town or in the neighboring countryside, would appear and testify on their behalf, often at great personal sacrifice. Bessie Bunker's mother was threatened with being prosecuted under the Contagious Diseases Acts if she tried to protect her daughter (*Shield*, 1 July 1871). In addition to their supportive presence at trials, relatives defended the women in other ways. Some relatives promised to take the women away if they were taken off the police register. Others, like Fanny Church-ward's mother and Mary Jeffries, physically defended their daughters from the police (*Shield*, 20 September 1873, P.R.O. Adm. I/6202, 23 September 1871). The parents of Mary Ann Ferris, Jane Jeffries, and Alice Osman were identified as "consenting parents" who encouraged their daughters in prostitution and ran brothels themselves (*W.D.M.*, 11 February 1871; *P.R.O.* Adm. I/6202, 23 September 1871; *W.H.I.*, 3 December 1870).

Some parents were not so sympathetic. The fathers of Mary Ann

Holman, Emma Edwards, Bessie Clarke, and Elizabeth Baker would not take them back (*W.D.M.*, 12 April 1870, 17 October 1870; *Shield*, 15 July 1871, 8 April 1873). Some could not afford to have them return home, as in the case of Mary Hayles' mother, who explained that her husband was an unemployed laborer (*W.H.I.*, 3 December 1870). The rejection of these marked women was often the consequence of social and economic constraints. In one case a young woman who had left prostitution and returned to her family was still required by the police to submit to examination. Threatened with the loss of her stepfather's job in a public company if she refused to sign the voluntary submission, she eventually complied, although it meant her exclusion from the family: "So at last I signed, and was then examined, and as father had said, I shouldn't stay at home as I was brought under the examination" (*Shield*, 12 November 1870).

In the face of glaring publicity, the women's support from neighbors, relatives, and friends inevitably crumbled. Many landladies experienced the same ambivalence toward subjected women as the woman's own relatives. A basic concern over public respectability recurs. What bothered respectable neighbors was not the "immorality" of a young woman so much as the notoriety gained by police visits and the economic sanctions that could result (*Shield*, 9 June 1877).

A significant portion of the local community was hostile to prostitutes from the start, although their antagonism may have been exacerbated by the police and the examination system. A petition to the Home Office in 1870 from forty-five inhabitants of the neighborhood surrounding the Southampton examining house complained that "their feelings have been outraged and scandalized, and their interest in many cases injured" by the placement of the examination house in their neighborhood (*P.P.*, 1871, xix, Q. 17350). In general, local "matriarchs" acted as the voice of righteous indignation in the neighborhood, objecting to the presence of "bad" women as well as the scandal of the examination in their vicinity. One woman commented that the "neighbours made it a rule to shut themselves indoors until it [examination hours] was all over" (*P.P.*, 1871, xix, Q. 17342). Another woman expressed concern that children had begun imitating examining procedures: "My little girl came to me the other day and asked me what the young women went into the examining house for; she understood they went in there to undress" (*P.P.*, 1871, xix, 17351).

Mothers were equally distressed over the invidious comparison their impressionable offspring drew between the greater affluence of prostitutes and the lesser income of respectable working women. Children outside the examination house were overheard discussing:

It is more than mother got who went out washing. My mother is out now, one little girl said, and will be tired to death. Wait a bit and I shall go as well, and my mother shall not go out to wash like that. . . . and they live better than we do. See how fine they dress, and they get more than we do (*P.P.*, 1871, xix, q. 12644).

One can only speculate on the feelings of certain groups in these working-class communities who remained silent in the midst of the C.D. Acts controversy. Young working women who were not prostitutes articulated very little public response to the Acts, although they may have participated in crowd activity on the streets, and some may have signed petitions against the Acts which were circulated in their neighborhoods. Like the indignant married women cited above, young single women who chose to eke out a pitiful though respectable living may well have resented the flamboyant dress and easy spending habits of prostitutes. Part of their reticence may also have stemmed from motives of self-preservation, since association with prostitutes rendered a woman's character suspect to the police and could lead to her name being placed on the registration list. One milliner who left Plymouth because of the system of police intimidation claimed that malicious neighbors contributed to this reign of terror by threatening "you with the Water Police." She also noted that the general neighborhood response to subjected women was condemnatory: "When girls are arrested, all look on them with disdain; some perhaps with pity."[30]

While police officers acknowledged that registered women subsequently experienced difficulty in obtaining respectable employment, their social exclusion from the general poor community may have more seriously disrupted the normal pattern of their lives. Of special significance was the abandonment of women by their lovers in the military services. At the height of legal resistance in Plymouth in the summer of 1870, seven men defended their women in court; they claimed they were living monogamously with the accused, although they acknowledged that the women had checkered pasts. But not all working men responded in this way. Ester Levi, Elizabeth Bond, Matilda Brown, and Lavinia Lambert all pleaded in court that their men had either abandoned them or refused to marry them until they were taken off the register (*W.D.M.*, 7 August 1870; *W.H.I.*, 2 September 1872, 2 May 1874; *P.P.*, 1871, xix, q. 8429). The metropolitan police seem to have actively harassed some of the men: Maria Barnett's fiancé, who was a sailor, was upbraided by Inspector Anniss for planning to marry a prostitute (*P.R.O.* Adm. I/6418, 30 October 1873). In addition police were known to report an enlisted man's liaison with a prostitute to his commanding officer (*P.P.*, 1881, vIII, App. 18).

By 1883, when the Contagious Diseases Acts were suspended, the character of prostitution in Plymouth and Southampton appears to have been distinctly altered. The women subjected to the Acts were clearly getting older; much larger numbers were in the over-thirty category. In the Devonport district, 106 out of 403 (26.3 percent) "known common women" were listed as thirty-one years and older for 1881, while there had been only 54 out of 557 (9.7 percent) in this age group in 1870. Southampton showed a similar trend: 4 out of 154 (2.6 percent) in 1870, as opposed to 20 out of 110 (18.2 percent) in 1881 (*P.P.*, 1882, LIII). Similarly, lock hospital records document the increasing recidivist rate of registered women admitted to the lock wards throughout the 1870's. Hospital authorities acknowledged that their rehabilitation program only worked effectively with first-timers— women who had not yet entered upon a professional career of prostitution.[31]

Contemporary reports confirm this trend toward professionalization. Both repealers and C.D. Acts authorities noted that women were staying longer in prostitution, but predictably they disagreed on the reasons for this trend. Police officials tended to stress the improved health and increased longevity of prostitutes under the Acts; repealers emphasized the stigma attached to being a registered woman, as well as the fact that women who remained in the districts profited from the system and bragged about being "Queen's women," i.e., sanctioned by the government. What the change does suggest is that prostitution had become more profitable; because of police surveillance the amateur dollymops had been "deterred" and a streamlined, rationalized "work force" resulted. Also, as prostitutes became public figures through the registration process, it became increasingly difficult for them to gain respectable employment and to move in and out of their other social identities.[32]

III

The history of the women of Southampton and Plymouth suggests the process by which working-class prostitutes were transformed into a specially identified professional class. But most of the accumulated evidence on subjected women presents a picture of poor women integrated rather than excluded from the community of the casual laboring poor. The eventual isolation of prostitutes from general lower-class life was largely imposed from above, although it received the passive acquiescence of the poor themselves.

It may well be that the experience of registered women was symptomatic of important long-term changes in working-class life: a growing inflexibility in social norms and habits and a restriction in occupational identities and personal mobility. The isolation of a separate criminal class may have been a necessary corollary to the increasing social and legal pressures placed upon the poor to adhere to a more rigid standard of public respectability. Thus, it could be argued that the Contagious Diseases Acts, by establishing an unusually effective system of police surveillance and public stigmatization, simply accelerated a process occurring more slowly elsewhere. National criminal statistics for the late nineteenth century lend support to this thesis. The changing composition of registered women anticipates the national trend toward a general narrowing down of "antisocial" behavior among a smaller but more readily identifiable group of women, as indicated by declining arrest rates for women for both summary and indictable crimes and by increased recidivism among women prisoners, who increasingly occupied older age categories.[33]

Some indications of the changing character and dimensions of prostitution may be observed as well. If criminal statistics for the early twentieth century and the post-World War I period are compared, in London, for instance, there was a notable decline in arrest rates for "known prostitutes," a change in the occupational background for those imprisoned, and increased recidivism among those imprisoned. In part this decline may be related to changes in social and sexual mores that altered the nature of the "demand" for prostitution. There is some evidence that the rigid Victorian double-standard system had broken down in the postwar years; observers noted that among young people extramarital sexual relations on a "noncommercial" basis had substantially replaced the need for prostitution.[34]

While a diminished demand for commercial sex may partially explain the apparent decline in prostitution, changing social and economic options for working-class women need to be examined as well. If the character of nineteenth-century prostitution was largely determined by limited economic opportunities for poor working women and by prostitutes' ability to reintegrate themselves into the general poor community, then two conditions would appear necessary for the transformation of lower-class prostitution: repressive public sanctions that would make the move into prostitution a different kind of choice than it had been when it constituted a temporary and relatively anonymous stage in a woman's life; and the economic transformation of the casual laboring poor community. The general trend in crime statistics cited above would indicate that police and judicial measures, as well as the efforts of moral reformers and educators, had had some visible impact on the social behavior of the poor. Furthermore, historians have argued that decasualization in the late nineteenth century and especially after World War I transformed the life style of the urban lower classes, affording the unskilled steadier incomes and higher real incomes. Despite high unemployment rates in postwar years, chronic casual poverty—which was the basic precondition for the kind of prostitution found in nineteenth-century Plymouth and Southampton—had largely been eliminated by industrialization, a rise in real wages, and a decline in the birthrate and in overcrowding.[35]

Nevertheless, it is unclear what the net effect of this improved living standard was for women. It may well have afforded women greater economic opportunity to support themselves, since the real wages for women substantially exceeded prewar levels and increased mechanization expanded their employment opportunities.[36] But it also may have made men more viable as supporters of the family, whether as husbands or fathers. The decline in mortality and birth rates and the easing of overcrowding may have helped strengthen the lower-class family unit, perhaps making it more possible for young women to remain at home. These developments may have further contributed to a privatized, home-centered culture and stimulated lower-class antagonism toward women who supported themselves as "public" women.

More stringent public sanctions against unrespectable social behavior as well as economic access to the means of maintaining a respectable life style seem to have had a decided impact on public prostitutes, poor working women, and working-class culture in general. Decasualization may have meant higher real incomes and greater economic security, but also a significant loss of autonomy. In addition, the lower strata of the working class would be permanently enclosed within city walls, within the home, and within the bounds of respectable social behavior, while the poverty that persisted would be more invisible, isolated, and desperately anonymous.[37] The history of

Southampton and Plymouth prostitutes suggests the early outlines of this process; the registration and confinement of prostitutes under the C.D. Acts and their ultimate isolation from the community of the laboring poor marked an important formative stage in the making of an outcast group.

# 5. *Image and Reality*

### The Actress and Society

### *Christopher Kent*

THE 1841 OCCUPATIONAL CENSUS LISTS 387 ACTRESSES IN ENGLAND AND
Wales and 987 actors. The 1911 census lists 9,171 actresses and 9,076
actors. This twenty-six-fold increase among actresses, and the altered
ratio of their numbers to actors', is remarkable evidence of the growth
of the stage as a profession for women.[1] Even in 1911, however, the
stage could not be regarded as a statistically significant source of female employment. Rather, the figures are an index of the theater's, and
particularly the actress's, growing significance for society: to Victorians
the profession of actress, like that of governess, had a symbolic importance as an occupation for women that transcended mere numbers.
It offered striking opportunities for independence, fame, and fortune,
and even for those outside it the stage incarnated fantasies, providing
vicarious release in the notion that here was an area of special dispensation from the normal categories, moral and social, that defined
woman's place. Indeed, a writer in the *Englishwoman's Review* remarked on the discrepancy between the rather lurid popular image
and the mundane reality:

The life of an actress is to the world at large a curious *terra incognita* peopled by
forbidding phantoms of evil or seductive visions of pleasure and success; as a
gifted woman's devotion to art, or the honest and laborious means by which she
earns her bread, the vocation of the actress is understood by few.[2]

This chapter explores the interplay of image and reality in the actress'
profession as it evolved from the Victorian period, through the Edwardian, up to the eve of World War I.

The division of this chapter proposes four distinct phases in the profession's development. The initial period, 1830 to about 1850, was one of nationwide economic and social unrest to which the prosperity of the theater was very vulnerable. A further complication was the artistic uncertainty that attended the defeat of the old patent theater monopolies. The profession was still dominated by theatrical families and it offered little to attract the outsider by way of economic, social, or artistic opportunities. From the 1850's to the 1870's, however, a marked recovery in the fortunes of the theater appears to have corresponded with a successful campaign for the patronage of the middle class and a significant opening up of the profession to outsiders. This development culminated during the 1880's in a period of intense and well-publicized debate over the status of the profession, in which the situation of actresses became the dominant theme. Finally, the fourth period, from about 1890 to 1914, saw a striking growth in the artistic quality and explicit social significance of the English drama which accorded actresses in particular artistic and social opportunities, and even political importance, unparalleled before or since.

Though the stage shared in the growing public esteem of the artistic professions, it still remained the least respectable of them. Women were caught between Victorian dictates of modesty and the public self-display that the theater demanded. Painting and writing were relatively private arts; acting, however, could not be done anonymously (except to the extent of assuming a stage name), nor could it be done in the home. "Respectability" is of course a question-begging term, and while it is evident that the public image and social acceptability of the actress improved somewhat during the Victorian period, and that the profession recruited from higher social ranks than previously, the relationship between these developments was not one of simple cause and effect.

Players optimistically referred to their occupation as "the profession," but it had no formal controls over recruitment, no institutionalized avenue of entry, no established qualifying standard, and no mechanism of self-government, though tentative steps were being taken by the end of our period to remedy these shortcomings. Meanwhile it was easy for outsiders to enter the profession, particularly newcomers of good family who were felt to raise its status. Even by Victorian standards players were inordinately sensitive about status. On the other hand, that outsiders were often amateurs who were not dependent on the stage for their livelihood ran contrary to the professional ideal. This dilemma was increasingly sharp among actresses by the end of the century. But other problems were also traceable to the absence of a homogeneous professional ethos. One finds evidence of a growing divergence between the traditional actresses, for whom acting was above all a livelihood into which they were born, and those actresses who specifically chose the stage as an avenue to social or economic advancement, as a means to artistic self-fulfillment, as an assertion of individual autonomy, or as a means of furthering the cause of women generally. Yet these very divergences gave the profession of actress peculiar importance, both in its projection of new images of women for society at large, and in its reality for the growing number whose profession it was.

I

Describing the life of her parents, who were provincial players in the 1830's, Adelaide Calvert remarked on the relative ease of entry into the theater at a time when the exhausting routine, low pay, and low social esteem lent it little attraction.[3] Provincial stock companies toured the regional circuits playing repertoires of truncated classics, melodramas, and farces in minor theaters and town halls for salaries averaging a pound or so a week. The even more precarious "fit up" companies strolled the countryside, ready to perform in stableyards and barns wherever an audience seemed possible. This vagabond world was chiefly inhabited by theatrical families who intermarried and commonly raised their children for the stage. Such families were economic units, maximizing their opportunities and resources and giving mutual support against a society which regarded them as suspiciously as it did the other "rogues and vagabonds," with whom the law had until very recently classified them. Indeed, the very Bohemianism of this way of life was the chief attraction to those outsiders who came within its orbit. This was the world unforgettably caricatured by Thackeray and Dickens in the Snevellici and Crummles families—the mother taking parts while raising a family whose members might first appear on stage well before the age of ten, as did Adelaide Calvert, the Terry sisters, Madge Robertson (Mrs. Kendal), and Marie Wilton (Mrs. Bancroft), who played pages, fairies, perhaps Little Eva in *Uncle Tom's Cabin,* or were even taken from the cradle backstage to play the stolen baby in the popular melodrama *Pizarro.*[4]

In such circumstances, belonging to a theatrical family was

clearly an advantage—particularly for actresses, whose careers tended to be significantly shorter than actors', beginning earlier and ending earlier. Because girls were preferred for both male and female child roles, demand for them was disproportionate: according to census figures, during the period from 1841 to 1911 the proportion of actresses below the age of twenty varied between 19 and 23 percent, while the equivalent for actors was only 5 to 8 percent. Even in 1841 actresses under twenty outnumbered actors under twenty.[5] In the absence of child labor or compulsory education laws the pathway to the stage was largely unobstructed for a girl born into a theatrical family.[6] A typical start was as one of the supernumerary fairies in the pantomimes that practically every theater put on at Christmas. The Victorian panto-mime was voracious of young girls. They were hired in swarms, especially for the major London production, where they were fastened to frames to make set pieces: in the all-important transformation scene great formations of spangled fairies, dazzling in the limelight, ascended by means of elaborate mechanisms, while solo fairies flitted down from the flies supported by wires and harnesses.[7] Most of these roles were purely decorative and fairly undemanding, though there were singing and speaking roles for a few. Many actresses born outside the profession got their start as children in pantomimes, usually on the initiative of parents anxious to increase the family income. (Their brothers were likely to be found in the maritime scene, lying on their backs beneath the wave cloth, agitating it with their arms and legs to simulate the tossing sea.) The early Victorian theater was very partial to precocious child performers (e.g., Ninetta Crummles, the stunted "Infant Phenomenon"), a situation that often led to exploitation of children by parents or guardians. The actor Ben Terry—no wicked father apparently—took up management to promote and profit from the talents of his young children, as did H. L. Bateman, and the father of Amy, Percy, and Julia Roselle.

Although a London reputation was the goal for those child actresses who made the transition to an independent adult career, the provincial stage was felt by most to offer the best preparation. One of the better provincial companies in the 1850's and 1860's was the Bristol and Bath Stock Company, where Marie Wilton, the Terry sisters, and Madge Robertson trained under James Chute's management (Barker, *NCTR*, p. 11). More commonly, however, provincial managers provided little training, and the young actress simply did what she could to acquire a useful repertoire of parts and learn the time-honored "business" attached to each. She was helped by opportunities to watch and work with London stars, who periodically toured the provincial theaters. She would also find her place in the complex hierarchy of "lines" that characterized the profession at this time. An agent's ad in the *Era* (4 March 1860) lists "Lady Characteristic," "First Walking Lady," "Old Woman," "Broad Chambermaid," "Singing Chambermaid," "Soubrette," and "First Burlesque" among the lines wanted. However, as Leman Rede remarked in his useful handbook *The Road to the Stage* (1836), the glamorous "First Tragedy" and fine lady roles were generally overcrowded, and he recommended that the neglected "Old Woman" offered the best opportunities to a young novice.[8]

Unless a young actress had unusual talents, connections, or luck, singing and dancing abilities were useful, because the common theatrical program, at least until the 1860's, contained three or even four pieces: perhaps a curtain-raising farce, a burlesque, a melodrama, and a tragedy. The short, lighter pieces (and the inevitable Christmas pantomime) often included singing and dancing. Because Covent Garden and Drury Lane in London held a monopoly on pure spoken drama, the minor theaters resorted to spicing their dramatic entertainment with music and dance (and horses, lions, water-filled tanks, and anything else that would draw) with such success that they created a popular taste to which even the patent theaters had to submit. Hence we have the oft-lamented "debasement" of the theater, which continued well past the abolition of the monopoly in 1844. The sorting-out or purification of the theater came in the latter part of the century, particularly with the growth of the music halls, which siphoned off some of that less-respectable part of the theater audience who were felt to encourage the illegitimate interpolations. This, in turn, prepared the way for wider middle-class patronage of the legitimate stage, a trend that would have important implications for the actresses' social situation.

No doubt there was some loss of status in the acting profession during the early nineteenth century as the upper classes withdrew much of their traditional patronage of the stage, and the increasingly dominant lower-class elements of the audience made known their demands and preferences, often vehemently, as they did in the Old Price riots of 1809 and the anti-French riots of 1849.[9] Within the profession itself, however, the traditional hierarchy of parts was still respected, from the First Tragedy at the top, down through the character and comic parts, to the singers and dancers at the bottom. (The operatic and ballet stage must be placed somewhat apart here, for it was a major beneficiary of the aristocratic patronage withdrawn from the regular stage; but it was dominated, especially in its remarkably highly paid upper reaches, by foreign prima donnas like Pasta, Grisi, Malibran, and Jenny Lind.[10]) The decline in status, or self-esteem, is best exemplified by W. C. Macready, who was generally acknowledged as the head of the profession in the 1830's and 40's and who frequently expressed his sense of shame in belonging to a profession unfit for a gentleman such as he (a Rugbeian) considered himself.[11]

But whatever its status, the stage still offered real economic opportunities, particularly for women, though most notably at the less exalted end of the professional spectrum. Thus, the remarkable musical comedienne Mme. Vestris could command as much as £40 a night on tour. Plaster casts of her shapely legs were on sale in London, for she made her reputation in "breeches parts"—male impersonation roles that enabled her to display more leg than female dress allowed.[12] (It will be recalled that Dickens' Miss Snivellici "always played some part in blue silk knee smalls at her benefit."[13]) Though her dramatic talent was modest, Vestris' entrepreneurial talent was considerable; she made and lost a good deal of money during her innovative career in theater management during the 1830's and 40's. Her contemporary, the versatile Fanny Kelly (so greatly admired by Charles Lamb), amassed during her acting career £20,000, with which she built her own theater and drama school (which unfortunately failed).[14]

The moral and social image of the theater received a boost with the renewal of royal support in the 1840's, when the new Queen and her Prince Consort often attended the theater. Victoria particularly favored certain actresses, such as Caroline Heath (Mrs. Wilson Barrett), who was later appointed Reader to the Queen, and Helena Faucit (Lady Martin), who married the biographer of the Prince Consort and became a frequent royal guest.[15] Miss Faucit, who acted with Macready and was one of the leading tragic actresses of her time, believed very firmly in the power of the stage as a moral influence, particularly in elevating her own sex. She considered it her duty "to put in living form before her audience the types of noble womanly nature as they have been revealed by our best dramatic poets, and especially by Shakespeare" (Martin, p. 166). She did so with some success; one critic remarked on "the contagious elevation of thought and purity of sentiment proceeding from this young lady, which, next to devotion itself, tends powerfully to confirm man in the paths of virtue" (Martin, p. 125).[16]

Among Helena Faucit's greatest admirers was George Eliot, who admitted to being inspired by her while writing Herr Klesmer's lectures on art and artists in *Daniel Deronda* (1876), a novel that is significant as one of the few serious literary treatments of the theatrical profession in the nineteenth century (Martin, p. 338). The novel takes place in the mid-1860's. Gwendolyn Harleth has chosen to become an actress rather than endure "the dead level of being a governess"[17] when she is forced to support herself. After she has enjoyed some measure of success as an amateur, Klesmer admonishes her for her dilettantish desires, and he upholds with pride the professionalism of the true artist, which transcends mere talent in its arduous pursuit of perfection. Although the novel supports artistic feminism, it also reveals some ambivalence in Eliot's attitudes toward the theater. The potentially corrupting effects of a life on the stage are clearly shown in the case of Mirah, Deronda's fiancée, who only escapes them when she leaves both the theater itself, for which she has been brought up, and her father, an actor who has debased his histrionic talents by using them to deceive his own family. Moreover, the novel makes it clear that the theatrical profession, whatever its artistic claims, still conferred a very questionable social position on its members: "the honour comes from the inward vocation and the hard-won achievement: there is no honour in donning the life as a livery," Klesmer tells Gwendolyn (I, 366).

*Daniel Deronda* was an inspiration to at least one intelligent actress. Alma Ellerslie read it (and *Sartor Resartus*) to fortify her idealism during her struggles.[18] By showing the stage to be a place of serious art that required intelligent commitment, George Eliot departed from the literary tradition of portraying players as feather-brained babblers, vacantly reciting their lines. Thackeray's Pendennis, infatuated by the beautiful Miss Fotheringay, earnestly asks her how she interprets the role of Ophelia—whether she was in love with Hamlet or not: " 'In love with such a little ojus wretch as that stunted manager of Bingley?' She bristled with indignation at the thought."[19] Yet Edmund Yates and George Henry Lewes, both of whom of were intimately connected with the theater, had the highest praise for Thackeray's characterization. Lewes commented that, generally speaking, the intelligence of actors and actresses was "below par."[20] In extenuation one obviously can point to the extremely unfavorable conditions prevailing in the theater at this time which could foster such an impression—the intellectual poverty of most contemporary plays and the inadequacy of rehearsals. As a sympathetic writer remarked:

A very different thing is that same drama, which yesterday afternoon perhaps only two or three of the dozen people employed in it knew a syllable about, to those who act and to the audience who sit in judgement thereon. To the former it is a miraculous achievement. To the latter, a disgusting stupidity. Yet perhaps no critic among the audience knows better than those whom he condemns, what it ought to have been.

("A Few Words about Actresses," p. 392)

The system was greatly at fault, the writer concluded. And, it must be added, the lack of formal education among most of those born to the stage was a further hindrance.

## II

Women born outside the theater showed increasing interest in the profession in the latter part of the century. One of them was Helen Taylor, a woman of considerable intelligence, the daughter of Harriet Taylor Mill and stepdaughter of John Stuart Mill. Fascinated since childhood with acting, she regarded the stage as a career offering both independence and an opportunity to apply her artistic and intellectual powers to some high purpose.[21] With the reluctant consent of her mother she took lessons with the leading comic actress, Mrs. Fanny Stirling, and in November 1856, under the assumed name "Miss Trevor," she entered the theater as a novice (though at twenty-five she was hardly young by actress standards). The short, secret period of her "experimental life" (as her mother hopefully called it) brought Helen Taylor into contact with the various levels of theater life, from established companies in Newcastle and Glasgow, to a precarious touring company.[22] Generously supported by her mother (she was paid £1 per week in Glasgow, but elsewhere nothing) she could afford comfortable accommodations and an elaborate wardrobe—actresses were expected to provide their own costumes—and even a servant. But by self-consciously living as economically as possible, she did get some sense of the relentless grind of the actress' life: the travel, the search for temporary lodging in a succession of strange towns, the desperate

*"The Poor Actress's Christmas Dinner,"* R. B. Martineau.

race to learn the next day's lines, the constant preparation, repair, and cleaning of costumes, the morning rehearsals—all this in addition to five hours of attendance every night at a theater that was often dirty and cold.

Helen Taylor was eager "to carry out my own ideas in the great parts"—Lady Macbeth and Portia appealed particularly to her —and she was indignant at the "atrocious trash" chosen by the managers (f. 41, 27 November; f. 164, 15 December 1856). She was also dismayed at the limited business assigned to her. The competition for parts was considerable; the theater in Sunderland listed ten actresses on one playbill, many of them novices like herself. She acquitted herself well in her few parts; in her debut she was greatly praised by the other actresses for her self-possession (which drew from Mrs. Mill the characteristic comment that it showed "what a low class they generally are connected with the theatre, as no well-bred young lady would show any, or feel much trepidation on such an occasion"; f. 131, 10 December 1856). Her experience soon made her aware of her ignorance of the "mechanical aspects" of acting, and she remarked on the advantages of those "habituated to the stage from childhood" (f. 71, 2 December 1856). She quickly lowered her sights and even accepted a pantomime part, to her mother's dismay. But whether her intellectual and artistic qualifications might prove the foundation of a successful career was not to be answered, for her mother's sudden death in 1859 terminated the experiment. She left the stage to become her stepfather's devoted secretary and a leading feminist.

Helen Taylor might have gone far had she continued her stage career. She was attractive, dignified, intelligent, and respectable; above all, the moment was propitious for respectability in the theater. Interestingly, she made her debut in the company of another novice, Henry Irving, who had made his professional debut in the same theater only two months earlier.[23] Irving was the harbinger of a new trend in the profession, the first (and greatest) of a group of outsiders who went on stage in the late 1850's and 1860's—Squire Bancroft, Charles Wyndham, and John Hare—and by their eventual knighthoods won for the stage the decisive mark of professional respectability.

The 1860's, a peculiarly transitional decade in the English theater both artistically and socially, were above all the decade of Tom Robertson. His carefully produced "teacup and saucer" dramas, moralistic social comedies with earnest monosyllabic titles (*Ours, Caste, School*), decisively confirmed the tendency to a new style of acting—

the underplayed, nonchalant, drawing-room style which became the orthodoxy for nearly a century and perhaps created as much as reflected the middle-class conception of gentility for a succession of generations. The correct rendering of Robertson's *nuancé* dialogues required a fairly intimate knowledge of polite society (and Robertson's elaborate and didactic stage directions made clear his doubts that most players had such knowledge [Watson, p. 412]). Edmund Yates, writing at this time on "the Social Position of Actors," had protested against the ungentlemanly sneers of the *Saturday Review* at the vulgarity of actresses, observing sarcastically: "You see, as a rule, women do not work in England except from sheer necessity, and actresses, women who go on the stage, have little experience of the life they sometimes have to portray" (*Temple Bar*, May 1863, p. 185). Fortunately for Robertson's plays, they were first performed by the company of the Prince of Wales Theatre, which included members such as Bancroft and Hare who had the requisite social credentials.

The "Robertsonian Revolution" was largely sponsored by an actress. The manager of the Prince of Wales was Marie Wilton; born of first-generation theater people, her unsuccessful father was the errant son of a good country family who, his daughter wrote, "in succumbing to the surface glitter of the stage . . . struck the fatal keynote to his destruction." Starting as a child actress—"When other children were cozily tucked up in bed, dreaming of their sunny lives . . . I was trudging by my father's side in all weathers to the theatre, where I had to play somebody else's child"—she followed the usual provincial apprenticeship and then came to London, where she won popular acclaim as burlesque "principal boy" at the Strand Theater (*The Bancrofts*, pp. 2, 3, 38). She was able to break out of this line when in 1865 she borrowed £1,000 from a relative, took over a shabby and unfashionably located little London theater, and redecorated it into a pink- and blue-draped, upholstered, and carpeted band-box; elegant and intimate, it was perfectly suited to the fastidiously staged drawing-room comedies of Robertson.[24] It was also perfectly suited to overcoming the antitheatrical prejudice of the respectable middle class (white lace antimacassars on the seats were the crowning touch). Miss Wilton soon married the gentlemanly Mr. Bancroft to form a theatrical partnership that brought them considerable artistic and tremendous social and financial success. By 1885 they were able to retire from the stage to a home in Mayfair, and a life of conspicious and punctilious gentility.

Women were not in fact uncommon in mid-Victorian theater management. One of the problems of the serious career actress was that, having reached a certain level of achievement and reputation, it was difficult for her to obtain the higher and more demanding roles that could satisfy her artistic ambitions without taking a theater of her own ("A Few Words about Actresses," p. 392). This was true in London, at least; an alternative was to remain in the provinces as a touring star. Theater management required some capital (though not necessarily a great deal) or a sponsor; there was of course risk involved, and managerial turnover was very high at some theaters. The St. James had at least four manageresses between 1854 and 1878, including Mrs. Seymour (Charles Reade's friend and later mistress) and the capable Mrs. John Wood.[25] At the Strand, Miss Swanborough was extremely successful in producing burlesques during the 1850's and 60's (Watson, p. 389). Another burlesque entrepreneur was Lydia Thompson, whose troupe of "British Blondes" toured the United States with considerable success in the 1860's and 70's.[26]

Many actresses were content to make a reasonable living in run-of-the-mill light comedy—which they could do so long as they retained their looks and vivacity. Some actresses were kept women, supported by "wealthy and dissipated men . . . for the gratification of their own selfish passions" ("A Few Words about Actresses," p. 392). Such "patrons" exerted influence over venal managers to promote the careers of such women at the expense of honest, self-supporting actresses. Alma Ellerslie's diary records a conversation with a man who asked her why she did not take a theater to advance her career; when she replied that such an undertaking required money, he remarked (significantly dropping into French), "*Vous pouvez toujours trouver de l'argent*" (Ellerslie, p. 117). Most actresses no doubt expected to marry eventually.[27] Marriage to an actor would probably mean continuing in the profession, with increased opportunities if he were successful or in management. But even a less advantageous professional marriage at least brought companionship, certain domestic economies, and some protection of respectability, all of which were probably very attractive to the ordinary actress, especially one born to the stage. But the *Stage Directory* (March 1880, p. 8) warned against the professional and domestic strains of actor-actress marriages, and it urged actors once married not to let their wives work and not to marry until they could afford to do this.[28] The married actress often continued to be billed as "Miss_____" because there was felt to be greater drawing power in the appearance of "availability" in an actress. Marriage outside the stage would more likely mean leaving it. Marriage to an actress was enough of a defiance of convention for most men, without allowing a wife to continue her career. However, the eccentric Henry Labouchere supported the career of his wife, Henrietta Hodson, in acting and management, and even the respectable Theodore Martin agreed on marrying Helena Faucit that "she was to be free to continue the practice of her art" (Martin, p. 320).

There were other occupations related to acting, to which the older actresses often gravitated. One was teaching acting and elocution (and not just to theater aspirants; clergymen and barristers were among the elocutionists' clientele). Another was giving readings, which had the double advantage of fulfilling artistic aspirations and conferring greater respectability; people who would not consider entering a theater would flock to a meeting or concert hall to hear Shakespeare, poetry, and novels read dramatically by Helena Faucit, Mrs. Stirling, or Fanny Kelly.[29] Although Emily Faithfull, the feminist journalist, publisher, and promoter of women's employment, was herself a lecturer and elocution teacher, the mid-Victorian feminist movement seems to have paid relatively little regard to the stage as a career for women, which probably reflects both the movement's concern with respectability, and the stage's want of it. Also, the stage hardly needed publicizing as a field for women's employment. Thus, the 1876 *Handbook of Women's Work* makes no mention of the stage, and from 1876 to the end of the century, the *English Woman's Review* was almost as taciturn; actresses rarely received the obituaries given to other prominent women. The few mentions the stage did receive were usually of a cautionary kind: in 1883 the plight of twenty young English girls "employed in the theatre" who were working in Paris and had to lodge in the dirty back room of a "hotel of very doubtful character" was noted in the *English Woman's Review* (15 September 1883). *Women and Work* (11 December 1875, p. 7) warned in its Guide to Employment that "women wishing to enter the dramatic profession should never answer anonymous advertisements in the papers," but should deal only with respectable and established agencies.[30]

If the 1860's witnessed the arrival of a genteel generation in the profession, the late 1870's saw many of its stage women already established in positions of influence. The great era of the actor-manager had begun. A number of changes were occurring within the theater, with important implications for the profession. The theater business was becoming more profitable, as evidenced by the spate of new London theaters built from the late 1860's on (Watson, p. 9). This prosperity seems to have been due initially more to fashion and the return of the affluent classes to the theater than to any improvement in the quality of the drama. There was a great expansion in the theater's potential audience, particularly in London, as improved transit services linked the West End with suburbia.[31] The playbill, which had been reduced to a double bill by Edmund Kean in the 1850's, was further reduced by the Bancrofts to a single main production. The practice soon became general (Watson, p. 99), and, along with longer runs, it made for better productions, which in turn increased the artistic self-respect of players. It also lightened the burden of rehearsal and study, giving more time for social life and other pursuits. The shorter programs permitted a later start, in step with the fashionable dinner hour, and an earlier finish. Other changes, such as the suppression of the pit (the traditional center of rowdiness), the introduction of orderly queuing, the increase in ticket prices, and the adoption of evening dress by the audience, were evidence of the growing gentility of the theater (Hudson, pp. 81–83). Prosperity also raised the profession's level of pay (for persons above the lowest ranks, at least), and there followed a decline in the demeaning practice of taking benefits to supplement earnings.[32]

Players were increasingly visible in "society." Society itself was becoming somewhat less rigid in its criteria of social acceptability, while the profession was becoming more socially acceptable. The Prince of Wales was an important influence in this loosening of the stays. In the 1860's he took over from his mother as chief royal patron of the theater, in which his tastes were fairly catholic, and his patronage more convivial than artistic. Lady St. Helier, one of the eminent society hostesses of the late nineteenth century recalled that until the 1870's "the stage was a part of the community which lived in its own little world, entirely absorbed with its own professional interests and having no communication with any society outside its boundaries."[33] She was one of the more adventurous hostesses who first opened her doors to actors and actresses.

Even the church, the oldest and firmest enemy of the profession, showed signs of a new attitude toward the theater. Purification replaced anathematization as the watchword among some clergymen, and a spate of pamphlets appeared in the late 1870's dealing with the moral reform of the stage. More advanced still was the Reverend

Stewart Headlam, a radical Church of England clergyman who in 1879 founded the Church and Stage Guild, the avowed aim of which was to break down the prejudices endemic in the church against the theater and theater people and to vindicate their worthiness.[34] Its original committee included Emily Faithfull, as well as Genevieve Ward and Mrs. Kendal, two of the most successful and respectable of their profession. The Guild caught on and soon attracted a large membership of clergymen eager to meet players in an uncompromising setting, players eager to meet sympathetic clergymen, and other persons who supported the rapprochement. The awkard truth, however, was that Headlam was drawn to the lost sheep of the music halls, particularly the spiritually neglected ballet girls of the Alhambra and Empire theaters for whom the Guild gave parties lasting until 4:30 A.M. There was too much frivolity and too little piety in all this for some of the Guild's earliest supporters, and Mrs. Kendal and a number of other actresses from the legitimate stage fell away, apparently unhappy at having to fraternize with the vulgar music-hall entertainers from whom their profession was, after all, striving so hard to dissociate itself (Bettany, pp. 100–103).

## III

Mrs. Kendal, who was a sister of Tom Robertson (and who proudly claimed that she never played opposite any man on the stage except her husband), created a stir in theater circles when in 1884 she was asked to give an address on the drama to the National Association for the Promotion of Social Science. She took the opportunity to deliver an optimistic homily on the moral and social position of the stage.[35] Generalizing from her own gratifying social ascent, she remarked that acting was at last being recognized as a profession, and that "the terms 'actor' and 'gentleman' may now be considered synonymous." "How many educated girls," she earnestly asked, "finding themselves through force of circumstances suddenly compelled to face the world on their own account, have turned with relief from the stereotyped position of a 'companion' or a 'governess' to the vista that an honourable connection with the stage holds out to them?" (Pemberton, p. 117). Not only were players becoming respectable, but respectable young women were becoming players. Mrs. Kendal's claims were scornfully dismissed by F. C. Burnand, the old Etonian editor of

*Punch* and a successful burlesque playwright. "Would any one of us wish our daughters to go on the stage?" he asked. "There can be but one answer to this. 'No!'" A well-brought-up girl would react to the stage in one of two ways, either recoiling in disgust at "life behind the scenes" and fleeing, or else succumbing to its corruption "until the fixed lines of the moral boundary have become blurred and faint." The only women who could resist the moral infection of the theater, he maintained, were those brought up in it under the protection of their parents. Like Mrs. Kendal, they developed a sort of immunity which enabled them to ignore its immoral influence.[36] Burnand's provocative article created a great stir in theater circles and a number of actors leapt forward to defend the honor of actresses. Interestingly, Burnand, a Catholic, twice married actresses, the second being his deceased wife's sister.[37]

The virtuous Mrs. Kendal was perhaps not fully aware of the terms on which actresses tended to be taken up by fashionable society. The social analyst T. H. S. Escott probably showed more accurate insight when he noted the strain of "prurient prudishness" and taste for "a *soupçon* of naughtiness" in society's stage-struck condition: "Actresses are taken into society not professionally but on an unreal footing of equality which makes them more diverting." Society was entertained by their pretensions, amused by actresses who "comport themselves with the mien of women to whom imperial sway is a second nature."[38] At the very time of Mrs. Kendal's address, a well-publicized breach of promise suit was being brought by the attractive actress Miss May Fortescue against Lord Garmoyle. Born May Finney, daughter of a London coal merchant who had gone bankrupt, she went on stage to support her mother and sister and joined the Savoy Theater company to appear in *Patience*, for which she received £6 per week. She met Lord Garmoyle "in society"; he proposed and she accepted. His parents, who regarded the stage as "sinful and profane," reluctantly consented, with the provision that she and her sister (who was preparing for the stage) immediately abandon it, which she did. However Garmoyle finally broke off the engagement under family pressure, explaining that "looking into her profession, she would not be received by his friends and relations." He admitted his breach of promise and offered to settle privately, but Miss Fortescue, who was "not simply a pretty brainless doll" (as she noted in a letter to him), insisted on going into court to vindicate her conduct publicly and to demonstrate her entire innocence in the matter. She then accepted £10,000 in damages. A leading article in *The Times* cited the case as proof that successful players were no longer "social cyphers," and noted that the amount was "no extravagant estimate of the worth in society's scales of the rank of countess, even if a generous valuation of the prospects of a theatrical career" (21 November 1884, pp. 4, 9).

Like all female Savoyards, May Fortescue had in W. S. Gilbert a jealous guardian of her reputation. Under his benevolent moral despotism in the 1880's, the theater came to be called the "Savoy Boarding School," because backstage visitors were virtually prohibited and the actors' and actresses' dressing rooms were located on opposite sides of the stage.[39] Gilbert had a number of young women in his charge, many of whom had not been born into the profession and were of good family—daughters of the clergy and of professionals. He was very conscious of the moral snares so luridly portrayed by Burnand (whose rather overdrawn picture was most applicable to "fast" variety theaters like the Gaiety—the Prince of Wales's favorite haunt), and he took his responsibilities very seriously as a "Dramatic Daddy," in one protégée's phrase, to his girls.[40]

By the 1880's the influx of women outsiders into the profession seems to have begun to catch up with that of men.[41] One important reason for this was the growing publicity given to players in the press. Like the empire, the stage was a realm where the popular press found glamor and excitement for its swelling readership. George Moore, a scathing critic of publicity-induced "Mummer-Worship," even suggested that the stage was attracting idle and cowardly young men who would not join the army or face the hardships of colonial life, and surplus young women who could not.[42] Mrs. Kendal complained of the "insatiable thirst for newspaper paragraphs" among her colleagues, and the increasingly undignified, personal style of theatrical journalism (Pemberton, p. 134.). Such writing was evident not only in journals specializing in theatrical matters, like Clement Scott's *The Theatre* (founded in 1878), with its photos of leading players, but also in the proliferating society and women's magazines, such as Ella Hepworth Dixon's *The Englishwoman* with its breathless, intimate interviews of "Stage Stars" by "Baroness von Zedlitz" (e.g., "She [Olga Nethersole] held out a warm, sensitive hand which, when I clasped it in mine, sent a current of sympathy straight to my heart and I at once realized that here was not only an artist to her fingertips, but a lovable woman" [August 1896, p. 434]).

Such publicity commonly emphasized the status and inde-

*A Widening Sphere*

pendence of the actress' life, and no doubt gave vicarious satisfaction to women who could either sympathize with it or censure it, as they chose. Although most of the leading actresses, at least Bancroft, Ward, and Kendal, were very respectability-conscious, one outstanding exception was the wayward Ellen Terry. She embodied a sort of Bohemian life-style, and she received a special social dispensation that made her the quintessential actress. Her checkered private life was condoned; she bore two illegitimate children, but society's attitude toward her behavior was summed up in Lady Salisbury's comment that it was "never immoral, only rather illegal" (Steen, p. 204). Her privileged position, her beauty, her common touch, and her talent combined to give her symbolic stature, in the phrase of her biographer, as "the Queen of Every Woman." She was no doubt the greatest single influence on young women eager to go on the stage, many of whom she directly encouraged: Violet Vanbrugh, Lena Ashwell, and Dorothea Baird, all from professional or clerical families, were three of the most notable. Her friend, the very proper Lewis Carroll, introduced Dorothea Baird to her only after cautiously seeking Mrs. Baird's permission and sympathetically but explicitly outlining Ellen Terry's unconventional "history."[43]

Many of the newcomers to the stage were fashionable amateurs, and Ellen Terry's encouragement of them offended some of her colleagues, who viewed them as a threat to their professional livelihood. The wings of the Lyceum, according to Kate Phillips (herself the daughter of a fox-hunting squire) "stank of debs and Debrett," as drawing-room dilettantes competed for walk-on parts. Managements often encouraged them because their families and admirers were "good for a block of stalls, or two or three boxes" (Steen, pp. 162–63). Also, they were indifferent to salaries and could afford to dress themselves well (especially for the increasingly popular "society" plays) at a time when most managements still required actresses to provide their own costumes. Ironically, while •they perhaps enhanced the social status of the profession by their association with it, they undermined its status as a profession by their amateur attitude.

An additional factor in the recruitment of actresses that became increasingly important in the final decades of the century was the virtual collapse of the old provincial stock companies, which also meant the disappearance of the traditional training ground where young actors and actresses had acquired versatility and discipline through the repertory experience. In the absence of recognized dra-

*"Ellen Terry as Lady MacBeth,"* J. S. Sargent.

matic academies, aspirants had more than ever to look to London, where minor parts in long runs provided much less experience, which in turn offered up yet another hostage to amateurism.[44] Another characteristic of this period was the continuing competition between professional beauties like Lily Langtry and Mrs. Cora Brown Potter, both of whom adopted the stage as a career in the 1880's and relied chiefly on their well-publicized looks and their connections (both women were friends of the Prince of Wales) for success. Lily Langtry made large sums—£60,000 in the 1880's alone, thanks largely to her American tours—and was able to go into management.

## IV

Although beauty and sponsorship were of perhaps greater importance to the success of an actress in the 1880's than at any time before or since, women of intelligence and artistic ideals also aspired to the stage. After ten years as a governess and lady's companion, Margaret McMillan decided to train for the stage in 1888, but instead she applied her voice training to exhorting dockers during their great strike that year, and she went on to become a pioneer member of the Independent Labour Party and a great educational reformer.[45] A much better-known socialist governess with ardent dramatic ambitions was Eleanor Marx. In 1882, after a struggle with her father, she took lessons with veteran actress Mrs. Herman Vezin, who saw signs of talent in her. Her sister Jenny, whose own earlier dramatic aspirations had been discouraged by parental concerns with respectability, encouraged her in hopes that she might have the "prospect of living the only free life a woman can live—the artistic one."[46] Eleanor was, of course, an admirer of Ellen Terry, and even when Mrs. Vezin finally concluded that she would never achieve "real greatness" on the stage, she persevered. Her few amateur performances, chiefly in her husband Edward Aveling's plays, drew mixed notices, however, and her very real contribution to the English theater and to the actress' profession lay in her work as propagandist and translator of Ibsen in the 1880's.[47]

Elizabeth Robins, a feminist actress and writer, had considered one of the major problems of her profession that there were so few challenging parts for women.[48] This complaint was answered by the rise of Ibsenism in the 1880's, and the subsequent efflorescence of the English drama in the 1890's, when H. A. Jones, Pinero, Wilde, Shaw, and Barrie in their different ways discovered the "new woman" and wrote her into the newly fashionable sexual problem plays. These plays were a boon to an upcoming generation of intellectual actresses like Janet Achurch (the first English Nora), Elizabeth Robins (the first Hedda Gabler), Florence Farr (the first Rebecca in *Rosmersholm*), and of course the queen of the female psychodrama, Mrs. Patrick Campbell, who created the parts Paula Tanqueray and Agnes Ebb-smith.[49] The older generation may have disapproved—Genevieve Ward called *Ghosts* "an exhibition fit only for an audience of doctors and prostitutes"—but such actresses were now sought out and fêted by the literary and artistic avant-garde, and some of them became intellectual confidantes to Shaw, Yeats, Wells, Bennett, and Henry James (Robins, p. 198). It was a heady time, and a far cry from Thackeray's Miss Fotheringay. When Janet Achurch produced Ibsen's *Little Eyolf* in 1896, with a cast that included herself, Elizabeth Robins, and Mrs. Patrick Campbell, the event epitomized the changed situation of women in the theater, not only as actresses, but as audience too (Hudson, p. 96). It was an experimental production and played four matinees; the matinee was itself a new feature of the period, offering a testing ground for experimental and minority drama, and matinee audiences tended to be predominantly women, who were more responsive to intellectually demanding plays than the tired businessman audience of the evenings. These serious women provided much of the audience for Shaw's didactic plays in the famous Vedrenne-Barker matinees at the Court Theater.[50]

The artistic and professional momentum generated in the 1890's was sustained until the eve of World War I as women became more prominent in the theater than ever before (or perhaps since), not only as actresses and audience, but as directors, producers, and playwrights. Janet Achurch, Elizabeth Robins, and Cicely Hamilton were playwrights as well as actresses. Florence Farr, Gertrude Kingston, Lena Ashwell, and Lillah McCarthy became actress-managers, with their own companies and the freedom to produce the experimental and intellectual plays that the much better known commercially-minded actor-managers tended to shun. In addition to this greatly increased level of professional participation and artistic responsibility among women in the theater, there was a growing sense of mutuality, reflected in organizations like the Theatrical Ladies Guild, founded in 1891 to assist needy actress-mothers with children's clothes, and struggling actresses with wardrobe.[51] Later the Three Arts Club was founded and promoted by actresses to provide residential and social centers not only for actresses, but for independent women in the other artistic professions as well, to free them from the drab and lonely lodgings that were such a terrible part of the young actress' life.[52]

Though the 1890's were the decade of the Ibsenite revolution, they were also the Naughty 'Nineties. If some of the ablest late-Victorian actresses were in the vanguard of feminism, the majority continued in their more traditional role of populating the fantasy world of the people, on and off the stage. Nowhere was this more successfully done than at the Gaiety Theatre, where George Edwardes staged a succession of extremely popular musical comedies—*The Shop Girl* (1894), *The Circus Girl* (1896), *A Runaway Girl* (1898)—filled with beautiful actresses. The legendary Gaiety Girls were the quintessence of all that was daring and exciting about actresses, and a godsend to the popular press, which breathlessly followed their saucy exploits and traced their fortunes.[53] And their fortunes were spectacular in some cases. In the last decades of the century a number of peers rushed in where Lord Garmoyle had feared to tread: wits joked about the "actressocracy" as the years 1884 to 1914 saw nineteen marriages between actresses and members of the English nobility, fourteen of whom were peers.[54] The phenomenon reflects more on the changing attitudes of the aristocracy than on the social acceptability of actresses. The fashion for such marriages perhaps indicated a sense of *après moi le deluge* in an era of declining landed incomes, since the actresses did not bring fortunes, unlike the more useful American heiresses, who were also in vogue.[55] But Arthur Wing Pinero, who dramatized the changing social status of actresses in *Trelawny of the Wells* (1898), offered a more cheerful eugenic interpretation of such marriages in his *The 'Mind-the-Paint' Girl* (1912), where a character compares the weedy, chinless aristocrats with the "strong frames, beautiful hair and fine eyes, healthy pink gums and big white teeth" of the musical comedy actresses, declaring that they will be "the salvation of the aristocracy."[56]

While these actresses cheerfully bore the burden of public sexual fantasy, smiling coyly out of a thousand picture postcards, and while a few of them actually realized off the stage the same fairy tale romances they portrayed on the stage, their more serious sisters were defining new roles for women both on the stage and off. Lena Ashwell, Cicily Hamilton, Elizabeth Robins, Decima and Eva Moore, Lillah McCarthy, Irene and Violet Vanbrugh, Sybil Thorndike, and May

Whitty were among the most active members of the Actresses' Franchise League, founded in 1908.[57] Its members marched and spoke out at suffrage demonstrations, but their most notable contribution was the publication and presentation throughout the country of a number of feminist plays and entertainments designed to spread the message and raise funds for the cause.[58] In the spring of 1913, when Miss May Etheridge married the future 7th Duke of Leinster at the Wandsworth Registry Office, militant members of the Actresses' Franchise League were contributing their skills in make-up and costuming to provide disguises for Grace Roe and other suffragette leaders who were dodging the clutches of the "Cat and Mouse" Act.[59] Image and reality neatly coincided: actresses had become prominent forces in society, as well as Society.

# 6. Women and Degrees at Cambridge University, 1862=1897

*Rita McWilliams-Tullberg*

IN 1837 THERE WERE ONLY FOUR UNIVERSITIES IN ENGLAND, NONE OF them open to women. The continental challenge to Britain's industrial might in the latter half of the nineteenth century lent urgency to demands from industrial centers for local universities attuned to their needs and willing to try educational experiments. By the end of Queen Victoria's reign, there were twelve universities and university colleges, all of which educated women to degree level and awarded them degrees.[1] Women were also allowed to study at Oxford and Cambridge, the oldest and most prestigious institutions; indeed, Cambridge was the first university to encourage women's studies. Yet after taking the same examination as men, they were not awarded the degrees they had earned. They left the ancient foundations with curious pieces of paper known as "certificates of degrees" and with no letters after their names, often to meet with mistrust and misunderstanding from a suspicious world.

The story of the admission of women to degrees at Cambridge is a telling illustration of masculine ambivalence toward women's struggle for emancipation. Since women clearly made progress toward the goals of economic and social independence during the second half of the nineteenth century,[2] it is sometimes assumed that men's attitudes developed simultaneously in a positive direction. The fierce resistance to women's enfranchisement in prewar Britain comes as something of a surprise, especially when one's reading has been confined to women's successes on the educational front. Women's successes were matched by a conspicious failure in the later nineteenth century to make progress toward the vote. It is therefore important to note that in the country's two most respected universities, finishing schools for the nation's leaders, attitudes to women's educational advances were often most restrictive. The conservatism of these two foundations was not a reflection simply of their greater age, but of their peculiar constitutions. Graduates who left Oxford and Cambridge did so not merely with a feeling of affection for their alma mater, but with a vote in the future administration of university affairs.[3] A refusal to share this power with women was one of the major reasons for denying them their degrees, and in this respect the women's degree campaigns at Oxford and Cambridge can be seen as microcosms of the national struggle for female enfranchisement.

The women's education movement shared with the suffrage movement and with other groups working for the social, economic, and legal rights of women a desire to free women from preconceived roles as subservient and incapable relatives of men. Yet the aims of particular groups were often at variance. While suffrage workers wanted votes for women, on the grounds that women could make good use of the power they would thus achieve, Cambridge women were not particularly eager to have a voice in the university's decision-making processes and, until the 1920's, they were prepared to bargain this potential privilege for something they regarded as more important —the equal recognition of academic work whether performed by a man or a woman. With the benefit of hindsight, we can doubt whether either group had a really clear grasp of what they intended to do with the vote or degree once obtained. Neither reform, while essential in itself, has proved to be the hoped-for springboard to female advancement. After the first flush of enthusiasm, women's political activity rapidly declined, and university-educated women were, and still are, largely to be found at low-status levels in a limited number of professions.

The two movements do demonstrate similarities in their tactics and in the opposition they faced. Both the suffragists and the women at Oxford and Cambridge believed that they could demonstrate, by hard work and good behavior, their maturity and suitability as voters and holders of academic honors. Unfortunately, their demonstrations of competence, whether as citizens or students, were not enough. Although Oxford men succumbed and gave their women degrees in the general confusion of enfranchisement in the immediate postwar years, Cambridge men remained unmoved, despite the academic achievements and the war work of their women students. It is also

*A Widening Sphere*

clear that the suffragists were no nearer to victory in 1905, when the Pankhursts burst on the scene, than they had been in 1866. The reforms that were successfully promoted by women and their friends in the late nineteenth century were largely concerned with woman in her domestic setting and sought to adjust the legal position of woman to the popularly approved role of superior moral being within the family. Meanwhile, too few men were convinced or frightened enough to offer her a share in power outside her home or immediate neighborhood. We should not, however, underestimate the factors which hindered women's advance but which were not specifically related to the "woman question." Constance Rover has written that the delay in getting the vote "was largely the result of the vicissitudes of party politics."[4] Degrees for Cambridge women were also sacrificed on occasion for the sake of other reforms. Nor is it easy to suggest tactics that would have led to an earlier success, though it is possible that bolder action in the early stages of the movement would have secured victory before objectors had time to organize their opposition.

From an early date it was recognized that public support could be lost by mixing appeals for greater educational opportunities with demands for other reforms in the status of women. Mrs. Josephine Butler acknowledged this at the start of her crusade against the Contagious Diseases Acts and withdrew from both the suffrage and the education movements.[5] Emily Davies, who founded Girton College, was originally involved with the Women's Suffrage Committee and took a leading part in the presentation of the 1866 petition to Parliament. But she too withdrew from active support during the early years of the Cambridge campaign, explaining that suffrage was a source of controversy and dissension even among women. "So on the whole, I think with Lady Goldsmid that 'We had better quietly withdraw and stick to our "middle-class"' (i.e., education)" [sic].[6] Nonetheless, the suffrage issue did impinge on the Cambridge struggle, because opponents refused to believe that this withdrawal was total,[7] and because it was assumed that Cambridge women wanted a voice in the running of university affairs in the same way they wanted to participate in national politics.

Our study is here confined to women's admission to Cambridge. The pattern of struggle was similar in Oxford and Cambridge in the nineteenth century, the universities taking turns to grant women some favor and deny them another. Only in the twentieth century, when the "woman question" was less of a cause per se and instead a strand in the universities' fight for continued independence while receiving government grants, did the two take separate courses. Oxford admitted its women students to degrees and university membership in 1920.[8] Cambridge, after several bitterly fought votes, gave women the titles of degrees and allowed them to take university posts, but it was not until 1948 that women were admitted to university membership. By then, the voting rights of nonresident graduates had been reduced to a token and the number of women residents at Cambridge was contained at a reassuringly low level.

I

Several early strands of reformist thought on the question of women's education are apparent. There was a small group inspired by the ideals of the French Revolution who believed women were human beings who shared a common humanity with men and who therefore should be allowed to develop their intellects. To this group were later added John Stuart Mill and his disciples, who decried the subjection of women to men and who strongly supported their enfranchisement. Other reformist groups stressed the importance of character training and solid learning in preference to showy accomplishments. Frederick Denison Maurice and Charles Kingsley, both early workers for improvements in women's education, could not accept the full consequences of women's emancipation, and they tended to consign women to secondary supporting roles within a morally renewed society. Such views, which became the popular refuge of many reformers as the century passed, were a source of great difficulty for Cambridge women because they implied a theory of "separate development." A third important factor was the growing public concern in the 1840's and 1850's for the quality of education given to both sexes and all classes, which manifested itself in three Royal Commissions[9] and many schemes for reform. Thoughtful opposition to women's education usually coupled it with the growth of free thought and moral laxity; opposition was otherwise based on men's wishes to see their domestic authority unchallenged by their womenfolk and was expressed either in the romantic terms of Ruskin's "separate spheres"[10] or as a question of "Man's Rights and Woman's Duties."[11]

Among women themselves the question of reform was one less of ideals than of practical urgency. The industrial revolution had produced in Britain a class of business and professional men who, in the second and third generations, had adopted codes of behavior that weighed heavily on their womenfolk. Middle-class girls were to be prepared not for married life but for the marriage market. Selling-points were thought to be personal appearance, accomplishments, submissiveness, and ignorance, which was usually described as innocence.

But demand, it was realized by mid-century, did not match supply. Not only did nature produce an excess of women over men, but the numbers of available men were further reduced by service in the army, navy, and colonies and by an apparently perverse desire of men to remain single. Trollope, in an exchange between Frank Greystock and his companion Herriot in *The Eustace Diamonds* (1873), echoed the opinion of the contemporary commentators who believed that the excess of females was exaggerated and that the reason men did not marry was because of foolish ideas about the financial burden of a wife and family.

That idea as to the greater number of women is all nonsense. Of course we are speaking of our own kind of men and women and the disproportion of the numbers in so small a division of the population amounts to nothing.[12]

To the suggestion that a man did not marry because he was afraid he could not feed his wife and family, Greystock replies, "The labourer with twelve shillings a week has no such fear" (Trollope, Ch. 24).

It was, however, true that the basis of middle-class wealth was often unsound and fortunes readily lost. Professional incomes were strained by the demands of middle-class life, especially where there were many girls in the family. Despite the fantasy that a middle-class girl had nothing to do but await the appearance of a rich suitor, her need to earn a living was often pressing. Unfortunately she had been taught to dread and despise such activity. Edward Carpenter has described the empty lives of his six sisters as they waited for marriage, a life of boredom that was nevertheless preferred to the prospect of earning a living.

It is curious—but it shows the state of public opinion of that time [1860's]—to think that my father, who was certainly quite advanced in his ideas, never for a moment contemplated that any of his daughters should learn professional work with a view to their living—and in consequence he more than once drove himself quite ill with worry. Occasionally it happened that, after a restless night of anxiety over some failure among his investments, and dread lest he should not be able at his death to leave the girls a competent income, he would come down to breakfast looking a picture of misery. After a time he would break out. "Ruin impended over the family," securities were falling, dividends disappearing; there was only one conclusion—"the girls would have to go out as governesses." Then silence and gloom would descend on the household. It was true; that was the only resource. There was only one profession possible for a middle-class woman—to be a governess—and that was to become a pariah.[13]

Many girls in this situation earned little beyond bread and board, and with some justification since they were often thoroughly incompetent as teachers. From the pathetic case histories gathered by the Governesses Benevolent Institution, which was founded in London in 1841 "to afford assistance privately and delicately to ladies in temporrary distress," it soon became clear that the status of governesses would not improve until it was recognized that education for all middle-class girls should be improved as an insurance against later distress.

This idea was put into effect by another group of women who were fortunate to have no financial worries but who suffered under prevailing convention which thwarted their every aspiration. They longed to be useful, instead of "dabbling in paints and music" like Carpenter's six sisters, who wandered aimlessly from room to room to see if by any chance "anything was going on" (Carpenter, p. 32). These women joined Maurice in founding Queen's College, London, in 1848, and in the following year another group opened Bedford College. The early histories of the two establishments are familiar;[14] they were responsible for training women who were to have a reforming influence on girls' schools. It was these schools which provided the pupils for the great experiments in Cambridge from the 1860's on. One special feature of Queen's College was the attention paid to testing students. The authorities felt examinations would help train women in disciplined study, and as college women took up work in a few girls' school, many of them also felt the need for a standard comprehensible to the public that would measure their students' progress.

The leader of the latter group was Emily Davies, founder of Girton College and sister of Maurice's close supporter, Llewelyn Davies. She was secretary of the Kensington Society, a ladies' discussion group with about fifty members, where women's questions were aired by such devotees of the cause as Helen Taylor, Sophia Jex-Blake, Barbara Bodichon, Frances Power Cobbe, Elizabeth Garrett, and Elizabeth Wolstoneholme. She had gained valuable experience helping her protégée, Elizabeth Garrett (Anderson), in her struggle as a woman

*A Widening Sphere*

to acquire full medical qualification in Britain. (For this story, see Manton, Part 1, pp. 17–163.) Above all, she had learned that although a woman could, without too much difficulty, buy herself an education of the highest quality, her chances of having her intellectual achievements attested were nil, and so, in consequence, were her chances of challenging the male monopoly of public life and the professions. During the 1850's, examinations for schoolboys had been started by the Royal College of Preceptors, the Royal Society of Arts, and Oxford and Cambridge. Though they were still a controversial feature of educational reform, they were seized upon both by those in the women's education movement who, like Miss Davies, were concerned with education as a means of demonstrating women's equality with men, as well as by those whose aims were more purely educational.

Emily Davies began making informal inquiries in the summer of 1862 at both Oxford and Cambridge regarding the position and attitude of authorities toward opening their Local Examinations to schoolgirls. Her Oxford correspondent, John Griffiths, Secretary of the Local Examination Delegacy, found the matter of examining young ladies quite beyond the university's sphere of duty (Griffiths to Davies, 22 July 1862, Girton Archives), and when Dr. Frederick Temple of Rugby was approached for his support, he stressed that girls should have "privacy and modesty."[15] He felt they would be harmed by competition. The reply that Emily Davies received from Cambridge was more encouraging. The Cambridge examinations, like those of Oxford, were not held at the university but in centers all over the country, administered by local committees. Since such committees would bear the heavy and novel responsibility of conducting the examinations, Davies was advised to secure their support.[16]

She found that there was much sentiment against the indelicacy of bringing together girls "of that rank"[17] whose families were not acquainted with each other. In addition, the Liverpool local committee strongly opposed the idea of examining girls on the grounds that the status of examinations would be ruined in the eyes of boy candidates. If Cambridge implicitly approved the identity of education for boys and girls, boys could be expected to prefer Oxford to such an "emasculated institution." The reply from the London committee was more encouraging, and after much delay it was possible to organize a "trial run" there with eighty-three candidates. The authorities at Cambridge had seen no objection in principle to girls using the examination papers, though the marking had to take place privately by arrangement with the examiners. The girl examinees acquitted themselves well in the circumstances and were found on the average equal to the boys in all subjects except arithmetic.[18] Davies made use of these results to illustrate the usefulness of examinations in monitoring the effectiveness of teaching.

Following this experiment and its concomitant requests that the examination be opened officially to girls, a syndicate appointed by Cambridge University to consider the matter reported that they could see no objection to the extension of the Local Examinations to schoolgirl candidates. The voting on the proposal was very close, 55 to 51 in women's favor, but the measure had not really aroused much interest or passion.[19] Emily Davies continued her efforts to open the Oxford Local Examinations to schoolgirls, but opposition there was too strong, especially after the Cambridge vote, and it was clear that Oxford was prepared to let its rival university take the risk of such a novel experiment. Her approach to Cambridge had been supported by a group of reformist young dons, including G.D. Liveing, Henry Fawcett, Robert Potts, J.W. Hales, and Thomas Markby. For the most part, Cambridge was indifferent, and even those men who expressed opposition did so on the grounds of the threat which examinations were thought to pose to a girl's modesty and health or from an opposition to examinations in general, rather than from a perception that their privileged position as men was endangered.

The movement for improved female secondary education recaptured public attention when in 1865, by the persistence of Emily Davies and her associates, girls' schools were included in the terms of reference of the Royal Commission on Secondary Education. Miss Davies hoped that revelations concerning the inefficiency of "ladies academies" would lead to improvements both in the school curriculae and in the training of teachers. In their report the commissioners described the state of middle-class female education as "unfavourable."

Want of thoroughness and foundation; want of system; slovenliness and showy superficiality; inattention to rudiments; undue time given to accomplishments and those not taught thoroughly or in any scientific manner; want of organisation.

(p. 548)

Any academic knowledge that it was felt girls should have was imparted by teachers who were simply not competent for their work. James Bryce, one of the most perceptive commissioners, who was familiar with Davies' views, blamed this on "the want of any institution for supplying a higher education to women" (p. 819) or training them as teachers. Davies gave evidence in person to the commissioners and also sent them a memorandum on the "Need for a Place of Higher Education for Girls," which lamented the absence of a "public institution for women analogous to the Universities for men," and she requested that in any recommendation concerning school endowments or other charities which the commission intended to make, the need for such an institution should not be overlooked. The matter lay beyond the commissioners' brief, but as Emily Davies had already in hand a scheme for a college for women up to university standard, the publicity was of great value.

When her college plans were discussed at a London conference in 1868, attended by over two hundred supporters of both sexes, it became clear that in the mind of the enlightened public there, the most daring feature of the scheme was not that women would be given the opportunity for higher learning but that they would be studying in a college, away from their homes and families (Anne Austin to Anna Richardson, 31 March 1868, Girton Archives). The idea had to be promoted with the utmost care and delicacy, and for this reason Davies planned to site her college in the country, where her students would have greater privacy. A group of Cambridge men who formed a committee to support the college scheme[20] pressed her to locate the college in Cambridge itself. Since only professors and heads of college were free to marry, the colleges were monastic communities in which a man was obliged to resign his fellowship on marriage. A young woman found within college precincts was likely to be arrested by the proctors on suspicion of prostitution. Nor was it yet clear that Cambridge University would give the new college the support and encouragement it required; perhaps London University would prove more generous. With these factors in mind, while openly declaring that her model was no less than Trinity College, Emily Davies insisted that her girls be housed midway between London and Cambridge, at Hitchin.

At the same time, a group of university men were passionately concerned with the quality of education given at both Oxford and Cambridge, and the way in which these ancient foundations exercised their authority over the whole spectrum of education for children and adults. Their concern was justified; on many counts the universities were failing in their responsibilities. Singled out for special criticism at Cambridge were the low standards of the Ordinary degree and the compulsory Previous Examination, the excessive emphasis placed on the study of Latin and Greek, and the exclusive association with the Established Church. Henry Sidgwick, leader of the Cambridge reformists,[21] soon found himself on a collision course with Emily Davies, who was prepared to accept every detail of education in its unreformed state. Only by following to the letter the educational courses laid down for men could women claim to be measured with men. Any divergence from this iron rule of "identity of conditions" would be interpreted by a skeptical public not as a step toward educational reform but as a sop to women's inferior intellects.[22]

An obligatory examination for all students at this time was the Previous Examination, which included a test of Latin and Greek. The Ordinary was a degree of supposedly "general" nature, and its standards were considerably lower than those of the Honours degree. Sidgwick fought a lifelong crusade against the poverty of the Previous and of the Ordinary degree, which he felt had a detrimental influence on academic standards both in the secondary schools and at Cambridge. In Sidgwick's view, students were often given an indifferent classical education where their time might have been spent more usefully on science and modern languages. He knew he would have a difficult task persuading the university and boys' schools to change, but in the new women's institutions, where there was no existing tradition of classical scholarship, Sidgwick felt his reformist ideas could be accepted. Davies, however, was quite unmoved by the academic objections to the quality of the university's examinations, and she accused her critics of wanting separate systems of education for boys and girls. Sidgwick and his supporters discovered that if they wished to experiment, a second women's college would have to be founded at Cambridge.

The opportunity arose in connection with the establishment of new examinations for more mature women run by Cambridge University. A group of women in the north of England, led by Anne Jemima Clough, planned a lecture series for women in the major northern towns and approached Sidgwick for suggestions of suitable lecturers. Sidgwick's choice was Hales, who had actively supported the movement for schoolgirls' examinations. The name of James Stuart was put forward by Josephine Butler and Sidgwick was asked to express his opinion of Stuart's suitability. He wrote that Stuart's studies had been mathematical rather than literary, that he was young and inexperienced, but that he was bright, eager, clever, wrote an effective English style, and had "a quaint simplicity and a naive independence of thought which, if it does not quite deserve the name of originality, is the next best thing to it."[23] Sidgwick's less than wholehearted support for Stuart was fortunately ignored, to the benefit of the University Extension Lecture Movement, which developed from these lectures. It blossomed under Stuart's leadership and gave educational opportunities to thousands of adults in the latter half of the nineteenth century.[24]

Anne Clough had been introduced into the London circle of women's educationalists by her brother, Arthur Hugh Clough, whose work was much admired by Sidgwick, and she soon became familiar with the various aims and plans of its members. Her own chief concern was for the plight of schoolmistresses, their isolation and lack of training in mental discipline. She was convinced that some form of examination was necessary to "test and attest" their knowledge and to give them a goal for their studies. Following a meeting held in London in December 1867 to discuss the establishment of a private association for examining governesses and teachers, an approach was made to a number of men at both Oxford and Cambridge, and though not present at the meeting, Sidgwick was soon involved.[25] The group's aim was for its responsibilities to be taken over by the universities, and in the early months of 1868 a Memorial was drawn up by the women in the north, asking Cambridge for its assistance in the matter. After some consideration, the university agreed that an examination calculated to test the higher education of women could be undertaken without inconvenience; it was to be more advanced than Local Examinations and on a level suited to the older candidates.[26]

Women in the north of England now had the benefit of lectures given by university men and examinations administered by Cambridge to chart their academic progress. Sidgwick reasoned that a similar system of lectures could most appropriately be started in Cambridge itself, in view of the ready supply of young, committed, and underemployed lecturing talent available in the university town. A group of dons, some with their wives, gathered at the home of Professor and Mrs. Henry Fawcett and discussed with some restraint what all understood was a novel and daring plan. According to Mrs. Fawcett, Sidgwick had discussed with his hosts his plan to accommodate women in Cambridge so that they could attend lectures, but the plans were not aired at the meeting for fear of shocking moderates there.[27]

Whether Sidgwick contemplated a residential scheme or not,

he soon received spontaneous applications from women outside Cambridge wanting to attend lectures, with the result that in 1871 he purchased a house in the center of town to accommodate women students. Anne Clough came to take charge of the house and promote the scheme that really interested her, the training and testing of middle-class teachers. The house of residence was run in conjunction with the Cambridge Lectures for Women, and it was assumed that the students would prepare themselves for the newly instituted Cambridge Higher Local Examinations. Yet some of the first students were awarded places after having completed these examinations. Individual study plans were mapped out for them, and from the beginning they included lectures at Tripos level. It is not clear whether Sidgwick had any plan regarding women, degrees, and their position at Cambridge, nor is it clear whether he had analyzed the long-term consequences of his liberal view that a first-class education should be offered to those women capable of benefiting from it.

Emily Davies, whose goals were clear, had opened her college for women in Hitchin in 1869. Her students had already started on the road to Tripos examinations. A curious mixture of vision and conservatism, she was among the last to allow any relaxation of rules of behavior for herself and her students, and she tacitly accepted differing moral codes for men and women. Yet in the field of intellectual emancipation, she insisted that women could only be judged in men's terms. As the idea of women's higher education took root, she grew increasingly afraid of "separateness," and repudiated every suggestion that women should start their own university instead of challenging the male exclusiveness of Cambridge. But there were many practical problems to be overcome before her aim of making the women's college a member foundation of Cambridge University could be achieved.

After a year's hard preparation it was felt that five Hitchin students, trained by Cambridge men who had traveled out to the college by train, were ready to take the Previous Examination. It was by no means certain that they would be allowed to use the university's examination papers, and on top of anxieties about their academic ability, students and staff had to face the possibility that they had spent a year preparing for an examination they would not be allowed to take. When approached, the Council of the Senate felt it was not within its province to permit the use of the papers, but it did not object to a private arrangement being made with the examiners.[28]

They proved cooperative, and, carefully chaperoned, the five students went to Cambridge to write their papers and to see for the first time something of the way of life of the university whose regulations dominated their studies. Fortunately the distractions did not prevent the women from success with their papers. When the question of Triposes arose, the Council took the same attitude: that the papers could be used on an informal basis and could be marked by the examiners privately if they agreed. An adequate supply of examiners were always found who were willing to look over the papers, but for a decade to come the use of examination papers by women was always to be surrounded by uncertainty.

When Sidgwick first entertained the idea of accommodating women students in Cambridge, he corresponded with Davies on the possibility of amalgamating their two schemes but found her unwilling to cooperate. She scoffed at the "other section" who "do not want degrees" and remained deeply suspicious of Sidgwick, whom she felt wanted special university courses for women.

If we could get information as to his ultimate objects, it might be a help in judging whether it would do at all for us to act in any sort of concert with him. As the matter at present stands, it seems best to steadily resist the oft-recurring attempts to draw us into partnership.[29]

She objected to the use made by Sidgwick's students of the Higher Local Examinations, which at this stage were for the exclusive use of women, and remained fixed in her views on the dangers of siting a college for women in the city. When Sidgwick discovered his diplomacy made little headway with the single-minded Davies, he decided they must go their separate ways. Davies and her students moved to buildings at Girton, a village then suitably distant from Cambridge, in Michaelmas 1873. In October 1875 Sidgwick's students moved from temporary quarters into Newnham Hall, on the edge of Cambridge but within walking distance of the men's colleges. Two of Sidgwick's students had successfully entered for the Moral Science Tripos in 1874,[30] but the college still accepted many women who could study for only short periods and who aimed at Higher Locals. While Davies insisted that her women pass the Previous and proceed to a Tripos within the appropriate time limit, Anne Clough, as Principal of Newnham, adopted a more flexible scheme that would meet the urgent demand for schoolteachers faster than was possible under the Girton regime. Firmly steered by Sidgwick, Newnham also allowed students to take Triposes without first having taken the Previous, though they had to prove themselves in the Higher Locals. As Cambridge-educated women returned to girls' schools as teachers and as the general standard of girls' education began to rise, the practice of admitting girls to Newnham solely for the purpose of taking Higher Locals was discontinued, and the patterns of education at Girton and Newnham became similar. That is, women came to Cambridge for the purpose of following degree courses.

During the 1870's the two women's colleges quietly expanded, while avoiding the limelight and rigorously ordering the lives of their students so as to give no cause for complaint. By 1879 Girton had received approximately one hundred students and Newnham, two hundred and thirty. Though their existence was in no way recognized by the university authorities and they were never certain that they could use the degree examination papers, the women were becoming a presence in university life. Some of the women who were successful in the Tripos stayed at their colleges as lecturers, but in the early years women were heavily dependent on men coming in to coach them. Such tutoring was not unwelcome as a source of income for many young dons. There was some reluctance to make the long journey out to Girton, but Sidgwick had less difficulty in persuading men to lecture to his young ladies in rooms conveniently situated in the middle of town. However, it soon became tiresome for some of these hard-pressed dons to repeat their lectures for the small numbers of women students who were preparing for a Tripos. A more economical solution, in terms of both energy and money, was to invite the young ladies, suitably chaperoned, to the Tripos lectures given for male undergraduates.

In 1880 a Girton student, Charlotte A. Scott, was informally bracketed with the 8th Wrangler in the first part of the Mathematical Tripos. This was a great success for women, coming as it did in a subject that was supposedly beyond their mental capacity. Scott's achievement occurred two years after London University had opened its degrees to women, and it highlighted the ambiguous position of female students in Cambridge, where they were taught and examined but in no way officially recognized. There is no record that the women's leaders intended to make an approach to the university at this time, but they were embarrassed into action by the appearance of a Memorial that had been circulated in the Newcastle area by Professor and Mrs. Steadman Aldis, calling on Cambridge to grant "to

*A Widening Sphere*

properly qualified women the right of admission to the Examinations for University Degrees and to the Degrees conferred according to the results of such Examinations" (University Library Collection, Cambridge Papers, Cam.b.500.8[16]). The petition, which had over eight thousand signatures, also suggested that Cambridge treated its women students rather shabbily. The women's leaders in Cambridge were most perturbed by the indelicacy of this approach; even the forthright Davies wrote to Mrs. Aldis and through friends tried to use her influence in the northeast to have the Memorial stopped.[31] Both Girton and Newnham were agreed that the university should not be antagonized by demands for recognition, but if, as it proved, the Memorial could not be halted, they should use the opportunity to remind the university of their worthiness to share in the academic cake. This, however, was the extent of their agreement.

Sidgwick hoped Girton and Newnham could make a joint approach, seeking the formalization of the existing system of examinations and the granting of a certificate to women successful in the Tripos. Davies was very annoyed by the suggestion that both Girton and Newnham students should receive the same certificates. Girton students studied for Triposes on the same conditions as men, while Newnham students followed a course adapted for them. Common certificates would only add to the confusion. She complained to Sidgwick, "people do not understand the difference [between Girton and Newnham] and I am worn to skin and bone trying to make them" (Davies to Sidgwick, 13 March 1880, Girton Archives). Girton, she said, would ask for degrees, and she believed such a request would have the support of the country clergy if the University Council approved the suggestion. According to Davies' report of their discussion, Sidgwick felt this might well be the case.[32] For him the insuperable objection to women seeking degrees on the same terms as men was the Latin and Greek of the Previous, but he declared, again according to Davies, that Newnham would "go for degrees" if compulsory Latin and Greek were abolished.

Sidgwick, however, had the ear of the university, and when the Senate appointed a syndicate to discuss the fifteen Memorials received on the question of admitting women formally to examinations and degrees, Sidgwick was its leading member. He was a much greater opinion-builder than he chose to admit, and opponents were not surprised when the syndicate's report reflected his own ideas on women's education at Cambridge.[33] The syndicate declined to discuss the question of degrees, for reasons they felt unable to explain. Their report proposed that the Tripos examinations be formally opened to women who had fulfilled the normal residence requirements and who had been recommended by their college. On the successful completion of their examination, they would be given a certificate and their names would be published in a class list, though separate from the men. They would be allowed to substitute certain passes in the Higher Local Examination for the Previous, and they would not be admitted to the Ordinary degree (*Reporter*, 1 February 1881).

The report was discussed in the Arts School on 11 February 1881 (*Reporter*, 15 February 1881). The vice chancellor, E. H. Perowne, felt that this was a step toward making woman identical with man instead of man's complement. G. F. Browne, a syndicate member who had strongly supported the opening of Local Examinations to women, believed that the power to discriminate between detail and principle, a logical method of statement, and a developed power of reasoning were not detrimental but advantageous to woman in her complementary role. Browne challenged Perowne and other objectors to show how they believed the Tripos would leave woman unsuited for her role in life. Leader of the university Tories, a group opposed to most forms of university reform, Perowne was described as an "angry, unbalanced man" who could occasionally give the women his help.[34] Browne was also a Tory and an unreliable friend who was later to elaborate his views on educating women for their special role in a scheme for a separate women's university.

Stuart wrote to Emily Davies warning her of Perowne's opposition and the possibility of a "strong whip" against the report. He feared that defeat would mean the end of any connection between Cambridge and the education of women (Stuart to Davies, 19 February 1881, Newnham Archives). John Peile, the university Liberal leader and a member of the Newnham Hall Company, was only a little less pessimistic. He did not think the proposal would be opposed on its own merits, "but the cry of the 'thin end of the wedge' will be raised just before voting and a defeat would be disastrous" (Peile to Davies, 13 December 1880, Girton Archives).

When the matter was put to the vote, it was passed by 366 "Placets" to 32 "Non-Placets," a result that astonished the women and their friends and delighted most of them, though Emily Davies remained unconvinced of its value. The vote proved to be a display of strength from women's supporters and a display of indifference or shortsightedness from the remainder. The formal admission of women to examinations in 1881 was later recognized as that "thin end of the wedge" Peile had mentioned, and women's opponents had cause to regret the concession that was granted. It bound women, though tenuously, to the university's form of education and residence requirements. Astute opponents, like Alfred Marshall, recognized the latter as the most dangerous concession, demanding as it did women's presence in Cambridge, where from an entrenched position they could make further attacks on university male-held privileges. On the other hand, the university had granted women very little—no membership, no degrees, not even the right to attend lectures, and more sanguine opponents rightly felt that the university retained the upper hand. Further, university men were as yet untouched by competition from women; their numbers were too small and their success too exceptional to pose a genuine threat.

## II

Attempts were again made in 1887 to persuade Cambridge to award women degrees, following Agnata Frances Ramsay's success in the Classical Tripos, where she alone was placed in the first class. The move began among Emily Davies' associates, who initially made little progress because they collided head-on with Sidgwick over the now familiar matters of the Previous and the Ordinary examinations. It was an object lesson for the cause's devotees; no headway could be made without Sidgwick's support. The fact that women had demonstrated their academic ability would not automatically result in university recognition. Miss Davies did find some encouragement among university men who resented Sidgwick's indiscriminate condemnation of the Previous and Ordinary,[35] but most of those in favor of the women's cause were prepared to follow Sidgwick's judgment.[36] After months of internal debate, the two factions reached a compromise allowing them to make a combined approach to the university.

Meanwhile, Sidgwick had been canvassing opinion on the "woman question," and the opposition that had first been expressed to him privately now came out into the open when it became clear that an approach would be made under his practiced and influential leadership. Sidgwick, however, was a distinctly unenthusiastic leader. Many Cambridge men who had supported the women since the days of the Local Examinations doubted the wisdom of the move, whether from a conviction that compulsory classics would soon disappear and that women had best wait until then, or out of respect for Sidgwick's position. The controversy also brought to light those among the women's earliest supporters, such as Marshall,[37] Browne, and Sedley Taylor, who now felt that the development of educational opportunities in Cambridge was going too far. Browne and Marshall were "opposed on principle to proceeding any further in the direction of admitting women to academic privileges."[38] For the first time, the fear of women's "interference" in men's affairs was expressed. If women took part in the government of Cambridge, it would cease to be fully responsive to the wants of men. Opponents found grounds for their fears in the adaptation of university regulations that Newnham had made to suit its students and for which it now sought official approval (*St. James Gazette,* 25 July 1887 and 2 November 1887). And when it was pointed out that women's numbers and therefore influence in the university's affairs could be limited, the opponents made the telling rejoinder that any restriction placed on women would be the source of future controversy and agitation. (The number of women resident in Cambridge at that time was about 200.)

As in most debates that accompany women's efforts to break into a man's world, the arguments used by men were not always reasoned, and the fact that discussions were carried on at a great seat of learning does not appear to have affected their logicality. It was possible for a Cambridge man simply to assert that women were better off without degrees and the matter needed no further explanation. On this occasion no one was ever pressed to expand his arguments; university men did not come forward in sufficient numbers to support the women's appeal, and in 1888 the Council voted by eight votes to seven not to appoint a syndicate to examine the matter.

Henry Jackson, who was often called upon to mediate between Emily Davies, whose line on women's education he favored, and Henry Sidgwick, whose enthusiasm for many reformist schemes he shared, blamed the Tories for the defeat of the women's case before the Council of the Senate. But he added in his letter to Davies,

I must confess however, that ever since Dr. Sidgwick's opposition became clear, I have had grave fears as to the *result;* and I am inclined to think that it is better for us to be beaten at the outset, than to be driven to refuse some unsatisfactory compromise at a later stage.

(Jackson to Davies, 14 February 1888, Girton Archives)

*A Widening Sphere*

It is interesting to speculate that women might well have won at least the titles of their degrees if only Sidgwick had given the move his wholehearted support. He was at the time more concerned with curriculum reform, and while a generous worker for the intellectual emancipation of women, he was too ready to believe that the world was populated by intelligent, liberal-thinking people like himself, and he failed to see that reasonableness was a very feeble weapon for a reformer.[39] What was needed was a touch of fanaticism and arguments that could easily be understood. Davies knew that this meant identity of conditions and not complex theories on the value of Greek in the education of young adults. Some years later Ann Rogers explained the matter for the Royal Commission on Secondary Education (1894) from the viewpoint of both an educator and a devoted worker for degrees for women in Oxford.

It is not possible to ignore classics in girls' education while the subject holds the place it does in boys' schools and at the universities; girls will not leave them alone. They feel that if they are to get the full good out of their university, they must study the subject in which men win most credit and in which the best teaching is to be procured. Those who direct their studies cannot make them the object of educational experiments beyond a certain limit nor will the general public think much of a course of work which is followed mainly or entirely by women.[40]

In her work on the women's emancipation movement, Ray Strachey described the late 1880's and early 1890's as a period of deadlock and discouragement.[41] The public was growing bored, irritated by and indifferent to emancipationist propaganda. This was particularly noticeable in the field of education. Great improvements had occurred following the Schools Inquiry Commission; good schools were opened for girls and there were many opportunities for higher education. London University had opened its degrees to women in 1878; the Scottish universities, the Royal Irish, Wales, Durham, and the new provincial universities and university colleges all awarded their degrees to women by 1895. With these successes came public complacency, then reaction. The second inquiry into secondary education, which opened in 1894, had little to say on the specific subject of girls' education beyond noting a "most marked" improvement in girls' schools, private as well as endowed. The universities were congratulated for producing a large supply of competent teachers—"no change has been more conspicious than this, nor any more beneficial" (Report, p. 15)—but were not called upon to make any greater contribution.

Only Henry Sidgwick's brother, Arthur, took the opportunity to explain to the commissioners how tenuous was the new foothold women had in the ancient universities.[42]

The authorities of the women's colleges never forgot the precariousness of their existence and they were extremely vigilant lest their students' behavior should give offence. Generally speaking, the students understood and accepted the limitations laid upon them by the college authorities, and college activities amply compensated for the lack of contact with the rest of the university. The seclusion, however, was harder for the colleges' women teachers to accept. These women were doing important work preparing their students for the university examinations, and they were often eager themselves to follow their lines of research. Their work was continually hampered by their isolation from other university teachers and their exclusion from all matters concerning the organization of Triposes; their enthusiasm for research was dampened by the absence of funds for advanced work. They were barred from university prizes, scholarships, and offices that would have helped to finance research. One major inconvenience was the restriction on their use of the university library, and the negative reaction to their request for a relaxation of this limitation was a clear warning of a growing reluctance to grant women further privileges.[43]

The frustrations that followed from a lack of security and recognition for women at Cambridge were heightened as more and more women throughout the country successfully completed university courses. Yet, after a quarter of a century in Cambridge, the pioneers of the women's colleges were reluctant to put their position to the test by asking for degrees. Both colleges, however, now had a large corpus of old students whose voices could not be ignored. Their practical difficulties in the teaching profession when in competition with women from other universities who had degree letters after their names initially formed the basis of the women's new appeal for admission to university membership and degrees.[44] A great deal of effort was made in the ensuing investigation to show that Cambridge women suffered a genuine disadvantage in not having a degree title, but cases of discrimination were difficult to prove and the argument was further weakened by many of the women's obvious preference for a degreeless Cambridge education over that offered by another university. The Girton/Newnham dispute over "identity of conditions" was muzzled so far as possible by the new guard, who saw it as the prime cause of their defeat in 1887–88. A large group of Newnham women accepted that there should be no special examination conditions for women, and on the Girton side, although Davies refused to work with Sidgwick, it was appreciated that the cause was lost without his influence. His views on the questions of the Ordinary and Previous would have to be swallowed.

When the Memorial asking for admission to university membership and degrees was first circulated in the early months of 1896, more than two thousand Cambridge men gave it their support. It seemed a foregone conclusion that women would be awarded their degrees and that discussions would simply cover the practical details of the arrangements. Yet in May 1897, after eighteen months of bitter dispute and unparalleled disruption of the university's academic life, at least three quarters of these men had changed their minds. The Cambridge women's decision to act at this point was a reflection of earlier activity at Oxford rather than of any general movement in the country. It is interesting to note that the mid-1890's is regarded by Strachey as a turning point in the fortunes of the women's suffrage movement (Strachey, p. 286). Over half of the members returned to Parliament in the 1895 election supported the principle of women's suffrage, but easily allowed themselves to be outmaneuvered whenever a suffrage bill was before the House. The response to the 1896 Memorial also reveals that women had a large measure of support that was not translated into votes for the women's cause. A comment made in the later stages of the struggle is timelessly appropriate; women owed their defeats "not so much to the strength of their enemies as to the supineness of their friends" (*Time and Tide*, 27 July 1923).

It is tempting to seek connections between the two movements, to hypothesize that the modest request for degrees at Cambridge was jeopardized because it was associated with the more advanced idea of women's suffrage. If the connection was made, it was seldom spoken about at Cambridge. Suffrage is rarely mentioned in the material remaining in the Girton and Newnham archives, giving some slight support to the generally accepted view that the two movements understood that their work was best kept separate (Strachey, p. 104).[45] Yet the small but influential group centered round the London homes of Mrs. Humphrey Ward and Mrs. Alice Stopford Green clearly thought Cambridge a bastion of "women's rights" ideas, particularly in regard to the odious question of the vote.[46] When Cambridge was considering giving women some further measure of recognition, Mrs. Green wrote a letter to *The Times* denouncing the duplicity of Cambridge women. She claimed the current agitation was a political tactic of "transparent dishonesty."

Unhappily at the very outset of the whole movement [for the higher education of women], the women whose professed aim was the pursuit of knowledge, timidly consented to a political alliance in which their own interests were and have ever since been, subordinate to the political action whose voice dominates all others.

(19 May 1897)

These specific accusations were largely ignored, though they may well account for the growing belief that women wanted to gain power in the university.[47] Some men clearly thought the issues of degrees and privileges could be kept separate by awarding women no more than degree titles. Yet when women, who had originally asked for degrees and university membership, said they were satisfied with the offer of degree titles, other opponents accused them of hypocrisy, and they had little defense against the charge.

Arguments against the women's gains are difficult to analyze;[48] implicit in all of them was the view that women should not have any say in decision-making processes and could therefore never be admitted to full and equal membership with men in the university. By far the most often used argument was one which in effect avoided any real discussion of the issues involved. The women's request was regarded yet again as "the thin end of the wedge," and therefore, irrespective of its merits, it could not be granted. It was held that Cambridge had a primary obligation to educate men. To give women full equality with men within the university was therefore unthinkable; yet to give them a measure of recognition on terms inferior to men would only lead to further "agitation" for university posts, fellowships in men's colleges and a share in endowments and in the government of the university.[49] This argument was persuasive because all Cambridge men had in mind some limit of numbers and privileges where women were concerned. It may well be the major reason why all but the most ardent supporters of the women's cause felt they must vote against any proposal for women's advancement.

Cambridge had been badly hit by the agricultural slump of the 1870's and 1880's, which had reduced rental incomes, yet the university and colleges found it difficult to attract the big industrial endowments needed to expand their overcrowded lecture rooms and laboratories and to employ more teachers. At the same time, it was feared that the

*A Widening Sphere*

university's whole academic reputation was spiraling downward and that the best students were going "elsewhere," to an Oxford which had recently rejected an appeal for degrees by its women students.[50] These fears were no doubt exaggerated, but Cambridge was in the doldrums in the 1890's, and there was fertile ground in which to propagate the claim that Cambridge as a mixed university would no longer be considered a serious academic institution and would quickly slide into irrevocable decline. The assumption at the root of this— that university education given equally to men and women was somehow inferior to that given solely to men—was rarely touched. Many Cambridge men were ambivalent. While rejecting the women at Girton and Newnham, they were certain that the Cambridge women's colleges were the best in the world. When elaborate schemes for a women's university were drawn up by opponents,[51] they received no widespread support, and few plans envisaged a total break between Girton, Newnham, and Cambridge University. The group wishing to remove women entirely from Cambridge was very small indeed.

Only one university man of any standing, professor of political economy Alfred Marshall, claimed that women were of inferior mental ability and unlikely to benefit from a Cambridge education.[52] On the other hand, the old view that the moral and mental differences between the sexes could not be accommodated if men and women followed similar educational courses was widely expressed, though it was now rare for God and the Bible to be mentioned as authorities for this belief.[53] The majority of subscribers to the belief in an education adapted to women's "special" needs and talents made the elementary error of overgeneralization, which women were well able to counter. Nor could much open support be found for the view that the presence of women in Cambridge would inevitably lead to immorality, though some attempts were made to depict a Cambridge filled with hoards of idle women distracting the studious men.[54] Opposition to residence per se was very limited.[55]

A weighty argument, though it was rarely clearly formulated, was known as the "evils of competition."[56] For some, the rejection of competition was based on outmoded views of "women worship" as preached by Ruskin and Tennyson; for others, there was a suspicion that women would compete with men for jobs.[57] The professions were thought to be very vulnerable to attack from women. If, as men had so often insisted, women had special "feminine" talents, medicine was an obvious profession in which they could display them. Women were taking over schoolteaching and even the instruction of young boys. They had already made certain encroachments on public offices at the local government level. Few of the academic staff at Cambridge could have privately failed to notice outstanding women who were passed over for university appointments and research opportunities. It seems likely, however, that these ideas were not based on accurate information on the state of the labor market but on rumor and hearsay, a desire by professionals to exaggerate their own exclusiveness, and the lack of an appointments board that could help to widen the horizons of both graduates and prospective employers. The professions favored by Cambridge men were still politics, the administrative branch of the Civil Service, the Bar, medicine and public school and university teaching (Rothblatt, pp. 259–67). Women were barred from all these careers except medicine and university teaching, and Cambridge women could neither take their first medical examinations nor be appointed to teaching posts at the university. The real prospect of Cambridge men being elbowed out of desirable jobs by Cambridge-educated women was hardly imminent, and the fear-of-competition argument, if genuine, would imply an unusual humility on the part of prospective medical men and academics if they felt women could outmatch them. Time has shown men to be adept in handicapping potential female competitors; in the 1890's the competition argument, though scarcely relevant to the Cambridge situation, was used with considerable effect.

After months of deliberation, the Women's Degree Syndicate produced a proposal giving women the titles of their degrees.[58] They were to continue to have an alternative to the Previous, but no provision was made for their official admission to lectures and laboratories, nor any extension made in the matter of prizes or the university library. The idea that women should be admitted to university membership and be eligible for appointments was not even discussed. The two months prior to the vote on this proposal found the university in a state of turmoil. *The Times* on 20 May 1897 reported that private friendships had been severely strained and that there was a degree of hostility "previously unknown" in the attitude of men toward the claims of the women. It is true that a great many men were drawn into the controversy without having any real interest in the matter and many cast their vote against the women simply out of annoyance that their request had led to such disturbance.[59] Ann Rogers attributes the virulent antifeminism of Cambridge men to the length of time (eighteen months) devoted to the debate. In contrast, when Oxford had discussed the matter, it had been "superficial, hurried and petty" (Rogers, p. 58).

Suspicions were raised before—and accusations publicly made after the women's defeat—that some senior members of the university were inciting the undergraduates to oppose women.[60] Much was made of a petition presented by over two thousand male students to the vice chancellor asking that women be kept out of the university and of the "open" Union debate in which a motion condemning the recommendations of the Women's Degree Syndicate was carried by 1,083 votes to 138. (The Cambridge Union is a closed debating society. On this occasion the exceptional step was taken of allowing all university members to attend, speak, and vote.) What is remarkable is that some M.A.s who would normally have been outraged at the idea of consulting an undergraduate used vocal student opposition as an unprecedented weapon against the women. Those undergraduates who gave the matter some thought described, for example, the inconveniences that arose in the laboratories when women students had to be given the best seats and a lion's share of the demonstrator's attention.[61] Women who were guilty of demanding equality while still insisting that they be deferred to no doubt presented a hopeless puzzle for the well-reared male undergraduate. The majority of students, however, cared little for the facts but found endless amusement in the bickering of their elders. Nonetheless, their siding with the women's opponents was due to more than chance; a rapid decline in the quality of students coming to Cambridge—including potential rowing blues—was spelled out for them by senior members and the press, and their own fears regarding their future in the "overcrowded professions" did the rest.[62] On 21 May 1897, M.A.s streamed to Cambridge from all parts of the land to cast their votes on the proposal to give women the titles of their degrees. The women lost by 1,713 votes to 662, and the undergraduates celebrated the defeat with a night of riotous bonfires, fireworks and fun.[63]


## III


It is indeed strange, in view of the violent feeling that had been aroused during the years of debate, that the defeat had no repercussions for the status of women in Cambridge. Two explanations can

*"The Women's Degree Question at Cambridge,"* The Illustrated Sporting and Dramatic News, *12 June 1897.*

be offered for this paradox; many who had voted against the women were inconsistent in their prejudices and, as mentioned previously, were quietly proud of "their" women; and second, teaching women at Girton and Newnham had for many years been a lucrative way to supplement a college stipend, and it gave work to "a large body of competent, but only partially employed teachers of the higher branches of learning" (*Westminster Gazette*, 15 May 1897). Following the defeat, the women's colleges continued with their business. They had been put sharply in their places, but their place, as they reflected with cautious amazement, was still in Cambridge. The defeats at Oxford and Cambridge did, however, represent an enormous failure by women to convince men in positions of influence and authority that their further advancement was justified, a failure which was repeated in the bitter and unhappy struggles that preceded women's enfranchisement in Britain.

At the time of the Cambridge debate, women working for the vote had received great encouragement from franchise bills introduced by Faithfull Begg (Conservative) in May 1896 and February 1897. The latter bill secured a majority of 71 at its second reading, only to be talked out on 7 July 1897 before reaching committee stage. Nonetheless, the defeat was regarded as a "theoretical victory" by suffragists (Strachey, p. 287), who on a wave of new optimism settled internal quarrels and renewed their efforts throughout the country.

The Cambridge defeat, however, produced no enthusiasm for continued struggle. Unlike suffrage workers, who had nothing to lose and everything to gain by continued agitation, Cambridge women were perched on the gunwale of the university boat and were therefore most reluctant to rock it. The defeat was interpreted for students as having fine character-forming properties, but the women's leaders were privately shocked at the crude antifeminism the campaign had revealed, particularly in its final stages. The matter was not raised again until 1919, when the initiative was taken by university men following the admission of women to degrees at Oxford. Full degrees and university membership were finally granted to Cambridge women in 1948 on the suggestion of two university men and under conditions that included limits on the number of women students. Only now, after a presence of one hundred years, are Cambridge women again beginning to ask for a fairer share in university benefits, which Emily Davies had once optimistically thought were denied them because of "some unfortunate accident."[64] Again, the initiative has not been entirely theirs.

Finally, there is a note of irony in the results of women's emancipation in Britain. The Victorian middle-class woman in financial difficulties was scarcely employable because she lacked training and qualifications. After training, one occupation was opened to her: teaching. We come then to the interesting hypothesis that better education for the middle-class woman was not simply the *sine qua non* of her eventual escape from the home and into employment but a relief work, a whole industry created for women. As such, the new educational opportunities were not the self-evident vehicle of emancipation they are sometimes thought to have been. Although women were allowed to rule in their own schoolrooms, they were confined there and little encouragement, legal or otherwise, was given to an educated woman who looked for an intellectually satisfying job outside teaching. In a recent study of the reception of female graduates into business and industry, Michael Sanderson reports only insignificant numbers of women graduates taking jobs there before World War I. The war did much to alter attitudes toward women in "men's" jobs, but Sanderson concludes that

growing points in the changing career opportunities of the inter-war years lay outside the universities which for the majority of their women members were too often a firm if constricting road back to the traditional occupation of teaching.[65]

This is not to suggest that the improvements in women's education in any way hindered emancipation, but the resulting emergence of a "women's" industry, complete with discriminatory wages and for the most part controlled by men, should not pass unnoticed.

In the early days of the emancipation movement, Mill warned that those whose power was based on "might is right" had never given an inch until "physical power had passed to the other side."[66] Mrs. Pankhurst tried, with some success, to change the balance of power. Cambridge women had no use for such tactics in the degree struggle, but it is also possible that they had forgotten what the struggle was really about. Mrs. Sidgwick made a telling admission as to the purpose of the education movement when she laid a foundation stone at Roedean in 1897. She described the growth in dignity and importance of the teaching profession, which was "no longer the refuge of the destitute, but the chosen vocation for its own sake and carefully prepared for"[67] (Newnham Archives).

Students do not seem to have been equipped for the realities of the male-dominated society they would face outside the walls of the women's colleges. There was a certain sense of elitism among Cambridge women; after all, if the degree was so necessary for a woman to make progress in a man's world, she could have got it elsewhere. Instead, a Cambridge education, with or without a degree, was seen as an end in itself. This idea was copied by many other university-educated women and, coupled with the liberal, nonspecialist nature of most studies, it led them to feel that they need not make active use of their training in fields other than teaching. Thus, although Mill was their redeemer, many women fell under the spell of Kingsley, Ruskin and Tennyson, who preached that improved education for women was simply a prelude to their exerting a higher moral influence within the narrow confines of family life and, by extension, the schoolroom.

The results of efforts to obtain higher education for women must have disappointed the real emancipationists, just as the results of enfranchisement have disappointed all who felt that votes for women would herald a new era of justice and influence for the second sex. Disappointment in both fields springs from a common failure to recognize that the roles of both men and women need adjustment. Efforts instead were concentrated on modernizing the role of middle-class women to meet the realities of changed economic and social conditions. Better education for middle-class girls followed by a "nice" career in teaching, where the hours and the holidays leave time for childrearing and household tasks has become the kind of accepted pastime that *petit point* was previously. It is an extension of women's traditional role and requires no sacrifices on the part of men.[68] A vote can be cast while shopping for the family's dinner, but for a woman to participate in political life requires a reallocation of household responsibilities which few men are prepared to accept. Much emancipationist effort, of which the Cambridge struggle is a significant example, has necessarily been concerned with symbols; only now are women uniting to demand the substance of their hard-won rights.

# 7. Victorian Masculinity and the Angel in the House

*Carol Christ*

ONE OF THE MOST STRIKING CHARACTERISTICS OF VICTORIAN LITERATURE is its preoccupation with an ideal of womanhood that we have come to call, after the title of Coventry Patmore's most famous poem, the angel in the house. As Patmore's title suggests, the angel brings a more than mortal purity to the home that she at once creates and sanctifies, for which her mate consequently regards her with a sentimental, essentially religious reverence. Historians of Victorian society have accounted for the period's idealization of woman by examining the century's religious and economic crises.[1] Religious doubt and the viciously competitive atmosphere of business combined to threaten the stability of many traditional religious and moral values. Experiencing at once the breakdown of faith and the dehumanizing pressure of the marketplace, many Victorian writers relocated those values in the home and in the woman who was its center. It was she who could create a sanctuary both from the anxieties of modern life and for those values no longer confirmed by religious faith or relevant to modern business. Furthermore, the horror that many Victorian writers felt at the crassness of the marketplace, the fear that Philistines, or worse, the populace, were coming to dominate the tone of society, led to a renewed emphasis on a notion of gentility which contained a courtly reverence for women. The need to maintain this reverence appeared even more urgent in the face of social forces that seemed to threaten it: the agitation for women's rights, the increase in prostitution, even the debilitating influence of French literature.

No doubt all of these historical explanations help to account for the particular kind of idealization of women in the Victorian period.

But curiously enough, despite the relationship that historians have claimed between the idealization of woman and the pressures the age brought to bear upon the Victorian man, no one has looked at the representation of maleness in those works of literature centrally concerned with the angel in the house. To be sure, images of women in those works have received much attention and criticism. Feminists starting with Virginia Woolf have shown the ways in which the ideal of the angel in the house in fact limits woman's political power and psychological freedom even while it apotheosizes her.[2] But no critic has investigated the images of maleness that may well explain what led certain Victorian writers to see the angel in the house as an appropriate mate. If, as Simone de Beauvoir argues in *The Second Sex*, men project ideals of woman that reflect values they themselves would like in some way to possess or incorporate, then the ideal of the angel in the house should tell us at least as much about the Victorian man as about the Victorian woman. Furthermore, the images of men those same writers depict should indicate the conception of manhood that their ideal of woman in some way fulfills. In this chapter I will be concerned with the conception of masculinity as it reveals itself in the works of two Victorian writers centrally concerned with the image of the angel in the house—Coventry Patmore and Alfred Lord Tennyson. By the analysis of representative literary works, I will show that each of these writers sees man's aggressiveness, and particularly his sexual aggressiveness, as dangerous and distasteful. The ambivalence with which each writer portrays man's aggressiveness explains much about his idealization of woman's passivity and asexuality. She represents an ideal freedom from those very qualities he finds most difficult to accept in himself.

I

Although the phrase "the angel in the house" has become a common name for the Victorian ideal of womanhood, few have paid attention to the poem from which it came. *The Angel in the House* is not a very good poem, yet it is culturally significant, not only for its definition of the Victorian sexual ideal, but also for the clarity with which it represents the male concerns that motivate fascination with that ideal. The principal passage in *The Angel in the House* that explains the character of sexual difference between men and women is

the poem that begins Canto V, "The Comparison." I will quote it in
its entirety.

Where she succeeds with cloudless brow,
    In common and in holy course,
He fails, in spite of prayer and vow
    And agonies of faith and force;
Or, if his suit with Heaven prevails
    To righteous life, his virtuous deeds
Lack beauty, virtue's badge; she fails
    More graciously than he succeeds.
Her spirit, compact of gentleness,
    If Heaven postpones or grants her pray'r,
Conceives no pride in its success,
    And in its failure no despair;
But his, enamour'd of its hurt,
    Baffled, blasphemes, or, not denied,
Crows from the dunghill of desert,
    And wags its ugly wings for pride.
He's never young nor ripe; she grows
    More infantine, auroral, mild,
And still the more she lives and knows
    The lovelier she's express'd a child.
Say that she wants the will of man
    To conquer fame, not check'd by cross,
Nor moved when others bless or ban;
    She wants but what to have were loss.
Or say she wants the patient brain
    To track shy truth; her facile wit
At that which he hunts down with pain
    Flies straight, and does exactly hit.
Were she but half of what she is,
    He twice himself, mere love alone,
Her special crown, as truth is his,
    Gives title to the worthier throne;
For love is substance, truth the form;
    Truth without love were less than nought;
But blindest love is sweet and warm,
    And full of truth not shaped by thought;
And therefore in herself she stands
    Adorn'd with undeficient grace,
Her happy virtues taking hands,
    Each smiling in another's face.
So dancing round the Tree of Life,
    They make an Eden in her breast,
While his, disjointed and at strife,
    Proud-thoughted, do not bring him rest.[3]

Patmore associates woman with a complex of traditionally feminine values—love, intuition, beauty, virtue. Each of these values, however, results from woman's lack of desire to act. When woman does succeed, it is with "cloudless brow," without the determination of effort, in common activities. But she fails with equal grace because she has no ego investment in success or failure. She is unaffected by others' blame or praise because she has no desire to achieve. Woman is naturally passive for Patmore, and the better off for it. Her growth, paradoxically, consists of a continual regression toward the more passive states of childhood and infancy. Even her intuition seems curiously undirected. Her wit does not track or hunt, both of which are acts motivated by a purpose; it "flies" and "hits," without the need for direction or intention on her part. It just happens. Man is truth, but woman is love which is not shaped by the directive agency of thought. Thus the happy virtues, which finally transform her to both Eden and the Tree of Life at the end of the poem, all result from an essential passivity, a lack of any desire to strive or to achieve.

Man, on the other hand, is defined precisely by the desire to achieve, but that desire brings him only anxiety and pain. Failure and success both lead to self-hatred. Despite all the agonies of faith and force he can summon, he often fails, and that failure leads to nothing but anger and despair. Success gives him no satisfaction either; "his virtuous deeds lack beauty," the true sign of virtue. In other words, there is an inherent ugliness about him that does not allow any amount of good-doing to prove him good. Furthermore, the images that Patmore uses for achievement and pride, dunghill and ugly wings, are so repulsive that they suggest a discomfort with the whole sphere of masculine action. He identifies manhood with the thought that forms and shapes, but he prefers the love he associates with womanhood that does not have that shaping capacity. Patmore thus shows an intense ambivalence in his definition of manhood. Man is defined by his capacity for action, aggression, and achievement, but that capacity is both frightening and unattractive. To reject that capacity would mean a loss of identity but to accept it leads to self-hatred. Woman, on the other hand, does not have either to venture or to worry about failure. She represents a possibility of freedom from impulses that man finds it difficult to accept in himself. The very ambivalence that the poem reveals about male achievement thus explains its idealization of feminine passivity; it frees woman from the obligation of accomplishment that man finds so burdensome.

Patmore's depiction of sexual situations in other parts of the poem displays an ambivalence toward sexual aggression similar to the ambivalence "The Comparison" displays toward masculine action. In Canto XI Patmore meditates about the sources of happiness and concludes:

> Who pleasure follows pleasure slays;
>   God's wrath upon himself he wreaks;
> But all delights rejoice his days
>   Who takes with thanks, and never seeks.
> (p. 126)

Patmore's reluctance to seek pleasure explains his attitude toward sexual aggression; the poem asserts that direct sexual overtures do women wrong. In the same canto I have just quoted, Felix presses Honoria's hand during a dance and feels "measureless remorse." Patmore continually asserts that even after marriage a husband must retain a ceremonious distance from his wife because

> she's so simply, subtly sweet,
> My deepest rapture does her wrong.
> (p. 71)

Patmore's treatment of Felix's proposal to Honoria reflects a similar ambivalence toward masculine sexuality. The first time Felix attempts to propose to Honoria, he is interrupted by the dog Wolf, which bursts into the room and "put[s] his nose upon her lap" (p. 104). In Canto XII, where Felix successfully proposes to Honoria, Patmore represents the proposal in violent animal and hunting images out of keeping with the tone and imagery of much of the rest of the poem. In the prelude that precedes the narrative of the proposal, Patmore represents the lover as a serpent gliding in the grass who

> fascinates her fluttering will,
> Then terrifies with dreadful strides.
> (p. 132)

The dominating metaphor of the prelude is a hunt in which the man pursues the woman until she is "chased to death, undone,/ Surprised, and violently caught" (p. 134). In the narrative itself Honoria is represented as a "pet fawn by hunters hurt." Although the tone of much of the prelude is playful and although Patmore implies that the woman slows down to be caught, nevertheless, the images of rapacity with which he represents male courtship are so inconsistent with the gentility of the rest of the poem that they suggest a discomfort with the sexual motivation of courtship. Patmore calls the man who finds more pleasure in the chase than in the woman a churl, and later in the poem Felix asserts that Frederick Graham, the unsuccessful suitor, is a more heroic figure than he is because his love has been its own reward.

Because of the ambivalence that the poem reveals toward male sexuality, even its idealization of woman becomes confused. Woman possesses power in Patmore's world by the exalted respect man has for her, which causes him to behave virtuously, and by her denial of her favors, which makes man strive to become worthy of her. Both of these sources of power are essentially passive. Because woman's power lies in withholding her acceptance until man is truly worthy, she in some way inevitably loses her moral ascendancy when she accepts a man as her lover:

> Ah, wasteful woman, she who may
>   On her sweet self set her own price,
> Knowing man cannot choose but pay,
>   How has she cheapen'd paradise;
> How given for nought her priceless gift,
>   How spoil'd the bread and spill'd the wine,
> Which, spent with due, respective thrift,
>   Had made brutes men, and men divine.
>
> (p. 79)

The money imagery in these lines shows Patmore's fear that women may be prostitutes who sell themselves to the highest bidder. Woman is an object of exchange, of which she herself controls the selling, that by its price assures the moral tenor of civilization. Because of Patmore's ambivalence about men's morality, that price can never be high enough. Patmore creates an ideal of womanhood to offer him a transcendence that in some way he is sure he can never attain. When woman accepts man, she loses the moral stature that is her power, and he is finally then free to become the beast Patmore fears he is.

There is one way for man to avoid this moral failure: to retain the distance of courtship in marriage. Patmore exalts that distance into an ideal of married love. Husband and wife must maintain

Circumference for moving clear,
None treading on another's train.
(p. 154)

In the final canto Patmore praises his wife for what seems a kind of frigidity. He begins by asking "Why, having won her, do I woo?" and replies that, although she is "as lowly as a wife can be," he woos her

Because her gay and lofty brows,
When all is won which hope can ask,
Reflect a light of hopeless snows
That bright in virgin ether bask;
Because, though free of the outer court
I am, this Temple keeps its shrine
Sacred to Heaven; because, in short,
She's not and never can be mine.
(p. 202)

Woman's frigidity assures man's continual striving for a higher morality as well as a conviction of his lack of it.

*The Angel in the House*, then, combines an idealization of woman's passivity with an ambivalence toward masculine action and an idealization of woman's purity with an ambivalence toward masculine sexuality. The combination itself suggests those male needs that motivated the worship of the angel. Patmore offers the image of the angel in the house both to his autobiographical hero, Frederick Graham, and to his reader as one means of transcending the tension over male achievement and male sexuality. Though man in Patmore's vision is disjointed and at strife, torn by the necessity of achievement and his denigration of it, the desire to touch a hand and the remorse for having done it, he can find and worship a creature that he conceives to be free from those conflicting desires and thus find some salvation from them. But the solution is a problematical one at best. *The Angel in the House* alternates between praising woman's superiority to man and asserting her absolute domination by him. The alternation suggests the difficulty of Patmore's position. The passivity and asexuality that proves woman's superiority to him puts him in the position of sole actor and sexual aggressor. Thus the very idealization through which he had sought to escape his ambivalence compels him to reenact the domination and sexual aggression that create such conflict. Patmore himself ultimately resolves the tension so evident in *The Angel in the House* and in its sequel, *The Victories of Love*, by turning to mystical religious poetry that allows him an unquestionably ideal realm for the erotic impulse. Yet it is that tension so evident in his early attempt to create an ideal of woman within the home that is typical of much Victorian literature.

## II

Alfred Lord Tennyson, like Patmore, believed in the redemptive power of "the maiden passion for a maid" to save men from the bestial elements within themselves. At the end of the *Idylls of the King*, Arthur asserts that he knows no more subtle master

> Not only to keep down the base in man,
> But teach high thought, and amiable words
> And courtliness, and the desire of fame,
> And love of truth, and all that makes a man.[4]

Many of Tennyson's poems—"Locksley Hall," "Edwin Morris," *Maud, The Princess,* and, of course, the *Idylls*—hold out the hope of the regeneration of the hero by his passion for a woman he idealizes. Because Tennyson's women most frequently fail at their task, it may seem that he has a very different vision of woman than Patmore, but such is not the case. By choosing the wealthier or more attractive suitor over the worthier hero, Tennyson's heroines merely fulfill Patmore's fear that women as commercial objects may give themselves to unworthy bidders. They fail, but they fail because Tennyson shares with Patmore the same exalted vision of their mission and the same fear that they may operate in the world by selling themselves. That woman who remains true to her ideal self, as Guinevere might have, has the power to do nothing less than motivate the creation of an ideal society.

Tennyson's concern with woman's mission seems to stem, like Patmore's, from a discomfort with male sexuality and male action. This discomfort is most evident in *The Princess*, the poem in which Tennyson is most explicitly concerned with sexual role definition. Most critics, understandably enough, have focused upon the poem's treatment of women's issues, evaluating its conservative or progressive qualities in the context of the age.[5] But both Tennyson's care to maintain woman's femininity and his final vision of androgyny depend very largely on a concern for man's feminization. In *The Princess* Tennyson, like Patmore, uses woman's purity and self-containedness to criticize man's sensuality and unsuccessful striving. Furthermore, he dramatizes a pattern of feminine identification in his portrayal of the Prince, which he never reverses as he does the masculine identification of Princess Ida.

The most ideal character in *The Princess* is the Prince's mother, whom Tennyson defines much like Patmore's angel in the house. She is a saint

> all dipt
> In Angel instincts, breathing Paradise,
> Interpreter between the Gods and men,
> Who looked all native to her place, and yet
> On tiptoe seemed to touch upon a sphere
> Too gross to tread, and all male minds perforce,
> Swayed to her from their orbits as they moved,
> And girdled her with music.
> (VII:301–308)

More significant than the similarity in the ideal of womanhood the two poets describe is the fact that Tennyson, like Patmore, uses that ideal to criticize man's failings. Woman possesses a purity, a self-sufficiency, a wholeness, but man, for Tennyson as for Patmore, is disjointed, never at peace, and that disjointedness results from his continual striving, his efforts and his failures. Woman, the Prince asserts in *The Princess* has

> Not a thought, a touch,
> But pure as lines of green that streak the white
> Of the first snowdrop's inner leaves; I say,
> Not like the piebald miscellany, man,
> Bursts of great heart and slips in sensual mire,
> But whole and one.
> (V:187–92)

The Prince's father, the least attractive character in the poem, suggests the potential destructiveness of those "bursts" and "slips." He defines himself in conventionally masculine terms: he does battle with men and pursues and dominates women. He asserts:

> Man is the hunter; woman is his game:
> The sleek and shining creatures of the chase,
> We hunt them for the beauty of their skins;
> They love us for it, and we ride them down.
> Wheedling and siding with them!
> (V:147–51)

In accordance with his sense of sexual identity, he wants to gain the Princess Ida for his son by doing battle with her father's knights and by taking her by force, convinced that "a lusty brace of twins" will cure her of her folly. The events of the poem reveal the inadequacy of the old king's response. The resolution of the poem owes nothing to the king's vision of martial and sexual conquest, which in fact alienates both the Prince and the Princess, but depends upon their mutual respect and compassion. Tennyson's portrayal of the king thus makes the aggressive masculinity the king represents appear as both an unattractive and an inadequate way of defining sexual identity.

The Prince makes it clear that he has taken his character from his mother and not from his father. He is initially described in feminine terms:

> blue-eyed, and fair in face,
> Of temper amorous, as the first of May,
> With lengths of yellow ringlet, like a girl.
> (I:1–3)

He suffers weird seizures in which the world suddenly seems an apparition and goes to claim his bride dressed up like a woman. To be sure, Princess Ida too reverses her sexual identification in taking upon herself masculine prerogatives in founding her college. The reversal of sexual identification of the two main characters of the poem suggests that the poem is concerned with the restrictiveness of both masculine and feminine sexual roles, and indeed it is. The poem ends with a vision of an androgynous society in which woman will become more masculine, man more feminine:

> in the long years liker must they grow;
> The man be more of woman, she of man;
> He gain in sweetness and in moral height,
> Nor lose the wrestling thews that throw the world;
> She mental breadth, nor fail in childward care,
> Nor lose the childlike in the larger mind.
> (VII:263–68)

Despite Tennyson's assertion of an androgynous ideal, however, he is far more careful to maintain the virtues of femininity than masculinity not only in the characterization of Ida, where we might expect him to do so, but in the characterization of the Prince himself. The reversal of the poem, in which the sexes take on their proper sexual roles, is accomplished not by the battle, in which the Prince has one of his seizures and is felled by Arac, but by the pity the women feel at the sight of the wounded and by their transformation of the college into a hospital. Ida falls in love with the Prince by tending him when he is sick, semiconscious, and delirious. The poem seems almost a reversal of the Sleeping Beauty legend; Ida wakes the Prince with a kiss, and that kiss makes her falser self slip from her like a robe and leaves her a true woman. The Prince does not seek Ida's love actively but wins it passively by awakening her womanly pity. She reverses her sexual identification in the course of the poem, but the Prince does not reverse his except in the projection he makes of the future in which he calls upon Ida to "accomplish thou my manhood." Despite its initial sexual reversal and apparent plea for an androgynous society, the poem is more careful to insure feminine than masculine elements in both its female and its male characters.

Feminist critics such as Kate Millett and Katharine Rogers see in *The Princess* an attempt to preserve true womanhood in reaction to the threat of feminine emancipation. Such a reading of the poem is correct, but Tennyson seems equally concerned with the feminization of men and the feminization of women. His concern suggests that, like Patmore, he idealizes certain feminine postures, not merely because he wants to keep women in their place, but because he finds such postures so attractive himself.

Tennyson shows a concern for man's feminization not only in *The Princess* but in other poems as well. In *In Memoriam* Tennyson praises Hallam for a

> manhood fused with female grace
> In such a sort, the child would twine
> A trustful hand, unasked, in thine,
> And find his comfort in thy face.
> (CIX:17–20)

Tennyson attributed to Christ a union of male and female qualities, of sweetness and strength, which he called the man–woman in him,[6] and he wrote in a late poem "On One Who Affected an Effeminate Manner":

> While man and woman still are incomplete,
> I prize that soul where man and woman meet,
> Which types all Nature's male and female plan.

It is true that Tennyson also praises the woman–man,[7] though not so frequently, and it is true that he is careful to say that he does not admire effeminacy. He instructs the one who affected an effeminate manner that "man–woman is not woman–man."[8] But he nonetheless repeatedly asserts the need for man to cultivate the feminine elements in himself as a corrective to the faults he sees in the purely masculine character. In some lines he later omitted from "The Dream of Fair Women," Tennyson looks forward to a time when the feminine character will have more control over civilization:

> In every land I thought that, more or less,
>   The stronger sterner nature overbore
> The softer, uncontrolled by gentleness
>   And selfish evermore:
>
> And whether there were any means whereby,
>   In some far aftertime, the gentler mind
> Might reassume its just and full degree
>   Of rule among mankind.[9]

In addition to the explicit concern with androgyny Tennyson's poetry repeatedly shows, it also exhibits a pattern of feminine identification in its preoccupation with a figure frequently called the isolated maiden. Critics have observed the number of poems—"Mariana," "Mariana in the South," "The Lady of Shalott," "The Palace of Art," "Oenone," "Fatima"—in which Tennyson returns to the figure of the isolated woman. Lionel Stevenson has explained Tennyson's fascination with the isolated maiden in Jungian terms.[10] It represents his anima, the personified image of his unconscious; and the evolution of the symbol in Tennyson's poetry provides an unintentional diary of Tennyson's own psychological evolution. I agree that the isolated maiden is undoubtedly a projection of Tennyson's unconscious, but I think the sex of the speakers has a more specific significance than Stevenson attributes to it. All of Tennyson's isolated maidens are cast in essentially passive situations. Oenone, Mariana, Fatima all wait and mourn for the lovers who have deserted them. The Lady of Shalott weaves in obedience to a mysterious spell; the speaker of "The Palace of Art" wanders through her house admiring her treasures. The activities the women engage in are merely cyclical, not directed toward the achievement of any goal. Like Patmore, Tennyson thus associates women with freedom from the demands or desires of action. Unlike

Patmore, Tennyson does not give that freedom any particular moral value. Oenone, Mariana, Fatima, and the Lady of Shalott are all unhappy victims of an externally imposed immobility, and the speaker of "The Palace of Art" is condemned for choosing a life of retreat. Tennyson's failure to give isolation any moral sanction suggests that he feels the responsibility for action more strongly than Patmore, however ambivalent he may be about it. Nevertheless, his continual return to women in passive postures reflects a deep attraction to such situations, an attraction expressed in his return to immobile and passive male protagonists as well—the Lotos Eaters, Tithonus, Merlin. Like Ulysses, Tennyson has not stopped his ears to the sirens. His attraction to such passive states explains his fascination with the isolated maiden. She represents for him an extraordinarily attractive though morally unsanctioned possibility of retreat from the world of male action.[11]

When we return to his portrayal of the male world of action, we can see why he was so attracted to the possibility of retreat. In *In Memoriam* and in *Maud*, Tennyson portrays the world as one of acute religious and social conflict in which it is impossible to find the opportunity to exercise the moral imperative to heroism. Man can find only doubtful religious sanctions within a social climate dominated by the aggressive competition in which personal gain seems the only consistent principle. Both the fear of action and the pattern of feminine identification and idealization are ways of responding to a world in which action has lost its religious imperative and seems to have gained meaning only from a Malthusian and Darwinian marketplace.

Despite the ambivalence about action and about masculinity that runs throughout Tennyson's poetry, he did repeatedly seek to create a heroic masculine ideal. And yet his lack of success at constructing a convincing male ideal suggests as clearly as the pattern of feminine idealization the difficulties that masculine action offered to him. King Auther, the most clearly ideal figure in Tennyson's poetry, seems both weak and asexual and takes for his sphere not the world of heroic quest but the humbler one of plowing the field, an activity essentially cyclical. The speaker of *Maud* resolves his disillusionment with the unheroic climate of the age by choosing to fight as a soldier in the Crimean War, but the conclusion of the poem is bombastic and unconvincing. Tennyson's attempts to commit himself to a world of action thus suggest the same difficulties as his retreats.

As with Patmore, Tennyson's fear of action is related to a fear of sexual energy. The principle that destroys both men and women in Tennyson's poetry is lust, capable in the *Idylls* of bringing about the collapse of an entire civilization. In "The Lady of Shalott," acting upon a sexual desire leads immediately to her death. Tennyson is far more aware than Patmore of the complexity of his ambivalence toward action and sexuality and of the social context that supports it, but despite their differences, the two writers resemble each other in the way in which they associate the ideal of the angel in the house with a fear and distrust of male action and sexuality. Thus both Patmore and Tennyson lead us to see that feminine idealization in Victorian literature, far from being an isolated phenomenon, takes its impetus from man's desire to escape burdens of action and sexuality made difficult to bear by the social climate of the age, and from his desire to incorporate a passivity and asexuality he assumed was woman's natural identity.

## III

We have seen that both Patmore and Tennyson sought to resolve an ambivalence about manhood in the idealization of the angel in the house. Other Victorian writers sought similar resolutions to their ambivalent feelings toward man's capacity for aggression. In *Sesame and Lilies*, for example, John Ruskin locates moral qualities in woman to compensate for man's naturally aggressive temperament. He addresses the girls of England:

There is not a war in the world, no, nor an injustice, but you women are answerable for it; not in that you have provoked, but in that you have not hindered. Men, by their nature, are prone to fight; they will fight for any cause, or for none. It is for you to choose their cause for them, and to forbid them when there is no cause. There is no suffering, no injustice, no misery, in the earth, but the guilt of it lies with you. Men can bear the sight of it, but you should not be able to bear it. Men may tread it down without sympathy in their own struggle; but men are feeble in sympathy, and contracted in hope; it is you only who can feel the depths of pain, and conceive the way of its healing.[12]

Charles Dickens finds a similar source of virtue in those heroines like Agnes Wickfield and Esther Summerson who resemble Patmore's angel in the house. Their capacity for selflessness and purity, for immersion in the cyclical round of daily activities, enables them to create a refuge from the selfishness and aggression of the male business world. To be sure, a number of female writers—most notably Charlotte Brontë and George Eliot—are also concerned with the ideal woman's capacity to contain sexual and aggressive energy, but their identity as women results in a very different pattern of ambivalence and resolution, which I am not concerned with here. The historical tensions of the age placed male writers in a unique position: faced with a society that valued and rewarded male aggressiveness, yet ambivalent about its value, they idealized certain feminine qualities to which they themselves were deeply attracted as an escape from their dilemma.

The desire to incorporate feminine qualities takes the form not only of the idealization of woman that I have been discussing but of a more feminine ideal of male behavior. We have seen a movement toward such an ideal in Tennyson's characterization of the Prince and in Patmore's characterization of the lover "who takes with thanks and never seeks." We can also see it in Dickens' preference for passive childlike protagonists and in his admiration for older, essentially motherlike men such as John Jarndyce, Mr. Brownloe, and Joe, who care for children and for the sick and helpless in ways that are self-abnegating and essentially feminine. The ideal of the gentleman that emerges in the prose of Arnold, Ruskin, and Newman also represents a more feminine ideal of male behavior. The posture of disinterested observation that Arnold recommends, Ruskin's emphasis in *Modern Painters* upon the delicacy, sensitivity, kindness, sympathy, and apparent reserve of the gentleman (*Works*, 7:343–62), and the ideal of the gentleman that Newman defines at the end of *The Idea of a University* all have in common with the heroes that we have discussed a retreat from the ideal of the man of action and an admiration for traditionally feminine virtues. Newman, for example, asserts:

Hence it is that it is almost a definition of a gentleman to say he is one who never inflicts pain. . . . He is mainly occupied in merely removing the obstacles which hinder the free and unembarrassed action of those about him; and he concurs with their movements rather than takes the initiative himself. . . . The true gentleman . . . carefully avoids whatever may cause a jar or a jolt in the minds of those with whom he is cast; . . . his great concern being to make every one at their ease and at home.[13]

By seeking to avoid the initiative, and by emphasizing the traditionally feminine virtue of taking care of people, Newman successfully avoids any ambivalence that he, like Patmore and Tennyson, may feel toward aggression. But as in Patmore's and Tennyson's poetry, the ideal of gentlemanly behavior that emerges in Newman ultimately suggests the same kind of inability to deal creatively with sexual energy. In the preface to *Pendennis* Thackeray complains that "since the author of *Tom Jones* was buried, no writer of fiction among us has been permitted to depict to his utmost power a MAN." Thackeray's complaint is reflected in the images of men created by the writers I have discussed. The fear of sexual energy seems to permit two alternatives of characterization and sexual identity: the man who gives way to his energy is a beast; the good man wishes to retreat from the world of male energy and action.

Interestingly, the writers of the Victorian period who have little difficulty in dealing with male energy—Thackeray and Browning—have much less difficulty in dealing with female energy. Browning values energy almost for its own sake. Furthermore, he portrays the sexual impulse as motivating his most creative character, Fra Lippo Lippi, while the failures in his world, like Andrea del Sarto, fail precisely because they do not commit themselves to either their creative or their sexual energies. Browning uses the criterion of commitment to energy of all kinds to judge his female as well as his male characters. The women of "Dîs Aliter Visum," or "The Statue and the Bust," or "Two in the Campagna" fail like their lovers through a failure of sexual energy. Although Browning does create ideally pure child heroines in Pippa and Pompilia, even they have greater energy than many of Dickens' heroines, and his dramatic monologues frequently portray the libidinous and aggressive energies of women like the speakers of "Count Gismond" and of "The Laboratory." Likewise, Thackeray's judgment of the male characters in the fiction of his age is reflected in his own fiction not only by a greater commitment to the portrayal of male energy but by his fascination, ambivalent though it is, with the female energy of a Becky Sharp and his satire of the ideal of passivity in his portrayal of Amelia Sedley.

Lionel Trilling has suggested that the nineteenth century set women up in the place of the eighteenth century's Noble Savage as a criterion for nobility and even for masculine strength.[14] The heroines we have been discussing certainly do not have a masculine strength, but, like the Noble Savage, they constitute a similar virtuous ideal that exists separate from the stress and corruption of masculine civilization. The angel in the house represents an ideal freedom from those desires and responsibilities many Victorian writers found most difficult to handle; it is both a symptom of their difficulty in dealing with the world of action and a strategy for retreating from it. I do not mean to imply that considerable fear of and hostility toward women did not help to generate the ideal of the angel in the house; I simply mean that the fear of woman's sexuality and of her power for action and aggression was matched and complicated by an equivalent fear of man's own. If woman in fact should be a sexual creature, what kind of beast should man himself become? It may seem difficult for us to see the angel in the house as a desirable identity, but many Victorian men obviously did, from the conflicts and difficulties of their own existence and from that "modesty of service" she provided them. The ideal was hardly a successful way of resolving those conflicts. In addition to the harm it did women, the ideal of the angel in the house left the man who embraced it in an impossible dilemma, for to him woman was both a perpetual reproach and a perpetual temptation. He was indeed "disjointed," as Patmore and Tennyson assert, because neither success nor failure could bring him rest.

# 8. Sex and Death in Victorian England

*An Examination of Age- and Sex-Specific Death Rates, 1840–1910*

*Sheila Ryan Johansson*

ALTHOUGH EVERYONE DIES, SOME PEOPLE MANAGE TO DELAY THE INEVI-
table by capitalizing on certain advantages. Those with the best
chance of living a long life are born to healthy, white parents in a
developed country. In addition, they eat sensibly, practice a safe profession, and live in a benign environment. But the greatest assist to
longevity is being born female, since the average woman in the Western world now tends to outlive the average man by the substantial
margin of six to seven years. It is not modern mortality statistics which
support the belief that females are either the second or the weaker sex.

At present the impression is widespread that the marked mortality advantage of the female sex is biologically-based, and thus
relatively immune to cultural factors. Surveys discussing sex-based
physiological differences always mention that fewer females than
males are conceived and born with genetic defects, and fewer females
than males die from infectious or stress-linked diseases throughout
life.[1] A comparative study of mortality rates among Catholic nuns and
brothers showed that even when men and women led the same kind
of life in a similar environment females still retained a substantial
mortality advantage over males.[2]

This was not always true in the past. As recently as 1900 male
and female mortality patterns differed much less than today; life expectancy at birth in some countries, for example Italy and Ireland, was
the same for both sexes.[3] This lack of a marked mortality differential
between males and females is usually attributed to the destructive
effects of pregnancy and childbirth on female health, an explanation
that seems plausible when we consider that as late as 1900 over half

[ 163

the women in Europe who had been married for at least twenty years had given birth to five or more children.[4]

But the close study of mortality patterns in Victorian England does not support this common belief. Analyzing cause-of-death patterns for males and females from 1840 to 1910 shows that the absence of a pronounced female mortality advantage had relatively little to do with the direct effects of parturition-related dangers. The early stages of the emergence of modern mortality contrasts between the sexes were primarily the result of a disproportionately rapid fall in deaths among women caused by tuberculosis. Moreover, women in the age groups where childbearing was most common were not the last females to show signs of a rapidly increasing mortality advantage over males. Instead it was young girls aged five to nineteen who were the last to achieve consistently lower death rates than their male counterparts. To understand these trends we must explore the impact of industrialization and urbanization on the life styles of girls and women as traditional forms of overt social and economic patriarchy gave way to the subtler forms prevailing today.

I

Victorian society seemed unusually committed to maximizing differences between the sexes. One used to hear it argued that Victorian forms of "patriarchy" chivalrously favored women by protecting them from the harsher aspects of life. (Such a generalization could implicitly refer only to middle- or upper-class women.) Presently it is more common to hear that Victorian culture was oppressive to women of all social classes. If "privileged" women were pampered, they were also expected to lead artificial and cramped lives that were full of anxiety-ridden dependence. Working-class women are presently thought of as having had to work as hard or harder than men in hazardous and ill-paid forms of work, particularly after industrialization introduced the factory system.

Ultimately, any favorable or unfavorable evaluation of the life styles of Victorian women must end with an exploration of "death styles." But we can appreciate the significance of historical data on age- and sex-specific mortality rates only by first familiarizing ourselves with modern data. In contemporary England, as we can see in Table 1, women have a life expectancy at birth of 74.7 years. This is

## TABLE 1
Age- and Sex-Specific Death Rates Per Thousand in England and India

| Age | England and Wales (1966) | | India (1958–59) | |
| --- | --- | --- | --- | --- |
| | Males | Females | Males | Females |
| 0–1 | 21.7 | 16.6 | 198.0 | 182.0 |
| 1–4 | .9 | .8 | 42.6 | 45.4* |
| 5–14 | .4 | .3 | 5.6 | 5.5* |
| 15–24 | 1.0 | .5 | 3.5 | 5.4* |
| 25–34 | 1.1 | .7 | 4.2 | 6.4* |
| 35–44 | 2.5 | 1.8 | 5.8 | 5.4 |
| 45–54 | 7.4 | 4.4 | 12.8 | 8.0 |
| 55–64 | 21.4 | 10.3 | 32.2 | 21.0 |
| 65–74 | 53.0 | 28.4 (65+) | 72.9 | 54.7 |
| 75–84 | 118.4 | 79.2 | | |
| 85+ | 242.4 | 197.1 | | |
| | (1963–65) | | (1951–60) | |
| Life Expectancy at Birth | 68.3 | 74.7 | 41.9 | 40.5 |

Source: *The United Nations Demographic Yearbook, 1967,* England and Wales p. 424, India, p. 418. For India the data is "provisional" and for rural India only.

Note: The figures show us how many *per thousand* of the population of given age groups died in the period indicated. Thus for every thousand *Englishmen* aged 45 to 54, 7.4 died in 1966. For women in the same age group only 4.4 per thousand died in that year.

* Age groups in which mortality rates for women are higher or very nearly equal to those of men.

a full 6.4 years longer than the life expectancy of the average man. If we compare death rates for each age group, we see that during every stage of life females enjoy much lower death rates than males. Differentials are particularly marked after the age of fifteen. This pattern of age- and sex-specific death rates is now so common that it constitutes the distinguishing feature of the *modern* mortality pattern. Life expectancy is high for both sexes, but it is much higher for females.

Age- and sex-specific mortality rates for rural India in the 1950's are also presented in Table 1. Obviously, mortality rates in India were higher than those in England for both sexes at all ages. But for our purposes the most important observation is that in several age groups females died more often than males. In fact, males had a slightly higher life expectancy at birth—41.9 years versus 40.5 years for females. This mortality pattern can be called *traditional* rather than *modern* because its features are usually found only in preindustrial

*Sex and Death in Victorian England*

countries. A traditional mortality pattern is one in which both males and females have relatively low and relatively equal expectations of life at birth. In addition, in many traditional societies females in certain age groups sometimes have higher death rates than males.

By 1840, even though England was the world's first and only mature industrial society, data provided by its new system of civil registration showed clearly that its mortality pattern was still more traditional than modern[5] (see Table 2). Although life expectancy at

## TABLE 2
### Age- and Sex-Specific Death Rates

*England and Wales in 1838–44*

| Age | Males | Females |
|-----|-------|---------|
| 0–1 | 205.1 | 154.4 |
| 0–4 | 70.7 | 60.4 |
| 5–9 | 9.3 | 9.0 |
| 10–14 | 5.0 | 5.5* |
| 15–24 | 8.0 | 8.3* |
| 25–34 | 9.6 | 10.1* |
| 35–44 | 12.5 | 12.4 |
| 45–54 | 17.8 | 15.5 |
| 55–64 | 31.4 | 27.8 |
| 65–74 | 66.1 | 58.8 |
| 75–84 | 144.9 | 132.0 |
| 85–94 | 296.5 | 275.5 |
| Life Expectancy at Birth, 1838–50 | 39.9 | 41.8 |

Source: Age-specific death rates: *Ninth Annual Report of the Registrar-General, England and Wales*, p. 177; Life Expectancy at Birth: *Supplement to the 65th Annual Report of the Registrar-General.*

* Age groups in which females died at rates equal to or higher than those for men.

birth for females was already 1.9 years higher than it was for males, there were several age groups in which women died more often than men, most notably between the ages of ten and thirty-four.[6]

Between 1840 and the end of the 1860's there were no sudden or dramatic departures from the pattern of age- and sex-specific death rates already established in the 1840's. But in the 1870's mortality began to decline for both sexes. By 1880 it was clear that women were benefiting slightly more from this trend than men. Death rates fell by

*A Widening Sphere*

five percent for males of all ages, but by nearly ten percent for women of all ages (see Table 3).

TABLE 3

Male Mortality Rates as a Percentage of Female Rates

| Date | All Ages | 0–1 | 5–9 | 10–14 | 15–19 | 20–24 |
|------|------|-----|-----|-------|-------|-------|
| 1841–50 | 109 | 117 | 103 | 94 | 89 | 105 |
| 1871–80 | 115 | 117 | 108 | 100 | 96 | 108 |
| 1901–10 | 119 | 119 | 97 | 95 | 107 | 119 |

| Date | 25–34 | 35–44 | 45–54 | 55–64 | 65–74 | 75+ |
|------|-------|-------|-------|-------|-------|-----|
| 1841–50 | 94 | 100 | 114 | 112 | 111 | 107 |
| 1871–80 | 109 | 119 | 128 | 122 | 114 | 108 |
| 1901–10 | 117 | 122 | 130 | 118 | 120 | 112 |

Within a general pattern of falling death rates for both sexes, men between the ages of thirty-five and seventy-five actually had rising death rates. But only women aged fifty-five to sixty-four were affected by this retrogression. These different trends meant that by 1880 the average female could expect to live 3.27 years longer than the average male. In addition, there were now no age groups in which death rates were higher for females than for males.

But before the modern mortality pattern could fully and finally establish itself, there was some partial retrogression for females between 1880 and 1901–10. This can be seen from the following table, in which male death rates in the usual five-year age groups are expressed as a percentage of female death rates in 1841–50, 1871–80, and 1901–10.[7]

First of all we see that in 1941–51 males (all ages) had death rates that were 9 percent higher than rates for females (all ages). By 1871–80 this male disadvantage had increased to 15 percent, and in 1901–10 to 19 percent. But the mortality advantage of girls aged five to fourteen over males of the same age was lost between 1871–81 and 1901–10. The relative deterioration was particularly marked for girls aged five to nine. Meanwhile, it is interesting to note, the mortality advantage of women aged twenty-five to forty-four (when the majority of women were married and giving birth) increased most substantially before the years 1871–80, not after the great decline of the birth rate that began in the late 1870's.[8] According to the Registrar General, the same pattern of progress would have characterized women aged twenty to twenty-four, had not age-misstatements distorted the true death rates for women in this age group (*75th Annual Report, Decennial Supplement,* p. xxv).

### TABLE 4
#### Age-Specific Mortality Rates for Males and Females in 1876–80
#### (With Percentage Change Between 1838–54 and 1876–80)

| | Males | | Females | |
| | | Percentage of | | Percentage of |
| Age | Mortality Rates | Change to 1880 | Mortality Rates | Change to 1880 |
| --- | --- | --- | --- | --- |
| All Ages | 22.2 | − 4.7 | 19.5 | − 9.7 |
| 0–4 | 67.2 | − 7.0 | 57.0 | − 8.2 |
| 5–9 | 6.4 | −30.0 | 6.0 | −33.0 |
| 10–14 | 3.5 | −32.2 | 3.6 | −35.2 |
| 15–19 | 5.0 | −30.2 | 5.1 | −35.3 |
| 20–24 | 6.8 | −27.7 | 6.3 | −30.3 |
| 25–34 | 8.7 | −12.9 | 7.9 | −24.3 |
| 35–44 | 13.5 | + 4.8 | 11.2 | −12.3 |
| 45–54 | 19.0 | + 3.6 | 14.9 | − 6.4 |
| 55–64 | 34.6 | + 9.1 | 28.9 | + 2.4 |
| 65–74 | 67.6 | + 1.2 | 60.2 | + 0.5 |
| 75–84 | 146.7 | − 0.4 | 132.3 | − 1.6 |
| 85+ | 304.1 | − 1.3 | 274.0 | − 4.9 |
| Life Expectancy at Birth | 41.35 | | 44.62 | |

Source: Noel A. Humphreys, "On the Recent Decline in the English Death Rate and Its Effect Upon Duration of Life," *Journal of the Statistical Society of London* XLVI (June, 1883), p. 207.

## II

In terms of changing cause-of-death patterns it is easy enough to understand why death rates fell for both males and females after the middle of the nineteenth century. But there is no agreement among scholars about what role social and economic conditions played in bringing about the changes. A comprehensive analysis of mortality changes is tricky and often impressionistic. In the case of male/female mortality differences it can also lead very easily into a critical evaluation of what it means to be born male or female, grow up as a boy or girl, and live through adulthood in the fashion generally expected of each sex.

Victorian statisticians, particularly the Registrar General, found this out very quickly. Since almost no nineteenth-century statisticians wanted to criticize or even question the nature of the male/female status quo, they could deal only partially and awkwardly with the death-rate differences between the sexes. This was evident in the *Second Annual Report of the Registrar-General,* written in 1839. The report began by noting that the most widely accepted explanation for the longer life span of the female (women at that point had only a 1.9 year advantage) was a belief that war, intemperance, and excessive fatigue extracted a heavy toll from adult males.[9] But, said the Registrar General, this was not an adequate explanation for the difference, since in the years when men did most of their drinking, fighting, and working, females had higher death rates than males. (Table 2 reveals that in the 1840's the mortality advantages of females were confined to the age groups birth to five and forty-five and older.)

Since the mortality patterns of the sexes were most different when cultural factors were least relevant, the Registrar General argued that something in the "very blood and brains" of males and females exerted a hidden influence on death rates. Moreover, this biological something appeared to give unsuspected strength to the weaker sex during the most vulnerable years of human existence—extreme youth and old age. This was a very embarrassing observation, since Victorian doctors were firmly convinced that females were inherently more physically delicate and sickly than males. Perhaps that is why the Registrar General quickly dropped this line of analysis (which was an early anticipation of later biological theories of mortality differences between the sexes) and began to consider why females died more often than males during girlhood and middle life.

In terms of *specific* causes of death the answer was simple and centered on the greater incidence of deaths from consumption (or tuberculosis) among women. It was the leading single cause of death for both males and females throughout the nineteenth century, but in the 1840's and 1850's about eight percent more women than men died from it. Only after the 1880's did tuberculosis become a disease that regularly struck more males than females. In mid-Victorian England around half (sometimes more) of all women aged fifteen to thirty-five who died were killed by some form of consumption. In contrast only no more than one percent of these women died from pregnancy or childbirth-related difficulties.[10] (In general, for every one thousand women giving birth, between five and ten died; this ratio remained almost constant until 1900.)

This is not to deny that pregnancy and childbirth were taxing and hazardous processes; they were, particularly when repeated year after year. But they were more likely to damage the health of a woman than to be the immediate cause of her death. Victorian doctors believed that pregnancy could lead to a flare-up or aggravation of consumption, but there were no statistics kept on this. Nevertheless, tuberculosis remained the most obvious health problem for nineteenth-century women, affecting most before they had reached the age of marriage and childbearing.

In explaining why, doctors had to use general medical theories. Medical science took the position that almost everyone was exposed to the sources of contagion. Whether or not an individual remained immune, recovered from a mild attack, or died depended on a combination of constitutional, environmental, and even what we would today recognize as psychological factors.[11] Sensitive and creative individuals (particularly geniuses) were believed to be especially susceptible to consumptive wasting. But because the female sex was considered to lack such types, other factors had to be more relevant. In terms of their environment women did not live in different climates or types of housing than men. The most likely environmental factor would have been a dietary deficiency of some sort. In particular a relative scarcity of meat and dairy products for females (both high protein sources) should have been considered potentially important. Prolonged states of depression and anxiety were also believed to trigger attacks of tuberculosis and to affect one's chances of surviving. Thus, Victorian doctors, and the Registrar General as well, should have considered whether or not women were less well fed than men, more unhappy and worried than men, or some combination of both. But if Victorian men were convinced of anything, it was that in their paradigmatically progressive society women were highly regarded and chivalrously treated. Protectiveness toward women was even considered one of the defining characteristics of a civilized society. Given this bias, it would have been difficult to suggest that many English women were miserable and malnourished.

Thus, we should not be surprised that accepted explanations for the high incidence of tuberculosis among women became centered on the dangers of corseting, and, to a lesser degree, the unhappy effects of an indoor sedentary life.[12] "Corseting" was an indelicate word, and it was often alluded to as "the compression of the chest by costume" (*Second Annual Report, p. 5*). In a reforming mood, the Registrar General repeatedly urged "persons of rank and influence" to lead women away from their foolish and dangerous dress customs. More conservatively, he did not urge influential people to encourage women to take more exercise once they had adopted new dress styles.[13] Making a culprit of the corset made it seem as if women themselves were responsible for dying so often from consumption; it also implied they could change this sorry state of affairs as easily as their frocks.

The vast majority of Victorian women were working class, and it is doubtful whether they passed most of their days tightly laced and dressed in style. They also got quite a bit of indoor and outdoor exercise in the course of their varied duties. But nowhere does the Registrar General acknowledge the differentiation of women into social classes. Refined and unnatural upper-class ladies, as well as their middle-class imitators, were regarded as typical for "the sex."

In his later reports the Registrar General abandoned his early attempts to explain feminine mortality patterns superficially in terms of social customs. Instead, increasing attention was paid to the descriptive analysis of detailed cause-of-death data. By 1901–10 the Registrar General published tables showing that except for the excess mortality among women caused by tuberculosis, there would never have been any age group in which females had higher death rates than males, from the beginning of civil registration to 1910.[14]

The one exception to this was the group of girls aged five to nine. From 1890 to 1910 they still had death rates that were one to two percent higher than those of their brothers, even when tuberculosis as a cause of death was removed. These young girls died more often than boys from diphtheria, pneumonia, measles, heart disease, and burns and scalds. The Registrar General commented only on deaths caused by the last category; that four times as many girls as boys died from burns and scalds was attributed to the fact that female clothing caught fire more readily than male clothing. It is equally possible that mothers conscripted their very young daughters as kitchen help, exposing them early to the hazards of fire and hot water.

But if the Registrar General ignored social class and refused to consider anything beyond clothing-related causes of mortality patterns for women, other statisticians did not. In the pages of the *Journal of the Statistical Society of London* an article occasionally appeared that threw some light on the broader social and economic causes of male/female mortality pattern contrasts. One of the earliest of them dealt with the comparative mortality of males of the aristocracy and gentry, as opposed to males of the professional classes (Anglican clergymen, barristers, and other professionals), as opposed to females of the upper classes (peerage and gentry families)—all from the ages of eighteen to sixty-one. Upper-class females had lower life expectancies than their brothers between the ages of eighteen and twenty-four. Up to age forty, during the childbearing years, they did as well or slightly better than their male counterparts; subsequently they achieved a definite mortality advantage that lasted through old age.[15]

Nowhere in the article did its author, Dr. William Guy, try to explain why unmarried girls, with every advantage, should die more often than their brothers, or why their mortality picture should improve (relative to their brothers') once marriage and childbearing had started.[16] Dr. Guy was interested only in explaining why middle-class males seemed to have a more favorable pattern of life expectancy at various ages than upper-class males. With unmistakable satisfaction, the author (himself a middle-class professional) concluded that the effects of idleness and dissipation combined to impair the health and shorten the lives of the most privileged group of males in England. Their "physical inferiority" served once again to remind him that "temperance, mental occupation and bodily exercise were the three principle ingredients of health" (Guy, p. 49).

Had Guy extended his analysis to upper-class females, he would have had to declare them physically superior to all males, at least after the first flush of youth had passed. Logically he might have also concluded that during the late teens and early twenties upper-class women died more often than their brothers because they were more idle and dissipated. In a different vein he could have argued that their ladylike life styles deprived them of physical and mental stimulation to such a degree that their lives were imperiled. But all such conclusions would have been unacceptable, and so the social background of female mortality patterns was left undiscussed.

But an article published in the 1850's indicated again that existence as a proper Victorian girl or matron could indeed be hazardous to one's health. Although no general studies of mortality patterns of middle-class women were ever published, Joseph Fox presented some data on comparative death rates among Quaker women and men. The Society of Friends was an eminently middle-class group, and Fox argued that his data could be extended very legitimately to most women of middling rank.[17] This was a remarkable admission in that Fox's figures, drawn from records kept by the Quakers themselves, clearly showed that at every age from five to sixty men had lower death rates than women (see Table 5). The author was struck by what he called *"the lower relative value of female life"* [author's italics]. He could find no good explanation for it beyond the harm done by the "luxuries and refinements which surround an educated class" (Fox, p. 222).

TABLE 5

Mortality Rates of Male and Female Quakers in the 1850's

| Age | Males | Females |
|---|---|---|
| 0–1 | 148.2 | 107.3 |
| 0–4 | 56.0 | 47.3 |
| 5–9 | 5.6 | 6.8* |
| 10–14 | 3.4 | 4.9* |
| 15–19 | 7.8 | 8.4* |
| 20–29 | 8.8 | 9.1* |
| 30–39 | 7.8 | 11.4* |
| 40–49 | 9.9 | 11.4* |
| 50–59 | 14.0 | 16.8* |
| 60–69 | 44.7 | 33.8 |
| 70–79 | 85.8 | 74.6 |
| 80–89 | 178.3 | 216.2* |

Source: Joseph Fox, "On the Vital Statistics of the Society of Friends," *Journal of the Statistical Society of London* (June, 1859), p. 220.

* Rates for females are higher than those for males.

Fox did not elaborate on this suggestion, and thus he subtly conveyed the impression that these fortunate women were being killed by kindness. But was chivalry so deadly, or were the physical hardships and psychological stress imposed on women of this class responsible? It is hard today to associate "physical hardship" with the phrase "middle-class female," but one has only to read the first sections of a novel like *Jane Eyre* (1847) to realize that some middle-class girls, even the daughters of clergymen, were systematically abused and underfed in girls' schools, and sometimes even at home. The conditions at Lowood School that Jane Eyre encountered were based on conditions which Charlotte Brontë and her sisters had experienced at the

Reverend Carus Wilson's Clergy Daughters' School (where they were sent after their mother's death). Two of Charlotte's sisters died there, after having contracted tuberculosis. Some historians have stressed that most Victorian middle-class children were often cruelly treated, and a recent article by Mary Hartman has graphically described how exceptionally sadistic this treatment could be for daughters who showed any sign of rebellion or any overt manifestation of sexuality.[18]

Until 1910 there were no other studies of middle-class women and their mortality patterns, so it is not now possible to say whether or not the fading of Victorian customs and the rise of feminism was accompanied by better treatment for girls of this class. In the meantime we can only note that male Quakers derived a much more substantial longevity advantage from their class position than did female Quakers.

## III

During the entire Victorian era no more than five to fifteen percent of the total population of England and Wales was middle or upper class in status.[19] Thus the age-specific death rates for the general population (which we have already considered) were very nearly equivalent to rates for the working class during this period. But we cannot relate working-class mortality patterns to the social and economic conditions that influenced them in a straightforward fashion. The ordinary men and women of England and Wales lived and worked in a remarkable variety of circumstances. The Registrar General in his frequent studies of occupational mortality was able to show that for males longevity was not a simple function of social class. In fact, men employed in a rural setting almost always had lower death rates than those employed in a primarily urban setting. Agricultural laborers, poor as they were, had a more favorable mortality pattern than doctors or tradesmen who lived and worked in a large city like Manchester.[20]

But rural/urban contrasts were not so simple for women as they were for men. In the 1870's some statisticians began to notice that those women aged fifteen to twenty-four, living in the outer ring of rural counties which surrounded London, had a death rate of 9.0 per thousand. But those women of the same ages who lived in London itself died at the rate of only 5.9 per thousand. The same unexpected rural/urban contrasts could also be found for women living in other

*A Widening Sphere*

parts of England. Statisticians concluded, without any confirming evidence, that some country girls who migrated to wicked, unhealthy cities found work but soon became ill. Thereupon they returned to their families in the country and died.[21] In this way London and other cities were blamed for excess rural mortality.

It is just as probable that girls and young women living in the countryside were often genuinely worse off than those in the city. The most rural part of Great Britain was Ireland. When Robert Kennedy, Jr., examined Irish mortality data for the nineteenth and early twentieth centuries he found that rural Irish women still had a life expectancy at birth that was lower than it was for men.[22] (The figures were twenty-nine years for women and thirty years for men.) But in Dublin urbanized Irish women had a life expectancy at birth of twenty-eight years; though lower than the figure for rural women, it was a full four years higher than the figure for men. Like most nineteenth-century cities, Dublin had overcrowded housing and poor sanitation facilities. Both conditions guaranteed that, irrespective of general levels of prosperity, proportionately more people would die from contagious diseases there than in the country. While this lowered life expectancy for both sexes, it is clear that Dublin's men were much more adversely affected than Dublin's women. In terms of age-specific death rates, once urban girls reached the age of sixteen they consistently had lower death rates than urban males; but rural women aged twenty-six to forty-five and fifty-six to sixty-five continued to remain at a distinct mortality disadvantage when compared to rural males of the same age (Kennedy, p. 128).

Kennedy explained this by noting that, while both rural wives and daughters were hard working and productive members of their families, neither their domestic nor agricultural labor brought any wages to the family coffers. Women in general were regarded as dependents; daughters were thought particularly expensive since they needed a dowry for marriage. In this poverty-stricken peasant economy the best of everything was saved for husbands and sons. "The best" included the lion's share of the food and all or most of the meat available. Both wives and daughters appear to have been undernourished. Perhaps in Ireland, as in other peasant countries around the world, females, particularly the youngest ones, were made to bear the brunt of any permanent or temporary food shortages (Oakley, p. 28). But in Dublin daughters could find work outside the home. Because they contributed a wage to the family economy, they were better treated.

Married women did not work outside the home as a general rule; this meant that if wives continued to be relatively underfed, at least they did not have to bear the burden of a heavy domestic and agricultural workload.

Rural England was not so desperately poor as rural Ireland, but there were areas in which traces of a male-favoring mortality pattern could be found. For example, when the most urbanized and industrialized areas in Cornwall are contrasted with those areas that remained relatively agrarian, isolated, and backward, we see that although rural males had death rates which were always lower than those for urban males, the same was not true for females.[23] In Table 6 age- and sex-specific death rates for an area in the agrarian Northeast of Cornwall are contrasted with some from a district in the industrial West during 1851–61. Over half the males in industrial Redruth were employed as

## TABLE 6
### Age-Specific Death Rates for Males and Females
### in Two Registration Districts
### 1851–61 *

| Age Group | Rural (Stratton) | | Industrial (Redruth) | |
|---|---|---|---|---|
| | Males | Females | Males | Females |
| 0–4 | 45.3 | 35.7 | 72.1 | 65.7 |
| 5–9 | 8.2 | 9.9 | 8.8 | 8.9 |
| 10–14 | 3.7 | 5.4 | 4.9 | 4.6 |
| 15–19 | 4.4 | 6.4 | 6.5 | 5.3 |
| 20–24 | 7.9 | 6.6 | 9.1 | 7.0 |
| 25–34 | 9.8 | 6.7 | 8.9 | 7.8 |
| 35–44 | 10.2 | 10.2 | 12.8 | 8.3 |
| 45–54 | 14.3 | 11.4 | 24.9 | 11.7 |
| 55–64 | 21.4 | 25.4 | 43.7 | 24.8 |
| 65–74 | 57.6 | 46.6 | 75.2 | 53.9 |
| 75–84 | 145.4 | 129.5 | 147.6 | 129.7 |
| Crude Death Rate | 20.1 | 19.1 | 23.0 | 19.6 |

Source: *Supplement to the 25th Annual Report of the Registrar-General*, p. lxxviii.

* When civil registration began, all the counties of England and Wales were divided into registration districts. Geographically these were usually identical to Poor Law unions. In the case of Stratton the district consisted of a small market town and its rural hinterland. Redruth, however, was a town in the middle of a densely settled area heavily dotted with mines. The whole registration district was industrial in character, and many of the men living there spent all or most of their working life in the mines.

copper miners. Most of them lived in the two unsanitary towns that had grown rapidly since 1820. Their occupation was one of the most dangerous in England, since it left very few men in good health after even a decade of steady employment.

In agrarian Stratton two-thirds of the adult male labor force were farmers or agricultural laborers. Both occupations were among the healthiest possible in nineteenth century England. In addition, the spread of contagious diseases was not a major local problem because Stratton had no large towns or districts of high population density in it or near it.

But for girls and women it seemed to make no difference whether they lived in a healthy rural district or a polluted and unsanitary urban one. In fact, for the five to nineteen age group the open sewers and polluted water of Redruth appeared to confer some positive benefits, since girls there had lower death rates than their Stratton counterparts. But a study of their employment patterns (using manuscript census data) shows instead that, as in Ireland, it was the relative availability of paid employment that probably made the difference.

In the data below we can see that as early as ten to fourteen, one third of the Redruth girls were already at work. They were employed primarily in mines (doing surface work) or in stores. Both occupations paid steady if low wages. But in Stratton only twenty percent of the girls that young were employed. Most of them worked as domestic servants who lived away from their parents and were paid little more than room and board.

TABLE 7

Percentage of Females Aged 10–14 Who Were Employed in 1861[24]

|  | Employed | Receiving Schooling | Doing "Nothing" |
|---|---|---|---|
| Redruth | 37 | 51 | 12 |
| Stratton | 20 | 51 | 29 |

If we look once more at Table 6 and compare the Stratton girls with their brothers, we gain some insight into how badly the rural girls must have been treated. Tuberculosis was the main cause of the unfavorable differential for females in the five to nineteen age groups; and, since both sexes lived in the same types of housing in the same climate, the diets of the girls and/or their general states of mind must have been considerably worse, at least among the poorest families.

About 40 percent of the household heads in Stratton were agricultural laborers. This work was the lowest paid of all major occupations in Cornwall, and agricultural wages were much below average in Stratton. Farm laborers lived on bread supplemented with an occasional bit of bacon or cheese. The wives and daughters of the Stratton farm workers fared even worse; they ate only bread and oatmeal. This protein-deficient diet surely contributed to the high death rates from consumption common among them.

Mining was a relatively well-paid occupation, and thus over half the household heads in Redruth had a standard of living well above subsistence. Miners' diets seem to have included a bit of meat or fish at lunch and dinner. Greater prosperity meant more food for everyone, including wives and daughters. Census data indicate that with very few exceptions wives did not work outside the home, and thus they were spared the double burden of a domestic and agricultural, or industrial, workload. Daughters could find work fairly early, as we have seen, and were not necessarily perceived as unproductive liabilities. All this meant better care, and less tuberculosis for girls, despite poor sanitary conditions.

In sum, adult males who were employed in the industrial sector of Cornwall's economy paid for their higher wages with shorter lives. Their womenfolk were the beneficiaries of this sacrifice. In rural areas, even backward and poverty-striken ones, male wage laborers could work in relative safety and live in a clean environment. But their good health was a product of sacrifices made by wives and daughters.

But how typical was the Cornish situation for England as a whole? Since the mass of regional data on age- and sex-specific death rates has never been analyzed systematically, this question cannot be answered at present. There were rural districts in England, and even in Cornwall, which showed no trace of a male-favoring mortality pattern by the middle of the nineteenth century. But there were English industrial areas which still did.[25] Although a large-scale survey of available mortality data is beyond the scope of this chapter, recent research in social history is beginning to indicate that the onset of industrialization was more beneficial to working-class women than we previously thought.

Peter Stearns has stressed that wherever industrialization or urbanization increased and diversified the jobs open to ordinary girls, they were able to emancipate themselves from parental care at an earlier age. This was important because they took better care of themselves than they received as dependents.[26] Cornish and Irish data indicate that the availability of relatively well-paid jobs, which girls could hold while remaining at home, also improved the care they received. In this light it is interesting to note that after around 1870, when compulsory education and technological changes dried up the supply of jobs for girls in their early teens, a mortality pattern emerged in which once more girls had higher death rates than their brothers (See Table 3).

By raising real wages industrialization also improved the conditions under which working-class wives were expected to survive. Higher standards of living meant more and better food for them. In addition, for the vast majority (as census data show) it was no longer necessary to bear the strain of a double workload. Only the wives of men whose unskilled jobs were least affected by industrialization continued to suffer from a pattern of semi-starvation well into the twentieth century. These unfortunate wives survived on bread and tea; any meat they might purchase was saved for their husbands.[27]

But do the optimistic generalizations about industrialization apply to that fraction of the female population which was *directly* employed in factories or other forms of industry? Everyone has read about the horrors of the early factory system. Workdays were extremely long and machines were hazardous. Conditions improved very slowly between 1840 and 1870, and they were still not good as late as 1910.[28] The health and safety of England's female industrial workers were probably imperiled as much and as often as for male workers. But women usually did not spend their entire adult lives in industry. Typically, the women who worked in factories were not women at all, but young girls. In most factory districts employment for women dropped off sharply after the age of twenty-four, as Victorian census data clearly show.

Since the majority of Englishwomen aged twenty-five to sixty-five were not employed full time in anything beyond their domestic capacity, the Registrar General never published data on occupational-specific mortality rates for women. Thus, we actually do not know to what extent factory work or other forms of industrial employment could raise or lower age-specific death rates. It was only in 1907, at the formal request of the *Journal of the Statistical Society of London*, that the Registrar General used the information on death certificates to provide some data on the comparative death rates among women employed in several major occupational groups.

These data appear to show that at the turn of the century

## TABLE 8
### Age-Specific Death Rates for Occupied Females[29]
### 1900–1907

#### Death Rates Per 1,000 Women Living at Each Age

| | 15–19 | 20–24 | 25–34 | 35–44 | 45–54 | 55–64 |
|---|---|---|---|---|---|---|
| **All Females:** | 3.2 | 3.9 | 5.4 | 8.8 | 14.3 | 27.4 |
| **Females employed as:** | | | | | | |
| Cotton Workers (Lancashire) | 2.3 | 3.0 | 3.3 | 4.7 | 8.3 | 19.8 |
| Domestic Servants (London) | 1.6 | 2.0 | 2.5 | 5.4 | 9.2 | 12.9 |
| Charwomen (London & Lancashire) | 3.2 | 6.2 | 6.4 | 8.4 | 9.8 | 10.8 |

women who worked in cotton factories had *lower* death rates than the general population of women. They even had a more favorable mortality pattern than did domestic servants above the age of thirty-five. Charwomen (cleaning ladies employed by the day) were far worse off at every age.

But because of the way death certificates were filled out, the Registrar General did not feel these data were valid.[30] His doubts were probably well-founded. When D. J. Collier attempted to investigate conditions in factories in 1914, and the influence these conditions had on accidents and death among female employees, company managers and doctors refused to speak to her or open their files.[31] All that can be said is that, in spite of the abundance of descriptive literature on the horrors of the factory system, there are actually no direct and specific data available on the extent to which the mortality patterns of employed women were adversely (or beneficially) affected.

This survey of age- and sex-specific mortality rates in Victorian England has raised more questions than it has answered. Despite the recent proliferation of literature on Victorian women, we do not know enough about them to relate fully the way they lived to the way they died. Not enough is known about the actual effects of intensive child-bearing on the health of adult women. We know almost nothing about the way young girls were raised and treated in comparison to their brothers. The influence of social class on female mortality patterns remains relatively unexplored. This area of investigation might contain a number of surprises, since the data on aristocratic girls and middle-class Quaker women seem to show that privileged women were not so well off as popular moralists would have us believe. It is be-

*A Widening Sphere*

ginning to look as if females employed as ladies, like men employed as copper miners, were engaged in a hazardous occupation that undermined their health and shortened their lives.[32] In this sense the reformist feminist movement, with its overwhelmingly middle-class character, was not another luxury for those who were already well off, but a necessity as essential to them as trade unions were to employed working-class women.

However inadequate the existing data are, they point to the conclusion that a strictly biological approach to understanding the emergence or existence of a female mortality advantage has serious limitations. Social and economic factors were important as well, and today they are making it more and more deadly to be male.

# 9. Sexuality in Britain, 1800=1900

### Some Suggested Revisions

### F. Barry Smith

OUR CURRENT NOTIONS ABOUT VICTORIAN SEXUALITY ARE IN A PROMISING
state of uncertainty. The traditional picture, composed in Victorian
times and reinforced during the first thirty years of this century, is now
beginning to break up. We are poised to ask new questions about
Victorian sexual behavior and to explore new sources for answers.
Probably there is much that we shall never know, for men, and women
more so, do not leave masses of clear-cut information about intimate
and important elements in their behavior, but we should be able to
discard the condescending stereotype we currently use.

This stereotype includes male dominance in the family, strict
differentiation of sex roles, separate standards of morality for males
and females, female coldness in marriage, and general silence about
sexual matters, all of it tainted by hypocrisy.[1] We can all supply
quotations and anecdotes to embellish this interpretation. Asides by
Thackeray, Charles Reade, and Mrs. Gaskell about the limitations set
by middle-class morality upon the artists' treatment of sexuality and
family life; the Veneerings, Podsnaps, and Pooters; the moralizing of
Old Humphrey and other Religious Tract Society hacks; and Mrs.
Lynn Linton's diatribes, add up to a formidable collection of assertions
of prudery and sexual coldness as norms. There are also memorable
absurdities of etiquette, like that recommended by Lady Gough in
1863:

The perfect hostess will see to it that the works of male and female authors be
properly separated on her bookshelves. Their proximity, unless they happen to
be married, should not be tolerated.[2]

It is also said that genteel reticence required the substitution of circumlocutions for straightforward nouns and adjectives: "enceinte" or "in an interesting condition" for pregnant, "nether limbs" for legs, "bosom" for breast, "private parts" for genitals, "retire to rest" for go to bed, "the serious disease" for syphilis, "the social evil" for prostitution, "fallen women" for prostitutes. Crinolines and tight corsets were employed to suppress the breasts and disguise pregnancy. The dress of respectable middle-class men became more drab than it has ever been before or since. Chaperonage of women during courtship is said to have become more strict during the 1850's. The dressing of piano legs is also alleged to have become common in the 1860's, although I have never seen it documented except satirically. It is unclear whether these alleged taboos were ever widespread, and whether Britain imported such fashions from France and the eastern United States.[3]

Indeed, when one begins to look for evidence for the stereotype, its insubstantiality becomes worrying. *Punch* lampooned prudery and American rectitude, and the equally widely read *Leader* and *Saturday Review* successively denounced it. One astute observer insisted that such behavior was imported from Boston and warned against such "vulgar gentility" in a treatise on correct manners intended for the middling sort.[4] The private lives of the novelists and critics who are commonly tapped for quotation do not fit. And their quotations are frequently extracted from a context of protest and exaggerated satire. Dickens, Wilkie Collins, Charles Reade, George Meredith, George Moore, Eliza Lynn Linton, George Eliot, George Gissing, D. G. Rossetti, Samuel Butler, J. M. W. Turner, Sir John Millais, J. M. Whistler, A. C. Swinburne, G. A. Sala, John Chapman, John Stuart Mill, G. H. Lewes, John Morley, and Henry Labouchere were each at odds with normal monogamy, and their various personal situations need to be remembered when their innuendoes and denunciations of Victorian proprieties are mentioned.[5]

The chronology of the stereotype is difficult too. Wingfield-Stratford's widely read book, *Victorian Tragedy*, effortlessly muddled its periods by constructing the "Tragedy" out of examples of prudery and male dominance drawn indiscriminately from the early eighteenth to early twentieth centuries. In reaction, Maurice Quinlan and Muriel Jaeger pointed out many years ago that Bowdlerism and "female delicacy" long predated the accession of Victoria. Yet the very titles of their books, *Victorian Prelude* and *Before Victoria,* and their arguments predicate the triumph of the Bowdlers and the Proclamation

Society, and the transmission with increased force into Victorian times of the taboos they characterize. "Victorian" becomes a datum by which they reify their interpretation of changes in manners. The transmission is more complicated than this. Just as Bowdlerism began long before the Bowdlers—Allan Ramsay was censored in the 1720's—so the victory of what is really a very old strand in British moralism was never complete and floods of unexpurgated literature, street ballads, music-hall songs, and shady advertisements continued throughout the century despite unflagging attempts at suppression. The Proclamation Society and its heirs succeeded only partially in bringing the grosser members of the aristocracy and other classes to obey its taboos. On the other hand, there does seem to have been a qualitative change in convention between about 1819 and 1830. The crude behavior and flagrant promiscuity of the aristocratic sets and their hangers-on at Holland House, Lansdowne House, Hertford House, and the Pavilion do seem to have become discredited toward the end of the 1820's and to have diminished. Henceforth promiscuity had to be less public. Quinlan, Jaeger, and Ford K. Brown have adduced several reasons for the change in the realm of pietistic and ethical pressures, but my reading of the evidence suggests that the reactions of the populace and the marines to the trial and death of Queen Caroline shook the aristocracy more than the efforts of the evangelicals. Among the laboring poor of London, at least, there also seems to have occurred a qualitative improvement in manners, accompanied by a lessening of the squalid brutality and cruelty that had characterized London street life in the eighteenth century. But this subject still awaits proper historical exploration.[6]

Other parts of the stereotype, especially the conspiracy of silence, the latent viciousness and sadism in male-dominated family relations, and the hypocrisy that greased the system of private villainy masked by public respectability, derive mainly from late-Victorian rebels, principally Samuel Butler, G. B. Shaw, Havelock Ellis, Edward Carpenter, A. C. Benson, Arnold Bennett, and Lytton Strachey. Their onslaught on what they declared to be the duplicity of their elders, delivered with memorable intensity, elegance, and wit, has shaped our imagination to the present. The impressive work of the 1960's by Peter Cominos, Steven Marcus, and Phyllis Grosskurth, each writing within the Butler-Ellis framework, has served to strengthen the received view that has come down to us. Indeed, the readiness with which historians and literary students accepted Marcus's *The Other*

*Victorians* may be explained largely by the manner in which his treatment of Acton and *My Secret Life* fit prevailing opinions.[7]

Nonetheless, *The Other Victorians* marks the breakthrough. Marcus's sensitive literary analysis of nineteenth-century pornographic material opens questions that historians had ignored. But there are difficulties, it seems to me, in accepting his methods of argument. Marcus relies on William Acton (1814–75), urologist and self-announced authority on prostitution and sexuality in the years between 1850 and 1880, for confirmation of the standard Victorian attitudes to sex. For example, Marcus quotes Acton's assertion that debility and insanity were inescapable penalties of masturbation and concludes that "the prevailing tone" of his work is "a characteristic Victorian tone. It is resonant of danger, doom and disaster . . . and tells us of a world hedged in with difficulty and pain, a world of harsh efforts and iron consequences."[8] This form of historical argument is common in literary circles. It consists of turning exegesis into historical evidence. The exposition begins by referring a literary text, the representativeness of which in time and place is unestablished, to an ideal type generalized from current fashions in literary interpretation. This happy conjunction itself becomes "evidence" which "proves" the historicity of the literary text and thereby transforms its fictional modes of thought and happenings into thoughts and events that actually occurred in the past. It is a superficially persuasive presentation, but it is not history.

There are, moreover, indications that Acton is both a less reliable guide to sexual behavior and a less representative example of medical opinion than Marcus and others have taken him to be. Acton's medical contemporaries, for instance, were skeptical about his claims. The *London Journal of Medicine* rejected "as mere fancy or gratuitous assertion" his claims about the health of prostitutes in *A Practical Treatise on Disease of the Urinary Organs in Both Sexes* (1851). The equally authoritative *Sanitary Review*, reviewing Acton's *Prostitution . . .* (1857), noted that his figures for hours of work of girls in the slop clothes trades (nineteen a day) were unbelievable and doubted his allegations about the amount of prostitution in London. The reviewer went on to remark that much of Acton's evidence was drawn from dubious reportage by scandalmongering journalists such as Bracebridge Hemyng and his collaborators and not always, as Acton implied, from his own experience.

The remarkable neglect or, where noticed, outright rejection of Acton's assertions by medical spokesmen raises questions about the views of the profession. At present we know very little about medical practitioners' opinions on any matter, let alone sexuality. Three eminent representatives of the profession, Sir James Paget, Sir Andrew Clark, and Sir Clifford Allbutt, are said to have advised "self-control," with sexual intercourse reserved for the purpose of procreation. Allbutt expressed what seems to have been their shared belief that "mere . . . physical gratification" was "certainly not . . . necessary to health in man or woman." But the context in which Paget's alleged advice was given, a lecture to medical students, suggests that he and his audience expected as doctors to have their patients engage them in full discussion of sexual behavior. He went on to say that prevailing lay opinion, and medical opinion too, was that "fornication" was good for body and mind and that patients expected their doctors to prescribe sexual intercourse. Certainly these three great men sound embattled by opinions that differed strikingly from theirs and Acton's[9] and by attitudes to sexuality that were less furtive than they wanted them to be.

Other informed observers distrusted Acton too. Jacob Bright, the Liberal M.P. and campaigner against the Contagious Diseases Acts, dismissed Acton "as probably the most illogical man who ever put pen to paper." Benjamin Scott, Chamberlain of the City of London and another campaigner against the Acts, quoted the "Judicial Statistics for 1863–68" to demolish Acton's assertions about the 80,000 prostitutes operating in London. (It is fair to add that the "Judicial Statistics" are pretty unreliable too.) Whenever we test Acton's assertions against other contemporary evidence, they begin to look shaky. His claim, for instance, that many part-time prostitutes were seamstresses and milliners is contradicted by two extensive and apparently careful surveys of the occupations of prostitutes. Authorities at the Glasgow Lock Hospital kept records of the 4,000 patients treated in the decade 1870–1880; over half were "mill-girls" and "domestic servants," and only 85 were "needlewomen." G. P. Merrick's files of twenty years' rescue work in London between 1870 and 1890 yield similar results: of 14,756 prostitutes he contacted, 5,823 (or 40 percent) called themselves "domestic servants," 1,122 "laundresses" formed the next largest group, and only 943 (or 6 percent) were "dressmakers."[10]

Acton's credibility is also diminished when he announces as scientific fact beliefs that common experience suggests are dubious and that objective inquiry into his Islington Dispensary practice (if not his Hanover and Cavendish Square ones) might have exposed as nonsense. Marcus quotes his testimony that genteel women of all classes (not simply the middle classes, as Marcus interprets it) have no sexual drive or need of sexual gratification, thereby exemplifying the alleged Victorian dictum that "ladies do not move." Even here, the recently published evidence about Fanny and Charles Kingsley suggests that Acton's experience was, at least, limited.[11] The view that females existed sexually only to satisfy male needs and that the material association was ultimately a cash relationship can also be extrapolated from Acton. Marcus seeks to establish the general applicability of this point by instancing "Walter" and his cash negotiations with prostitutes and servant girls in *My Secret Life,* although these are casual encounters with distinct class and legal connotations.[12]

The emphasis in current writing on Acton and "Walter" has renewed the old tradition of the Victorian Tragedy and obscured the important fact that a great many Victorian families and liaisons in widely differing classes, times, and local situations were richly happy. But then, as Tolstoy noted, harmonious families resemble one another and are not very interesting to outsiders. James and Ellen Watson, the radical publicists; George Julian and Mary Harney, the Chartists; W. E. and Mary Gladstone; the Brownings; William and Catherine Booth; Charles and Mary Booth; the Darwins; the Kingsleys; the Amberleys; William and Mary Howitt; W. J. and Emily Linton, the Mazzinian republicans; Tom and Fanny Hughes; Richard and Mary Oastler; George and Josephine Butler, formed intensely happy families and this happiness must have had at least some basis in their parents' mutual sexual satisfaction. Our knowledge of these families also suggests that they were united by much more than mere monetary (or the lack of it) bonds: in each case the husband and wife shared social values and jointly participated in working for their common public aim. That strict demarcation of male and female roles usually "proved" by quotations from "The Princess" or Ruskin's *Sesame and Lilies* seems in practice to have been breached, especially among the working classes, by female preachers and political reformers, street cleaners, wives who controlled the family finances in Scottish textile villages, London costers, and rural unlicensed "wise woman" medical practitioners. Much of what Acton wrote is simply irrelevant to this world of happy families and independent women. It is worth asking, in view of his "turbulent" childhood, his decision to take such an unusual path in medicine, and his vivid, imaginative, novelistic prose, whether much of his purported sound information is really private fantasy. Certainly we need more than Acton's works to provide convincing reference points for Walter's sexual extravaganza.

Marcus's preoccupations with *My Secret Life* are literary, but his use of the book as a document about behavior in the past raises difficulties for the historian akin to those associated with Acton. In 'Walter's' case, Marcus validates the actors' perceptions and motives by referring to Dickens. Yet the fact remains that action in *My Secret Life* occurs in filmy London streets and houses, imprecise in time and place. The total isolation of the narrative from secular happenings against which its obsessively deployed minutiae could be checked raises important questions for the reader. 'Walter's' reports of conversations ring true, as do many of his encounters with clubmen, servant girls, and prostitutes, yet the total narrative of repeated easy, rapid, sexual conquests and unflagging physical prowess ultimately becomes incredible. It seems to me that *My Secret Life* must be handled gingerly as a historical document, indeed treated as a total fiction, until we know more about its author, or authors, its provenance, and its relation to known historical relationships and events. At the very least, we need to demote it from the place it has come to occupy as a standard guide.

The vagueness that envelops *My Secret Life* afflicts our general understanding of nineteenth-century sexuality. We know almost nothing about actual sexual practices. We have no chronology of changes in customs and beliefs. We have hardly begun to differentiate sexual and marital behavior by class or by religion. We know next to nothing about the effects of sexual and marital practices on social cohesion or dysfunction. Even the impact of sexual customs on the crude birthrate is little explored. Yet there is precise and extensive information in census returns, reports of inquests and divorce actions, mothercraft books, and medical journals that remains largely untapped.

There exist two other sets of writing on sexuality which greatly exceed Acton in their sales and accessibility to a range of readers. Historians will have to consider these materials more seriously than they have done so far. The authors of both sets agree in proclaiming a single standard of morality for both sexes and they argue for joyous heterosexuality, for contraception, for easier divorce, and in some cases, for promiscuity. The first set contains the often-named but little-read line of neo-Malthusians, launched popularly by Richard Carlile and continued through the century by Robert Dale Owen, Dr. Charles Drysdale, Annie Besant, Charles Bradlaugh, and through to Marie Stopes. The important feature of this literature is that it was simply and attractively written, it was cheap, and it must have been disseminated very widely. Carlile's *Every Woman's Book* sold 10,000 copies within five months of publication in 1828. Over 165,000 copies of Dr. Knowlton's *Fruits of Philosophy* were published in 1876–77. Thirty-five thousand copies of Annie Besant's *Law of Population* were sold within a year of publication in 1878. Twenty thousand more sold in the United States during that year and it had already been translated into Dutch. My copy of Drysdale's *Elements of Social Science* (dated 1887, first published 1854) is the 65,000th issue of the 26th edition.[13] Respectable men apparently kept their distance from Drysdale and other doctors in the Malthusian League, but nonetheless their teachings must be considered in any discussion of "official" medical opinion about sexuality and contraception in the nineteenth century.

Carlile's argument sets the pattern for subsequent literature. He declared that every healthy woman after the age of puberty felt, in some degree, the passion of love—a declaration far removed from the doctrine that ladies never move. Persons who abstained from such a natural and enjoyable function as sexual intercourse were likely to join the ranks of priests and cranky celibates who resisted other natural appetites and became embittered and "useless for civil life." Females did differ physiologically from males, but not to a degree that incapacitated them from engaging in civil life; moreover "all experience" suggested that when females received education and opportunity equal to that of males, their mental and creative capacities proved also to be equal. But the immediate block to the pursuit of equality and the release of mental power, the fear of pregnancy, had to be removed. Carlile straightforwardly suggested the use of douches, vaginal sponges, and withdrawal. He remarked, on what evidence I do not know, that the vaginal sponge was "common with the females of the more refined parts of . . . Europe and with those of the Aristocracy of England. An English Duchess . . . never goes out to dinner without being prepared with the sponge . . . French and Italian women wear them fastened to their waists."[14]

Carlile, Drysdale, and the rest are never prurient. Their sober message was that self-restraint expressed through contraception—in which "the considerable, manly act" of withdrawal was prominent, and cheap—and family responsibility were the only humane answers to the Malthusian crux. Abstinence, as recommended by Malthus, they denounced as cruel, while infanticide and crude abortion were both inhumane and dangerous. Contraception, they argued, would reduce what they believed, probably rightly, to have been a horrifyingly high rate of infanticide and abortion. Moreover, by limiting the number of children in working-class families, contraception was the key to that private independence and public respectability which lay at the heart of nineteenth-century radical ambitions.[15]

The good sense of these radicals is also shown by their dismissal of masturbation and nocturnal emissions as causes of insanity and debility. Dr. Knowlton, whose pamphlet was frequently reprinted in Britain, remarked that it was "truly astonishing to what a degree of mental anguish this disease [the medical name for nocturnal emission was gonorrhea dormietium] gives rise in young men." Knowlton and Robert Dale Owen, for example, allowed that masturbation and seminal emissions were esthetically unpleasing, but agreed that such behavior did no demonstrable physical harm.[16]

Historians now need to ask who studied this material and who followed its advice. We know where it was sold: free-thought and radical booksellers in English and Scottish towns stocked it and advertised titles for sale in the radical press. In January 1834, for example, Henry Hetherington's *Poor Man's Guardian* advertised the tenth edition of Owen's *Moral Physiology* at 1s. per copy: "This work . . . is of the first importance, not only as a reply to Malthus, but also as supplying to every father and mother of a family the knowledge by which, without injury to health, or violence to the moral feeling, any further increase which is not desired may be prevented." G. J. Holyoake's *Reasoner* for October 1855 advertised works published by Turner in Stoke-upon-Trent, including *Matrimony* (3d.), *Love and Parentage* (3d.), and *Marriage and Parentage or the Reproductive Element in Man* (10d.). Ernest Jones's *People's Paper* recommended the *Elements of Social Sciences* in July 1857. Bradlaugh's *National Reformer* for August 1869 has advertisements for the French edition of *Elements of Social Science*, Palmer's *Principle of Nature* (1s.), and Owen's *Moral Physiology*. Booksellers like the Watsons, Holyoakes, Edward Truelove, and the Watts family advertised and sold contraceptive devices. "Indecent" booksellers, like the one in Bristol whose conviction for selling the Knowlton pamphlet provoked the Bradlaugh-Besant challenge in 1876, were probably the most numerous and effective disseminators of information, to males at least, about sex and methods of family limitation. Condoms were also available from barbers, surgeons, and itinerant charlatans and were sold at taverns and public resorts.[17]

From C. J. Welton, Marriage and Its Mysteries, *40th ed. 1907 (1st ed. 1889).*

We shall need a great deal more family reconstruction, census-data analysis, and local historical studies of sales of sex literature and contraceptives before we can make confident statements about the impact of this material on the crude birth rate. Family reconstruction work is rapidly emerging from its antiquarian phase and appears ready to supply information about differences in family formation between social strata and the relative fertility rates of particular groups within parishes and towns. Dr. E. A. Wrigley has shown that family limitation was practiced in one preindustrial community, and the present general figures we have for York, Ashford, Nottingham, rural Lancashire, and Preston in 1851 show that the average of the number of children in the family was about 1.9, a figure very close to the 2.1 that has been calculated for preindustrial families. Allowing for the variables of fertility and child mortality, it still seems plausible that family limitation methods continued to be employed through the decades of transition.[18]

The growth of the urban, commercial economy may well have caused some people to turn to family limitation and its literature. From the status of the vendors, presumably it was an amalgam of people such as those with radical proclivities and free-thinking, privatized ethics, blocked upwardly mobile artisans—and self-employed men and their wives, and "uneasy" middle-class people, who studied physiology and sought to practice equality within the family. These careful individuals seem the most likely to have used withdrawal and to have experimented with douches and sponges and, after the 1870's, to have tried spermicides and rubber condoms. William James Linton, the wood engraver, and his common-law wife, both radical Republicans, purchased Robert Dale Owen's *Moral Physiology* from Watson's shop, read it, and apparently practiced contraception; although "accidents," as Emily described them, kept happening. Between 1841 and 1854 they ended up with seven children after planning to have four. Their case is a reminder that raw data and size of families are not simple indicators of recourse to contraceptive methods. The Lintons observed equality between the sexes and of parents with children. Stricken with poverty, illness, and death, their household was nevertheless happy and free.[19]

When, how, and to what extent the merchant, professional, churchgoing ranks adopted contraception is a further question. The evidence produced by J. A. and Olive Banks in *Feminism and Family Planning in Victorian England*, the pother in the middle-class press about delayed marriage and "race suicide," and the renewed persecution of radical publicists culminating in the Bradlaugh-Besant trial of 1877 suggest that the crucial decade was the 1870's. These years mark the turning point in the modern British birthrate. If this is so, it is another instance of that process in nineteenth-century Britain by which humane, sensible reforms were developed by the self-instructed ranks and subsequently filtered upward to the propertied strata. But at this heady point it is worth adding that the crude gynecology of the century, worsened by the crazes for hysterotomy and laporatomy that swept the medical profession in the later part of the period, may have reduced the size of doctor-employing, middle- and upper-class families as effectively as the devices respectable spokesmen for the profession so vehemently condemned.

A second set of writings has hitherto been little noticed by historians and demographers, but it could illuminate many nineteenth-century beliefs about sex and sexual practices. This is the subterranean stream of popular writings, often by medical hacks and charlatans, titillating sexual curiosity and working upon anxieties about impotence, sterility, the pox, and menstruation. Advertisements for advice and nostrums appear in widely read radical and sporting sheets throughout the century, usually beside the "police news," and their adjunct pamphlets appear to have been best-sellers. The advertisements usually enjoin worried readers to send descriptions of their symptoms together with a fee (usually 4s. 6d. but sometimes as high as a guinea), upon receipt of which the doctor undertook to send advice, pills, and lotions. The latter were normally cheap mercury compounds. The response must have been extensive, for advertisements for innumerable differently named practitioners at addresses throughout the country recur throughout the century. Take two representative samples at a forty-year interval. In the *Northern Star* during May 1842 a Mr. Wilkinson of Bedford was advertising "medical advice" and the "genuine Widow Welch's Female Pills." In the same issues Messrs. Perry of Liverpool and Manchester extolled the virtues of "Perry's Purifying Specific Pills" and "Perry's Concentrated Defensive Essence," while Messrs. Bruce and Holloway of London announced the rival claims of "Bruce's Samaritan Pills," "Bruce's Tonic Mixture," "Bruce's Female Tonic Pills," and Mr. Holloway was launching the long lucrative career of "Holloway's Pills." Mr. Brodie was competing, too, with his "Purifying Vegetable Pills." He also recommended *The Secret Companion*, an invaluable compendium containing "observations on marriage, with proper directions for the removal of all disqualifications." *Bell's Life in London and Sporting Chronicle* for January 1880 contains notices of Clarke's Pills, at "4s. 6d. a box or 60 stamps," for "discharges from the urinary organs," available from Mr. F. J. Clarke, High Street, Lincoln; "Red Cross Pills," "warranted not to contain mercury," and allegedly from Paris; "Grimuad's Vegetable Matico"; and "Brou's Injection."[20] The companion pamphlets to the medicaments, usually by a named, allegedly qualified person, describe symptoms of venereal disease and menstrual difficulties and laud their author's particular methods of cure. The booklets also carry, incidental to this information, helpful, reasonably accurate physiological expositions, but take for granted acquaintance with the basic facts of sex and copulation. The booklets I have seen are uniformly silent about contraception, doubtless because the authors were careful not to offend the law too blatantly, but also possibly because they believed that their readers were already acquainted with withdrawal at least. I suspect that many of these shady practitioners sold condoms and fitted pessaries, but I have no evidence of this. Pessaries, moreover, were normally fitted in the earlier nineteenth century for disorders in the womb rather than as contraceptives.[21]

The prodigious circulation of this literature has not been appreciated. Samuel Solomon of Liverpool, M.D., Member of the University and College of Physicians, Aberdeen, published his *Guide to Health, or Advice to Both Sexes* in at least sixty-six editions between 1782 and 1817, and new printings kept appearing into the 1870's; each edition after 1800 probably ran to over 30,000 copies. Sales of the *Guide to Health* were reputed at the time to be second only to those of the *Rights of Man*. And, over time, they probably exceeded them. *Man and Woman* by Horace Goss, M.D., Surgeon, Great Queen Street, Lincoln's Inn Fields, ran through at least five editions in the 1850's. It was regularly advertised in the radical *Sheffield Free Press,* together with Goss's *On Self-Inflicted Miseries and Disappointed Hopes* with 70 Coloured Engravings on Steel, price 2/6 . . . or 40 postage stamps."

Dr. Solomon, like Doctors Goss, Brodum, Ramsay, and others of their trade, fished both sides of the stream. He recommended male and female enjoyment in intercourse and noted that intercourse was "natural" and that orgasms made the participants happy and loving to each other. Yet he warned that "over-indulgence" created overexcitement of the physical organism, and that the excessive loss of seminal

*A Widening Sphere*

fluid occasioned by over-indulgence led to physical and mental exhaustion. So, while intercourse was "exstacy," "excessive venery" resulted in "lassitude, weakness, numbness, a feeble gait, headache, convulsions of all the senses, dimness of sight and dulness of hearing, an idiot look, a consumption of the lungs and back, and effeminacy." And because over-indulgence weakened the sensation of particular "exstacies" it produced "a perpetual itch for pleasure," with inevitable debility. The remedy was to write for Dr. Solomon's "Cordial Balm of Gilead," apply muriatic quicksilver, and sleep on a hard mattress. Females had to be especially careful during sexual play because their blood, according to available medical opinion, was more "capillary and lymphatic" than that of males. This condition made them more excitable and insatiable than males and therefore more vulnerable to "exhaustion" and degeneration of their sexual organs. For ladies with this problem Dr. Solomon had a "Special Cordial Balm of Gilead," at 10s. 6d. a bottle, obtainable at market towns throughout Great Britain.[22]

The absence of explicit advice about physiological differences between the sexes, sex play, intercourse, and pregnancy may be significant. Presumably Dr. Solomon and his fraternity were unusually well informed about the sexual proclivities and fears of their contemporaries, especially among the looser gentry and laborers who read the sporting journals and the respectable middle-class and artisan radicals who read the *Gauntlet, Northern Star, Sheffield Free Press,* and *Reynolds Weekly Newspaper.* Had there been money to be made from such advice, Dr. Solomon and company would have purveyed it. Or perhaps we may conclude that rudimentary sexual knowledge was widespread among both males and females in these strata and that the inferences about disastrous innocence on wedding nights, which are very hard to document anyway, even in biographies of Ruskin, can be drawn from a narrow band within the religious upper-middle class?

The advertisements and popular medical literature harp throughout the century on masturbation and the evils of sexual daydreaming, but the emphasis changes between the first three decades and the last three. Masturbation in the earlier period seems mostly to have been related to male adults. Dr. John Roberton's warning is typical:

from the commencement of the disgusting habit of self-pollution . . . there is seldom any desire for sexual intercourse . . . at length, there is induced a general lassitude, with a weariness, often approaching to pain, in the loins; the bowels become constipated, often in alarming degree; the face becomes pale and cadaverous, and the body in general flabby or emaciated, with coldness in the extremities. Then occurs trembling hands, dim eyes, confused indistinct hearing, if not entire deafness, frequent and violent headache, drowsiness, without the power to sleep, all attempts at which are interrupted by the most frightful dreams; and in this stage . . . the patient becomes terrified to go to bed, lest sudden death should be his fate; and, during the day is tired, fretful, terrified and discontented, he knows not for what; with violent palpitations of the heart; and although he seems sensible of the causes of his distresses, is unable to abandon his habits, particularly while in bed. A complete state of imbecility, both of body and mind, at length ensues. . . .[23]

Roberton seems to be a shining example of the gainful adaptation of private repression to public anxiety.

After 1870 warnings against masturbation concentrate on infants and young people. Whereas in the earlier period children appear to have been regarded as innocent of sexuality and its attendant lust, toward the end of the century this behavioral category seems to have been soured. The change coincided with the discovery of adolescence, among boys at least—even properly reared ones—as a special period of sexual unrest. It is strange, given that *Jane Eyre* provided a classic account of adolescence in 1847, that the Victorians retained the traditional notion of an abrupt transition from childhood to adulthood. Adolescence is a rare word in Victorian writing, and the notion, especially with its modern post-Freudian accretions, scarcely figures in the diaries and fiction of the period. "Puberty" does appear occasionally but only in its strict physiological sense. The absence of the notion of adolescence makes conservative Victorians' attitudes toward protection of young people in factories and to the age of consent more comprehensible. They were not being simply callous when they asserted that adulthood began at twelve or thirteen and that "adults" should be permitted to protect themselves.

From the late 1860's on, medical spokesmen and purity publicists agreed that infants and children did show sexual curiosity, that they masturbated and had erections. Much earnest thought and ingenuity was given to prevention. "Strict supervision," belts, and punishment for infringements of an unspoken code were resorted to by worried parents and schoolmasters, although the actual spread of these attitudes, especially outside the middle classes, remains unexplored. Such anxieties were not restricted to Protestant Britain. In France, for example, doctors working in insane asylums seem to have been even readier than their British colleagues to remove the clitoris from "libidinous" patients. The operation succeeded, too, for, like most

*A Widening Sphere*

self-fulfilling prophecies, it proved that masturbation, if it did not initiate insanity in imbeciles, certainly worsened their condition: as a doctor reported after one such operation, "the patient was watched and her libidinous propensities gradually decreased, and her mental powers slowly improved." "Strict supervision," especially at night, was a normal procedure at most asylums, poor houses, and refuges for the destitute.[24]

Warnings against masturbation and nocturnal emissions were published throughout the century, but preoccupation with them appears to have been become endemic among medical men and the clergy, especially school chaplains, between 1870 and 1914. Dozens of "cautions to young men," originating as hygiene and purity talks and sermons, were published during these years. This fearmongering coincided with a strengthening of the militaristic "anti-intellectual manly purity" code of the middle- and upper-class schools and universities.

"I would to God I could keep silence," Reverend Richard Armstrong told his young men's meeting at Hope Street Chapel, Liverpool, in 1887. But "I am now convinced that . . . solitary vice . . . so honeycombs society, so saps the health, the happiness, the moral force of tens of thousands, convinced also that so much of this is brought about by sheer ignorance and thoughtlessness, that every man who is awake to the facts is bound to speak out."[25]

Priscilla Barker, who with her husband "worked for Purity and Chastity for many years," offered numerous examples of the degenerative effects of masturbation among girls:

Another victim came under my notice whose infatuating habit betrayed itself in sweaty, clammy hands, stinking feet, and mouth always full of saliva. I felt compelled to question her, for her own sake, and she confessed that as a child living in the quiet country, her chief delight was to go and sit up in a tree for hours, to gratify her sinful pleasure, under the pretence of cracking nuts.[26]

Whatever the remote causes, the rhetoric and urgent tone of the homilies disclose a failure of nerve and call to mind Armstrong's "Germanic race" closing ranks against insurgent foreign nations and lesser breeds. Embedded in the sermons is a notion that only a chaste leadership can survive challenge from the infidel lower orders. Servants given to self-abuse, Priscilla Barker affirmed, were impertinent and slovenly.[27] The Reverend Ashington Bullen linked sexual pollution with the wrecking of the family, and thence inevitably with social chaos and the fall of the Empire.[28] These admonitions overshadowed the youth of the late-Victorian rebels mentioned earlier who helped to draw the stereotype of Victorian sexuality. I do not think their rebellion can be understood without setting it in the context of repression; this context is especially important in view of the frightful social risks imposed on middle- and upper-class male homosexuals after 1885.

Lytton Strachey was never more destructively ahistorical than when he remarked that we knew too much about the Victorians. Much myth and prejudice about their political and social behavior has recently been dissolved with the aid of new questions and new evidence. The myths about their sexual behavior will take longer to dislodge. Our notions are always likely to be colored by the vivid evidence about abnormal sexuality and irregular liaisons, while mutually happy relationships that were taken for granted then as now have vanished for want of record. But at least we are becoming aware of the complexities and gaps in our knowledge. We have arrived at the point where, at least, if we know too little about the Victorians, we know enough to be wary of what Lytton Strachey and other literary men have said about them.

# 10. The Women of England in a Century of Social Change, 1815–1914

## A Select Bibliography, Part II

~

### Barbara Kanner

IN ADDITION TO PROVIDING USEFUL SOURCES, THE INTENTION OF THIS bibliography[1] is to support the case for studying the social position of English women by questioning the relationships existing between the various social and intellectual changes that transformed national life in the nineteenth and early twentieth centuries and the changes that occurred in the roles, attitudes, and activities of women during that period. A major argument for this focus is that it avoids flat description of women's behavior in their immediate milieu in favor of an attempt to analyze the meaning and function of women's roles within the wider matrix of English society. Social historians are beginning to include this focus, and the thesis that societal and sex-role change are interdependent, in their analytical schema.

The problems involved in selecting sources for this bibliography have not arisen from a shortage of primary and secondary works about Victorian and Edwardian women, because a large number of books and articles of varying quality are available.[2] But problems do abound in finding reliable and scholarly writings, because too few are systematic, historically oriented studies that focus *directly* on questions about women's—as opposed to exclusively men's—responses to social readjustments and social thought. Perhaps we should say that there has been a fairly widespread neglect of the element of sexual differentiation in historical analyses of the consequences of social change.[3] And yet, there has been no denial of a dichotomy in the impact of social change upon the two sexes.

In a valuable essay J. A. and Olive Banks suggest this point through their exploration of the neglect of women's movements involving feminism in studies of nineteenth-century activities for social reform. "It might not indeed be too fanciful," they write, "to ascribe the neglect of feminism on the part of historians to their more general neglect of genuine *social* history."

1. J. A. and Olive Banks, "Feminism and Social Change—A Case Study of a Social Movement," in George K. Zollschan and Walter Hirsch, eds., *Explorations in Social Change*. Boston, 1964, p. 548.

More recently, Brian Harrison credited "current trends" toward the growth of "social" history with stimulating the attention of modern scholars to questioning Victorian sexual attitudes and behavior (notably from the time of Steven Marcus's *The Other Victorians, SBS* item 236), an area in which women as much as men are investigated:

2. Brian Harrison, "Underneath the Victorians," in *Victorian Studies* 10 (1967), 239–62, p. 241. An important article.

Also supporting the ideal of the responsibility of social history to expand scholarly inquiry to include the social significance of sex roles, Natalie Zemon Davis, in her paper for the Second Berkshire Conference on the History of Women in 1974, urges:

that we should be interested in the history of both women and men, that we should not be working only on the subjected sex any more than an historian of class can focus on peasants. Our goal is to understand the significance of the *sexes*, of gender groups in the historical past. Our goal is to discover the range in sex roles and in sexual symbolism in different societies and periods, to find out what meaning they had and how they functioned to maintain the social order or to promote its change.[4]

3. Natalie Zemon Davis, " 'Women's History' in Transition: the European Case," in *Feminist Studies* 3 (1976), 83–103, p. 90.

Recent social histories, then, are beginning to propose and to answer questions for those who are interested in studying women's roles and behavior in relation to social dynamics, and for those who, reversing the order, have concluded that "many unfamiliar aspects of nineteenth century society spring to view" when questions about women's position—either sexually differentiated or in a social relation to men—are investigated by historians (quoted phrasing from Harrison, p. 262, entry 2).

*A Widening Sphere*

The problem of quality of sources persists, however, in the sense that we require scholarship that deeply informs our understanding not only in theory but also in the context of time, place, and circumstances, and in the sense that we must insist on at least an attempt to answer, with sufficient supportive evidence, *why* and *how* changes transpired within the female population in reciprocity with trends in general society. The introduction to the first part of this bibliography (*SBS*, 173–77) is largely concerned with encouraging and exemplifying this critical viewpoint. Questions of methodology, semantics, evidence as replacement for assertion, and the importance of attention to the factor of social class are included among the suggestions for critique.

The questions and problems that formulated the categories of inquiry for Part I pertain largely to traditional areas of social studies: employment, education, population trends, social service attending socioeconomic distress, political activity, and the law. The question of "climate of opinion," another standard subject, is also included in order to convey the ideas of women's nature and condition and status as communicated in contemporary books and articles. Starting with this familiar ground assists the argument that not only are questions about women's roles and activities within their society integral to general social development, but that sources for studying this integration are at hand and awaiting use.

Most of the categories developed for this chapter, Part II, are deliberately focused on questions that are less attended by historians. These questions are involved more with women's private than public concerns—as "public" suggests "extra-domestic" and as "private" indicates connection with home and intimate aspects of experience, thought, and behavior expressed away from public view.[5] On no account, however, is the relational tie joining women's personal condition and status to their social activity and position intended to be cut. On the contrary, and in consideration of the extent to which the private, personal image of the nineteenth-century English woman was in her own time inextricably related to her social place and role, it would be inaccurate to segregate the private sphere entirely from social connection and interpretation. It is true that the Victorians themselves differentiated private from public life. But it is important to remember how at least for a large segment of the population private behavior was subject to social judgment because it was among the important criteria for acceptance to or rejection of membership in higher circles of society: linkage between the domestic and the social spheres being an acknowledged feature in nineteenth-century social placing. We can learn from Leonore Davidoff's excellent study of the ideas and "blue prints" of formalized nineteenth- and early twentieth-century Society the details of how it was Society that constituted the "linking factor *between* the family and political and economic institutions."

4. Lenore Davidoff, *The Best Circles: Society, Etiquette and the Season.* 1973, pp. 14–15.[6]

As a subject for close historical study, then, the nineteenth-century English family deserves the scholarly attention it has not yet received from social historians. Historical demographers, interested primarily in measuring events such as births, marriages and deaths against the background of the structure of the populations in which they took place, have begun to contribute to our understanding of the family as a basic unit of social activity in England's past. On this concern, E. A. Wrigley writes:

Most children pass their formative years in a family, learning there those forms of conduct, values and attitudes of mind which make the continuation of society possible. The process of socialization is very largely a family matter, and the study of family structure and relationships sheds much light on the behavior of society at large. Demography and the study of society, therefore, whether in the present or the past, have many points of contact.

5. E. A. Wrigley, *Population and History.* Toronto, 1969, p. 11.

But the history of the family as a basic unit in society will not in itself satisfy the requirements of understanding in detail the roles of wives and mothers and spinsters of the different social classes vis-à-vis other family members, let alone neighbors and the national community, unless we insure that studies include specific evaluations of the female role in marriage and household, in family work and family welfare, and, equally important, in relating changes in these roles to developments in wider society. Among the developments in the nineteenth century were the processes and effects of rapid industrialization, population expansion and movement, modernization, and the growth of cities. One result of historical-sociological analyses of these phenomena is that cultural and social determinants emerge as having perhaps equal weight with politics and economic conditions in forming interpretations of change or continuity. However, the kinds of developments that are studied need to be expanded to include those that touched private lives as much as general society and family group status. Not the least of the developments still requiring attention include those that affected the treatment and improvement of the health of the people, and the scientific discoveries along with the social-science theories that, incidentally, maintained strong ties with social attitudes and social philosophy. It is surely important to examine how nineteenth-century developments in anthropology and biology, along with new theories in sociology and eugenics, either combined or clashed over the years so that ideas and social policies related to women, for example, became subjects for highly articulated controversy. An illustration of this is suggested by the strong polemical pamphlet of physician and neo-Malthusian Charles V. Drysdale, who writes:

It is continually cast up against advanced women by Imperialists and Eugenists that education and freedom unfit them for their divine function of motherhood. . . . But before women apologize . . . it would be well for them to consider a little more fully what have been the results of this passive maternity in the past, not only for themselves but for the commnuity and the Empire.

6. Charles V. Drysdale, *Freewomen and the Birth-Rate.* 1911, pp. 1–2.

Another example of a comparatively unexplored development concerns the numerous organized groups that were formed around social issues and that promoted social and moral reform. Whether or not questions about women were the direct focus of these organizations— as they were in the groups formed to abolish the Contagious Diseases Acts and to combat the "white slave traffic" and to gain the enfranchisement of women and to form guilds or unions of working women of different occupations and classes—women were well represented in the vast network of societies, associations, clubs, leagues, and cooperatives. Like the family, the organized unit and its members deserve historical treatment in terms of the interaction of the personnel within the group and within the social process. As well as expanding our knowledge about the more intimate aspects of female roles, this kind of study should provide evidence of how women combined their private and public identities in behalf of group causes, and how they did so increasingly as the years of our period wore on.[7]

The main subject headings of the categories for this bibliography are: I. "The Family and Marriage: Relations and Roles in Home and Household"; II. "Sickness and Health Care: Self-Help, Midwives, and Doctors"; III. "Science, Social Science, and Their Social Application"; and IV. "Organizations: Protection, Solidarity, and Reform." The number of entries is unavoidably limited by space, so that titles have been omitted that have potential value to some readers. The arrangement of titles under the headings and subheadings is also imperfect because some of the books and articles consider a number of topics in the same volume. To remedy this somewhat, an attempt has been made at cross-referencing by entry number throughout this chapter, and by entry number following "SBS" for relevant items in Part I. The close relationship of the various subjects we are considering confirms the actual artificiality of the categorical separation made necessary by the demands of rational bibliographical treatment of research sources.

To give a sense of development over time of the phenomena covered in each section, the presentation is mainly chronological. However, some titles will be listed out of place for purposes of emphasis or discussion. With regard to periodical entries, the name of the journal, rather than author, will appear first to allow for the chronological order to be maintained in presenting a series of articles for the same category. This is largely a space-saving device. In an attempt to condense the number of periodical references, the articles cited below begin mainly with 1867. For earlier material the reader can consult Eugenia Palmegiano's excellent periodicals bibliography that covers some of the same subjects with which we are dealing:

7. Eugenia M. Palmegiano, "Women and British Periodicals, 1832–1867: A Bibliography," the entire issue of *Victorian Periodicals Newsletter* (VPN). March, 1976. Included are periodicals specifically addressed to females; annuals and manuals; seventy magazines and twelve newspapers. Palmegiano concludes that "Victorians did not have a stereotype about the female and the more that writers sought to delineate approximate behavior for the sex, the more confused they seemed" (p. 3). And, ". . . the research uncovered almost no concern about the behavioral patterns of men in the particular male roles of husband, father or son." (p. 6)

The main libraries consulted for this bibliography include, in London, the British Museum Reading Room; the Fawcett Society Library; the Institute of Historical Research and the Library at London University; the Wellcome Institute of the History of Medicine Library, Museum and Archives; and the British Library of Political and Economic Science. At Essex University, the Oral History Project of Paul Thompson and Thea Vigne, "Family Life and Work Experience, Before 1918," was seen and discussed. In California, the main collections utilized were at the University Research Library and Bio-Medical Library of University of California at Los Angeles and the Sutro Library (Pamphlet Collection) in San Francisco.

## I  Marriage and Family: Relations and Roles in Home and Household

8. Michael Anderson, *Family Structure in Nineteenth Century Lancashire*. Cambridge, 1971,

is the one exception to J. F. C. Harrison's admonition in:

9. *The Early Victorians, 1832–1851*. 1971:

> It is a sad comment on British historiography that while we have a great many studies of political parties, trade unions and religious bodies, there is not a single history of the basic unit of British life, the family. Until some attempt has been made to fill this gap it is impossible to write with assurance about family life in the nineteenth century. . . . (p. 73)

These books, published in the same year, not only call attention to a great historical void, but also demonstrate at least one approach to how it can be filled: Anderson's close study is a sociological history of working-class family experience in the cotton towns and villages of the county of Lancashire, where questions of town-country contrasts, industrial impact on social and family structure, and kinship relationships are of immediate relevance.[8] Aside from Anderson's book, which will be discussed in a different context below, it would seem that Harrison's observation is all too true. Modern historically oriented writings on the history of the nineteenth- and early twentieth-century English family consist mainly of chapters, sections, paragraphs, and statements within studies having a different major focus; general surveys of the English social scene, or specialized investigations such as: historical demography; social class; childhood; women in English society; historical analysis of a region or city; literary history including family reading; and intellectual history—largely "ideas and beliefs." A consequence is that these subjects have become intrinsic aspects of "family history" and are used, too often, as replacements for thorough studies of a complex social institution. For the student and researcher of the Victorian and Edwardian periods, the absence of detailed, book-length studies—whether they are similar to Anderson's or are based upon different theoretical foundations—remains a problem. For those interested in investigating questions of change in women's family roles and social status over the century, it creates particular difficulty.

A varied selection of contemporary and historical writings that discuss aspects of English family life, including references to female roles, forms the basis of the bibliography that follows. First is a brief summary of some representative historical statements that give an idea of the popular portrayal of the family, with a brief discussion of the newer approaches being advocated for family history.

A.  Historical and Sociological Perspectives and
     Background of the Victorian Family

The centrality of the family in the English social system has not been considered a point for debate. An unchallenged view is:

10. G. M. Young, *Victorian England: Portrait of an Age.* 1936; rpr. 1953:

> Who are these Victorians? By what mark do we know them? What creed, what doctrine, what institution was there among them which was not at some time or other debated or assailed? I can think of only two: Representative Institutions and The Family. (p. 150, 1953 ed.)

Implying that questions about Family should logically pertain to the full social spectrum, Young writes in

———, *Victorian Essays.* 1962:

> As you go downwards [in the social scale], the family, the home, counts for less and less until it breaks up altogether . . . this division, this contrast, between the households where the children are cared for and those where they are left to shift for themselves. . . . They were the children of the underworld and will be the fathers and mothers of the underworld. (p. 123)

This awareness of social contrasts is expressed by:

11. H. L. Beales, "The Victorian Family," in Harman Grisewood, ed., *Ideas and Beliefs of the Victorians.* 1949:

The Victorian family won a reputation for itself as a noble social institution, upon whose continuance depended all that was fine and stable in British civilization (p. 343). . . . The Victorian family was, as near as might be, a self-sufficient unit. Every Englishman's home was his castle. In its sanctities and privacy a man might escape from the trials of the outer world and be safe from its prying eyes. The family was indeed a kind of estate, like, say, the British Empire, and subject like it to the benevolent despotism of its lord and master. For it *had* a lord and master, and his ways were expected to be authoritarian (p. 344). . . . The clear impression that emerges is that of established routine, of a division of labor between man and woman that correlates with known social habits, known ambitions and prestige values, and approved positives and negatives of personal behavior. . . . But what of the family down in the social scale? (p. 347)

The very poor family? This is the concern with family expressed by:

12. Llewellyn Woodward, *Age of Reform, 1815–1870.* 1936; 1962.

Woodward notes that despite the conventional reverence for the family, pauper families were separated in the workhouses established by the New Poor Law:

> Married women of good character were to be put with the aged, though nothing was said about unmarried women or young girls (p. 454). . . . Until 1842 parents had no right to see their own children in the same workhouse. . . . The [Poor Law] board advised that the children—between 40,000 and 50,000 of them in 1848—should be sent to special poor-law schools. Within the next twenty years most pauper children between the ages of five and fourteen were brought up in these large, barrack-like places. (p. 455)

The effects of industrialism on the middle and working classes are contrasted by

13. Harold Perkin, *The Origins of Modern English Society, 1780–1880.* 1969:

> While the Industrial Revolution was providing more work for working-class women both inside and outside the home, it was taking it away from their well-to-do sisters. Just as domestic industry was a partnership in which the wife assisted the husband, so too most businesses and professions and trades in the old society were partnerships in which the husband and wife worked as a team. . . . (p. 158)

This situation changed completely for middle-class women, claims Perkin, with

the rise of the "perfect lady," the Victorian ideal of the completely leisured, completely ornamental, completely helpless and dependent [on husband-father] middle-class wife or daughter, with no function besides inspiring admiration and bearing children. (p. 159)

Undoubtedly, contemporary observers who wrote down their impressions assisted in communicating this view of the middle-class woman. One sure influence was:

14. Hyppolyte Taine, *Notes on England.* 1872, in French and English. 1958 edition trans. E. Hyams as *Taine's Notes on England.* Fair Lawn, 1958.

Taine complains:

An English girl wants to marry only for love . . . she creates a romance in her imagination and this dream is part of her pride, of her chastity. . . . To marry is to give oneself wholly and forever. . . . But in her private romance the English girl is still English, that is to say positive and practical. . . . She wants to be her husband's helper. . . . A woman's husband is her lord, and very often he takes that title very seriously. (pp. 76–79, 1958 ed.)

With more insight into sociocultural concepts underlining middle-class women's roles in marriage,

15. Walter E. Houghton, *The Victorian Frame of Mind.* New Haven, 1957; 1964,

writes:

whether a sacred temple or a secular temple, the home as a storehouse of moral and spiritual values was as much an answer to commercialism as to declining religion. Indeed, it might be said that mainly on the shoulders of its priestess, the wife and mother, fell the burden of stemming the amoral and irreligious drift of modern industrial society. (p. 348, 1964 ed.)

The domestic function is probably the most well-documented generalization about the family role of nineteenth-century middle-class Englishwomen. The theme of woman-in-the-home dominates in contemporary books, magazine articles, and household manuals, with emphasis on idealization of the role and with instruction for accomplishing its requirements.[9] More recently, historians have reviewed this nineteenth-century domestic literature with analytical objectivity. Outstanding in utilizing these particular sources and in evaluating ideology, behavior requirements, and performance of women in affluent families is:

16. Barbara Stein Frankel, "The Genteel Family: High Victorian Conceptions of Domesticity and Good Behavior," Ph.D. diss., Univ. of Wisconsin, 1969.

*A Widening Sphere*

The contemporary observers who recognized the importance of the ritualized social life of their peers were acutely aware of the Victorian woman's problems, and her direct relationship to the reformation of social behavior (p. 18). . . . Because leisure was so essential for the nurturing of the gentle graces, many etiquette writers directed their works toward the woman in the household. . . . It was the feminine role to represent the family socially to engineer its social life while the menfolk manoeuvred its financial one.[10] (p. 58)

17. Leonore Davidoff, "The Rationalization of Housework," in S. Allen and D. Barker, eds., *Dependence and Exploitation: Work and Marriage*. 1976.

One of the rewards of a superior position [husband-father] within a hierarchical structure is the protection of the superordinate from potentially polluting activities. The ultimate nineteenth century ideal became the creation of a perfectly orderly setting. . . . This process must be recognized as a relational aspect of social stratification. It should not be substituted for an analysis of the distributive aspects of inequality. Drawing attention to the part such interaction plays in the maintenance of stratification, however, emphasizes the way the system was divided along *both* class and sex lines.[11]

Relying most heavily on domestic manuals for English housewives of the less-affluent social segment, is

18. Patricia Branca, *Silent Sisterhood: Middle Class Women in the Victorian Home*. 1975.

Branca claims that these "mute" and "inarticulate" housewives can be brought out of darkness by historians who, using as sources housekeeping, cooking, home-medicine, and child-care manuals, will "rescue the Victorian middle-class woman from the realm of myth and bring her into the light of reality" (p. 6). Branca denies that the phrase "the perfect lady" either typifies or describes numerically the life-style, behavior, or aspirations of most Victorian middle-class women.

The relationship between women's family roles and their expected sexual behavior has been asserted but not deeply studied.[12] There is suggestion of this relationship in

19. Duncan Crow, *The Victorian Woman*. 1971.

As part of the grand strategy for civilizing society so that it became safe for the rising middle classes it was deemed necessary to tame the savagery of sex. . . . The way to achieve this most effectively . . . was to bar sex as far as possible from everyday life. . . . from the respectable household. . . . Silence was important . . . sex could be dematerialized by ignoring it. (p. 25)

More pointedly in the case of women:

20. Martha Vicinus, ed., *Suffer and Be Still: Women in the Victorian Age.* Bloomington, 1972. Introduction. Hereafter: Martha Vicinus, ed., sBs.

Regarding the upper middle class:

> Before marriage a young girl was brought up to be perfectly innocent and sexually ignorant. The predominant ideology of the age insisted that she have little sexual feeling at all, although family affection and desire for motherhood were considered innate. . . . In her most perfect form, the lady combined total sexual innocence, conspicuous consumption and the worship of the family hearth. (p. ix)

21. Francoise Basch, *Relative Creatures: Victorian Women in Society and the Novel.* New York, 1974.

> Thus the woman, the very ideal of mother and wife, source of all virtue and purity, appeared as the good conscience of Victorian society. Poets, moralists and philosophers embellished the domestic and family role of the woman with a universal and transcendental dimension. But the mutation of the Eve myth into the Mary myth, of temptress into redeemer, implied a fundamental process of desexualization of the woman, who was bit by bit deprived of her carnal attributes. (p. 8, paper ed.)[13]

The sexual mores among the aristocracy have been described as somewhat more relaxed but have been only individually detailed. On more solid ground is the study of women's roles in the making of aristocratic family relationships:

22. Peter Laslett, *The World We Have Lost.* 1965.

> Family relationships kept the whole [political] institution in working order, and the genealogical interrelationships between manor houses were extensive, complicated and meticulously observed. (p. 183)

23. F. M. L. Thompson, *English Landed Society in the Nineteenth Century.* 1963.

> There was a strong matriarchal undercurrent beneath the surface of male ascendancy and manly virtues. . . . From marriage the landed aristocrat might hope for both love and good fortune. It was the mothers with marriageable daughters who largely determined the field of selection, and contrived suitable combinations (p. 18). . . . By marrying his daughters into the established nobility, many a man of new wealth smoothed the path of respectability (p. 19). . . . In an ambitious family, resources would be mobilized behind the daughters, the instruments of family advance (p. 100). . . . a new family [could be] firmly tied into the fabric of established society. . . . (p. 129)

Perhaps the most important generalization we can make from the forty years of writing represented in this brief survey is that the structure and sex-role arrangement in families of all English social classes have responded to changing social conditions and social thought. On the dynamics of change from the mid-Victorian period to the early twentieth century, O. R. McGregor observes:

24. O. R. McGregor, "The Victorian Family: Illusion and Reality," in *Divorce in England*. 1957. (SBS, entry 78.)

> The middle-class mid-Victorian family which nowadays attracts the melancholy nostalgia of moralists was annihilated by external pressures and internal tensions. The sense of economic security and expansiveness which had cradled it in the good years after 1850, dissolved in the years of falling prices and imperial adventure after the seventies. . . . Then, as now, parents' duty to their offspring was not fulfilled unless they secured for them an adult station in the social hierarchy no lower, or if possible, higher than that in which they were reared. . . . by the seventies well-stocked nurseries conflicted with established social habits and parental obligations. (p. 81)

No doubt a close relationship existed between a developing attitude toward reducing family size and the trend toward social sanction of women's more open participation in activities outside the home. There is no historical study on the positive aspects of this relationship, though we can rely upon the analysis of J. A. and Olive Banks, *Feminism and Family Planning in Victorian England* (1964), (*SBS*, entry 15), that feminist agitation was not a prime cause in this aspect of change.[14] What, then, *is* the historical explanation for the shift from alleged social policy underlining the home as a cloister for pure Victorian maidens and matrons, to the wider acceptance after the 1880's that there was

> beginning to be provision for respectable women to meet in public places. . . . Cafés, the growth of tea rooms, the use of buses, even the provision of public lavatories for women, were . . . important in freeing middle-class women from the strict social ritual. . . . These social changes were as important in undermining the ideal of social duty and the domination of the home as the growing claims of the Suffrage movement. (Davidoff, *The Best Circles*, p. 67, entry 4)

An explanation, supplementing that of economic questions and demographic change in the direction of smaller families, is offered by:

25. Paul Thompson, *The Edwardians: The Remaking of British Society*. Bloomington, 1975.

> All the changes in the twentieth-century family thus took place in the context of a weakening of the formal authority of moral and social hierarchy, and a pervasive official lip-service to the concepts of democracy and individualism. (pp. 298–99)

It would seem that the McGregor-Davidoff-Thompson kind of questioning of interaction between family roles and socioeconomic and social-thought process is as basic, and perhaps more crucial, to our understanding of both family structure and family change than is the straight questioning of the family strictly in terms of its own internal, hierarchical, and interpersonal or role relationships.

Both of these approaches are used by Michael Anderson in *Family Structure in Nineteenth Century Lancashire.* Anderson focuses intensively on one area, Lancashire, considered to have typified industrializing Britain and whose villages sent a high proportion of migrants to Preston: "the town was in most relevant ways typical of the larger towns of the area" (p. 19). Anderson uses such sources as manuscript census returns and enumerators' manuscript books to get a carefully weighted sample of households. From these and other materials he is able to estimate valuable information, including the extent to which married sons and daughters settled near their parents; the percentage of offspring who left their parents' household; and the nature of the impact caused by insufficient income in different family groups. Anderson interprets data from at least two main vantage points: (1) the individual family members' perceptions of family/kinship relations, and (2) the way impersonal, concrete conditions imposed themselves upon relationships. In sociological terminology he speaks of "phenomenal" (the former) and "structural" (the latter) viewpoints. An example of his analytical style is taken from Chapter 10:

I am suggesting that the frequency of critical life situations and the almost complete absence of viable alternatives to the kinship system (and to some extent to neighbors) as sources of help in solving the problems which ensued from these crises, were, at the structural level, and to a very considerable extent at the phenomenal level also, key factors encouraging members of the Lancashire Victorian working class to make such great efforts to maintain relationships with kin. Although they were largely free from the economic and normative constraints which, in the rural areas, made terminating relationships with family and kin such a precarious and consequently rare business, yet, because they faced other problems of social welfare, for migrants, of accommodation and information, they could not exist for long at an optimum level of satisfactions without some kind of assistance from others. Kin were the major source of assistance. . . . this was so because they were, in the longer run, the only source of assistance which even began to promise an adequate (if qualified) predictability of response at a cost which could be met with the resources available. (pp. 160–61)

No doubt some historians are uncomfortable with Anderson's writing style, while they admire his method of using and analyzing data. Sociological semantics, it may be thought, can tend to obscure rather than reveal important facets of psychological implications in family functions and relationships. Nevertheless, it remains that Anderson's study has provided more data and interpretation of working-class family experience in a particular region and in a particular point in time and circumstances than we have previously received; and the knowledge gained covers the life-style, residence patterns, and internal relations against a background of socioeconomic conditions in the immediate family environment. No family members are neglected; thus the roles and conditions of women are woven logically into the interpretive scheme. One brief example:

where mothers did work they may very well have been so much improving the standards of living of their families that the betterment of the family's satisfactions outweighed in the minds of the children the greater degree of neglect suffered by themselves and by their home. (p. 74)

For a wider acquaintance with Anderson's studies and approach, see his:

26. "The Study of Family Structure," in E. A. Wrigley, ed., *Nineteenth Century Society: Essays in the Use of Quantitative Methods for the Study of Social Data.* Cambridge, 1972; "Household Structure and the Industrial Revolution," in Peter Laslett and Richard Wall, eds., *Household and Family in Past Time.* Cambridge, 1972; "Family, Household and the Industrial Revolution," in Michael Anderson, ed., *Sociology and the Family.* 1971.

For comments relating historical-sociological approaches to family history, see:

27. *Journal of Social History:* Neil Smelser, "Sociological History: The Industrial Revolution and the British Working-Class Family," 1 (1967), 17–36.
28. *British Journal of Sociology:* O. R. McGregor, "Some Research Possibilities and Historical Materials for Family and Kinship Study in Britain," 12 (1961), 310–17.

An excellent introduction to the field of history of the family which discusses a variety of approaches in addition to the sociological is:

29. Tamara K. Hareven, "The History of the Family as an Interdisciplinary Field," in Theodore K. Rabb and Robert I. Rotberg, eds., *Family in History: Interdisciplinary Essays.* New York, 1973.

See also:

30. Michael Gordon, ed., *The American Family in Social Historical Perspective.* New York, 1973. Introduction. Hereafter: Michael Gordon.
31. *Journal of Marriage and the Family:* Lutz K. Berkner, "Recent Research on the History of the Family in Western Europe," 35 (1973), 395–405.

Some representative historical-sociological studies that can assist in developing a history of the Victorian-Edwardian family and can provide a background of living conditions, housing problems, and interpretations of demographic data are in the following listing. It should be noted that the heaviest attention has been given to the working classes.[15]

32. W. M. Williams: *The Sociology of an English Village: Gosforth.* 1956; *A West Country Village: Ashworth: Family Kinship and Land.* 1956. Current sociology with historical references. Traditional community patterns holding into the twentieth century.
33. Richard Hoggart, *The Uses of Literacy: Changing Patterns in English Mass Culture.* 1957. See Ch. 2, "There's No Place Like Home." Changes in working-class culture from about 1910.
34. Michael Young and Peter Willmott, *Family and Kinship in East London.* 1957. See "Husbands and Wives, Past and Present."
35. Frank Musgrove, *The Family, Education and Society.* 1966. The family as an educational institution.
36. Margaret Stacey, *Tradition and Change: A Study of Banbury.* 1960. Historically oriented background for family in England and roles of women.
37. Richard Titmuss, *Essays on the "Welfare State."* 1963. Ch. 5, "The Position of Women." Ch. 6, "Industrialization of the Family."
38. Clarice S. Davies, *North Country Bred, A Working-Class Family Chronicle.* 1963. A sociologist's analysis of her own and her husband's family from early nineteenth century.
39. *Victorian Studies:* D. Spring, "Aristocracy, Social Structure, and Religion in the Early Victorian Period," 6 (1963), 263–80; H. J. Dyos, "The Slums of Victorian London," 11 (1968), 5–40; J. A. Banks, "Population Change and the Victorian City," ibid., 277–89; J. A. Banks, "The Way They Lived Then; Anthony Trollope and the 1870s," 12 (1968), 177–200.[16]
40. Francis Collier, *The Family Economy of the Working Classes in the Cotton Industry, 1784–1833.* Manchester, 1965 from the 1921 ed.
41. *Population Studies:* J. Matras, "Social Strategies of Family Formation: Data for British Female Cohorts Born 1831–1906," 19 (1965–66),

*A Widening Sphere*

167–81; P. Laslett, "Size and Structure in the Households of England over Three Centuries," 23 (1969), 199–223.

42. Anthony S. Wohl: *International Review of Social History:* "The Bitter Cry of Outcast London," 13 (1968), 189–245;[17] *Andrew Mearns, the Bitter Cry of Outcast London, with Leading Articles from the Pall Mall Gazette.* Leicester, 1970; "The Housing of the Working Classes in London, 1815–1914," in S. D. Chapman, ed., *The History of Working-Class Housing.* 1971.

43. Lynn Lees, "Patterns of Lower-Class Life: Irish Slum Communities in Nineteenth Century London," in S. Thernstrom and R. Sennett, eds., *Nineteenth Century Cities: Essays in the New Urban History.* New Haven, 1969.[18]

44. *Journal of Social History:* P. Laslett, "The Comparative History of Household and the Family," 4 (1970), 75–87; G. Stedman Jones, "Working-Class Culture and Working-Class Politics in London, 1870–1900," 7 (1974), 460–508.

45. *International Review of Social History:* R. Smith, "Early Victorian Household Structure: A Case Study of Nottinghamshire," 15 (1970), 69–84.

46. Mark Girouard, *The Victorian Country House.* Oxford, 1971.

47. Gareth Stedman Jones, *Outcast London: A Study in the Relationship Between Different Classes in Victorian Society.* 1971.

48. Robert Roberts, *The Classic Slum: Salford Life in the First Quarter of the Century.* Manchester, 1971.

49. Edward Shorter: *Journal of Interdisciplinary History:* "Illegitimacy, Sexual Revolution and Social Change in Europe, 1750–1900," 2 (1971), 237–72; *Social Science Quarterly:* "Capitalism, Culture and Sexuality: Some Competing Models," 53 (1972), 338–56; *American Historical Review:* "Female Emancipation, Birth Control and Fertility in European History," 78 (1973), 604–40. See critique of Shorter's contentions in *Comparative Studies in Society and History:* Joan W. Scott and Louise A. Tilly, "Women's Work and Family in Nineteenth Century Europe," 17 (1975), 36–64, n. 71, 55–56. See also Shorter's *The Making of Modern Society.* New York, 1975. And review: *New York Review of Books:* Christopher Lasch, "What the Doctor Ordered," 22 (Dec. 11, 1975), 50–54. See also the other reviews by Lasch in the same journal on similar questions: "The Family and History," ibid. (Nov. 13, 1975), 33–38, and "The Emotions of Family Life," ibid. (No. 27, 1975), 37–42.

50. R. S. Neale, *Class and Ideology in the Nineteenth Century.* 1972.

51. Peter Laslett and Richard Wall, *Household and Family in Past Time.* 1972. See especially: Laslett's Introduction; W. A. Armstrong, "A Note on the Household Structure of Mid-Nineteenth Century York in Comparative Perspective," and Michael Anderson, entry 26.

52. *American Historical Review:* Standish Meacham, "The Sense of Impending Clash: English Working-Class Unrest Before the First World War," 77 (1972), 1343–64.[19]

53. Martha Vicinus, ed., *SBS:* M. J. Peterson, "The Victorian Governess: Status Incongruence in Family and Society"; H. E. Roberts, "Marriage, Redundancy or Sin"; P. N. Stearns, "Working-Class Women in Britain, 1890–1914."

54. H. J. Dyos and Michael Wolff, eds., *The Victorian City: Images and Realities.* 1973. Hereafter: Dyos and Wolff. See especially E. E. Lampard, "The Urbanizing World," and J. A. Banks, "The Contagion of Numbers" in Vol. I; A. S. Wohl, "Unfit for Human Habitation"; G. Himmelfarb, "The Culture of Poverty"; and E. Trudgill, "Prostitution and Paterfamilias" in Vol. II.

55. Enid Gauldie, *Cruel Habitations: History of Working Class Housing, 1780–1918.* 1974.

56. Ann Oakley, *Woman's Work: The Housewife Past and Present.* New York, 1974. Especially Ch. 2, "Women's Roles in Pre-Industrial Society," and Ch. 3, "Women and Industrialism."

57. Patricia C. Otto, "Daughters of the British Aristocracy: Their Marriages in the Eighteenth and Nineteenth Centuries." Ph.D. diss., Stanford University, 1974.

58. Raphael Samuel, ed., *History Workshop Series: Village Life and Labour.* 1974. Based upon the History Workshop Pamphlets, Ruskin College, Oxford.[20]

59. Peter J. Ambrose, *The Quiet Revolution: Social Change in a Sussex Village, 1871–1971.* Sussex, 1974.

60. Mary S. Hartman and Lois Banner, eds., *Clio's Consciousness Raised: New Perspectives on the History of Women.* New York, 1974. Hereafter: Hartman and Banner. See especially Laura Oren, "The Welfare of Women in Laboring Families: England, 1860–1950," and Patricia Branca, "Image and Reality: The Myth of the Idle Victorian Woman."

61. Hugh McLeod, *Class and Religion in the Late Victorian City.* 1974.

62. Alan Armstrong, *Stability and Change in an English Country Town: A Social Study of York, 1801–1851.* 1974. Household and family structure; marriage and fertility; servant questions discussed.

## B. Oral History of the Family

The most extensive use of oral history methods to investigate the history of the Edwardian family is represented by the Essex University project "Family Life, Work and the Community Before 1918," conducted by Paul Thompson and Thea Vigne.[21] Tape-recorded interviews with a quota sample of five hundred women and men drawn from the 1911 census were the major basis of Thompson's research for his social history, *The Edwardians* (entry 25).

63. *Social Science Research Council Newsletter:* Paul Thompson, "Memory and History," No. 6 (June 1969), 17–18.
64. *Oral History* (Journal of the Oral History Society): Paul Thompson and Thea [Thompson] Vigne, "On Family Life, Work and the Community Before 1918: the Essex Project," 3 (Spring 1975), 2–3.

The interviews, documented in indexed tapes and transcriptions, have contributed new insights into twentieth-century childhood: the social position of children in those years between the mid-1880's and World War I.

65. *New Society:* Thea [Thompson] Vigne, "A Lost World of Childhood," (1972), 20–23.

> we are collecting the memories of childhood and youth, recollected by up to 500 people, aged between 102 and 67, who live in conurbations, towns and villages in all regions of England, Scotland and Wales. The interviews are "directed"—in that, in addition to the valuable and spontaneous recollections of childhood, we get answers to specific questions: behavior at meals, tasks in the home, bedtimes, bathing and washing, discipline and play, religious and social training, and relationships with parents. (p. 21)

66. *Oral History:* Thea Vigne, "Parents and Children, 1890–1918; Distance and Dependence," 3 (Fall 1975), 6–13 (Special Family History issue).

Paul Thompson quotes extensively from the interviews for his discussions of urban life, social distinctions, women workers and housewives, life-styles, sexual behavior, crime and deviance, and other questions in *The Edwardians*[22] (respondents are anonymous or are given pseudonyms to preserve confidentiality) and in:

67. Paul Thompson, "Voices from Within," in Dyos and Wolff, Vol. I.

Concerned with questions of comparing the accuracy and value of oral history documents to traditional historical documents (newspapers, correspondence, autobiography, transcriptions of Royal Commissions hearings, statistics, etc.), Thompson and others have written at length in:

68. *Oral History: An Occasional New Sheet,* No. 3: Brian Harrison, "Oral History and Recent Political History," (1972), 30–48; *An Occasional New Sheet,* No. 4: Paul Thompson, "The Interview in Social History," (1972), 1–55 (including discussion). See also *Oral History:* John Mar-

shall, "The Sense of Place, Past Society and the Oral Historian," 3 (Spring 1975), 19–25.

According to Thompson and Vigne, the oral history family studies outside the field of family history may assist in reinterpreting social mobility and stratification. In discussing the conventional belief that labor aristocrats, the upper ten or fifteen percent of the manual workers, were in their style of life closer to the middle classes than to average laborers, Thompson writes:

Yet only one family has so far been found which clearly fits this description. It seems possible that the pattern of individual occupational mobility, and therefore of social structure, was rather more flexible in this period than has been assumed. On a question such as this an interview survey of individual and family occupational careers, together with accounts of perceived class relationships, could therefore contribute to a major re-interpretation. ("Memory and History," p. 18, entry 63)

Because historians investigating women's family experience have found such questions as social stratification and emulation of life-styles extremely important, the Thompson–Vigne set of structured, recorded interviews are of considerable value. Respondents reveal not only close details about their role-oriented behavior but also their feelings about this behavior. Oral records, then, comprise evidence for the different social classes that is not otherwise obtainable. Surely, a very large number of the respondents would have remained historically inarticulate. Although sociological studies, statistical inquiries, and censuses of the late nineteenth and early twentieth centuries are indispensable,[23] the new emphasis on oral history should continue to enhance historical writing about that period.

## C.   Autobiographies and Diaries

With respect to detailing family experiences, authors of autobiographies to some extent resemble respondents in oral interviews. In any case, their testimonies are usually given some weight in historical interpretation. How much weight? Largely because of the various motives behind voluntary autobiographical writings and because of the possibility of faulty memory, historians have often expressed skepticism about their historical validity. But contemporary autobiographies, diaries, and journals—when supported by collaborative evidence—have nevertheless been considered helpful in understanding the past. In the case of Victorian and Edwardian women writing about their family-life experiences and relationships, these sources are extremely welcome. The following autobiographical references listed are very few in comparison with the considerable number available for our own period.[24] Because we want to emphasize women's views, only women authors are included here, but it should be clarified that autobiographies of men can shed useful light on women's roles, status, and behavior in family life.[25] Many more of the women represented the upper and middle classes than the lower. The obvious explanation is that they had more education, leisure time, and incentive. Yet, this is a question that is still to be investigated, just as the existence of possible unpublished privately printed and undiscovered autobiographies, diaries, and journals should be investigated. The selection below reflects the disproportionate representation of authors by class, but working-class and lower-class rural women authors are included. Very well-known women have been omitted intentionally because their autobiographies are already familiar.

69. Fanny Alford, *Reminiscences of a Clergyman's Wife.* 1860.
70. Mary Ann Ashford, *Life of a Licensed Victualler's Daughter.* 1844.
71. Beryl Lee Booker, *Yesterday's Child: 1890–1909.* 1937. Middle-class life.
72. Jean Curtis Brown, *To Tell My Daughter.* 1948. End of Victorian era.
73. Lucy Lyttleton Cameron, *Life of Lucy Lyttleton Cameron.* 1862. Includes diary.
74. Mary Toulmin Carbery, *Happy World.* 1941. Victorian childhood in Herts.
75. Mary Cowden Clarke, *My Long Life.* 1896. Upbringing. Marriage.
76. Katharine Chorley, *Manchester Made Them.* 1950. Rising business family.
77. Clara Clarkson, *Merrie Wakefield.* Wakefield. 1971. From diaries, 1811–1899.
78. Carolyn Clive, *From the Diary and Family Papers of Mrs. Archer Clive, 1801–1873.* Ed. by Mary Clive. 1949.
79. Celia Davies, *Clean Clothes on Sunday.* Suffolk. 1974.
80. Margaret Llewelyn Davies, *Life as We Have Known It, by Co-Operative Working Women.* 1931. See especially, Mrs. Layton, "Memories of Seventy Years." Childhood. Domestic service. Working-class wife and mother.
81. Eleanor Farjeon, *A Nursery in the Nineties: Portrait of a Family.* 1935. Jewish middle class.

82. Maude M. C. Ffoulkes, *My Own Past. 1915; All This Happened To Me.* 1937. Childhood in the 1880's.

83. Grace Foakes, *My Part of the River.* 1974. Life near the Thames among ethnic groups of working class, circa 1901.

84. Angela Sylvia Forbes, *Memories and Base Details.* 1921. Upper class. Relationships with governesses.

85. Eliza Fox, *Memoir.* 1869. Girlhood in Chichester to 1820.

86. Ida Gandy, *A Wiltshire Childhood.* 1929. Early twentieth century.

87. Margaret Jeune Gifford, *Pages from the Diary of an Oxford Lady, 1843–1862.*

88. Mary Vivian Hughes, *A London Family, 1870–1900; A Trilogy:* "A London Child of the Seventies"; "A London Girl of the Eighties"; "A London Home of the Nineties." 1946.

89. Diana Holman Hunt, *My Grandmothers and I.* 1960. Granddaughter of the artist.

90. Louise Jermy, *Memories of a Working Woman.* Norwich. 1934. Ladies' maid.

91. Annie Kenney, *Memories of a Militant.* 1924. With the suffragettes.

92. Sonia Keppel, *Edwardian Daughter.* 1958. Family life and family roles.

93. Florence Ada Keynes, *Gathering up the Threads.* Cambridge. 1950. Family biography and details of personal life.

94. Sybil Lubbock, *The Child in the Crystal.* 1939. Domestic scene and "The Season." Dedicated to her childhood governess.

95. Mary MacCarthy, *A Nineteenth Century Childhood.* 1924. Upper middle class.

96. Sybil Marshall, *Fenland Chronicle: Recollections of William Henry and Kate Mary Edwards Collected and Edited by Their Daughter.* 1967. Rural lower class.

97. Dorothy Nevill, *Reminiscenses of Lady Dorothy Nevill.* 1906.

98. Jane Ellen Panton, *Leaves from a Life.* 1908; *More Leaves from a Life.* 1911; *Most of the Game.* 1911. Childhood 1850's. Domestic and social life.

99. Muriel Jardine Parsloe, *A Parson's Daughter.* 1935. A "tomboy."

100. Winifred Peck, *A Little Learning; or, A Victorian Childhood.* 1952.

101. Dorothy S. Peel, *A Stream of Time, 1805–1861; 1933; Life's Enchanted Cup.* 1933.

102. Alice Wykeham-Martin Pollock, *Portrait of My Victorian Youth.* 1971.

103. Margaret Powell, *Below Stairs.* 1968. Working class. Born 1910.

104. Gwendolen Mary Darwin Raverat, *Period Piece: A Cambridge Childhood.* 1952.

105. Jean Rennie, *Every Other Sunday: The Autobiography of a Kitchen Maid.* 1955.

106. Emily Shore, *Journal of Emily Shore.* 1891. 1830's. Diary of family life.

107. Ethel Smyth, *Impressions That Remained.* 1919. Composer and suffragette.

108. Angela Thirkell, *Three Houses.* 1931. Late nineteenth century.

109. Helen Thomas, *As It Was: A World Without End*. 1931; 1956; 1972. Marriage, sex, family, childbirth. Rural.
110. Dorothy Thompson, *Sophia's Son: The Story of a Suffolk Parson, 1841–1916*. Sensitive recollections of the author's life. Valuable.
111. Flora Thompson, *Lark Rise to Candleford*. 1939. Rural working-class life. Useful social history.
112. Anne Tibble, *Greenhorn: A Twentieth Century Childhood*. 1973. Born 1905. Rural working-class family.
113. Laura Troubridge, *Life among the Troubridges*. 1966. Journal entries.
114. Ellen Nelly Weeton, *Journal of a Governess, 1807–1825*. 2 vols. 1936; 1939.
115. Molly Weir, *Shoes Were for Sunday*. 1972.
116. Katherine West, *Inner and Outer Circles*. 1958. London family, early 1900's.
117. Agnes Elizabeth Weston, *My Life among the Bluejackets*. 1909. Establishes retreats for sailors on leave.
118. Florence White, *A Fire in the Kitchen: The Autobiography of a Cook*. 1937.

D.  Contemporary Writings on Marriage and Family

The Victorians were probably more family conscious than any generation of English history. Perhaps this is why their writings on the subject of family hardly fall into the category of objective studies. Rhetorical, admonitory, religiously inspired, advisory, complaining, historical, curious, humorous, and moralistic are adjectives that best describe most of the books at least until the last quarter of the century. From about the 1880's more objective questions were posed about the institution of marriage and family, and to a large extent this may be attributed to the spread of ideas and discoveries from the social sciences—especially anthropology, evolutionary biology, and sociology; from the questions raised by investigators of socioeconomic and population questions (see note 23); and from reduction in family size. The knowledge of internal structure, roles, behavior, and practical matters of family living that we do have derive largely from very numerous writings on the home: how to regard it, manage it, and maintain it and its occupants. This may be called the literature of "manuals": the genre of "how to." And it included instructions and suggestions for the intimate relations of husbands and wives, parents and children. The easy availability of these books and articles is fortunate for the historian of Victorian middle-class family life. Their use has already been illustrated by Frankel, Davidoff, and Basch; extensively by Branca (entries 16–18 and 21) and in superb contextual argument by:

119. J. A. Banks. *Prosperity and Parenthood*. 1954. (See *SBS*, entry 109.)

However, it is very important to be cautious in using manuals and advisory books. These publications were often peddled for profit and infused with fantasy (see Davidoff, entry 4, p. 18), though autobiographies provide a check. With regard to marriage manuals describing and prescribing for marital relations and "sex hygiene," it is well to heed the warning by Carl Degler in his important article:

120. *American Historical Review:* "What Ought to Be and What Was: Women's Sexuality in the Nineteenth Century," 79 (1974), 1467–90:

> historians need to recognize that the attitudes of ordinary people are quite capable of resisting efforts to reshape or alter them. (p. 1490)

The selected titles listed in the sub-categories below offer a guide to what Victorians and, later, Edwardians were aware of in terms of "what ought to be," and to a still questionable extent of "what was."

a. CONVENTIONAL CONTEMPORARY APPROACH TO
   MARRIAGE QUESTIONS[26]

121. John Ovington, *The Duties, Advantages, Pleasures and Sorrows of the Marriage State*. 1813.
122. William Cobbett, *Advice to Young Men and (incidentally) to Young Women, in the Middle and Higher Ranks of Life, in a Series of Letters, Addressed to a Youth, a Bachelor, a Lover, a Husband, a Father, a Citizen or a Subject*. 1829.
123. John Brindley, *The Immoralities of Socialism. Being an Exposure of Mr. Owen's Attack upon Marriage*. Birmingham, 1840.
124. Henry and Augustus Mayhew, *Whom To Marry and How To Get Married: or, The Adventures of a Lady in Search of a Good Husband*. Illus. G. Cruikshank, 1847.
125. Martin F. Tupper, "Of Marriage," in *Poetical Works*. 1850. Typical "Tupperism."
126. William B. Mackenzie, *Married Life: Its Duties, Trials, Joys*. 2nd ed. 1852.
127. Anon., *The Yelverton Marriage Case: Thelwall Versus Yelverton (Comprising an Authentic and Unabridged Account of the Most Extraordinary Trial of Modern Times)*. 1861.

128. John Cassell, *Social Science*. 1861. Changing ideas on marriage discussed in "prize essays."

129. *Temple Bar:* "Marriage Not a la Mode," 9 (1863), 506–21; "Young Husbands and Wives," 26 (1869), 498–506; "To Those About to Marry by an Unmarried Cynic," 34 (1871–72), 364–69; "Why We Men Do Not Marry," 84 (1888), 218–23.

130. John Maynard, *Matrimony: or, What Marriage Is, and How to Make The Best of It*. 1866.

131. Mary Taylor, *The First Duty of Women*. 1870.

132. *Chamber's Edinburgh Journal:* "Matrimony by Advertisement," 47 (1870), 753–56; "The Matrimonial," 56 (1879), 689–92; "Domestic Harmony," 57 (1880), 93–95; "The Coming Domestic Evolution," 81 (1903–1904), 289–91; "The Domestic Tyrant," 82 (1904–1905), 545–48.

133. John Cordy Jeaffreson, *Brides and Bridals*. 2 vols. 2nd ed. 1873.

134. John W. Lea, *Christian Marriage: Its Open and Secret Enemies in England at the Present Day*. 1881.

135. Frances Power Cobbe, *The Duties of Women*. 1881; 1884.

136. James Baldwin Brown, *The Home in Its Relation to Man and to Society*. 1883.

137. *Fortnightly Review:* M. Cookson, "Morality of Married Life," 18 (1872), 397–412; G. H. Lewis, "Marriage and Divorce," 43 (1885), 640–53; C. Black, "On Marriage: A Criticism," 53 (1890), 586–94; W. H. Mallock, "Marriage and Free Thought," 56 (1891), 259–78; J. H. Schooling, "The English Marriage-Rate," (statistical), 69 (1901), 959–68.

138. Mona Caird, *Is Marriage a Failure?* 1888; *The Morality of Marriage, and Other Essays*. 1897. See also; Harry Quilter, *Is Marriage a Failure?* 1888. Collection of letters on Caird's *Is Marriage a Failure?* published in the *Daily Telegraph*.

139. Maud Wheeler, *Whom to Marry, or, All About Love and Matrimony*. 1894.

140. Marie Corelli, Lady Jeune, Flora Annie Steel, Susan, Countess of Malmesbury, *The Modern Marriage Market*. 1898.

141. *Contemporary Review:* F. P. Cobbe, "Wife-Torture in England," 32 (1878), 55–87; D. M. Mulock, "For Better or Worse," 51 (1887), 570–76; W. J. K. Little, "Marriage and Divorce: the Doctrine of the Church of England," 68 (1895), 256–70; S. Gwynn, "Bachelor Women," 73 (1898), 866–75; M. Loane, "Husband and Wife Among the Poor," 87 (1905), 222–30.

142. Harry Horseman, *The Husband To Get and To Be. Homely Homilies for the Home. The Young Man's Model and the Young Woman's Ideal*. Paisley, 1901.

143. Emily Anna Acland, *Marriage as the Foundation of the Home: An Address to Women*. Oxford, 1902.

144. Edward J. Hardy, *What Men Like in Women, and What Women Like in Men*. 1906.

145. Maud C. Braby, *Modern Marriage and How To Bear It.* 1908.
146. Cicely Hamilton, *Marriage as a Trade.* 1909. Wifehood and mother-hood considered as a means of livelihood.

b. CONTEMPORARY SOCIAL-HISTORICAL PERSPECTIVE

147. Friedrich Engels, *The Origin of the Family, Private Property and the State.* 1884; 1891. Prefaces to these editions include discussion of anthropological writings.
148. Frances Elizabeth Hoggan (physician), *The Position of the Mother in the Family: in Its Legal and Scientific Aspects.* 1884.
149. Jane H. Clapperton, *Scientific Meliorism and the Evolution of Happiness.* 1885. Discusses marriage, heredity, the domestic system.
150. Havelock Ellis, *Women and Marriage: or Evolution in Sex.* 1888. The changing status of women.
151. C. J. M. Letourneau, *The Evolution of Marriage and the Family.* 1891.
152. Edith Ellis, *A Noviciate for Marriage.* 1891.
153. Edward Westermarck: *The History of Human Marriage.* 3 vols. 1892; *The Origin and Development of the Moral Ideas.* 3 vols. 1906. See Vol. I, "Subjection of Wives"; Vol. II, "Marriage," Chapter 40; "Free Love-Adultery," Chapter 42.
154. Charles H. Pearson, ed., *National Life and Character: A Forecast.* 1893. Chapter V, "The Decline of the Family," by E. C. Parsons.
155. Edward Carpenter, *Marriage in a Free Society.* Manchester, 1894.
156. Bernard Bosanquet, eds., *Aspects of the Social Problem by Various Writers.* 1895. See "Marriage in East London" by Helen Dendy.
157. *International Journal of Ethics:* J. H. Muirhead, "Is the Family Declining?" 7 (1896), 33–35.
158. Charlotte Perkins Gilman: *Women and Economics.* 1899: 1906; (*SBS*, entry 287) *Concerning Children*, 1901; *The Home: Its Work and Influence.* 1904.
159. Stanton Coit, ed., *Ethical Democracy: Essays in Social Dynamics.* 1900. See J. H. Muirhead, "The Family," and V. Zona, "Women as Citizens."
160. George Elliott Howard: *A History of Matrimonial Institutions, Chiefly in England and the United States, with an Introductory Analysis of the Literature and the Theories of Primitive Marriage and the Family.* Chicago, 1904; *The Family and Marriage: An Analytical Reference Syllabus.* Lincoln, 1914.
161. Helen Dendy Bosanquet, *The Family.* 1906. Chapter VI, "The Family and the State in England." Economic significance of the family unit.
162. Elsie Clews Parsons, *The Family: An Ethnographical and Historical Outline with Descriptive Notes, Planned as a Text Book.* 1906.
163. William C. D. Whetham and Catherine D. Whetham, *The Family and the Nation: A Study in Natural Inheritance and Social Responsibility.* 1909.

164. Charlotte Wilson, *The Economic Disintegration of the Family*. 1909.
165. George Bernard Shaw, *Getting Married*. 1909. Preface, "The Revolt Against Marriage."
166. James Corin, *Mating, Marriage and the Status of Women*. 1910.
167. Ellen Key, *Love and Marriage*. Trans. A. C. Chater. 1911. Introduction by Havelock Ellis.
168. *Royal Historical Society of London, Transactions:* O. Browning, "The Evolution of the Family," n.s. 6 (1892), 87–107; W. Cunningham, "The Family as a Political Unit," 3rd ser. 6 (1912), 1–17.
169. John M. Gillette, *The Family and Society*. 1914.
170. Willystine Goodsell, *A History of the Family as a Social and Educational Institution*. New York, 1915.

C. "MARRIAGE MANUALS": ADVICE ON THE

INTIMATE DETAILS OF MARRIED LIFE

171. William Whateley, *Directions for Married Persons: Describing the Duties Common to Both, and Peculiar to Each*. 1804.
172. Samuel Solomon, *A Guide to Health, or, Advice to Both Sexes*. . . . 1810. (60th ed.) Takes female sexual passion for granted.
173. Henry T. Kitchener, *Letters on Marriage, on Causes of Marital Infidelity and the Reciprocal Relations of the Sexes*. 2 vols. 1812.
174. Michael Ryan, *The Philosophy of Marriage in Its Social, Moral and Physical Relations*. . . . 1831. A medical lecture with implications for marital life.
175. Arthur Freeling, *The Young Bride's Book: Being Hints for Regulating the Conduct of Married Women, with a few Medical Axioms*. 1839.
176. Pye Henry Charasse, *Advice to a Wife on the Management of Her Own Health*. 1842. Editions to 1893.
177. Anon., *Human Physiology for All: Being a Full and Free Discussion on Various Topics Connected with the Human Frame*. . . . *Courtship, Marriage, Pleasure, Amusements*. . . . 1848.
178. Priscilla Barker, *The Secret Book, Containing Instructions for Women and Young Girls*. Brighton, 1868; 1870; 1888.
179. Samuel R. Wells, *Wedlock: or, The Right Relations of the Sexes: Disclosing the Laws of Conjugal Selection, and Showing Who May, and Who May Not Marry*. New York, 1869.
180. John W. Kirton, *Happy Homes and How to Make Them: or, Counsels on Love, Courtship and Marriage*. Birmingham, 1870.
181. George H. Napheys, *The Physical Life of Woman*. 1872.
182. John H. Kellogg, *Plains Facts about Sexual Life*. Southampton, 1882.
183. Job Flower, *A Golden Guide to Matrimony; or Three Steps to the Altar, with Six Qualifications for Wedded Life: And All Its Secrets Revealed*. 1882.
184. Annie Besant, *Marriage as It Was, as It Is, and as It Should Be*. New York, 1879.

185. Lionel Weatherly, *The Young Wife's Own Book: A Manual of Personal and Family Hygiene, Containing Everything that the Young Wife and Mother Ought to Know.* . . . 1882. Medical approach.

186. *Journal of Mental Science:* G. H. Savage, "Marriage in Neurotic Subjects," n.s. 29 (1883–84), 49–54. Marriage won't cure Hysteria.

187. Elizabeth Blackwell, *The Human Element in Sex: Being a Medical Enquiry into the Relationship of Sexual Physiology to Christian Morality.* 1885.

188. W. J. Ramsey, *The Wife's Handbook.* 1886.

189. H. A. Allbutt, *The Wife's Handbook: How a Woman Should Order Herself during Pregnancy, in the Lying-In Room: and After Delivery with Hints.* . . . *and Other Matters of Importance to Be Known by Married Women.* 1886. Dr. Allbutt's references to "the Wife's Friend" refer to pessaries for contraception. These are mentioned in advertisements as inventions of W. J. Rendell (1885) and as recommended by Allbutt.

190. Augustus K. Gardner, *The Conjugal Relationships as Regards Personal Health and Hereditary Well Being.* . . . Glasgow, 1892.

191. Annie S. Swan, *Courtship and Marriage, and the Gentle Art of Home-Making.* 1893.

192. T. R. Allinson, *A Book for Married Women.* 1894.

193. James B. Ryley, *Words of Advice to Young Wives.* 1895.

194. George Bainton, *The Wife as Lover and Friend.* 1895.

195. Lyman B. Sperry, *Confidential Talks with Husband and Wife.* Edinburgh, 1900.

196. H. Senator and S. Kaminer, eds., *Health and Disease in Relation to the Married State; A Manual.* Trans. J. Dulberg. 2 vols. 1904.

197. G. R. M. Devereaux, *The Marriage Guide, Including the Language of Love.* . . . 1907.

198. Margaret Stephens, *Woman and Marriage: A Handbook.* 1910.

199. Laurence Housman, *The Immoral Effects of Ignorance in Sex Relations.* 1911.

200. Leopold Loewenfeld, *On Conjugal Happiness. Experiences, Reflections and Advice of a Medical Man.* . . . 1912.

201. William L. Howard, *Plain Facts on Sex Hygiene.* 1913.

202. Bernard M. O. Hancock, *Problems for the Married.* 1913.

203. Guy T. Wrench, *The Healthy Marriage. A Medical and Psychological Guide for Wives.* 1913.

204. Mary Scharlieb, *What It Means to Marry.* 1914. Physician's advice. Questions of sex.

205. Walter Heape, *Preparation for Marriage.* 1914.

d. ON MOTHERHOOD[27]

206. *Saturday Review:* E. L. Linton, "Modern Mothers," 25 (1868), 268–69.

207. F. E. Hoggan, *The Position of the Mother in the Family in Its Legal and Scientific Aspects.* Manchester, 1884.
208. W. Carr, *The Ideal Mother.* 1886.
209. Alice J. S. Ker, *Motherhood.* Manchester, 1893.
210. Edward R. Sullivan, *Woman, the Predominant Partner.* 1894.
211. Jane Ellice Hopkins, *The Power of Womanhood: or, Mothers and Sons. A Book for Parents and Those in Loco Parentis.* 1899.
212. Elizabeth M. S. Chesser, *Woman, Marriage and Motherhood.* 1913.
213. Catherine G. H. Gallichan, *The Age of Mother-Power.* 1914.
214. Women's Cooperative Guild, *Maternity: Letters from Working Women.* 1915.

e.  ON CHILD CARE AND TRAINING[28]

215. Ann H. Taylor, *Practical Hints to Young Females on the Duties of a Wife, and a Mother and a Mistress of a Family.* 3rd ed. 1815.
216. Anon., *Hints to Parents.* 5th ed. 1827. "In the spirit of Pestalozzi's method."
217. Anon., *The Mother's Oracle for the Health and Proper Rearing of Infants.* 1833.
218. Thomas Bull, *Hints to Mothers, for the Management of Health during the Period of Pregnancy, and in the Lying-In Room.* . . . 1837. Medical advice.
219. Adelaide S. Kilvert, *Home Discipline: or, Thoughts on the Origin and Exercise of Domestic Authority.* 1841.
220. John C. Hudson, *The Parent's Handbook.* . . . 1842.
221. John T. Conquest, *Letters to a Mother on the Management of Herself and Her Children in Health and Disease.* . . . 1848. Medical approach. Valuable source.
222. Alfred Fennings, *Every Mother's Book: or the Child's Best Doctor.* Cowes, 1856. Medical advice.
223. D. H. F. Routh, *Infant Feeding.* 1876. Physician's theories.
224. Elizabeth Blackwell, *Counsel to Parents on the Moral Education of Their Children.* . . . 1878. Physician relates moral life to health.
225. O. S. Fowler, *Love and Parentage, Applied to the Improvement of Offspring.* Manchester, 1880.
226. George Black, *The Young Wife's Advice Book: A Guide for Mothers.* 1880.
227. Ward and Lock, *Children and What to Do with Them.* 1881.
228. Rhoda E. White, *From Infancy to Womanhood: Instruction for Young Mothers.* 1882.
229. H. A. Allbutt, *Every Mother's Handbook . . . with Instructions for Preliminary Treatment of Accidents and Illness.* 1897.
230. Clare Goslett, *Things We Must Tell Our Girls. Written for Working Mothers.* 1911.
231. A. S. Acland, *Child Training: Suggestions for Parents and Teachers.* 1914.

# f. ON PEDIATRICS:[29] CONTEMPORARY AND HISTORICAL

232. *Lancet:* A. Hess, "On the Necessity of Practical Instruction in the Treatment of Diseases of Children," 1 (1849), 341–42; M. A. Baines, "Infant Alimentation; or, Artificial Feeding, as a Substitute for Breast-Milk, considered in its Physical and Social Aspects," 1 (1861), 33–34; "Baby-Farming," 1 (1869), 507–508; Editorial, "The Problems of Infant Birth and Infant Feeding," 1 (1911), 1145–46; E. C. Pritchard, H. R. Carter, and W. O. Pitt, "Breast-Feeding: the Value of the Test-Feed," 2 (1911), 677–80.

233. *British and Foreign Medico-Chirurgical Review:* "On Hospitals for Children," 5 (1850), 362–71; E. Ballard, "Baby Killing," 45 (1870), 346–70.

234. *Pediatrics:* F. H. Garrison, "History of Pediatrics," 1 (1923), 1–170. See especially 84–124 and 125–30. See also Arthur F. Abt, *Abt-Garrison History of Pediatrics.* Philadelphia, 1965.

235. *Archives of Pediatrics:* A. Hymanson, "A Short Review of Infant Feeding," 51 (1934), 1–10.

236. *Archives of the Diseases of Childhood:* A. H. Gale, "A Century of Changes in the Mortality and Incidence of the Principle Infections of Childhood," 20 (1945), 2–21.

237. *Bulletin of the History of Medicine:* J. Rendel-Short, "Infant Management in the Eighteenth Century," 34 (1960), 97–122. See also Rendel-Short's *The Father of Child Care: Life of William Cadogan, 1711–1797.* Bristol, 1966.

238. Claire Elizabeth Fox, "Pregnancy, Childbirth and Early Infancy in Anglo-American Culture: 1675–1830," Ph.D. diss., Health Sciences, Univ. of Pennsylvania, 1966.

239. Elizabeth Raine Lomax, "Advances in Pediatrics and Infant Care in Nineteenth Century England," Ph.D. diss., Health Sciences, Univ. of California, Los Angeles, 1972.

240. Ann Roberts, "Feeding and Mortality in the Early Months of Life: Changes in Medical Opinion and Popular Feeding Practices, 1850–1900," Ph.D. diss., Hull Univ., 1973.

241. Janet Blackman: *Mother and Child:* "Baby Scales and Tin Openers: Improvements in Child Health in Our Recent Past," (Dec. 1973), 15–17; *Bulletin of the Society for the Social History of Medicine:* "Child Health and Diet in the Nineteenth Century," 13 (Feb. 1974), 10–12.

# g. THE HOME AND HOUSEHOLD MANAGEMENT[30]

242. William Cobbett, *Cottage Economy.* 1831.

243. Mrs. William Parkes, *Family Secrets, or, Hints to Those Who Would Make Home Happy.* 3 vols. 1841.

244. Thomas Webster (and Mrs. W. Parkes), *An Encyclopaedia of Domestic Economy*. 1844.
245. Alexis Soyer, *The Modern Housewife or Ménagère*. 1849; 1853 rev.
246. John H. Walsh, *A Manual of Domestic Economy Suited to Families Spending from One Hundred to One Thousand Pounds a Year*. 1856.
247. Isabella Beeton, *Mrs. Beeton's Book of Household Management*. 1861. Many reprints to 1969. See review, *New York Times Book Review*, by Steven Marcus, 14 (Dec. 1969), 56–57. Most comprehensive, popular, and used guide to all aspects of maintaining home, children, household.
248. *The English Matron: A Practical Manual for Young Wives*. 3rd ed. rev. by James Hogg, 1861.
249. Cre-Fydd, *Cre-Fydd's Family Fare. The Young Housewife's Daily Assistant on All Matters Relating to Cookery and Housekeeping*. 1864.
250. Eliza Warren: *How I Managed My House on Two Hundred Pounds A Year*. 1864; *How I Managed My Children from Infancy to Marriage*. 1865; *Comfort for Small Incomes*. 1866.
251. Mrs. Pedley, *Practical Housekeeping*. 1867.
252. Charles L. Eastlake, *Hints on Household Taste in Furniture, Upholstery, and Other Details*. 2nd ed. rev. 1869.
253. *Cassell's Household Guide: Being a Complete Encyclopaedia of Domestic and Social Economy*. 4 vols. 1869–1871.
254. S. S. Wigley: *Home Comfort and Beauty*. 1876; *Our Home Work*. 1876; *Simple Lessons in Domestic Economy*. 1878.
255. Florence Cady, *Household Organization*. 1877. Important discussion on "the servant problem" and a "philosophical" view of social behavior.
256. Augusta Webster (Cecil Home, pseud.), *A Housewife's Opinions*. 1879.
257. H. L. Hamilton, *Household Management for the Labouring Classes*. 1882.
258. J. J. Pope, *Number One and How to Take Care of Him*. 1883.
259. James Baldwin Brown, *The Home in Its Relation to Man and to Society*. 2nd ed. 1883.
260. James R. Miller: *The Perfect Home*. 1884; *Secrets of Happy Home Life*. 1894; *The Home Beautiful. The Wedded Life*. 1904.
261. Samuel Smiles: *Happy Homes and Hearts That Make Them, or, Thrifty People and Why They Thrive*. 1884, rev. ed.; *Character*. 1888.
262. *Sylvia's Family Management*. 1886; 1898 ed. "for working people."
263. Jane Ellen Panton: *Homes of Taste: Economical Hints*. 1890; *From Kitchen to Garret: Hints for Young Housewives*. 1890; *Leaves from a Housekeeper's Book*. 1914.
264. Dorothy C. Peel, *The New Home: Treating of the Arrangement, Decoration and Furnishing of a House of Medium Size to Be Maintained by a Moderate Income*. 1898. See also, "Homes and Habits" in G. M. Young, *Early Victorian England, 1830–1865*. Vol. I. 1934.

265. Hugh C. Davidson, ed., *The Book of the Home, A Practical Guide to Household Management.* 8 vols. 1905.
266. Louise Creighton, *The Economics of the Household.* 1907.
267. Florence B. Jack, *The Woman's Book: Contains Everything a Woman Ought to Know.* 1911.

h. ON SERVANTS:[31] CONTEMPORARY AND HISTORICAL

268. Samuel Adams (and Sarah Adams), *The Complete Servant: Being a Practical Guide to the Peculiar Duties and Business of All Descriptions of Servants.* . . . 1825.
269. M. A. Baines, *Domestic Servants as They Are and as They Ought to Be.* 1859.
270. Mary Motherly, *The Servants Behavior Book.* 1859.
271. Henry G. Watkins, *Friendly Hints to Female Servants.* 1867.
272. *Contemporary Review:* R. F. Littledale, "High Life Below Stairs," 22 (1873), 559–79.
273. Rose M. Crawshay, *Domestic Service for Gentlewomen: A Record of Experience and Success.* 1874.
274. *Cornhill Magazine:* E. L. Linton, "On the Side of the Maids," 29 (1874), 298–307; J. M. Capes, "On the Side of the Mistresses," ibid., 459–68.
275. *Chamber's Edinburgh Journal:* "The Domestic Servant Difficulty," 59 (1882), 329–31; "Revolution Below-Stairs," 63 (1886), 28–30; "Domestic Service," 83 (1905–1906), 166–68.
276. *Fortnightly Review:* E. Salmon, "Domestic Service and Democracy," 49 (1888), 408–17.
277. *Nineteenth Century:* C. E. Stephen, "Mistresses and Servants," 6 (1879), 1051–63; E. A. M. Lewis, "A Reformation of Domestic Service," 33 (1893), 127–38; G. S. Layard, "Doom of the Domestic Cook," 33 (1893), 309–19; C. Black, "The Dislike to Domestic Service," ibid., 454–56; E. B. Harrison, "Domestic Servants: Mistress and Maid," 53 (1903), 284–89.
278. *Macmillan's Magazine:* "Domestic Service," 34 (1876), 182–85; S. Brodhurst, "A Plea for the Domestic Servant," 80 (1899), 284–87; F. W. Harberton, "The Domestic Problem," 82 (1900), 276–81 ("that we are on the brink of a revolution in our daily lives owing to the impossibility of finding female servants").
279. Emily James, ed., *Englishwoman's Yearbook and Directory, 1899–1900.* 1900. Session on the "Scientific Treatment of Domestic Service."
280. Dorothy Marshall, *The English Domestic Servant in History.* 1949.
281. E. S. Turner, *What the Butler Saw: Two Hundred and Fifty Years of the Servant Problem.* 1963.
282. Jonathan Gathorne-Hardy, *The Rise and Fall of the British Nanny.* 1972.
283. Leonore Davidoff: *New Society:* "Above and Below Stairs," 24 (1973),

*A Widening Sphere*

181–83; *Journal of Social History:* "Mastered for Life: Servant and Wife in Victorian and Edwardian England," 7 (1974), 406–28.

284. Frank Dawes, *Not in Front of the Servants: Domestic Service in England, 1850–1939.* 1973. See review, Lee Holcombe, *Victorian Studies,* 19 (1975), 121–22.
285. Pamela Horn, *The Rise and Fall of the Victorian Servant.* Dublin, 1975.

i. ON SOCIAL BEHAVIOR AND ETIQUETTE ( COURTESY BOOKS ):
   CONTEMPORARY AND HISTORICAL

286. Anon., *The Female Instructor: or, Young Woman's Companion: Being a Guide to All Accomplishments which Adorn the Female Character.* 1811.
287. Charles W. Day (Agogos, pseud.), *Hints on Etiquette and the Uses of Society.* 1834; 1839.
288. Elizabeth Whately, *English Life, Social and Domestic, in the Middle of the Nineteenth Century, Considered in Reference to Our Position as a Community of Professing Christians.* 1847.
289. G. E. Sargent, *Domestic Happiness: Home Education, Politeness and Good Breeding.* 1851.
290. James Hogg, *The Habits of Good Society.* Edinburgh, 1860.
291. Eliza Cheadle, *Manners of Modern Society.* 1872.
292. Theresa Grey, *Idols of Society: or Gentility and Femininity.* 1874.
293. Samuel Beeton, *All About Etiquette.* 1879.
294. *Girl's Own Paper:* A. Holt, "Etiquette for Ladies and Girls," 1 (1880), 211–12, 407; S. F. A. Caulfield, "Good Breeding: as Shown in Conversation," 5 (1883), 38–40; "Good Breeding: Shown When Travelling," ibid., 98–99; "Etiquette in Walking, Riding and Driving," ibid., 474–75.
295. (Lady) Colin Campbell, *Etiquette of Good Society.* 1893; 1912.
296. Cecil W. Cunnington, *The Perfect Lady.* 1948.
297. Charles Gibbs-Smith, *The Fashionable Lady in the Nineteenth Century.* 1960.
298. Peter Fryer, *Mrs. Grundy, Studies in English Prudery.* 1963.
299. Alison Adburgham, *A Punch History of Manners and Modes, 1841–1940.* 1961.
300. Joan Wildeblood and Peter Brinson, *The Polite World: A Guide to English Manners and Deportment from the Thirteenth to the Nineteenth Century.* 1965.

II  *Sickness and Health Care: Self-Help, Midwives, and Doctors*

Any consideration of the questions of health and health care of women in nineteenth- and early twentieth-century England should proceed from two vantage points: the socioenvironmental and the medical-physiological-psychological. With the former approach the main concern is the interaction of women as members of socioeconomic groupings, with factors in their environment affecting health. With the latter approach the main concern is with the special physiological features and problems of the female sex in the context of the kind of health care available to them at the time. Until now, there remains a drastic shortage of thoroughly detailed studies of health and health care questions about English Victorian and Edwardian women. There is none to compare with the historical discussions about American women,[32] for example:

301. G. J. Ben Barker-Benfield: *Horrors of the Half-Known Life: Male Attitudes toward Women and Sexuality in Nineteenth Century America*. New York, 1976; also: *Feminist Studies:* "The Spermatic Economy: A Nineteenth Century View of Sexuality," 1 (1972), 45–74, rpr. in Michael Gordon.

302. Carroll Smith-Rosenberg: *Social Research:* "The Hysterical Woman: Sex Roles and Role Conflict in Nineteenth Century America," 39 (1972), 652–78; *Journal of American History:* "The Female Animal: Medical and Biological Views of Woman and Her Role in Nineteenth Century America," 60 (1973), 332–56; "Puberty to Menopause: The Cycle of Femininity in Nineteenth Century America," in Hartman and Banner.

303. *Journal of Interdisciplinary History:* Ann Douglas Wood, " 'The Fashionable Diseases': Women's Complaints and Their Treatment in Nineteenth Century America," 4 (1973), 25–52, rpr. in Hartman and Banner.

304. *Journal of Interdisciplinary History:* Regina Markell Morantz, "The Perils of Feminist History," 4 (1974), 649–60. Includes a critique of Wood's article, entry 303; "The Lady and Her Physician," in Hartman and Banner.

305. John S. Haller and Robin M. Haller, *The Physician and Sexuality in Victorian America*. Urbana, 1974.[33] Review: *Journal of the History of Medicine:* V. L. Bullough, 29 (1974), 429–31.

Although the health care experiences of English women were undoubtedly different from those of Americans in many ways, there were similarities also. It is probably correct to interpret that studies for both England and the United States can demonstrate how questions of women's physical condition were related in the nineteenth and early twentieth centuries to questions of women's social position and to social attitudes and policies that guided opposition to their

even limited opportunities in education, employment, and enfranchisement (see category III).


A.  Social-Environmental Approach to Women's
    Health and Health Care

In the absence of health studies focused directly on women's
concerns, we can rely for helpful background on contemporary and
modern historical analyses of the prevalence of disease and of the
preventive public-health measures and medical therapies that were
applied. Special studies have focused on urban sanitary conditions,
on housing, and on questions pertaining to infant welfare.[34] One
valuable source is:

306. George Rosen, "Disease, Debility and Death," in Dyos and Wolff.
     Vol. 2:

> "Fever," the portmanteau term that included typhoid, typhus, and relapsing
> fevers was a problem of major concern among physicians during the earlier
> nineteenth century. Indeed, from a public-health and medical viewpoint, the
> history of the Victorian city is to a considerable degree a history of "fever,"
> the consequence of inadequate or absent community and personal hygiene.
> (p. 629)

Concerning rural conditions, Gilbert writes especially about poor rural
women:

307. Bentley B. Gilbert, *The Evolution of National Insurance in Great
     Britain.* 1966. Ch. 1, "The Eighties and the Nineties"; Ch. 2, "The
     Condition of the People."

> environmental sanitary conditions and knowledge of health care were no
> better in the country than in town. The river flowing from Chippenham
> was full of sewage and the local residents did not seem to care ... informa-
> tion of the most elemental rules of infant care simply did not exist. For
> obstetrical attention the poor never went to a licensed midwife, and if a
> mother died in childbirth the baby was allowed to die and was buried with
> her. (p. 90)

The question of mortality rates has been discussed in terms of class
and sex differentials, although it is difficult at this time to be explicit
about death rates for each of the different social classes and for the
causes of death for the different time periods over the century (see

Chapter 8, this volume). Looking at mortality figures for some local areas and stressing class differentials, Thompson tells us in *The Edwardians* (entry 25):

Expectation of life in middle-class Hampstead was fifty years at birth, but in working-class Southwark only thirty-six years. In Edinburgh, Manchester and many other cities the general death rates for the most prosperous wards were half those of the poorest. (p. 18)

Concerned with rates of mortality for the two sexes, Ansell tells us in:

308. Charles Ansell, *On the Rate of Mortality at Early Periods of Life, at the Age of Marriage, the Number of Children to a Marriage, the Length of a Generation, and Other Statistics of Families in the Upper and Professional Classes [Compared with Other Classes].* 1874.

Comparing the mortality of the two sexes as shown by the "Upper Class" experience . . . the mortality of females is materially lower than among males. . . . By the "English life" tables (poor classes) . . . at all ages between nine and thirty-eight the mortality among the females somewhat exceeds that among males. (p. 26)[35]

Considering the population as a whole, see:

309. D. V. Glass, *Population Policies and Movements in Europe.* 1940.

In 1841, according to the official life tables, the expectation of life at birth in England and Wales was 40.19 years for males and 42.18 years for females. By 1891–1900 this had risen to 44.13 and 47.77 years for males and females respectively, no doubt influenced by the development of public health and sanitation measures in the intervening period, from 1848 onwards, though neo-Malthusians regarded the decline in mortality as primarily dependent upon the decline in the birth-rate. (pp. 14–15)[36]

The causes of the improvement in mortality rates continue to be debated as they were argued in the previous century, with arguments attributing advances in medical science perhaps still more numerous than those defending other causes as the explanation. Very ably representing the latter is:

310. *Population Studies:* T. McKeown and R. G. Record, "Reason for the Decline in Mortality in England and Wales during the Nineteenth Century," 16 (1963), 94–122. A valuable article discussing specific diseases contributing to the death rate, medical and public health therapies that were applied, and environmental conditions including improvement in living standards. The authors conclude that the

lowered death rate was mainly a "response to an improvement in the environment" (p. 95).

Not mentioned in this article, and generally neglected in discussions of health questions, is the considerable extent to which appeals were made to women in the home to create this improved environment. Emphasis in writings and manuals on health is on keeping "sanitary houses" and "nursing the home to health." The improved environment did not create itself: a large body of literature testifies to the participation of those in charge of domestic sanitation, diet, housekeeping, and home nursing. Aside from informing the historian of the measures advised and the responsibilities of women in the home, the self-help literature offers considerable information about the problems involved. The following listing, divided into categories of sample foci of these writings, represents but a small selection from a vast catalog of writings directed largely to a female readership.

B. Self-Help toward Health and Healthy Houses[37]

311. Andrew Combe, *The Principles of Physiology Applied to the Preservation of Health and to the Improvement of Physical and Mental Education.* 1834; 14th ed. 1852, James Coxe, ed. Combe is physician and phrenologist.
312. Thomas John Graham, *Modern Domestic Medicine.* 2nd ed. 1837.
313. Allman Company, *The Family Physician and Guide to Health.* 1846.
314. Jabez Hogg, *The Domestic Medical and Surgical Guide.* 1853.
315. George Wyld, *Health and Comfort: Their Attainment and Preservation. Intended for Distribution among the Working Classes.* 1856. Physician.
316. Elizabeth Blackwell, *How to Keep a Household in Health.* 1870. Physican's address before the Working Women's College.
317. George Wilson: *Sanitary Defects in Villages and Country Districts and How to Remedy Them.* 1876; *Healthy Life and Healthy Dwellings.* 1880; *Hygiene and Sanitary Science.* 1883. Physician.
318. Robert K. Philip, *Domestic Medicine and Surgery.* 1878.
319. Lionel A. Weatherly, *Lectures on Domestic Hygiene.* Birkenhead, 1882. Physician.
320. Frederick A. Bond, *Sanitary Houses and How to Select One.* 1882.
321. Mrs. Hinton Dothie, *Health in the Home: Lectures to Working Women.* Greenock. 1886 (third thousand printing).
322. Gustave Jaeger, *Essays in Health Culture.* 1887.
323. Joseph MacGregor Robertson, *The Household Physician: A Family*

*Guide to the Preservation of Health . . . with Chapters on Food and Drugs and First Aid in Accidents and Injuries.* 1890. Medical advice.

324. Guy Rothery: *Healthy Households: A Plain Guide to Sanitation in the Home.* 1892; *Sanitary and Social Questions of the Day.* 1897.

325. A London Physician, *The Ladies' Physician, A Guide for Women in the Treatment of Their Ailments.* 1895.

326. Anna M. Galbraith, *Hygiene and Physical Culture for Women.* 1895. Physician.[38]

327. John H. Kellogg, *The Home Handbook of Domestic Hygiene and Rational Medicine.* 1896 (thirtieth thousand edition).

328. Cassell and Company, *Cassell's Family Doctor by a Medical Man.* 1897.

329. Clare Goslett: *The Battle of Life Health Tracts.* 1904; *The Science of Home Life.* n.d. (for the National Health Society).[39]

330. Peter Whalley, *Secret Remedies: Or How to Save on Doctors' Bills.* 1910.

331. Elizabeth Chesser, *Perfect Health for Women and Children.* 1912.

332. John K. Mitchell, *Self Help for Nervous Women: Familiar Talks on Economy in Nervous Expenditure.* 1909.

333. Lawrence Wright, *Clean and Decent: The Fascinating History of the Bathroom and the Water Closet.* 1960. Bibliography.


C.   The Medical Context: Obstetrics, Gynecology,
     Medical Psychology

The gynaecological literature of the first half of the nineteenth century is immense; of the latter half, gigantic. . . . While in the first half of the century gynaecology was still essentially medical in scope and the bulk of the literature was concerned with clinical and speculative observations, in the latter half of the century, the introduction of embryology, histology, cellular pathology, bacteriology and aseptic surgery enriched and also encumbered the literature. . . . (see p. vii)

334. James Vincent Ricci: *One Hundred Years of Gynaecology, 1800–1900.* Philadelphia, 1945; *The Development of Gynaecological Surgery and Instruments: A Comprehensive Review of the Evolution of Surgery and Surgical Instruments for the Treatment of Female Diseases from the Hippocratic Age to the Antiseptic Period.* Philadelphia, 1949:

the three indispensable requisites for adequate surgery: anaesthesia, antisepsis and haemostasis were finally discovered . . . operative gynaecology awaited these three essentials. (p. 279)

Because medical and surgical science in the fields related to medical care for women developed along these lines over the nineteenth century, Ricci calls the Victorian years gynecology's "greatest century." For the early period the development of surgical techniques for ovariotomy, removal of ovarian cysts, for fibroid uterus, repair of vesico-vaginal fistula, and vaginal hysterectomy are reported as having saved many lives, while techniques in obstetrics, with and without instruments, along with the development of Caesarian section are said to have saved great numbers of children as well as mothers.

Also reviewing the half-century 1850–1900 is:

335. J. M. Munro Kerr, R. W. Johnstone, and M. Phillips, *Historical Review of British Obstetrics and Gynaecology*. Edinburgh, 1954.

> The British obstetricians of the period included men of great mental distinction under whom both knowledge and practice developed steadily and with high credit. And if surgery, with anaesthesia on the one hand and asepsis on the other, has seemed to steal the limelight, let us not forget it was to an obstetrician that anaesthesia owed its rapid progress, and that another obstetrician had come within a hair's breath of discovering the cause of puerperal infection . . . twenty years before Lister. (p. 42)

The historian can be grateful for these clear surveys of developments in nineteenth-century medicine—a discipline that was not only very complex in its own science but also highly complicated in its interdependence with the other life sciences that were developing during the period. The changes or advances are not easy for the layperson to evaluate, not only for lack of training, but also for the temptation to employ hindsight and therefore harsh judgments—despite the knowledge that twentieth-century medical theory and practice is in most aspects extremely different from that of the nineteenth. Undertaking critical analysis of technical details is therefore perilous for the specialist outside the medical field. The careful historian, however, does have an advantage in being able to rely upon contemporary sources that detail and explain collaborations and controversies among the Victorian medical specialists that permit reasonable consideration of attitudes and behavior of physicians against the background of social-intellectual developments. Furthermore, the questions historians ask about the medical treatment of women go beyond appraisal of technique and physical results of the attempted remedies into areas that include questions of women's experiences and reactions in treatment, and of doctors' social as well as professional attitudes toward female patients. (See, for example, Wood, the Hallers, and Barker-Benfield, entries 332, 334, and 336, who rather convincingly reveal many Victorian medical men as self-styled guardians of the moral code and as eager experimenters in perhaps over-zealous surgery schedules for women.)

The main purpose of this select bibliography, then, is to exemplify theories, approaches, diagnoses, and remedies that were applicable to Victorian and Edwardian women in both private and charity-hospital medical practices. The major attitude underlying the suggestions of sources is that the study of medical care for women is such an uncharted area for social historians that the medical writings listed here should be read firsthand by persons interested in the subject. Following the implications in the foregoing statements of Ricci and Kerr, the listing of references proceed from developments that helped to advance the obstetrical-gynecological fields to questions focused more directly on theory and practice in obstetrics, gynecology, and medical psychology during the previous century.

## D.  Anesthesia and Antisepsis

336. Robert Ferguson, *Essays on the Most Important Diseases of Women.* 1839.
337. Edward Rigby, Jr., *A System of Midwifery.* 1844.
338. James Y. Simpson, *Account of a New Anaesthetic Agent as a Substitute for Sulphuric Ether in Surgery and Midwifery.* Edinburgh, 1847.
339. *British and Foreign Medico-Chirurgical Review:* E. Murphy, "Chlorophorm in the Practice of Midwifery," 2 (1848), 518–20.
340. James H. Aveling, *An Address to Mothers Commending the Use of Chlorophorm.* Sheffield, 1853.
341. Oliver Wendell Holmes, *The Contagiousness of Puerperal Fever.* Boston, 1855.
342. John Snow, *On Chlorophorm and Other Anaesthetics: Their Action and Administration.* 1858. Dr. Snow anesthetized Queen Victoria in her deliveries in 1853 and 1857.
343. *Obstetrical Society of London, Transactions:* C. Kidd, "On the Value of Anaesthetic Aid in Midwifery," 2 (1860), 340–61; also 5 (1864), 125–41.
344. Ignaz P. Semmelweis, *The Aetiology, Concept and Prophylaxis of Childbed Fever.* 1861. See also W. Japp Sinclair, *Semmelweis, His Life and His Doctrine.* Manchester, 1909.
345. I. B. Brown (younger), *On Safe Delivery from the Pains of Labour; or, Painless Parturition with Full Mental Consciousness.* 1889.
346. G. M. Foy, *The Discovery of Modern Anaesthetics.* 1889.
347. Joseph Lister, *Scientific Papers.* New York, 1910. See also: Rickman Godlee, *Lord Lister.* 1917; C. J. S. Thompson, *Lord Lister: The Discoverer of Antiseptic Surgery.* 1934.

348. Walter Radcliffe, *Milestones in Midwifery*. Bristol, 1967. "fever was by far the biggest problem that the new lying-in hospitals had to contend with" (pp. 64–65).


E.  Hospitals[40]


349. Anon., *An Account of the British Lying-In Hospital for Married Women . . . from Its Institution in November 1749 to December 1807*. 1808.

350. Augustus Bozzi Granville, *A Report on the Practice of Midwifery at the Westminster General Dispensary During 1818*. 1819.

351. William Hardwicke, *Report of the Medical Institution and Private Dispensary, 32 Hatton Garden*. 1848. Treated "unmarried females," "nervous cases," married women, "especially those in humble position," middle-class also.

352. Florence Nightingale: *Notes on the Sanitary Conditions of Hospital Wards*. 1859; *Notes on Hospitals*. 1863; *Introductory Notes on Lying-In Institutions*. 1871. See also *Obstetrical Society of London, Transactions*: C. C. Rowling, "The History of the Florence Nightingale Lying-In Ward, King's College Hospital," 10 (1868), 50–58.

353. James Edmunds, *The British Lying-In Hospital and the Ladies Medical College*. 1868.

354. Thomas Ryan, *History of Queen Charlotte's Lying-In Hospital from Its Foundation in 1752 to the Present Time*. 1885.

355. *British Medical Journal:* J. W. Ballantyne, "Plea for a Pro-Maternity Hospital," 1 (1901), 813–14.

356. Ralph B. Cannings, *The City of London Maternity Hospital*. 1922.

357. Brian Abel-Smith, *The Hospitals, 1880–1948; A Study in Social Administration*. 1964.

358. F. N. L. Poynter, ed., *The Evolution of Hospitals in Britain*. 1964. See Alistair Gunn, "Maternity Hospitals."

359. Gwendoline Ayers, *England's First State Hospitals, 1867–1930*. Berkeley, 1971.


F.  Development of the Medical Profession in Britain


360. Robert M. Kerrison, *An Inquiry into the Present State of the Medical Profession in England*. 1814.

361. *Association Medical Journal:* G. M. Stansfeld, "Statistical Analysis of the Medical Profession in England and Wales," n.s. 31 (March 1856), 253–56.

362. *Lancet:* "The Medical Practitioners' Bill: An Act to Regulate Qualifications of Practitioners in Medicine and Surgery," 2 (1858), 124–29.

363. *Obstetrical Society of London, Transactions:* "On the Founding of the Obstetrical Society of London (1859)," 1 (1859), v–xiv:

We might get something like a fair idea of the importance of obstetric practice in this country from the fact that of all the women delivered in England and Wales, no less than one in every one hundred and eighty nine, died in childbirth. The number of still-born children was over 22,000 a year. The chief business of an Obstetrical Society would be to diminish this mortality. . . ." (Dr. Tyler Smith)

364. Henry W. Rumsey, *On the State of Medicine in Great Britain and Ireland.* 1867.

365. William Dale, *The Present State of the Medical Profession in Great Britain and Ireland.* Dublin, 1875.

366. Robert B. Carter, *Doctors and Their Work, or Medicine, Quackery and Disease.* 1903.

367. *British Medical Journal Symposium: Fifty Years of Medicine.* 1950.

368. Charles Newman, *The Evolution of Medical Education in the Nineteenth Century.* 1957.

369. E. S. Turner, *Call the Doctor: A Social History of Medical Men.* 1958.

370. *Bulletin of the History of Medicine:* M. Brightfield, "The Medical Profession in Early Victorian England, as Depicted in the Novels of the Period, 1840–1870," 35 (1961), 238–56.

371. F. N. L. Poynter, ed.: *The Evolution of Medical Practice in Britain.* 1961. See H. J. Walkin, "The Rise of Obstetrics in British Medical Practice and the Influence of the Royal College of Obstetricians and Gynaecologists." Also *Medicine and Science in the 1860s.* 1968.

372. *History:* S. W. F. Holloway, "Medical Education in England, 1830–1858: a Sociological Analysis," 49 (1964), 229–324.

373. Ruth Hodgkinson, *Origins of the National Health Service: Medical Services of the New Poor Law, 1834–1871.* Berkeley, 1967.


G.   Women Physicians[41]


374. *Lancet:* "Female Medical Students," 2 (1861), 116, Miss Garrett refused as a pupil by London Hospital; "Lady Physicians," 1 (1862), 698, report of a meeting to admit ladies to the medical profession. Negative; "Female Physicians," 1 (1862), 17, editorial against women in medical practice; "Female Apothecaries: To the Editor," 2 (1862), 409, "the realms of medicine being threatened with an invasion of amazons"; "Female Apothecaries: To the Editor," ibid., 496, "the society of apothecaries cannot refuse any person . . . who conforms"; "The Female Students Question," ibid., 657, "The medical profession is . . . the least adapted to the female nature."

375. James Edmunds, *Inaugural Address Delivered for the Female Medical Society, October 3, 1864.* [1864.] Problem of diverting "lady practitioners" from duties of maternity, etc.

376. *British Medical Journal:* "Female Dispensers," 2 (1867), 579–80. Female chemists are all right but not female doctors.

377. Thomas Markby, *Medical Women.* 1869.

378. Charles R. Drysdale, *Medicine as a Profession for Women.* 1870.

379. *Obstetrical Society of London, Transactions:* "Special Meeting Relative to Admission of Female Practitioners to the Fellowship of the Society," 16 (1875), 65–83; "Annual Address" (including question of women as Fellows), 44 (1903), 56–57.

380. *International Review:* J. B. Chadwick, "The Study and Practice of Medicine by Women," 7 (1879), 445–72.

381. Sophia Jex-Blake, *Medical Women: A Thesis and a History.* 1886.

382. Elizabeth Blackwell, *Pioneer Work in Opening the Medical Profession to Women.* 1895. (*SBS*, entry 290).

383. Isabel Thorne, *Sketch of the London School of Medicine for Women.* 1905.

384. Martha Wollstein, *History of Women in Medicine.* 1908.

385. *New Statesman:* F. Murray, "The Position of Women in Medicine and Surgery," 2 (1913–14), Special Supplement, xvi–xvii.

386. *Annals of Medical History:* K. Campbell Hurd-Mead, "An Introduction to the History of Women in Medicine," n.s. 5 (1933), 1–27; 171–96; 281–305; 390–408; 484–504; 584–600. See also Hurd-Mead's *A History of Women in Medicine.* 1938.

387. Louisa Garrett Anderson, *Elizabeth Garrett Anderson, 1836–1917.* 1939.

388. Enid Bell, *Storming the Citadel: Rise of the Woman Doctor.* 1953.

389. Edythe Lutzker: *Women Gain a Place in Medicine.* 1969; see also *Proceedings of the Twenty-Third International Congress of the History of Medicine:* "The London School of Medicine for Women," 1 (1974), 357–66; see also "Medical Education for Women in Great Britain," M.A. thesis, Political Science, Columbia Univ., 1959. Relates the progress of women in medicine from the passage of legislature in 1858.

## H.   Midwives and Man-Midwives: Controversy

390. Philip Thicknesse, *The Danger and Immodesty of Employing Men-Midwives.* 1772; as John Blunt (pseud.), *Man-Midwifery Dissected.* 1793.

391. J. R. Pickmere ("Proprietas"), *An Address to the Public on the Propriety of Midwives Instead of Surgeons Practicing Midwifery.* 1826.

392. *Lancet:* "Observations on the Impropriety of Men Being Employed in the Business of Midwifery," 12 (1827), 118–19, a review of the book by the same title by Hunt and Clark, 1826; E. Moore, "Statistical Report of Pauper Midwifery Cases: To the Editor of Lancet," 1

(1862), 307, for the Bethnal Green district; W. Powell, "Midwifery Statistics," 1 (1862), 343, Powell as resident accoucheur, London Hospital, questions Moore's figures, gives his from his records; A. Meadows, "Lecture on the History of Midwifery," 1 (1872), 637–41;"The Midwives Act," 1 (1912), 550, effect of new regulations governing midwives.

393. Samuel Dickson, *The Destructive Art of Healing, or, Facts for Families*. 3rd ed. 1853. See pp. 39–45 for warnings by this physician against male practitioners at childbirth. (Chief complaints against the medical profession concern the "overuse" of instruments as opposed to midwives, who were not permitted to use instruments.)

394. Percival Willughby, *Observations on Midwifery*, edited from the manuscript by Henry Blenkinsop. Warwick, 1863. Rpr. Yorkshire, 1972. William Harvey's contribution to midwifery. One hundred fifty cases from seventeenth century.

395. Francis Harvey Champneys, *Midwives in England, Especially in Relation to the Medical Profession*. 1865.

396. John Stevens, *Man-Midwifery Exposed, or, The Danger and Immorality of Employing Men in Midwifery Proved: And the Remedy for the Evil Found*. 1865.

397. *British Medical Journal:* J. H. Aveling, "The Obstetrical Society of London and Midwives," 1 (1874), 153–54; "The Registration of Midwives," 2 (1893), 71, 127–28. Testimony from Select Committee, House of Commons.

398. *Contemporary Review:* C. J. Cullingworth, "The Registration of Midwives," 73 (1898), 394–402. The chief antagonism expressed by male physicians from at least the seventeenth century is that midwives have not been given scientific or technical knowledge or training and are therefore dangerous.

399. Stanley B. Atkinson, *The Office of Midwife in England and Wales Under the Midwives Act, 1902*. 1907. By this time many midwives have been professionally trained.

400. Francis Henry Champneys, *Midwives in England Epecially in Relation to the Medical Profession*. 1907–1908. A St. Bartholomew's Hospital Report.

401. *Maternity and Child Welfare:* M. O. Haydon, "English Midwives in Three Centuries," 3 (1919), 407–9.

402. Herbert K. Spencer, *The History of British Midwifery from 1650–1800*. 1927.

403. *Annals of Medical History:* W. F. Mengert, "The Origin of the Male Midwife," n.s. 4 (1932), 453–65.

404. James H. Aveling, *English Midwives, Their History and Prospects*. 1967. (Original edition 1872.)

405. Jean E. Donnison: "The Development of the Profession of Midwife in England from 1750–1902," Ph.D. diss., London Univ., 1974. The most thorough coverage of the subject. See also *New Society:* "The Sex of Midwives," 26 (Nov. 1973), 275–76.

# I. Obstetrical Care[42]

406. Thomas Denman, *An Introduction to the Practice of Midwifery*. 2nd ed. 1800. Physician-Accoucheur to Middlesex Hospital.

407. Marshall Hall, *Commentaries on Some of the More Important of the Diseases of Females*. 1827. Climacteric period holds dangers. And "The female sex is far more sensitive and susceptible than the male, and extremely liable to those distressing affections which for want of some better term have been denominated as nervous" (p. 2).

408. *London Medical Gazette:* E. Rigby, "An Historical Analysis of the English Midwifery Forceps," 7 (1831), 456–61; E. W. Duffin, "Description of a New Shield Pessary," 7 (1831), 807–11, "All females object, but practitioners have approved it"; Dr. Ramsbotham's Report of Cases that Occurred in the Eastern District of the Royal Maternity Charity," n.s. 13 (1851), 583–84, 711–13.

409. *British and Foreign Medico-Chirurgical Review:* "Obstetrics a Science, Midwifery an Art," 4 (1849), 501–10.

410. John Roberton, *Essays and Notes on the Physiology and Diseases of Women and on Practical Midwifery*. 1851. Hospital experiences. Ideas on hysteria. Midwives. Mesmerism in use.

411. Fleetwood Churchill, *On the Diseases of Women: Including Those of Pregnancy and Childbed*. 1857.

412. William Acton, *Functions and Disorders of the Reproductive Organs* ... 1857. Review in *Lancet:* 1 (1857), 556–57.

413. F. R. C. S. *The Speculum: Its Moral Tendencies*. 1857.[43]

414. George Morant, *Hints to Husbands: A Revelation of the Man-Midwife's Mysteries*. 3rd ed. 1857.

415. Robert Gooch, *On Some of the Most Important Diseases Peculiar to Women*. 1859. Robert Ferguson, ed., with Preface. Chap. II, "The Disorders of the Mind of Lying-in Women." Discusses "thoughts on insanity as an object of moral science." Reviews the issue of use of the speculum, prudery, contagious diseases, etc.

416. *Obstetrical Society of London, Transactions:* W. T. Smith, "On the Abolition of Craniotomy from Obstetric Practice in All Cases Where the Foetus is Living and Viable," 1 (1859), 21–52; P. H. Harper, "The More Frequent Use of the Forceps as a Means of Lessening both Maternal and Foetal Mortality," 1 (1859), 142–85.

417. John Hall Davis, *Parturition and Its Difficulties, with Clinical Illustrations and Statistics of 13,783 Deliveries*. 1865. These deliveries were in the Royal Maternity Charity, 1842–1864, where he supervised. Describes complications and gives statistical analysis.

418. *British Medical Journal:* J. H. Davis, "Progress of Obstetric Medicine Education," 1 (1868), 46–47, counts 588 members of the Obstetrical Society of London. Admits deficiencies of training; J. B. Hicks, "A Case of Caesarian Section," 1 (1868), 285–86, 321–24, 503–4.

419. James Y. Simpson, *Clinical Lectures on the Diseases of Women*. 1872. For craniotomy discussion, see pp. 512–27.

420. Graily Hewitt, *Pathology, Diagnosis and Treatment of the Diseases of Women*. 1872. 2 vols. Surgical appliances for uterine support discussed Vol. I, 456–58. Many women wore them permanently in the absence of medical knowledge of surgical repair.

421. *Obstetrical Journal of Great Britain and Ireland:* A. L. Galabin, "The Effects of a Frequent and Early Use of Midwifery Forceps Upon the Foetal and Maternal Mortality," 5 (1877–78), 561–68.

422. Henry Allbutt, *Evil Produced by Over-Bearing and Excessive Lactation*. 1880.

423. *British Gynecological Journal:* A Meadows, "Ought Craniotomy to be Abolished?" 2 (1887), 308–21.

424. John Glaister, *Dr. William Smellie and His Contemporaries*. Glasgow, 1894. See also R. W. Johnstone, *William Smellie the Master of British Midwifery*. Edinburgh, 1952.

425. James H. Aveling, *The Chamberlens and the Midwifery Forceps*. 1882.

426. Alfred Lewis Galabin, *A Manual of Midwifery*. 1900. "Up to the last few years, the mortality of Caesarean section has been so high as to restrict the operation. . . . British statistics gave a mortality of about 84 per cent" (p. 698).

427. Elizabeth Blackwell, *Essays in Medical Sociology*. 2 vols. 1902. Childbirth and sex: injury from "too frequent lesions" resulting from childbirth affects sexual life.

428. Herbert Thoms, *Classical Contributions to Obstetrics and Gynecology*. Springfield, 1935.

429. *American Journal of Obstetrics and Gynecology:* B. M. Anspach, "The Contributions of Great Britain to Gynecology and Obstetrics," 30 (1935), 459–66.

430. John H. Young, *Caesarean Section. The History and Development of the Operation from the Earliest Times*. 1944.

431. Walter Radcliffe, *The Secret Instrument. Birth of the Midwifery Forceps*. 1947; *Milestones in Midwifery* (entry 409).

432. Isaac Flack (Harvey Graham, pseud.), *Eternal Eve: The Mysteries of Birth and the Customs that Surround it*. 1950; rev. 1960. Aimed for general and wide readership, emphasizing the abnormal and sensational. Informative, but has thin documentation and therefore raises questions.

433. Roger Fulford, ed., *Dearest Child: Letters between Queen Victoria and the Princess Royal*. 1964; *Dearest Mama: Letters between Queen Victoria and the Crown Princess of Prussia, 1861–1864*. 1968. Includes sensitive expression of feelings about childbirth experiences of the Queen as mother and grandmother.[44]

# J. Gynecological Care

434. John Robertson, *Treatise of Menstruation*. 1748. Author was librarian to the Royal Society for the Improvement of Natural Knowledge.[45]
435. *Lancet:* F. Lavagna, 'On the Efficacy of Injections of Liquid Ammonia in Amenorrhoea," 2 (1824), 165–69, 265–69, 418–19; E. Tilt, "Nature and Treatment of the Various Forms of Ovaritis; with Cases Illustrating their Connection with Painful Menstruation, Hysteria, Sterility, Pelvic Inflammation and Ovarian Dropsy," 1 (1849), 338–41, 399–401; S. Edwards, "Dysmenorrhoea, and Its Treatment by Caustic to and Dilatation of the Uterine Neck," 1 (1849), 396–98; W. E. Fothergill, "Dysmenorrhoea," 2 (1912), 1015, identifies dysmenorrhoea as "painful menstruation" and considers it normal.
436. Samuel Ashwell, *A Practical Treatise on the Diseases Peculiar to Women*. 1844. Claims that sedentary life of many women contributes to illness.
437. Edward Tilt: *On Diseases of Menstruation and Ovarian Inflammation . . .* 1850. Includes discussion of hysteria; *On the Preservation of the Health of Women at the Critical Periods of Life*. 1851. Mothers cautioned toward the "right management" of daughters' menstruation; *The Change of Life in Health and Disease: A Practical Treatise on Nervous and Other Affections Incidental to Women at the Decline of Life*. 1857. Menopause is a critical period that has to be understood and managed.
438. *London Medical Gazette:* A. Hannover (trans. E. Hansen), "Essay on Menstruation in Some of Its Psychological and Pathological Relations," 13 (1851), 626–32, 797–800, 969–76.
439. Isaac Baker Brown (elder), *On Some Diseases of Women Admitting of Surgical Treatment*. 1854. Pioneer in surgical treatment for diseases of the reproductive organs.
440. Thomas R. Leadam, *The Diseases of Women Homeopathically Treated*. 2nd rev. ed. 1874.
441. Hugh Campbell, *Outlines of Medical and Surgical Electricity*. 1875.
442. Thomas Skinner, *Homeopathy in Its Relation to the Diseases of Females*. 1875.
443. Robert Lawson Tait, *Diseases of Women*. 1877. Discusses results of poor gynecological treatment. Expresses attitudes toward sexual practices.
444. *Obstetrical Journal of Great Britain and Ireland:* J. H. Aveling, "The Spaying of Women: A Note Historical and Philological," 6 (1878–79), 617–21; T. Savage, " On Oophorectomy," 8 (1880), 257–66.[46]
445. Thomas Spencer Wells, *The Revival of Ovariotomy*. 1884.
446. James H. Aveling, *British Gynecology Past and Present*. 1885.
447. William Japp Sinclair, *On Gonorrhoeal Infection in Women*. 1888.

448. Horation R. Bigelow, *Gynaecological Electro-Therapeutics.* 1889.
449. *British Gynaecological Journal:* H. M. Jones, "The Use and Abuse of Massage in Gynaecological Practice," 5 (1889–90), 89–105.
450. Francis H. Champneys, *On Painful Menstruation.* 1890.
451. George B. Massey, *Electricity in the Diseases of Women.* 2nd ed. 1890.
452. John C. Webster, *Puberty and Change of Life.* Edinburgh, 1892.
453. T. C. Allbutt, W. S. Playfair, and T. W. Eden, eds., *A System of Gynaecology.* 1896; rev. ed. 1906. Claim such rapid progress in the ten years between editions that very much had to be rewritten, especially on surgery. See Playfair's "The Nervous System in Relation to Gynaecology."
454. Alexander D. L. Napier, *The Menopause and Its Disorders.* 1897.
455. Andrew F. Currier, *The Menopause.* New York, 1897. English references.
456. James C. Burnett, *The Change of Life in Women.* 1898. Homeopathic.
457. *New Hampshire Medical Society, Transactions:* A. P. Chesley, "History of Ovariotomy," 64 (1900), 85–92.
458. H. MacNaughton-Jones, *The Relation of Puberty and the Menopause to Neurasthenia.* 1913. Also in *Lancet:* 1 (29 March 1913), 879–81.
459. Thomas W. Eden and C. Lockyer, eds., *The New System of Gynaecology.* 3 vols. 1917. Most chapters written by 1914. Aim of this work is to reflect the changes in gynecological medicine over the nineteenth century.

K. Gynecological Surgery and Moral Ideas
   Related to Medical Psychology[47]

Looking at the predominance of the emotional nervous element in the female; looking also at the peculiarities of the sexual organs, it would rather be anticipated that irritation of these organs would be more likely to derange the nervous centers in the female than irritation of the sexual organs of the male. (Graily Hewitt, Vol. 2, p. 126, entry 420. Hewitt devotes four chapters to nervous disorders connected with uterine irritation.)

In all large asylums you will find cases of insanity combined with if not resulting from uterine irritation and disease. (James Y. Simpson, p. 20, entry 419)

460. Isaac Baker Brown (elder), *On the Curability of Certain Forms of Insanity, Epilepsy, Catalepsy and Hysteria in Females.* 1866. Review, *Lancet:* 5 (1866), 485–86. Baker Brown recommended clitoridectomy for the stated ailments and also for "habitual masturbation," which was at the time considered not only immoral but also causing insanity or at least ill health. Baker Brown operated on women in his private hospital, The London Surgical Home. (Ricci writes that the twenty beds were always occupied.) Publicity about Baker Brown's practice brought

heated controversy in medical circles about his procedures. Argumentation in the Obstetrical Society of London led to his being removed from membership. Baker Brown claimed that even those among his vocal critics were themselves performing the operations.

461. *Obstetrical Society of London, Transactions:* Argumentation on Baker Brown and on clitoridectomy: 8 (1866), 360–84; 9 (1867), 61–62.

462. *Lancet:* On Baker Brown and clitoridectomy: 1 (1866), 699, 718–19; 2 (1866), 51–52, 114, 495, 560–61, 616–17, 639, 667–69, 678–79, 697–98, Baker Brown's defense, 709–11, 736–37; 1 (1867), 28–30, 427–29, formal charges against Baker Brown and his reply, 429–41, report of the Society and expulsion of Baker Brown; a sidelight: "Barbarous Chastity," clitoridectomies among Nubian women, 2 (1867), 165–66.

463. *British Medical Journal:* The Baker Brown controversy on clitoridectomy: 2 (1866), 705–8, 728–30; 1 (1867), 18–19; 395–410, the Obstetrical Society report in full with quotations of speakers, including description of the surgery.

464. John Scoffern, *The London Surgical Home: Being a Popular Statement of the Operations Therein Performed by Mr. Isaac Baker Brown.* 1867.

465. *Journal of Mental Science:* "Report on the Progress of Psychological Medicine: Dr. Ullersperger reviews "Clitoridectomy as a Remedy Against Hysteria, Epilepsy, and Mental Derangement Consequent on Masturbation," 14 (1868), 272–73; E. H. Hare, "Masturbatory Insanity: History of an Idea," 108 (1962), 2–25.

466. *International Medical Magazine:* A. Eyer, "Clitoridectomy for the Cure of Certain Cases of Masturbation in Young Girls," 3 (1894–95), 259–62.

467. Eric John Dingwall, *The Girdle of Chastity.* 1931.

468. *Journal of the American Medical Association:* J. Duffy, "Masturbation and Clitoridectomy: A Nineteenth Century View," 186 (1963), 246–48. Discusses sewing machine as a sexually stimulating instrument when in operation.

469. *Journal of the History of Ideas:* R. H. Macdonald, "The Frightful Consequences of Onanism: Notes on the History of an Illusion," 28 (1967), 423–31.

470. Alex Comfort, *The Anxiety Makers: Some Curious Preoccupations of the Medical Profession.* 1967. Concern with moral conduct spilled over into the field of medical hygiene, Comfort demonstrates. Portrays medical men fostering and reinforcing sexual anxiety as "a main driving power behind ethical and religious life." Behavior that had once been "abominable" became in the nineteenth century "unhealthy." Scanty documentation and brevity mars this provocative book.

471. *Bulletin of the History of Medicine:* H. T. Englehardt, Jr., "The Disease of Masturbation: Values and the Concept of Disease," 48 (1974), 234–48.

472. Vieda Skultans: *Madness and Morals: Ideas of Insanity in the Nineteenth Century.* 1975. See also *New Society,* "The Moral Managers,"

27 (1974), 573–74. Nineteenth-century writers called on moral force as antidote to insanity: individuals must take responsibility for their mental illness.

## L.   Gynecology-Physiology Related to Medical Psychology

473. *Lancet:* Dr. Clutterbuck, "Lectures on the Diseases of the Nervous System," 12 (1827), 737–43, hysteria of uterine origin; "Abuse of the Cold Douche in Insanity," 1 (1860), 130; J. H. Jephson, "Contraction of Abdominal Walls Due to Hysteria," 2 (1862), 52.

474. Thomas Laycock: *A Treatise on the Nervous Diseases of Women, Comprising an Enquiry into the Nature, Causes and Treatment of Spinal and Hysterical Disorders.* 1840. Factor of the reproductive organs in the state of mind.

475. *Journal of Psychological Medicine:* "Statistics and Pathology of Mental Diseases," 1 (1848), 57–71, "mental diseases are much more prevalent in this country among women than men"; T. O. Ward, "Case of Double Consciousness Connected with Hysteria," 2 (1849), 456–61; Dr. Webster, "Insanity from Chlorophorm Employed in Parturition," 3 (1850), 269–70; "Woman in Her Psychological Relations," 4 (1851), 18–50; "Woman in Her Social Relations Past and Present," 9 (1856), 521–44; "Charlotte Brontë: A Psychological Study, 11 (1858), 295–317; "On Puerperal Insanity," 12 (1859), 9–38.

476. Walter Johnson: *An Essay on the Diseases of Young Women.* 1849; *The Morbid Emotions of Women: Their origin, Tendencies and Treatment.* 1850.

477. Robert Brundell Carter: *On the Pathology and Treatment of Hysteria.* 1853. Anticipates Freud in dealing with repressed sexuality as a factor in causation and rejecting older concept of hysteria as a chiefly physical disease caused by uterine pathology. (Hysterical symptomology in men was regarded as "hypochondriasis.") In dealing with masturbation and sexual licentiousness, however, Carter is a typically moralistic Victorian, *On the Influence of Education and Training in Preventing Diseases of the Nervous System.* 1855.

478. *Obstetrical Society of London, Transactions:* R. Hodges, "On a Case of Hysteria Simulating Natural Labour," 1 (1859), 339–40; W. S. Playfair, "On Removal of the Uterine Appendages in Cases of Functional Neurosis," 13 (1891), 7–24.

479. *Journal of Mental Science:* S. W. D. Williams, "Cases Illustrating the Action of Amenorrhea as a Cause of Insanity," 9 (1863), 344–53; "Sex and Insanity," 18 (1873), 231–32, statistics on ratio of male-female "lunatics"; W. W. Ireland, "Relation of Diseases of Women to Insanity," 29 (1883), 425; Dr. Hammond, "The Bicycle in the Treatment of Nervous Diseases," 38 (1892), 612, bicycle prescribed for hysteria, neurasthenia, sexual perversion, and abnormal sexual appetite;

A. Walk, "Some Aspects of the 'Moral Treatment' of the Insane up to 1854," 100 (1954), 807–37.

480. *British Medical Journal:* J. Althaus, "Lecture on the Pathology and Treatment of Hysteria," 1 (1866), 245–48, based upon 820 cases; T. Laycock, "Contributions to a New Chapter in the Physiology and Pathology of the Nervous System," 1 (1868), 187–89; H. Maudsley, "Illustrations of a Variety of Insanity," 1 (1868), 387–88; M. D. Macleod, "Address on Puerperal Insanity," 2 ( 1886), 147–48, 409–10; R. E. Evans, "Case of Neurasthenia Treated by Hypodermic Injections of Nerve Extract," 2 (1893), 1321–22; E. L. Ash, "Treatment of Neurasthenia," 1 (1913), 390; T. R. Glynn, "The Bradshaw Lecture on Hysteria in Some of Its Aspects," 2 (1913), 1193–98.

481. Frederick C. Skey, *Hysteria . . . Six Lectures.* 1867. Important work.

482. C. Handfield Jones, *Studies in Functional Nervous Disorders.* 1870.

483. *Obstetrical Journal of Great Britain and Ireland:* E. H. Trenholme, "Correlation of the Psychological and Physiological Forces," 5 (1877–78), 439–46; R. J. Halton, "On Some Forms of Severe Mental Disturbance in Connection with Non-Puerperal Uterine Derangements," 6 (1878–79), 209–21; T. Wilson, "On the Influence of Maternal Shock in the Production of Foetal Monstrosities," 8 (1880), 331–35.

484. *Brain:* G. H. Savage, "Uterine Displacement Corrected and Insanity Cured," 1 (1878–79), 270–72.

485. *British Gynaecological Journal:* C. H. F. Routh, "On the Etiology and Diagnosis, Considered Especially from a Medico-Legal Point of View, of those Cases of Nymphomania which Lead Women to Make False Charges Against Their Medical Attendants," 2 (1887), 485–511; L. Tait, "Note on the Influence of Removal of the Uterus on Sexual Appetite," 4 (1888–89), 310–17; "Discussion on a Case of Insanity Cured by Pessary," 5 (1889–90), 483; R. Barnes, "On Correlations of the Sexual Functions and Mental Disorders of Women," 6 (1890–91), 390–413, 416–30.

486. Daniel Hack Tuke, *A Dictionary of Psychological Medicine.* 1892.

487. *Contemporary Review:* T. C. Allbutt, "Nervous Diseases and Modern Life," 67 (1895), 210–31.

488. Maurice Craig, *Psychological Medicine.* 1905.

489. G. Zilboorg, with G. W. Henry, *A History of Medical Psychology,* New York, 1941.

490. Denis Leigh, *The Historical Development of British Psychiatry.* Oxford, 1961.

491. Richard Hunter and Ida Macalpine, *Three Hundred Years of Psychiatry,* 1535–1860. 1963. "Medical attitudes put moral obliquity on mental illness, one of the roots of the stigma attached to insanity" (p. 932).

492. L. S. Hearnshaw, *A Short History of British Psychology, 1840–1940.* 1964.

493. Ilza Veith, *Hysteria: The History of a Disease.* 1965. Valuable.

494. William Parry-Jones, *The Trade in Lunacy.* 1972.

M.    Mesmerism and Hypnotism[48]

495. James Braid, *Neurypnology; or, The Rationale of Nervous Sleep, Considered in Relation with Animal Magnetism.* 1843; rev. ed. 1899.
496. *The Zoist.* Journal of Cerebral Physiology and Mesmerism. 1843 ff.
497. Thomas Capern, *Pain of Body and Mind Relieved by Mesmerism.* 1861.
498. Albert Moll, *Hypnotism.* 1890. Considers use in childbirth.
499. Ernest Hart, *Hypnotism, Mesmerism and the New Witchcraft.* 1893.
500. J. Milne Bramwell, *Hypnotism, Its History, Practice and Theory.* 2nd ed. 1906.
501. Hugh C. Miller, *Hypnotism and Disease: A Plea for Rational Psycho-Therapy.* 1912.
502. Eric Dingwall, *Abnormal Hypnotic Phenomena.* 1967. Part II, "Hypnotism in Great Britain."
503. *The Listener:* Jonathan Miller, "Mesmerism," 90 (1973), 685–90.
504. *Journal of the History of Ideas:* F. Kaplan, "The Mesmeric Mania; the Early Victorians and Animal Magnetism," 35 (1974), 691–702.


III    *Science, Social Science, and their Social Application*

505. Bert James Loewenberg, *Darwinism: Reaction or Reform?* New York, 1957.

> Once man was swept into the evolutionary orbit, the logic of science became applicable to all forms of human activity. . . . Hence the logic of science and the dynamics of evolution applied to mind, to morals, and to society. This was the Darwinian revolution. . . . not in science alone; it was a revolution in man's conception of himself and his works. . . . The Darwinian synthesis permeated every sector of thought. (p. 1)

That the publication of Darwin's theories was a catalyst in launching new developments in biology and psychology and in charting new paths for anthropology and sociology has been supported by scholarly defenders since the nineteenth century.[49] On the question of psychology:

506. J. C. Flugel, *A Hundred Years of Psychology.* 1933; 1970:

> in so far as Darwinism was accepted, psychology was itself compelled henceforward to adopt the evolutionary point of view. (p. 95) . . . The individual mind could no longer be considered in the artificial isolation of the philosopher's study. . . . the developmental aspect of consciousness of behavior . . . could no longer be lost sight of. From now onwards, psychology was

related not only to philosophy . . . and to physiology . . . but to the general study of life. (p. 99)

Regarding biology:

507. Charles Singer, A *History of Biology to About the Year 1900*. 1959.

> The whole of modern biology has been called a commentary on *Origin of the Species* (1859), . . . the generations to which the *Origin* was delivered followed Darwin blindly. The last decade of the nineteenth century showed some reaction. This lasted until the discovery of Mendel's work (genetics) ushered in a new era. (p. 311)

On anthropology and the rise of evolutionary anthropological theory:

508. Marvin Harris, *The Rise of Anthropological Theory*. New York, 1968:

> Competition, progress, perfection, expansion, struggle, conquest—these were themes, dynamic and optimistic, which awaited a joining with the biological interpretation of history. The fusion of all these diverse elements into one grand scientific theory was the achievement of Herbert Spencer and Charles Darwin. (p. 105) . . . It is almost impossible to read [Darwin's] *Descent of Man* (1871) without being struck by its almost total advocacy of the struggle for survival as the means of understanding sociocultural evolution. (p. 120)

The labels Darwinism and Social Darwinism have prevailed since the nineteenth century among social scientists and in public opinion[50] as the identifying terminology for theories that link the biological determinations represented in Darwin's writings with the theoretical constructs that were employed in attempts to define sociocultural evolution. On the aims of Social Darwinists:

509. *Journal of the History of Ideas:* J. A. Rogers, "Darwinism and Social Darwinism," 33 (1972), 265–80. Rogers concludes that "Social Darwinism . . . wanted to view society through Darwin's vision of the animal world. . . . [and to have] Darwin's belief in biological progress linked to Spencer's belief in social progress" (p. 265).

The practical task of interpreting the translation of Darwinian thought into social theory has been and remains a complex undertaking. This question is explored in the superb study:

510. Gertrude Himmelfarb, *Darwin and the Darwinian Revolution*. New York, 1959; 1962. "It [*Origin*] did not revolutionize . . . beliefs so much as give public recognition to a revolution that had already occurred. It was belief made manifest, revolution legitimized" (p. 452, 1962 ed.).

and also in

511. *Philosophy of Science:* K. E. Bock, "Darwin and Social Theory," 22 (1955), 123–34. Bock asserts the "need of discriminating between perspectives that are blatantly Darwin ('biologism') and others that have subtler and more elusive roots" (p. 132).

This theme is closely detailed in the important book:

512. J. W. Burrow, *Evolution and Society: A Study in Victorian Social Theory.* 1966.

and in

513. Maurice Mandelbaum, *History, Man and Reason: A Study in Nineteenth Century Thought.* Baltimore, 1971.
514. *Victorian Studies:* Entire issue 3 (Sept. 1959); R. J. Halliday, "Social Darwinism: A Definition," 14 (1971), 388–405.

Notwithstanding the permeation of Darwinism in late nineteenth-century thought, conflict and controversy reigned among the anthropologists and sociologists as their theories and prescriptions irregularly accommodated or clashed with traditional views about mankind and social processes. Gertrude Himmelfarb has observed (entry 510):

In the spectrum of opinion that went under the name of Social Darwinism almost every variety of belief was included. . . . some complained because it exalted men to the level of supermen and gods; others because it degraded them to the state of animals. Political theorists read it as an assertion of the need for inequality . . . alternatively as an egalitarian tract. (p. 431)

A uniting principle, however, concerned the mutual aspiration to develop the social sciences into structured disciplines:

515. *American Historical Review:* R. N. Soffer, "The Revolution in English Social Thought, 1880–1914," 75 (1970), 1938–64.

from the 1880s until 1914 there was in England a genuine, vital revolution in the contents of methodology and purposes of social thought. An inductive behavioral science bent on effecting practical sociology overthrew deductive social theory that assumed inherent laws of human nature and society. (p. 1938)

But in:

516. *Journal of British Studies:* R. N. Soffer, "New Elitism: Social Psychology in Pre-War England," 8 (1969), 111–40:

> The social psychologists, like other social evolutionists, could not give up the idea of progress though it contradicted their analysis of human nature in society. (p. 126)

The theme and idea of "progress" permeates the writings of the mid- and late-nineteenth-century anthropological and sociological writings with important ramifications for questions about women. For example, when "the evolution" of matriarchal structures of early societies to the patriarchal forms of recent times was traced, the trend was invariably attributed to "advance in civilization." This and similar questions are the concern of Elizabeth Fee, who discusses social anthropological theory and its application in social thought:

517. *Feminist Studies:* E. Fee, "The Sexual Politics of Victorian Social Anthropology," 2 (1973), 23–40, rpr. in Hartman and Banner.

> Social anthropology demonstrated that the idealized family in the Victorian middle class was dictated by no law of nature, that monogamous marriage was only one of various human sexual possibilities, and that women were not necessarily born only to domestic and decorative functions. (p. 24)

But in reviewing the writings of Maine, Bachofen, McLennan, Lubbock, and Herbert Spencer, she concludes that the assertions of these early social scientists nevertheless assured that:

> patriarchalism was now inextricably linked with the progress of civilization; Victorian culture and its attendant social relations represented the capstone of all evolution. Male superiority, then, was sanctified not by nature but by civilization. (p. 38)

By the 1880's argumentation on questions of women's intellectual and physical nature as well as their domestic, social, and political roles (past and present) began to rely perhaps as much on social science investigations and findings as on the traditional outlook, religion, myth, irrational prejudice and socioeconomic status. The extent to which the new sciences preserved myths and beliefs is still not precisely estimated.[51] The first section of the bibliography (entries 147–71) includes nineteenth- and early twentieth-century sociological and statistical surveys representing the investigative aspect of sociological work that focused mainly on the need for amelioration of the social ills disclosed.[52] The following sections on social science relate almost exclusively to more theoretical developments in the various categories of study that are tied to questions about roles, status, and responsibility of Victorian and Edwardian women. Because the interests, attitudes, and techniques of the nineteenth- and early twentieth-century social scientists were generally so similar as to be overlapping, the subheadings that follow have been assigned for convenience and clarity more than accuracy. There is little resemblance between mid-twentieth-century social science disciplines and nineteenth-century counterparts. Limits of space allow only a brief listing, considering the number of sources available.

A. Anthropology and Sociology

518. Herbert Spencer: *Social Statics.* 1850. (*SBS,* 38). Endorses the idea that a society based upon individual freedom requires individual liberty of women. By the second edition, 1864, Spencer changed his view in accordance with theories of social and biological evolution; *Westminster Review:* "The Social Organism," 17 (1860), 90–121; *Principles of Biology.* New York, 1864; *The Study of Sociology.* New York, 1873; *Principles of Sociology.* 3 vols. 1876, 1904. See Vol. I, Part III, "Domestic Institutions." See also Robert Carneiro, *The Evolution of Society: Selections from Herbert Spencer's Principles of Sociology.* Chicago, 1967. Introduction.

519. J. J. Bachofen, *Das Mutterecht.* Stuttgart, 1861. On the early supremacy of women in early primitive societies. Claims that this "gynaecocracy" evolved to patriarchy. Friedrich Engels refers to this theory in his *Origin of the Family.* Entry 147. See also the translated edition of Bachofen: *Myth, Religion and Mother Right: Selected Writings.* Trans. R. Manheim. Princeton, 1967.

520. Henry Sumner Maine: *Ancient Law.* 1861. Claims that the patriarchal system was the original, universal social system;[53] *Quarterly Review:* "The Patriarchal Theory," 162 (1886), 181–209.

521. J. F. McLennan: *Primitive Marriage: An Inquiry into the Origin of the Form of Capture in Marriage Customs.* Edinburgh, 1865; *The Patriarchal Theory.* 1885.

522. John Lubbock: *Pre-Historic Times.* 1865; *Origin of Civilization and the Primitive Condition of Man.* 1870. Theory of wife capture.

523. Edward B. Tylor: *Researches into the Early History of Mankind.* 1865; *Primitive Culture.* 1871; *Nineteenth Century:* "The Matriarchal Family System," 40 (1896), 81–96.

524. Lewis Henry Morgan, *Ancient Society*. 1877.

525. Eliza Burt Gamble, *The Evolution of Women: An Inquiry into the Dogma of Her Inferiority to Man*. 1894. Rev. ed. Westport, Conn., 1975, entitled *The Sexes in Science and History*. A critique of Bachofen, Lubbock, McLennan, Morgan (all of whom she calls "naturalists") and Darwin's *The Descent of Man*.

526. Herman H. Ploss, Max Bartels, and Paul Bartels, *Woman: An Historical, Gynaecological and Anthropological Compendium*. 3 vols. 1885, 1887; 1927 (in German); ed. and trans. Eric Dingwall. 1935. Dingwall claims that this work was utilized in England from the first edition. It is a very valuable work with important photographic illustrations. Editions must be compared to comprehend additions and changes. Vol. 1 rpr. as *Femina Libido Sexualis*. New York, 1965. Vol. 3 has lengthy bibliography.

527. Emma H. Woodward, *Men, Women and Progress*. 1885. Ch. 14, "Women and Evolution."

528. *Sociological Papers*: E. Westermarck, "On the Position of Woman in Early Civilization," 1 (1905), 145–60. See also Westermarck on history of marriage, entry 167. This collection of *Papers* was published in three volumes, 1905–1907, by the Sociological Society of London, founded in 1903. Articles on eugenics will appear below.

529. L. T. Hobhouse, *Morals in Evolution*. 1906. Part I, Ch. 4, "Marriage and the Position of Women." Important sociologist of the period.

530. George Chatterton-Hill, *Heredity and Selection in Sociology*. 1907. Necessity of studying biology as a preliminary for sociology.

531. Agnes Grove, *The Human Woman*. 1908.

532. *Sociological Review*: S. K. Ratcliffe, "Sociology in the English Novel," 3 (1910), 126–35; G. Spiller, "Darwinism and Sociology," 7 (1914), 232–53.

533. E. J. Schuster, *The Wife in Ancient and Modern Times*. 1911.

534. Jean Finot, *Problems of the Sexes*. 1913. "According to Darwin, man is only a woman who has finished the cycle of her evolution."

535. Elsie W. Clews Parsons, *The Old-Fashioned Woman: Primitive Fancies about the Sex*. 1913. Social science comment.

536. C. Gasquoine Hartley, *The Truth about Woman*. 1913. See especially "Sexual Differences in Mind and the Artistic Impulse in Woman."

537. *Quarterly Review*: E. Colquhoun, "Modern Feminism and Sex-Antagonism," 219 (1913), 143–66. "The keynote of the new relations" is the word "individualism."

B. Evolutionary Biology

538. Jill Conway, "Stereotypes of Femininity in a Theory of Sexual Evolution," in Martha Vicinus, ed., *SBS*:

The guiding rule of the early social sciences ... required sociologists to develop their discipline on the basis of a biology in which the significance of sex differences was far from clear. (p. 140) . . . in the English interpretation of Weismann's *germ-plasm* theory we have a perfect case study of the way in which sexual stereotypes could be adapted to new scientific formulations. The inheritance of acquired characteristics [had] permitted Spencer to explain the existing stereotypes of female character, . . . [but] once environmental factors were removed (by Weismann) as major sources of variation, evolutionary theorists were compelled to look for other explanations of the supposed psychic differences between the sexes and other ways to explain . . . the inferiority of women. (p. 142)[54]

539. Elizabeth Fee, "Science and the Woman Problem: Historical Perspectives," in Michael S. Teitelbaum, ed., *Sex Differences: Social and Biological Perspectives*. New York, 1976.

Physical anthropologists also hewed to the evolutionary line. Seeking to measure comparative intelligence, they [developed] a "science" that came to be known as craniology. . . . Male brains developed considerably with civilization, while women's brains had grown only slowly. (p. 194) . . . During the 1890s, craniology investigation began to give way before . . . criticisms. . . . Laboratory testing . . . [measured] what human brains could do, rather than . . . what they weighed. (p. 208)

540. Patrick Geddes and J. Arthur Thompson, *The Evolution of Sex*. New York, 1880. A study of sex differentiation and its significance in social evolution. Describes the existing state of knowledge about how sex differences occur, leading to conclusions (mainly Geddes') on how the social position of women coincided with a preordained evolutionary design. Defends inheritance of acquired characteristics against Weismann's theory of germ-plasm, just being formed.

541. August Weismann: *Essays upon Heredity and Kindred Biological Problems*. Oxford, 1889; *The Germ-Plasm: A Theory of Heredity*. 1893. See entry 538 and note 54.

542. Harry Campbell, *Differences in the Nervous Organization of Man and Woman: Physiological and Pathological*. 1891.

543. *Popular Science Monthly:* "Biology and Woman's Rights," 14 (1878–79), 201–13; W. K. Brooks, "The Condition of Woman from a Zoological Point of View," 15 (1879), 145–55, 347–56; E. Delauney, "Equality and Inequality in Sex," 20 (1881–82), 184–92.

544. *Fortnightly Review:* C. Lombroso, "The Physical Insensibility of Woman," 57 (1892), 354–57.

545. *American Journal of Obstetrics:* R. T. Morris, "Is Evolution Trying to do Away with the Clitoris?" 26 (1892), 847–58.

546. *The Monist:* G. Ferrero, "The Problem of Woman, from the Bio-Sociological Point of View," 4 (1893–94), 261–74; L. Ward, "The Exemption of Women from Labor," 4 (1893–94), 385–95, answer to Ferrero.

547. *Liverpool Medical-Chirurgical Journal:* J. Oliver, "Women, Physically and Ethically Considered," 9 (1899), 219–26.

548. *Gunton's Magazine:* M. K. Sedgwick, "Some Scientific Aspects of the Woman Suffrage Question," 20 (1901), 333–34.

549. F. H. A. Marshall, *The Physiology of Reproduction.* 1910. Discusses controversies among biologists on sex characteristics.

550. J. Arthur Thomson, *The Position of Woman: Biologically Considered.* 1911.

551. W. Bateson, *Biological Fact and the Structure of Society.* Oxford, 1912.

552. Laurence Housman, *The 'Physical Force' Fallacy.* 1913.

553. Walter Heape, *Sex Antagonism.* 1913.

554. *Journal of Endocrinology:* G. W. Corner, "The Early History of the Oestrogenic Hormones," 31 (Feb. 1965), iii–xvii.[55]

555. *Past and Present:* R. M. Young, "Malthus and the Evolutionists: the Common Context of Biological and Society Theory," No. 43 (May 1969), 109–45.

556. F. G. Young, "The Evolution of Ideas about Animal Hormones," in Joseph Needham, ed., *Chemistry of Life.* Cambridge, 1970.

C. Science and Social Science Views of Woman's Mind and Nature

557. James Allan MacGrigor: *The Intellectual Severance of Men and Women.* 1860; *Anthropological Review:* "On the Real Differences in the Minds of Men and Women," 7 (1869), cxcv–ccxxi; *Woman Suffrage Wrong in Principle and Practice.* 1890.

558. Herbert Spencer, *Education: Intellectual, Moral and Physical.* 1861.[56]

559. *Journal of the Anthropological Society of London:* L. O. Pike, "On the Claims of Women to Political Power," 7 (1869), xlvii–lxi.

560. *Popular Science Monthly:* H. Spencer, "Psychology of the Sexes," 4 (1873–74), 30–38; G. T. W. Patrick, "The Psychology of Woman," 7 (1895), 209–25.

561. Edward Clark, *Sex in Mind and Education.* Boston, 1874. See also *American Quarterly:* J. L. Trecker, "Sex, Science and Education," 26 (1974), 352–66.

562. *Fortnightly Review:* H. Maudsley, "Sex in Mind and in Education," 21 (1874), 446–83; E. G. Anderson, "Sex in Mind and Education, A Reply," ibid., 582–94.

563. *Blackwood's Magazine:* H. Cowell, "Sex in Mind and Education, a Commentary," 115 (1874), 736–49.

564. Thomas S. Clouston, *Female Education from a Medical Point of View.* Edinburgh, 1882.

565. *International Review:* "The Intellectuality of Woman," 13 (1882), 123–36.

566. John Thorburn, *Female Education from a Physiological Point of View.* Manchester, 1884.

567. Henry Maudsley, *The Pathology of the Mind.* 1886. This is the 3rd ed. of the second part of *Physiology and Pathology of the Mind.* 1868, rev.

568. *Nineteenth Century:* G. J. Romanes, "Mental Differences Between Men and Women," 21 (1887), 654–72. Brain weight.
569. J. F. Nisbet, *Marriage and Heredity: A View of Psychological Evolution.* 1889. Unlike other acquired characteristics, mental states may be transmissible.
570. *Westminster Review:* A. Bulley, "The Political Evolution of Women," 134 (1890), 1–8.
571. *The Monist:* E. D. Cope, "On the Material Relations of Sex in Human Society," 1 (1890–91), 38–47.
572. *Lancet:* J. C. Browne, "An Oration on Sex in Education," 1 (1892), 1011–18.
573. Karl Pearson, *The Chances of Death and Other Studies in Evolution.* 2 vols. 1897. Anatomical statistics disproved relation between brain size and intelligence.
574. Laura Hansson, *Studies in the Psychology of Woman.* Chicago, 1899.
575. *Nineteenth Century:* A. Sutherland, "Woman's Brain," 47 (1900), 802–10.
576. L. T. Hobhouse, *Mind in Evolution.* 1901.
577. Alice E. Lee, *Data for the Problem of Evolution in Man. A First Study of the Correlation of the Human Skull.* 1901.
578. Helen Bradford Thompson, *Psychological Norms in Men and Women.* Chicago, 1903. See also Viola Klein, *The Feminine Character.* 1949. (*SBS,* entry 69), Chapter 6, "First Investigations in Experimental Psychology: Helen B. Thompson." Excellent discussion. (Hereafter Klein, *Feminine Character.*)
579. *Westminster Review:* J. Swinburne, "Feminine Mind Worship," 158 (1902), 187–98.
580. Charles G. Leland, *The Alternate Sex, or the Female Intellect in Man, and the Masculine in Woman.* 1904.
581. Emmet Densmore, *Sex Equality: A Solution to the Woman Problem.* 1907.

## D.   Eugenics and "Race Improvement"[57]

582. Francis Galton: *Hereditary Genius: An Inquiry into its Laws and Consequences.* 1869. On women: why their names are omitted here (p. 3). Female influence is inferior to that of the male in conveying ability through heredity. But "it appears to be very important to success in science that man should have an able mother"—her influence (p. 196); *Record of Family Faculties.* 1884. Traces ancestry to forecast the mental and bodily faculties of children and to further the science of heredity; *Natural Inheritance.* 1889. Marriage selection; *Eugenics: Its Definition, Scope and Aims.* 1905; *Foundations of Eugenics.* 1907. Urges improvement of the quality of man in society— society being "a complex organism, with a consciousness of its own."

583. *Contemporary Review:* G. Darwin, "On Beneficial Restrictions to Liberty in Marriage," 22 (1873), 412–26; F. Galton, "A Theory of Heredity," 27 (1875), 80–95; W. Hutchinson, "Evolutionary Ethics of Marriage and Divorce," 88 (1905), 397–410; S. S. Sprigge, "Mating and Medicine," 96 (1909), 578–87; H. S. Shelton, "Eugenics," 101 (1912), 84–95, considers the "state endowment of motherhood"; H. Ellis, "Eugenics and Genius," 104 (1913), 519–27.

584. *Nature:* J. L. Avebury, "Review of McLennan's Studies in Ancient History," 15 (1876), 133; F. Galton, "The Possible Improvement of the Human Breed," 64 (1901), 659–65.

585. *Fortnightly Review:* F. Galton, "Good and Bad Temper in English Families," 48 (1887), 21–30; A. R. Wallace, "Human Selection," 54 (1890), 325–37, anti-legislative eugenics. See entry 515, Soffer: "not without opposition did the eugenicists subvert theory and method to a priori exclusively elitist ends" (p. 1955); K. Pearson, "Woman and Labour," 61 (1894), 561–77, "A study of the more advanced women's journals . . . shows how deeply women are interested in problems of heredity"; J. Sully, "The New Study of Children," 64 (1895), 723–37; M. Crackenthorpe, "The Friends and Foes of Eugenics," 92 (1912), 740–48; E. Alec-Tweedie, "Eugenics," 97 (1912), 854–65.

586. G. A. Gaskell, *The Social Control of the Birth Rate and Endowment of Mothers.* 1890.

587. Victoria Woodhull, *The Rapid Multiplication of the Unfit.* 1891.

588. S. A. K. Strahan, *Marriage and Disease: A Study of Heredity and the More Important Family Degenerations.* New York, 1892.

589. Karl Pearson: "Variation in Man and Woman," in *Chances of Death* (entry 573), 1897. Refutes Havelock Ellis on this subject; *National Life from the Standpoint of Science.* 1905; *The Scope and Importance to the State of the Science of National Eugenics.* 1911; *The Problem of Practical Eugenics.* 1912; *Eugenics and Public Health.* 1912; *Darwinism, Medical Progress and Eugenics.* 1912; *The Groundwork of Eugenics.* 1912.

590. Robert R. Rentoul: *Race Culture: or, Race Suicide? A Plea for the Unborn.* 1906; *Proposed Sterilization of Certain Mental and Physical Degenerates.* 1913. Includes "sexual degeneracy," dypsomania.

591. *Sociological Papers:* F. Galton, "Eugenics: Its Definition, Scope and Aims," 1 (1905), 45–89; F. Galton, "Restrictions in Marriage," 2 (1906), 1–47; W. McDougall, "A Practicable Eugenic Suggestion," 3 (1907), 53–104.

592. Morrison I. Swift, *Marriage and Race Death.* New York, 1906.

593. C. W. Saleeby: *The Creed of Eugenics, Biology and History.* 1908; *Parenthood and Race Culture.* 1909; *Methods of Race-Regeneration.* 1911; *Woman and Womanhood: A Search for Principles.* 1912; *The Progress of Eugenics.* 1914.

594. John B. Haycraft, *Darwinism and Race Progress.* 1908.

595. *Eugenics Review:* J. W. Slaughter, "Selection in Marriage," 1 (1909–10), 150–62; M. Sharlieb, "Adolescent Girlhood Under Modern Conditions, with Special Reference to Motherhood," ibid., 174–83; A. Ravenhill, "Eugenic Ideals for Womanhood," ibid., 265–74; E. M. Hughes, "Sex Teaching in Girls' Schools," 2 (1910–11), 144–46; L. Murray, "Woman's Progress in Relation to Eugenics," ibid., 282–98; R. J. Ewart, "The Aristocracy of Infancy and the Conditions of Its Birth," 3 (1911–12), 143–75; R. D. Kingham, "Ellen Key's *Love and Marriage* from the Viewpoint of Eugenics," ibid., 178–79; A. F. Tredgold, "Marriage Regulation and National Family Records," 4 (1912–13), 74–90; L. Darwin, "Notes on the Report of the Royal Commission on Divorce and Matrimonial Causes," ibid., 363–72; M. R. Thomson, "Women and Eugenics: A Review of Olive Schreiner's *Woman and Labour,*" ibid., 307–12; A. M. Carr-Saunders, "A Criticism of Eugenics," 5 (1913–14), 316–42; J. A. Cobb, "The Problem of the Sex Ratio," 6 (1914–15), 157–63.

596. *Sociological Review:* G. Chatterton-Hill, "Race Progress and Race Degeneracy," 2 (1909), 140–51, 250–59; C. W. Saleeby, "Obstacles to Eugenics," ibid., 228–40, and E. M. D. Marvin, "Reply," 400–401; M. Atkinson, "The Feminist Movement and Eugenics," 3 (1910), 51–56; J. M. Tayler, "Heredity and the Social Outlook," 4 (1911), 131–40; J. A. Hobson, "Olive Schreiner: *Woman and Labour,*" ibid., 149; B. L. Hutchins, "The Position of Women, Active and Ideal," ibid., 360; L. T. Hobhouse, "The Value and Limitation of Eugenics," ibid., 281–302.

597. Sidney Webb, *Eugenics and the Poor Law.* 1909.

598. E. F. Pinsent, *Social Responsibility and Heredity.* 1910.

599. James A. Field, *The Progress of Eugenics.* Cambridge, Mass., 1911.

600. Havelock Ellis: *The Problem of Race-Regeneration.* New York, 1911; *The Task of Social Hygiene.* 1912. "The breeding of men lies largely in the hands of women."

601. *Lancet:* "The International Eugenic Congress," 2 (1911), 1345; J. G. Adami, "A Study in Eugenics: 'Unto the Third and Fourth Generation,'" 2 (1912), 1199–1204; "Darwinism, Medical Progress and Eugenics," ibid., 1525; L. Darwin, "The Need for Eugenic Reform," 2 (1913), 1324–25.

602. *Quarterly Review:* A. F. Tredgold, "The Study of Eugenics," 217 (1912), 43–67.

603. William C. W. Whetham and C. D. Whetham, *Heredity and Society.* 1912.

604. Mary Scharlieb, *Womanhood and Race Regeneration.* 1912.

605. John E. Gorst, *Education and Race Regeneration.* 1913.

606. Bernard Semmel, *Imperialism and Social Reform: English Social-Imperial Thought,* 1895–1914. 1960. Ch. 2, "Social Darwinism: Benjamin Kidd and Karl Pearson."[58]

## E.   Studies of Sex, Sexology

607. Russell T. Trall, *Sexual Physiology: A Scientific and Popular Exposition of the Fundamental Problems in Sociology*. Glasgow, 1866.
608. Elizabeth O. G. Willard, *Sexology as the Philosophy of Life: Implying Social Organization and Government*. Chicago, 1867.
609. Richard von Krafft-Ebing, *Psychopathia Sexualis* (trans. of 7th German ed., C. G. Chaddock). 1892. Recent editions to 1965.
610. Edward Carpenter: *Sex-Love, and Its Place in a Free Society*. Manchester, 1894; *Love's Coming of Age: A Series of Papers on the Relations of the Sexes*. Manchester, 1896; *The Intermediate Sex: A Study of Some Transitional Types of Men and Women*. 1908.
611. Havelock Ellis: *Man and Woman: A Study of Human Sexual Characters*. New York, 1894; *The Evolution of Modesty*. Leipzig, 1899; *Studies in the Psychology of Sex*. 7 vols. New York, 1897–1928; *My Life*. 1940; 1967. See also *Psychological Review:* D. G. Brinton, "Review: Havelock Ellis, *Man and Woman*," 1 (1894), 532–34; ibid. "Review: Havelock Ellis, *Evolution of Modesty*," 6 (1899), 134–45; Isaac Goldberg, *Havelock Ellis: A Biographical and Critical Study*. 1926; Viola Klein, *Feminine Character*. Ch. 3, "The Biological Approach: Havelock Ellis"; *Encounter:* V. Brome, "Sigmund Freud and Havelock Ellis," 12 (1959), 46–53; ibid. A. Calder-Marshall, "Havelock Ellis and Company: Lewd, Scandalous and Obscene," 37 (1971), 8–23. Ellis's orientation was biological and anthropological. His insights were based on scholarship, on self-study, and on his experiences with women while he was a hospital student on midwifery duty. Ellis regarded sex as the "central problem of life."
612. J. Arthur Thomson and Patrick Geddes: *Moral Evolution of Sex*. 1896; *Problems of Sex*. 1911. Important reference.
613. John Allen Godfrey, *The Science of Sex: An Essay Towards the Practical Solution of the Sex Problem*. 1901.
614. James Foster Scott, *The Sexual Instinct: Its Use and Dangers as Affecting Heredity and Morals*. New York, 1902.
615. William H. Walling, *Sexology*. 1904.
616. Otto Weininger, *Sex and Character*. 1906. See also Klein, *Feminine Character*. Ch. 4, "A Philosophical Approach: Otto Weininger."
617. William I. Thomas, *Sex and Society: Studies in the Social Psychology of Sex*. Chicago, 1907. See also Klein, *Feminine Character*. Ch. 10, "A Sociological Approach: W. I. Thomas."
618. August Forel: *The Sexual Question: A Scientific, Psychological, Hygienic and Sociological Study for the Cultured Classes*. 2nd rev. English adaptation. 1908; *Sexual Ethics*. 1908.
619. Ernest Rumley Dawson, *The Causation of Sex: A New Theory of Sex, Based on Clinical Materials*. 1909.

620. E. H. Kirch, *The Sexual Life of Woman in Its Physiological, Pathological and Hygienic Aspects.* Trans. Eden Paul. 1910. Influential work
of the period.
621. *Psychological Bulletin:* H. Thompson Wooley, "A Review of the Recent
Literature on the Psychology of Sex," 7 (1910), 335–42.
622. Friedrich W. Foerster, *Marriage and the Sex Problem.* Trans. Meyrick
Booth. 1911.
623. Walter Heape, *Sex-Antagonism.* 1913.
624. Robert Michels, *Sexual Ethics: A Study of Borderland Questions.* 1914.
625. F. W. Stella Browne, *Sexual Variety and Variability among Women,
and their Bearing Upon Social Reconstruction.* [1915.] For the British
Society for the Study of Sex Psychology, formed 1914, pub. no. 3.
626. Laurence Housman, *The Relation of Fellow-Feeling to Sex.* [1917.]
British Society for the Study of Sex Psychology, pub. no. 4.
627. Magnus Hirschfeld, *The Sexual History of the World War.* New York,
1934.
628. H. L. Beales and Edward Glover, "Victorian Ideas of Sex," in Harman
Grisewood, *Ideas and Beliefs of the Victorians.* 1949.
629. Peter T. Cominos, "Innocent Femina Sensualis in Unconscious Conflict," in Martha Vicinus, ed., *SBS.*[59]
630. R. S. Neale, "Middle Class Morality and the Systematic Colonizers,"
in Neale's *Class and Ideology in the Nineteenth Century.* 1972. Critical
of Steven Marcus' and Peter Cominos' approach to questions of sexuality, entry 50.

F.  Early Twentieth-Century Psychoanalysis
and Psychiatry: Beginnings[60]

631. Josef Breuer and Sigmund Freud: *Studies on Hysteria.* Trans. A. A.
Brill. New York, 1912, from the 1885 German ed.; also trans. by
James Strachey in collaboration with Anna Freud, 1957. Usually
considered the starting point of psychoanalysis.
632. Sigmund Freud: *Selected Papers on Hysteria and Other Psycho-
neuroses.* Trans. A. A. Brill. New York, 1909; *Three Contributions to
the Sexual Theory.* Trans. A. A. Brill from the 1905 German ed. 1910;
also trans. as: *Three Essays on the Theory of Sexuality* by James
Strachey. 1949; 1962.
633. Thomas D. Savill, *Lectures on Hysteria.* 1909.
634. *Brain:* J. A. Ormerod, "Two Theories of Hysteria," 33 (1911), 269–
87; B. Hart, "Freud's Conception of Hysteria," ibid., 339–66.
635. Bernard Hart (and other contributors): *Subconscious Phenomena.*
1911; *The Psychology of Insanity.* 1912. Objectifies "prudery" and
other Victorian attitudes, and interprets in psychological terms the
phenomena behind them. Represents the beginning of modern psychological explanation.

636. *Lancet:* "Modern Views of Hysteria," 1 (1911), 951–52; F. W. Mott, "Heredity and Insanity," ibid., 1251–59; F. P. Weber, "The Association of Hysteria with Malingering: The Phylogenetic Aspects of Hysteria as Pathological Exaggeration of Tertiary Sex Characters," 2 (1911), 1542–43; "Review: *Selected Papers . . .* by Sigmund Freud," 1 (1913), 1105; "Discussion: The Medical Society of London on the Treatment of Neurasthenia," 2 (1913), 1469–72, 1542–44, 1557–58.

637. *The Practitioner:* Constance E. Long, "Psychoanalysis," 93 (1914), 84–97.

638. Ernest Jones: *Papers on Psychoanalysis.* New York, 1916; *Free Associations: Memories of a Psychoanalyst.* New York, 1959.

639. Joseph Jastrow, *Freud: His Dream and Sex Theories.* New York, 1932; 1948. See also Klein, *Feminine Character,* Ch. 5, "The Psychoanalytical Approach: Sigmund Freud"; also Gregory Zilboorg, *Sigmund Freud: His Exploration of the Mind of Man.* 1951; Fritz Wittels, *Freud and His Time.* 1956; Philip Reiff, *Freud: The Mind of the Moralist.* New York, 1959; Vincent Brome, *Freud and His Early Circle: The Struggles of Psychoanalysis.* 1967. See appendix: "Havelock Ellis and Freud."

640. *Bulletin of the History of Medicine:* W. Riese, "An Outline of a History of Ideas in Psychotherapy," 25 (1951), 442–56.

641. *International Record of Medicine:* W. Riese, "The Impact of Nineteenth Century Thought on Psychiatry," 173 (1960), 7–19. The importance played by "evolutionary thought."

642. Franz Alexander, S. Eisenstein, M. Grotjahn, eds., *Psychoanalytic Pioneers.* 1966. See Edward Glover, "Psychoanalysis in England."

463. Jean Baker Miller, ed., *Psychoanalysis and Women.* 1973. Critical, psychoanalytic approach by a practicing psychiatrist.

644. Juliet Mitchell, *Psychoanalysis and Feminism.* 1974. Valuable, balanced evaluation. Includes historical background. See review: *New York Review of Books:* C. Lasch, "Freud and Women," 21 (Oct. 3, 1974), 12–17. See comment also on the anthology: Jean Strouse, ed., *Women and Analysis: Dialogues on Psychoanalytic Views of Femininity.* New York, 1974.

## IV  *Organizations: Protection, Solidarity and Reform*[61]

Throughout the nineteenth century, women's names appeared on lists of subscribers to charitable organizations and in the membership roles of associations and societies representing a wide variety of causes and interests. The question of women's active participation in philanthropic groups is raised in:

645. *International Review of Social History:* F. K. Prochaska, "Women in English Philanthropy, 1790–1830," 19 (1974), 426–45:

> there is no reason to suppose that women were more often inactive than their male counterparts. . . . Leisured women were the backbone of the expanding system of district visiting, and it might be argued that the system would have been unworkable without them. . . . In the early decades of the nineteenth century women worked all over England in lying-in charities, asylums for the deaf, blind, destitute, and insane, soup kitchens. . . . (p. 431)

Concerning women's charities that focused upon aiding, reforming, and "rescuing" discharged women prisoners, destitute or "delinquent" girls, and prostitutes, see:

646. S. Barbara Kanner, "Victorian Institutional Patronage: Angela Burdett-Coutts, Charles Dickens and Urania Cottage, Reformatory for Women, 1846–1858," Ph.D. diss., Univ. of California, Los Angeles, 1972. See also: *SBS*, entries 115–18; 120–30; 133–97; 204; 214–27; 230; 234–35.

Charitable societies of the early nineteenth century invariably maintained ties to organized religion.[62] See:

647. *The Historical Journal:* O. Anderson, "Women Preachers in Mid-Victorian Britain: Some Reflexions on Feminism, Popular Rebellion, and Social Change," 12 (1969), 467–84.

See also:

648. Michael Hill, *The Religious Order.* 1973. Ch. 9, "The Role of Women in Victorian Society: Sisterhoods, Deaconnesses and the Growth of Nursing."

> sisterhoods in this sense are the first signs of incipient feminism among women of the middle class. One of the most frequent Protestant accusations against sisterhoods . . . was that they were exerting a subversive influence on familial authority. . . . There were, at the same time, widely perceived demographic factors which made some form of autonomous role for women an urgent necessity. . . . The relationship between sisterhoods and secular female occupations is one of mutual reinforcement. (pp. 10–11)

Michael Hill discusses the relationship between "changes in secular role-definition" (p. 271) for Victorian women and the roles and organized activities these women assumed under religious auspices. Changing secular role-definition may perhaps be understood best as a response to great changes in socioeconomic, demographic, and environmental conditions that accompanied the rapid growth of population, cities, and industry, as well as more liberal trends in government and in social ideas about individual liberty. The growth and development of voluntary organizations may be seen as responses to the same set of circumstances. Increasingly, over the century, women became members of established organizations or they founded groups of their own. The goal of ameliorating defined social problems was widely articulated by some women's groups, while others were openly implementing the expanding opportunities for women in employment and in public life. The publications of the organizations in which women were active reveal that, invariably, dominant social attitudes were incorporated into organizational goals and methods. A good example is the expressed concern within many of these groups with questions about cleanliness and abhorrence of disease and disease-related behavior—particularly prostitution. Societies promoting sanitation and public health tended to incorporate ideas of "social hygiene" as well as "social purity" so that social reform and moral reform were very often closely related. Relevant also were the ideas publicized by eugenicists interested in "race-regeneration" and the practices advocated by the many medical specialists who recommended the development of moral attitudes along with their suggested health regimens.

The following listing represents a very small sampling of associations, societies, leagues, guilds, and alliances to which both married and unmarried Victorian and Edwardian women of the various social classes donated their time and energies. An important question that remains largely unattended is the illogical concurrence, in writings about this period, of the stereotype of "the idle middle-class woman" and factual details of the very large number of organizations that demanded and received the services of this same segment of the female population.

A.   Labor and Professional Organizations

649. Society of Female Artists (Society, of Lady Artists): *Catalogue of First to Fifty-First Exhibition.* 1857–1906.
650. Women's Trade Union League (Women's Protective and Provident League): *Annual Reports.* 1875–1921; *The Women's Union Journal,* 1876–1890; Quarterly Report and Review. 1891; *The Women's Trade*

*Union Review (journal), 1891–1919;* G. M. Tuckwell, *Women's Opportunity.* 1906.

651. Women's Co-operative Guild: Public Papers (series). Manchester, 1897; R. Nash, *Reduction of Hours of Work for Women.* 1898; I. O. Ford, *Women as Factory Inspectors and Certifying Surgeons.* (Investigation Papers.) 1898; Margaret L. Davies, *The Women's Co-Operative Guild, 1883–1904.* Kirkby Lonsdale. 1904; Margaret Bonfield, *The National Care of Maternity.* 1915; see also Catherine Webb, *The Woman with a Basket: The History of the Women's Co-Operative Guild, 1883–1927.* Manchester, 1927.

652. National Union of Women Workers of Great Britain and Ireland (Central Conference of Women Workers, Central Conference of the National Union of Women Workers): *Official Report of the Central Conference of Women Workers, 1893.* Leeds. 1894; *Report of the Annual Meeting of the General Committee of the National Union of Women Workers.* 1895; *Handbook and Report, 1910/11–1949/50.* 1911–50.

653. Women's Industrial Council: *The Women's Industrial News* (journal), 1895–1919; *London Borough Councils and the Welfare of Women Workers.* 1903; *Technical Education for Women and Girls.* 1905; L. W. Papworth and D. M. Zimmern, *Women in Industry: A Bibliography.* 1915; Clementina Black, ed., *Married Women's Work.* 1915. See also Leonore Davidoff, "The Employment of Married Women in England and Wales, 1850 to 1950," M.A. thesis, Univ. of London, 1956.

654. Guild of Women Binders: *Bookbinding by Women.* 1898; *Catalogue of Bindings by the Guild of Women-Binders.* 1900; *The Bindery that Jill Built.* 1901; see also Joyce M. Bellamy and John Sackville, *Dictionary of Labour Biography.* 1972; Lee Holcombe, *Victorian Ladies at Work.* Camden, Conn., 1973. Excellent study of middle-class working women. Includes information about women's organizations.


B. Temperance Organizations


655. National Temperance League: *Women's Work in the Temperance Reformation: Being Papers Prepared for a Ladies Conference Held in London, May 26, 1868 with an Introduction by Mrs. S. C. Hall.* 1868; *The Ladies National Temperance Convention of 1876.* 1876; R. Rae, ed., *The National Temperance League Annual for 1880.* 1881; *The Temperance Record* (journal), 1903–1907.

656. British Women's Temperance Association: *Annual Reports* [from] *1876–7; The British Women's Temperance Journal, 1886–1892,* continued as *Wings 1892–1925* (also the official journal from 1903 of the Women's Total Abstinence Union); Louisa Stewart and Jessie A. Fowler, eds., *Memoir of Margaret Bright Lucas, President of the*

British Women's Temperance Association. 1890. See also Brian Harrison: *Drink and The Victorians: The Temperance Question in England, 1815–1872;* "State Intervention and Moral Reform," in Patricia Hollis, ed., *Pressure from Without in Early Victorian England.* 1974. Hereafter Brian Harrison, "State Intervention."

## C. Clubs for Girls and Women

657. Metropolitan Association for Befriending Young Servants (M.A.B.Y.S.): *Report, 1875.* 1877.
658. Girls' Friendly Society (G.F.S.): C. J. Hawksley, G.F.S. *What Does It Mean?* 1883; *Friendly Work (journal), 1883–1894;* S. M. Hill, *Our Work and Its Fame.* 1891; A. L. Money, *History of the Girls' Friendly Society.* 1897; *Friendly Work for Friendly Workers.* 1902. See also *Past and Present:* Brian Harrison, "For Church, Queen and Family: The Girls' Friendly Society, 1874–1920," No. 61 (1973), 107–38.
659. Young Women's Christian Association (Y.W.C.A.): *Our Own Gazette (and Y.W.C.A. News) 1884–1928; The Time and Talent News, 1891–1911; Our Outlook (journal), 1908–1919.*
660. Women's Institute: Mrs. Phillipps, *Dictionary of Employments Open to Women.* 1898. See also J. W. Robertson Scott, *The Story of the Women's Institute Movement.* Idbury, Kingham, Oxon, 1925.
661. Federation of Working Girls' Clubs (Factory Helpers' Union), *Girls' Club Journal, 1909–16;* see also Maude Stanley: *Nineteenth Century:* "Clubs for Working Girls," 25 (1889), 73–83; *Clubs for Working Girls.* 1890.
662. Mothers' Union: C. M. Hallet, *How to Begin and Carry on a Branch of the Mothers' Union.* 1909; M. Palmer, *Mothers' Union Work.* 1910.

## D. Anti-Contagious Diseases Acts Organizations[63]

663. Ladies National Association for the Repeal of the Contagious Diseases Acts: *Manifesto.* 1869. Also printed in *Daily News:* December 11, 1869; *First Annual Report of the Ladies National Association.* 1870. *Reports* continuous to 1915; Josephine Butler, *An Appeal to My Countrymen.* 1870; see also Millicent Fawcett and E. M. Turner, *Josephine Butler, Her Work, Principles and Their Meaning for the Twentieth Century.* 1927; J. L. and Barbara Hammond, *James Stansfeld: A Victorian Champion of Sex Equality.* 1932; Glen Petrie, *A Singular Iniquity.* 1971; *Bulletin of the Society for the Study of Labour History:* Jean L'Esperance, "Middle-Class Women, Working-Class Men and Working-Class Women: A Case Study of the Campaign to Repeal the Contagious Diseases Acts," No. 26 (Spring 1973),

9–14; Judith R. Walkowitz, "'We Are Not Beasts of the Field': Prostitution and the Campaign Against the Contagious Diseases Acts, 1869–1886," Ph.D. diss., Univ. of Rochester, 1974. A valuable study of the Acts and the campaign in sociohistorical context. Excellent bibliography; Brian Harrison: "State Intervention"; "Josephine Butler" in J. F. C. Harrison, B. Taylor, and I. Armstrong, eds., *Eminently Victorian.* 1974.

664. National Vigilance Association for the Defence of Personal Rights and for the Amendment of the Law in Points Wherein it is Injurious to Women: *Annual Reports, 1871–1885; The Factory [Health of Women] Bill.* 1874; *Journal of the Vigilance Association in Defence of Personal Rights, 1881–1886.* Continued as *Personal Rights Journal, 1886–1903;* William Shaen, *The Protection of Young Girls: Observations on the Report of the Select Committee of the House of Lords, on the Law Relating to the Protection of Young Girls in England.* 1882. See also W. A. Coote, *A Romance of Philanthropy: Being a Record of Some of the Principal Incidents Connected with the Exceptionally Successful Thirty Years of the National Vigilance Association.* 1916.

E.  "Social Purity" Societies

665. The Social Purity Alliance: *Annual Reports, 1873–1890.*
666. Moral Reform Union: *Annual Reports, 1882–1897.* See also Brian Harrison, "State Intervention."

F.  Suffrage Organizations

667. National Society for Women's Suffrage: *First–Sixteenth Annual Reports.* Manchester, 1868–1883; *Opinions of Women on Women's Suffrage.* 1877; *The Work of the Central Committee: A Sketch.* Westminster, 1893; *Opinions of Leaders of Religious Thought on Women's Suffrage.* 1896.
668. National Union of Women's Suffrage Societies: *Report of the Annual Meeting.* Westminster, 1889–1916; *The Common Cause* (journal), 1909–1918; Margaret Robertson, *Working Men and Woman Suffrage.* 1912; Millicent Garrett Fawcett, *Women's Suffrage: A Short History of a Great Movement.* 1911; F. C. Ring, *Women's Suffrage and Temperance.* 1913; *A Brief Review of the Women's Suffrage Movement Since Its Beginning in 1832.* 1913; See also Ray Strachey: *Women's Suffrage and Women's Service: The History of the London National Society for Women's Service.* 1927; *Millicent Garrett Fawcett.* 1931.[64]
669. Women's Social and Political Union (National Women's Social and Political Union): *Annual Report 1907–1914; Annual Conference Re-*

port *1905–1907; Votes for Women* (journal), 1907–18; *The Suffragette* (journal) 1912–15. See also: *SBS entries* 466, 475–76, 483, 494–98; Antonia Raeburn, *Militant Suffragettes.* 1973; *Contemporary Review:* T. F. Hale, "F. W. Pethick-Lawrence and the Suffragettes," 225 (1974), 83–89; Andrew Rosen, *Rise Up Women: The Militant Campaign of the W.S.P.U., 1903–1914.* 1975. The best modern history of this organization.

670. Women's Freedom League: *The Vote* (journal), 1909–33; Margaret Bondfield and Teresa Billington-Greig, *Sex Equality vs. Adult Suffrage.* 1907; Teresa Billington-Greig and Maude Fitzherbert, eds., *Women's Freedom League Occasional Papers.* 1909; F. W. Pethick-Lawrence, *Women's Fight for the Vote.* 1910; Teresa Billington-Greig, *The Militant Suffrage Movement.* 1911; Charlotte Despard, *Woman in the Nation.* 1913; Marion Holmes, *A.B.C. of Votes for Women.* 1913. See also Stella Newsome, *Women's Freedom League, 1907–1957.* 1957; David Morgan, *Suffragists and Liberals: The Politics of Woman Suffrage in England.* 1974.

## G. Other Organizations

671. Newcastle Ladies' Anti-Slavery Association: *A Concise View of Colonial Slavery.* 1830.

672. Bristol and Clifton Ladies' Anti-Slavery Society: *Special Report from January 1851 to June 1852.* 1852.

673. Reformatory and Refuge Union: *Fifty Years of Child-Saving and Reformatory Work, 1856–1906.* 1906.

674. Ladies' Sanitary Association: E. S. Griffiths, *Sketch of the Work of the Ladies' Sanitary Association from Its Commencement in October 1857 to December 1865.* 1865; *Annual Reports, First through Thirty-Eighth, 1857–1894.* 1894; *Report of the Ladies' Sanitary Association to the Seventh International Congress of Hygiene and Demography.* 1891; *Fraser's Magazine:* W. Richardson, "Woman as a Sanitary Reformer," 102 (1880), 667–83.

675. National Union for Improving the Education of Women of All Classes: *Journal of the Women's Education Union.* 1873–81.

676. The Malthusian League: *The Malthusian* (journal). 1879–1921: A. Vickery, "Certain Points in Which the Population Difficulty Affects the Life and Happiness of Women," 8 (1916), 52–54; "Eleventh Annual Meeting of the Malthusian League: Speeches by Mrs. Annie Besant, Dr. Alice Vickery, Mrs. Snowden, Miss Thornton Smith, Mr. Hember and Others," 10 (1888), 50–52; Pamphlets, Leaflets, Tracts. 1885–1915.

677. Salvation Army: *Heathen England.* 1879; *War Cry* (journal). 1880 to the present; *Sowing and Reaping: Being a Review of the Salvation Army in 1897.* 1898; W. T. Stead, *Mrs. Booth of the Salvation Army.*

1900; *Betsy Bobbet . . . Being the Annual Report of the Women's Society and Rescue Work of the Salvation Army.* 1905; see also Pamela Search, *Salvation Century, 1864–1964.* 1964; Bernard Watson, *A Hundred Years' War.* 1964.

678. British Women's Emigration Society: Mrs. Joyce, *Emigrant's Rest for Women and Children.* 1887; *The Imperial Colonist: Organ of the British Women's Emigration Society and the South African Expansion Committee* (journal), 1902–1927.

679. National Society for the Prevention of Cruelty to Children (Children's League of Pity): *The Children's League of Pity Paper: 1893–1911; The Ways of Child Torturers, Illustrated.* 1909. See also Leslie George Housden, *The Prevention of Cruelty to Children.* 1955.

680. Child Study Society (British Child Study Association): *The Paidologist* (journal), 1899–1907; *Proceedings of the Hampton Wick Conference, June 24, 1902.* 1902; *Child Study* (journal), 1908–1920.

# *Notes*

## INTRODUCTION
### New Trends in the Study of the Victorian Woman

1. One of the principal difficulties in analyzing Victorian domesticity is the variety of conflicting sources, which were often more prescriptive than descriptive of actual conditions. For a discussion of middle-class married women, based upon household manuals, health guides, and etiquette books, see Patricia Branca, *Silent Sisterhood: Middle Class Women in the Victorian Home* (Pittsburgh: Carnegie-Mellon University Press, 1975).

2. See the groundbreaking work by J. F. C. Harrison, *Robert Owen and the Owenites in Britain and America* (London: Routledge and Kegan Paul, 1969) for a discussion of women leaders of millennial sects. See also Olive Anderson, "Women Preachers in Mid-Victorian Britain: Some Reflexions on Feminism, Popular Rebellion, and Social Change," *The Historical Journal*, 12 (1969), 467–84.

3. See, however, Elizabeth Fee, "The Sexual Politics of Victorian Social Anthropology," *Clio's Consciousness Raised*, eds. Mary Hartman and Lois W. Banner (New York: Harper and Row, 1974), pp. 86–102.

4. For a discussion of the impact of the rise in the total number of servants during the nineteenth century, see J. A. Banks, *Prosperity and Parenthood: A Study of Family Planning among the Victorian Middle Classes* (London: Routledge and Kegan Paul, 1954), pp. 70–102, and *Annals of Labour: Autobiographies of British Working Class People, 1820–1920* (Bloomington: Indiana University Press, 1974), pp. 135–74.

5. J. A. and Olive Banks, *Feminism and Family Planning in Victorian England* (Liverpool: Liverpool University Press, 1964), p. 27.

## 1.  VICTORIAN WIVES AND PROPERTY
### Reform of the Married Women's Property Law, 1857–1882

1. Great Britain, Hansard, *Parliamentary Debates*, 3rd Series, cxcv, 765—hereafter referred to as Hansard with the series number preceding the

name and the volume and column numbers following; Frances Power Cobbe, *Life of Frances Power Cobbe by Herself* (London: Richard Bentley, 1894), II, pp. 70–71.

2. Millicent Garrett Fawcett, *What I Remember* (New York: Putnam, 1925), p. 62.

3. So far as I know, there are only two works that deal with married women's property rights in historical and nontechnical terms. One is the excellent study by A. V. Dicey published in his *Lectures on the Relation between Law and Public Opinion in England during the Nineteenth Century* (London: Macmillan, 1920). The other is Mary Beard's somewhat mistitled *Woman as Force in History, A Study in Traditions and Realities* (New York: Macmillan, 1946), which deals at length, *inter alia*, with the law affecting married women's property, especially on the American scene, and accuses feminists of misunderstanding or at least misstating the law. Beard fails, I think, to do justice to this subject for two reasons. First, she does not give due weight to the fact that the language and the underlying assumptions of the common law were a powerful psychological depressant to women. Second, she does not study in detail the extent to which equity had in practice superseded the common law, and therefore fails to prove her contention that the common law did not in fact inflict great material injury upon married women. I believe that it was both the psychological burden of the law and the practical hardships arising under it that stirred up feminists to fight for reform in the United States, as in England.

There are a good number of specialized legal treatises on the property rights of married women generally and on the Married Women's Property Acts individually, among which the following may be mentioned: Otto Kahn-Freund, "Matrimonial Property and Equality before the Law, Some Sceptical Reflections," *Revue des droits de l'homme*, IV (1971), 493–510; H. Lesser, "Acquisition of *inter vivos* Matrimonial Property Rights in English Law, A Doctrinal Melting Pot," *University of Toronto Law Journal*, XXIII (1973), 148–214; Joseph Haworth Redman, *A Concise View of the Law of Husband and Wife as Modified by the Married Women's Property Acts* . . . (London: Reeves and Turner, 1883); and Sir Arthur Underhill, *The Law Reform (Married Women and Tortfeasors) Act 1935 and the Unrepealed Sections of the Married Women's Property Acts 1882 to 1908 as Amended* (London: Butterworth, 1936).

There are, in addition, a good number of works that deal with the legal status of women generally and which include material on the law relating to married women's property, among them: James Bryce, "Marriage and Divorce under Roman and English Law," in his *Studies in History and Jurisprudence* (New York: Oxford University Press, 1901), II, 782–859; *A Century of Family Law, 1857–1957*, ed. R. H. Graveson and F. R. Crane (London: Sweet and Maxwell, 1957); Arthur Rackham Cleveland, *Woman under the English Law* . . . (London: Hurst and Blackett, 1896); Sir Alfred Denning, "The Rights of Women," in his *The Changing Law* (London: Stevens and Sons, 1953), and *The Equality of Women* (Liverpool: Liverpool University Press, 1960); Olive W. Stone, "The Status of Women in Great Britain," *American Journal of Comparative Law*, XX (1972), 592–621; Richard Lawrence Travers, *Husband and Wife in English Law* (London: Duckworth, 1956); Moss Turner-Samuels, *The Law of Married Women* (London: Thames Bank, 1957); and J. J. S. Wharton, *Exposition of the*

*Laws relating to the Women of England* . . . (London: Longman, Brown, Green and Longmans, 1853).

Finally, works on the history of English law in general are helpful in studying the changing legal position of women in historical perspective. A classic is Sir William Holdsworth's monumental *History of English Law* (London: Methuen and Boston: Little, Brown, 1923–66).

4. Holdsworth, I, 262–63, 443–45, 634–38, 646–49, IX, 375, XV, 103–4, 125–38, 176–79, 205; Edward Jenks, *A Short History of English Law* . . . (6th ed., London: Methuen, 1949), pp. 192, 218, 246–47, 250–66, 295–98, 306, 311, 314–18, 347–88.

5. The description of the married women's property law that follows is a greatly abbreviated and simplified account of a very complex body of law. For it I have drawn heavily on the works cited in note 3.

6. Special Report from the Select Committee on the Married Women's Property Bill, British Parliamentary Papers, 1867–68, VII, 365–67, 420; hereafter this report is referred to as Select Committee on Married Women's Property Bill with appropriate page numbers, and the Parliamentary Papers are referred to as *P.P.* with appropriate dates and volume and page numbers; 3 Hansard, CXCI, 1023; "The Political Disabilities of Women," *Westminster Review*, XCVII (1872), 60.

7. "The Legal Position of Women and Its Moral Effects," *Meliora*, VIII (1865), 93–102; Cobbe, II, 213–14; Frances Power Cobbe, *Criminals, Idiots, Women and Minors. Is the Classification Sound? A Discussion on the Laws concerning the Property of Married Women* (Manchester, 1869).

8. See Alice Acland, *Caroline Norton* (London: Constable, 1948); Jane Gray Perkins, *The Life of Mrs. Norton* (London: John Murray, 1910); David Cecil, *Melbourne* (Indianapolis: Bobbs-Merrill, 1954), pp. 219–31 and passim; and Clarke Olney, "Caroline Norton to Lord Melbourne," *Victorian Studies*, VIII (1965), 255–62.

9. See Hester Burton, *Barbara Bodichon, 1827–1891* (London: John Murray, 1949); Barbara Stephen, *Emily Davies and Girton College* (London: Constable, 1927); Matilda Betham-Edwards, *Mid-Victorian Memories* (London: John Murray, 1919), and *Reminiscences* (London: George Redway, 1898); and Evelyn Sharp, *Hertha Ayrton, 1854–1923, A Memoir* (London: Edward Arnold, 1926).

10. See, for example, the largely unfavorable comment by Margaret Oliphant, "The Laws concerning Women," *Blackwood's Edinburgh Magazine,* LXXIX (1856), 379–87 (authorship per *Wellesley Index*), and the sympathetic article by Caroline Frances Cornwallis, "Capabilities and Disabilities of Women," *W.R.*, LXVII (1857), 42–72 (authorship per *D.N.B.*).

11. Caroline Frances Cornwallis, "The Property of Married Women, Report of the Personal Laws Committee (of the Law Amendment Society) . . . ," *W.R.*, LXVI (1856), 331–60 (authorship per *D.N.B.*); Burton, pp. 40–41, 61–65; Stephen, pp. 40–41.

12. Burton, pp. 59–60, 66–70; Stephen, pp. 41–43; Ray Strachey, *"The Cause," A Short History of the Women's Movement in Great Britain* (London; G. Bell and Sons, 1928), pp. 71–73; "Property of Married Women," *English Woman's Journal*, I (1858), 58–59.

13. Strachey, p. 73; "Property of Married Women," *E.W.J.*, I, 58–59; 3 Hansard, CXLI, 120–21; Mary Howitt, *Mary Howitt, An Autobiography,* edited by Margaret Howitt (Boston and New York: Houghton Mifflin,

1889), II, 116. The petition is printed in Burton, pp. 70–71, and in Cornwallis, "The Property of Married Women," pp. 336–38.

14. *The Times,* 2 June 1856; Burton, p. 63; Stephen, p. 41; 3 Hansard, CXLII, 1273–84.

15. *Speech of Sir Thomas Erskine Perry at the Annual Meeting of the Married Women's Property Committee, 4th February 1880* (Manchester, 1880).

16. 3 Hansard, CXLVII, 373–415, 718–75, 1226–67, 1534–1603, 1717–60, 1785–1851, 1866–90. See O. R. McGregor, *Divorce in England, 1857–1957* (London: Heinemann, 1957).

17. 3 Hansard, CXCII, 1371; Select Committee on Married Women's Property Bill, 365, 376, 415, 419, 421, 424, 426, 429; *P.P.,* 1862, XLIV, 515–16.

18. "Property of Married Women," *E.W.J.,* I, 59; Strachey, pp. 75–76, 89; Burton, p. 72.

19. References to Mr. and Mrs. Jacob Bright occur frequently in contemporary accounts, but I do not know of a biography of either. The *D.N.B.* contains a brief sketch of Jacob Bright.

20. Schools Inquiry Commission, *P.P.,* 1867–68, XXVIII, Part 4, Minutes of Evidence, pp. 740–47; Elizabeth C. Wolstenholme, "The Education of Girls, Its Present and Its Future," in *Woman's Work and Woman's Culture, A Series of Essays,* ed. Josephine E. Butler (London: Macmillan, 1869), pp. 290–330; Helen Blackburn, *Women's Suffrage, A Record of the Women's Suffrage Movement in the British Isles with Biographical Sketches of Miss Becker* (London: Williams and Norgate, 1902), passim.

21. See Lawrence Ritt, *The Victorian Conscience in Action, The National Association for the Promotion of Social Science, 1857–1886,* Ph.D. diss., Columbia University, 1959.

22. Select Committee on Married Women's Property Bill, 355, 375; National Association for the Promotion of Social Science, *Sessional Proceedings* (London, 1867–68), pp. 189–98.

23. For press comment on Mill's work and on the debates and action in Parliament, see: "Married Women's Property," *All the Year Round,* XXIV (1870), 89–93; Matthew Browne, "The Subjection of Women," *Contemporary Review,* XIV (1870), 273–86; Margaret Oliphant, "Mill on the Subjection of Women," *Edinburgh Review,* CXXX (1869), 572–602 (authorship per *Wellesley Index*); Arthur Hobhouse, "On the Forfeiture of Property by Married Women," *Fortnightly Review,* XIII (1870), 180–86; Sir Henry Taylor, "Mr. Mill on the Subjection of Women," *Fraser's Magazine,* new series, I (1870), 143–65; "The Property of Married Women," M, XII (1869), 51–60; "Women's Rights," *Saturday Review,* XXIX (1870), 662–64; "Married Women and Their Property," *Spectator,* XLI (1868), 488–89; "The House of Commons on Wives' Property," s, XLII (1869), 470–71; "The Peers and the Married Women," s, XLIII (1870), 772–73; "The Subjection of Women," *W.R.,* XCIII (1870), 63–89.

24. 3 Hansard, CXCI, 1023–24; Select Committee on Married Women's Property Bill, 380–91, 401–15; *The Times,* 15 June 1868.

25. 3 Hansard, CXCII, 1361–62, 1374, CXCV, 760, CXCVIII, 986, CCI, 891, CCII, 614; Select Committee on Married Women's Property Bill, 375–76, 421–24, 431–32.

26. *P.P.*, 1867–68, III, 375–78; 3 Hansard, CXCI, 1015–24, 1367–69, 1376–78; Select Committee on Married Women's Property Bill, 341–45.

27. 3 Hansard, CXCV, 760–69, 794–98, CXCVIII, 405, 979–87; *P.P.*, 1868–69, III, 427–34, VIII, 771.

28. 3 Hansard, CCI, 878–92; *P.P.*, 1870, II, 657–60, 671–78.

29. *P.P.*, 1870, II, 663–70; 3 Hansard, CCIII, 397, 1488.

30. 3 Hansard, CCXIV, 670, 679. For a press account of this case and comment on it, see *The Times*, 11–14 March 1878.

31. 3 Hansard, CCXLIII, 306, 853; *The Times*, 24 January 1879.

32. *Annual Register*, 1870, p. 80.

33. National Association for the Promotion of Social Science, *Transactions*, XIV (1870), 242–44, 549–52; XIX (1875), 265–69; XXI (1877), 241–46; XXIII (1879), 205–6; XXIV (1880), 181–202, 270; XXV (1881), 248–49.

34. Strachey, pp. 274–75; *The Times*, 24 January 1879 and 5 February 1880.

35. *P.P.*, 1873, III, 59–66; 3 Hansard, CCXIV, 667–89.

36. *P.P.*, 1874, III, 265–66, 269–70; Hansard, CCXVIII, 607–14.

37. *P.P.*, 1877, IV, 25–30; 3 Hansard, CCXXXIII, 1404–19, CCXXXV, 1736–37.

38. Millicent Garrett Fawcett, "The Women's Suffrage Movement," in *The Woman Question in Europe*, ed. Theodore Stanton (New York and London: Putnam, 1884), p. 25.

39. *P.P.*, 1880, V, 77–83, 89–91; 3 Hansard, CCLII, 1533–45, 1548–53.

40. *P.P.*, 1881, IV, 53–61, IX, 661–726; 3 Hansard, CCLVII, 551–89, 706–14, CCLX, 687–88, 1179–81, 1521–27, CCLXI, 1438–40, CCLXII, 1751.

41. 3 Hansard, CCLVII, 714; *P.P.*, 1881, IV, 37–51, IX, 655–58.

42. *P.P.*, 1882, IV, 11–22; 3 Hansard, CCLXVII, 316–17, CCLXX, 616–18, CCLXXIII, 1603–12, 1844–47.

43. For press comment on the Act, see Ralph Thicknesse, "The New Legal Position of Married Women," *B.E.M.*, CXXXIII (1883), 207–20 (authorship per *Wellesley Index*); "The Married Women's Property Act (1882)," *Chambers's Journal*, 4th series, XIX (1882), 819–21; "Moneyed Wives," S, LVI (1883), 9–10; and *The Times*, 21 November 1882 and 1 January 1883.

44. Dicey, pp. 388–89; Holdsworth, XV, 223. The Law Amendment (Married Women and Tortfeasors) Act of 1935 (25 & 26 Geo. 5, c. 30), the first major amendment of the Act of 1882, replaced the term "separate property" with the phrase "married woman's property." "It is supposed that this was a concession to feminist feeling that a man and his wife being separate persons (and not one as considered by the old Common Law) it was as anomalous to speak of a wife's separate estate as it would be to speak of a husband's," Underhill, p. 24.

45. *P.P.*, 1884, V, 153, 157; 3 Hansard, CCLXXXVII, 839.

46. *P.P.*, 1893–94, V, 233; 4 Hansard, XV, 870; Dicey, p. 392; Jenks, p. 313; Underhill, pp. 16–19, 25–26, 37–38.

47. The eighteen bills introduced included ten measures of broad reform applying to England and five to Scotland; the two bills that led to the limited Act of 1874 for England; and Raikes's bill of 1870. The five that were passed into law were the Acts of 1870, 1874, and 1882 for England, and the Acts of 1877 and 1881 for Scotland. Of the thirteen bills not passed, three were introduced but did not obtain a second reading; six received a

second reading and then were dropped; three were read a second time and were considered by select committees but were not proceeded with further during the session in which they were introduced; and one—Raikes's bill of 1870—was defeated.

## 2. THE FORGOTTEN WOMAN OF THE PERIOD
### Penny Weekly Family Magazines of the 1840's and 1850's

1. See Guinevere L. Griest, *Mudie's Circulating Library and the Victorian Novel* (Bloomington: Indiana University Press, 1970), p. 79. Dickens' novels in shilling monthly parts generally sold fewer than 50,000 copies.

2. Circulation figures throughout are taken from Richard D. Altick, *The English Common Reader* (Chicago: University of Chicago Press, 1957), Appendix C.

3. Both the *London Journal* and the *Family Herald* survived into the twentieth century, but as literacy spread they became lighter in tone. By the 1870's and 1880's they were read almost exclusively by servants, shopgirls, and the wives of unskilled laborers.

4. *London Journal*, 1 (1 Mar. 1845), 16; hereafter *LJ*.

5. "Popular Literature of the Day," *British and Foreign Review*, 10 (1840), 243.

6. Britain in 1851 had thirteen million people above the age of fifteen. Altick, pp. 166–72, discusses conflicting claims about literacy; the guesses range from 60 percent to 75 percent, but literacy was defined in minimal terms. I have based my calculation on the suppositions that between seven and eight million could actually read and that each of the 750,000 purchased copies of the two leading magazines was seen by three or four people, making a readership of around two and a half million. Of course some people took in more than one penny magazine. *Cassell's Family Paper* and *Reynolds's Miscellany*, which were similar, respectively, to the *Family Herald* and the *London Journal*, sold between them almost another half-million.

7. *Master Humphrey's Clock*, the pseudo-magazine that included *The Old Curiousity Shop*, was also, not so incidentally, Dickens' only try at weekly rather than monthly parts, but each part cost threepence instead of a penny. See Thomas M. Hatton and Arthur H. Cleaver, *A Bibliography of the Periodical Works of Charles Dickens* (London: Chapman and Hall, 1933), p. 163, and Altick, p. 384.

8. Interestingly enough, the illustration of the composing machine that decorated the title of the first number showed it operated by two women: machine composition allowed the replacement of expensive unionized typesetters with cheap female labor. The *Family Herald* was initially issued on four newspaper-sized pages. This version ran for twenty-two weeks beginning on 17 December 1842. With the issue for 13 May 1843 the magazine format was adopted and the numeration began again with Vol. 1, No. 1.

9. Alvar Ellegard, *The Readership of the Periodical Press in Mid-Victorian Britain* (Göteborg, 1957); part II, repr. in *Victorian Periodicals Newsletter*, No. 13 (1971), 22. See also Altick, p. 360.

10. My discussion of class is indebted to John Burnett, *A History of the Cost of Living* (Harmondsworth, Middlesex: Penguin, 1969), Ch. iv; J. F.

C. Harrison, *The Early Victorians 1832–1851* (London: Weidenfeld and Nickolson, 1971), Chs. ii, iv; and Leone Levi, *Wages and Earnings of the Working Class* (London: John Murray, 1867).

11. William Rathbone Greg, *Why Are Women Redundant?* (London: N. Trübner, 1869), p. 24.

12. William Anderson Smith, '*Shepherd*' *Smith the Universalist* (London: Sampson Low, 1892), p. 101 and passim.

13. Margaret Dalziel, *Popular Fiction 100 Years Ago* (London: Cohen and West, 1957) devotes a chapter entitled " 'The Most Popular Writer of Our Time' " to G. W M. Reynolds.

14. Robert Louis Stevenson, "Popular Authors," *Random Memories and other Essays* in Vol. XII of *Works*, Vailima Ed. (London: Heinemann, 1922), p. 333. Reade's *London Journal* serial was subsequently published in three volumes as *White Lies* (1857) and reissued as *The Double Marriage or White Lies* (1868).

15. Accurate figures about the finances of penny magazines are hard to discover. When the *Penny Magazine*'s sales had declined to 40,000 its publisher remarked that the number was "scarcely remunerative"; quoted in Altick, p. 335. Six weeks after the *Family Herald* began publication its editor was guessing that they needed 20,000 weekly to pay; a little over a year later he was saying that "if it could only get up to 100,000, it would be a capital property"; see Smith, pp. 221, 230. One contemporary estimate of expenses is discussed in Louis James, *Fiction for the Working Man 1830–1850* (London: Oxford University Press, 1963), pp. 31–32.

16. The pioneering *Penny Magazine* (1832–45), published by the Society for the Diffusion of Useful Knowledge and strictly limited to factual material, attained at one time a circulation of 200,000 copies. It could not survive in competition with the magazines that printed fiction; the year of its demise coincides with that of the *London Journal*'s birth.

17. James, p. 40, for the *London Journal* figure; information on James Biggs, publisher of *Family Herald*, from F. Boase, *Modern English Biography*, Vol. I.

18. Smith, p. 166.

19. *The London Pioneer*, 1 (14 Jan. 1847), 593, to 2 (10 June 1847), 115; hereafter *Pioneer*.

20. *Pioneer*, 1 (11 Mar. 1847), 723.

21. *Pioneer*, 1 (1 Apr. 1847), 755.

22. *Pioneer*, 3 (19 Aug. 1848), 294.

23. "The Rights of Women," *Family Herald*, 6 (6 May, 1848), 12; hereafter *FH*.

24. John Wilson Ross, "The Love-Match," *LJ*, 1 (17 May 1845), 178–80.

25. "Edmund Merton," *LJ*, 2 (1 Nov. 1845), 125–27, is a particularly interesting story on this pattern; the superior suitor is rejected because he is the half-caste son of an army officer. The extreme case makes it obvious that blood is a poor measure of worth.

26. "The English Peeress and the Irish Peasant Girl," *LJ*, 2 (13 Dec. 1845), 218–21.

27. *LJ*, 1 (1 March 1845), p. 16.

28. In districts where child labor was particularly important it was common for a man to wait until a woman had proved her fertility before proposing marriage; see William Acton, *Prostitution* . . . (London: John Church-

ill, 1857), p. 71. There were many long-standing common-law marriages in the lower class. They often grew simply from an inability to afford the parson's fee; every so often a clergyman would announce a date for performing the ceremony free and regularize dozens of unions. See E. Royston Pike, *Human Documents of the Industrial Revolution in Britain* (London: Allen and Unwin, 1966), p. 326.

29. In the 1851 census the excess of females over males in Great Britain was more than half a million. There were 85,000 fewer males aged 20 to 24 in 1851 than males aged 10 to 14 in 1841, though the death rate in the intervening ages was greater for women than for men. One man in ten had left the country, either temporarily or permanently, as he approached marriageable age. See *The Census of Great Britain in 1851* (London: Longman, Brown, Green, and Longmans, 1854), pp. 5, 35–36, and B. R. Mitchell and Phyllis Deane, *Abstract of British Historical Statistics* (Cambridge: Cambridge University Press, 1962), p. 12.

30. *FH*, 1 (17 Feb. 1844), 648.

31. Cheap publishers sometimes found it necessary to clean up novels originally published for the middle class. *The Mysteries of Old St. Paul's* (London: G. Vickers, 1841) was a penny-issue plagiarism of W. H. Ainsworth's *Old St. Paul's*. The names of the characters are altered but the plot remains the same except that the plagiarist, unlike Ainsworth, preserves the chastity of the heroine—a shopkeeper's daughter. See James, p. 92.

32. "Walter," of *My Secret Life*, considered any unaccompanied working-class woman fair game.

33. *FH*, 1 (28 Oct. 1843), 395.

34. *FH*, 13 (19 May 1855), 44.

35. *The Vicar of Wakefield*, which was still popular (it had been published in penny numbers around 1836), is the obvious prototype.

36. *FH*, 1 (14 Oct. 1843), 353–55.

37. By "B. W.," *FH*, 1 (13 May 1843), 1–4.

38. The opinion that we have taken as nearly universal was disseminated in such works as William Acton, *The Function and Disorders of the Reproductive Organs* . . . , 4th ed. (London: John Churchill, 1865), and "Prostitution," *Westminster Review*, 53 (1850), 448–506. The latter reveals quite clearly the aura of guilt and evil surrounding even legal pleasure: "Women whose position and education have protected them from exciting causes constantly pass through life without ever being cognizant of the prompting of the senses. Happy for them that it is so!" (pp. 456–57), William Rathbone Greg was the author of this article; it is reprinted in *Prostitution in the Victorian Age: Debates on the Issue From 19th Century Critical Journals*, ed. Keith Nield (Farnborough: Gregg International Publishers, 1973). Carl Degler, in "What Ought To Be and What Was: Woman's Sexuality in the Nineteenth Century," *American Historical Review* 79 (Dec., 1974), 1467–90, demonstrates that there was not so general a concensus as has been thought: mid-century medical opinion was, in fact, divided on the subject of women's sexual desires. Degler argues that Acton et al. wrote proscriptively rather than descriptively. (For a detailed discussion of Acton, see Chapter 9, this volume.—Ed.)

39. *LJ*, 9 (31 Mar. 1850), 64.

40. *FH*, 13 (1 Mar. 1856), 699.

41. *LJ*, 9 (31 Mar. 1849), 62.

42. "The Maiden Tribute of Modern Babylon," *Pall Mall Gazette*, 6, 7, 8, and 10 July 1885.

43. By "J. P. H.," in four parts, *LJ*, 10 (16 Feb. 1850), 378–11 (16 Mar. 1850), 28; no part appeared on 9 Mar.

44. *LJ*, 9 (26 May 1849), 184.

45. John Wilson Ross's essay on "Woman," *LJ*, 1 (22 Mar. 1845), 53, dwells on the exceptional virtue of the female sex, with the corollary that since woman is superior to man she is, of course, too wise to coarsen herself with public life.

46. *LJ*, 10 (14 Apr. 1849), 96.

47. *FH*, 1 (14 Oct. 1843), 365.

48. Conservative social reformers like W. R. Greg believed that to get women out of the labor market would necessarily raise men's wages. Though it is possible that mass-magazine fiction is moved by a similar spirit, the stories never make a point of the message, as those in *Eliza Cook's Journal* or the *Alexandra Magazine* sometimes do.

## 3. FEMINISM AND FEMALE EMIGRATION, 1861–1886

1. *Saturday Review*, 12 November 1859.

2. Recent studies of Victorian women have made little more than passing reference to female emigration societies: for example, M. Jeanne Peterson, "The Victorian Governess: Status Incongruence in Family and Society," *Victorian Studies*, xiv (1970), 7–26, and J. A. and Olive Banks, *Feminism and Family Planning in Victorian England* (Liverpool: Liverpool University Press, 1964), pp. 28–33. An official centenary history of the emigration societies by Una Monk, *New Horizons: A Hundred Years of Women's Migration* (London: h.m.s.o., 1963), provides useful information, but unfortunately is unannotated and uncritical in approach.

3. The *English Woman's Journal*, founded by Bessie R. Parkes in 1858.

4. Martineau "Female Industry," *Edinburgh Review*, cix (1859), 293–336. On the influence of Martineau's article see Josephine Kamm, *Rapiers and Battleaxes: The Women's Movement and its Aftermath* (London, 1966), p. 45.

5. See, for example, J. D. Milne, "Remarks on the Industrial Employment of Women," *Transactions: N.A.P.S.S.* (1857), 531–38; B. R. Parkes, "The Market for Educated Female Labour" (1859), 727–28; J. Boucherett, "The Industrial Employments of Women" (1859), 728–29; J. Crowe, "Report of Society for Promoting the Employment of Women" (1861), 685.

6. The Society was headed initially by Jessie Boucherett and Jane Crowe, and its formation was soon followed by the establishment of branch societies in Edinburgh, Dublin, and other provincial towns, all affiliated with the Social Science Association. Crowe, t.n.a.p.s.s. (1861), 685; s.p.e.w., *Annual Report* (1879), 3–4.

7. In 1865 Dorothea Beale observed that out of 100 fathers of her pupils at Cheltenham Ladies' College, 83 were military officers, "private gentlemen," clergymen, or medical men, and the rest were civil servants, lawyers, bankers, merchants, and manufacturers. t.n.a.p.s.s. (1865), 275. Similar conditions prevailed at Queen's College, Miss Buss's North London Colle-

giate School, and Bedford College, all secondary schools founded between 1848 and 1853. C. A. Biggs, T.N.A.P.S.S. (1879), 442–44.

8. E. Davies, "On Secondary Instruction as Relating to Girls," T.N.A.P.S.S. (1864), 403 (reprinted in a separate pamphlet [London] 1864, p. 23); see also her evidence to the Taunton Commission, "Report of Schools Inquiry Commissioners," v, *P.P.*, (1867–68), XXVIII (Pt. IV), p. 246 QQ. 11293, 11370–71.

9. J. Boucherett, T.N.A.P.S.S. (1861), 685–86; A. B. Corlett (1862), 612–13; Corlett and P. Blyth (1863), 698–707. Emily Faithfull gave a boost to women's opportunities in the printing industry by establishing the Victoria Press, run for and by women; it obtained orders for most feminist works, especially the *Victoria Magazine*. By 1860 Faithfull had apprenticed nineteen female compositors and found that other printers were planning to admit women. Faithfull, T.N.A.P.S.S. (1860), 819–20.

10. T.N.A.P.S.S. (1860), 814–15. Louisa Hope thought that this class, too eager for the "peacockism of education," would be better off "as cottagers' or tradesmen's wives and mothers, or as household servants." T.N.A.P.S.S. (1860), 399–401.

11. M. S. Rye, *Emigration of Educated Women* (London: Faithfull, 1861), pp. 3–5, 14; B. R. Parkes, *Essays on Women's Work* (London: Alexander Strahan, 1865), p. 66.

12. Rye, pp. 2–14; Monk, pp. 1–3. A summary of Rye's paper appeared in T.N.A.P.S.S. (1861), 686.

13. The formation of the F.M.C.E.S. in May 1862 was accompanied by a stream of letters in *The Times*, mostly in support. In December 1861 Emily Faithfull had publicized the aims of the proposed Society, and in April Rye herself began to write regular letters acknowledging subscriptions and explaining the Society's intentions. *The Times*, Dec. 4, 1861; Dec. 6, 1861; April 7, 1862; April 9, 1862; April 25, 1862; April 29, 1862; June 21, 1862.

14. In 1849 both Governesses Benevolent Institution and Hyde Clarke's proposed National Benevolent Emigration Fund for Widows and Orphan Daughters of Gentlemen, Clergymen, Professional Men, Bankers and Merchants turned to emigration as an outlet for gentlewomen, but were discouraged by reports that such women would be unable to find respectable employment in the colonies. See my unpublished Ph.D. thesis, "A Study of Middle-Class Female Emigration from Great Britain, 1830–1914" (University of British Columbia, 1969), pp. 120–24.

15. As *The Times* argued, all prospective emigrants, no matter what their destiny, must possess "an industrial training and domestic accomplishments even more than they are likely to want in this country" (28 April 1862). These "domestic accomplishments" might reasonably be expected to predetermine, to some extent, a woman's future career abroad, a realization which was not lost on later female emigration societies.

16. By 1861 the ratio of women to men in England and Wales was 1,053 to 1,000, showing a marked increase from the 1851 ratio of 1,042 to 1,000. The greatest "excess," 209,663, occurred between the ages of 20 and 29. Between 30 and 39 it was 107,380, and between 40 and 49, 56,231. B. R. Mitchell, *Abstract of British Historical Statistics* (Cambridge: Cambridge University Press, 1962), p. 6, Table 2; General Report, Census, England and Wales, (1861), *P.P.*, (1863), LIII Pt. 1 (3221), Appendix, p. 115, Table

70. For a concise discussion of the causes of the sex disparity see Banks, pp. 27–29.

17. First published in the *National Review* in 1862, Greg's essay was reprinted in his collection, *Literary and Social Judgements* (London: Bungay, 1868, 2nd ed. 1869) and as a separate pamphlet in 1869. Greg was a moderate Liberal in political and social matters, but by the sixties he showed signs of increasing conservatism; see the "Memoir" by his wife in Greg, *Enigmas of Life* (London: Kegan Paul, 1891).

18. Caroline Chisholm had revolutionized the methods of "protected" emigration to Australia for working-class women and families during the forties and fifties. Margaret Kiddle, *Caroline Chisholm* (Melbourne: Melbourne University Press, 1950).

19. "What Shall we do with Our Old Maids?" *Fraser's Magazine*, LXVI (1862), 60–75; reprinted in *Essays on the Pursuits of Women*, (London: Faithfull, 1863).

20. *Hints on Self Help; A Book for Young Women* (London: S. W. Partridge, 1863), pp. 42–48.

21. "Social Science," *Victoria Magazine*, July 1863, 282–83; see also Oct. 1863, 571, and A. Houston, *On the Emancipation of Women from Existing Industrial Disabilities, Considered in its Economic Aspect* (inaugural lecture as Whately Professor of Political Economy, Dublin University, 1862), pp. 30–34.

22. Taylor herself had emigrated to New Zealand and returned to England after fifteen successful working years. Hammerton, Ch. IV; Joan Stevens, *Mary Taylor: Friend of Charlotte Brontë* (Auckland: Auckland University Press, 1972).

23. Taylor, *The First Duty of Women* (London: Faithfull, 1870), p. 43.

24. The Society obtained some influential support and achieved the status of a fashionable charity. Both Lord Shaftesbury and Lord Brougham promoted it, and Shaftesbury became its first president. Shaftesbury to Barbara Bodichon, 25 July 1862; Bodichon to Shaftesbury, 26 September 1862; Rye to Bodichon, 7 October 1862, Fawcett Library, Autograph Collection, Vol. II, Pt. A, F.M.C.E.S., *First and Second Reports*, London, 1861–62 and 1872. Anthony Trollope was well acquainted with the Society and created a fictional equivalent, the "Female Protestant Unmarried Women's Emigration Society," in *Phineas Finn* (London: Virtue, 1869), Chap. 41.

25. See, for example, the letters of Caroline M. Heawood, Melbourne, 25 March 1862, J. M. Cary, Dunedin, 18 October 1863, and Catherine Brough, Cape Town, 20 March 1863, who reported "I am far worse off than ever I was in England; it is next to impossible to obtain employment and the pay is so low that though I have had two temporary engagements I have not earned enough to pay my board, lodging and washing." F.M.C.E.S., *Letter Book No. 1* (Fawcett Library), pp. 15–18, 101–104.

26. Rye's early reading had included Susanna Moodie's famous account of her experiences as an immigrant's wife in the Canadian backwoods, *Roughing it in the Bush* (first published 1852), which effectively illustrates the painful process by which a genteel woman adapted to the crude physical and social conditions of a primitive environment. Moodie stressed that for the impoverished middle class emigration was "an act of severe duty," because to remain independent, "they cannot labour in a menial capacity in

the country where they were born and educated to command," (Toronto: McLelland Steward edition, 1962), pp. xv, 166, 236–37, E. A. Pratt, *Pioneer Women in Victoria's Reign* (London: G. Newnes, 1897), p. 23.

27. Rye, T.N.A.S.S. 1862, pp. 811–12. This was an elaboration of her earlier plans proposed in 1861 in her *Emigration of Educated Women*, pp. 9–11.

28. Only eight of the one hundred women Rye accompanied were governesses. These proportions were deemed admirably suitable by Roger Therry, an ex-judge of the N.S.W. Supreme Court, who added that Rye had "wisely and successfully extended her zeal and exertions to the introduction of a much more needed class in the Colony—domestic servants." *Reminiscences of Thirty Years Residence in N.S.W. and Victoria* (London: Sampson, Low and Son, 1863), pp. 430–31.

29. Report of F.M.C.E.S. meeting of 1 November 1862 prior to Rye's departure for New Zealand, in *The Times*, 3 November 1862; F.M.C.E.S., *First Report*, 1861–62, p. 7; Rye to Bodichon, London, 25 September 1862, Redfern, Sydney, 20 May 1865, Fawcett Library, Autograph Collection, Vol. II, Pt. A. After 1865 Rye made several trips to Canada, and from 1869 she organized a system of Canadian emigration for young "waifs and strays," a scheme designed to thwart the growth of prostitution in Britain. Pratt, pp. 30–37; Monk pp. 6–7, 119–21.

30. Compiled from lists of emigrants in F.M.C.E.S. *Reports* (First, 1861–62; Second, 1862–72; Fifth, 1880–82; Sixth, 1882–85); there is no trace of surviving copies of the third and fourth reports covering the period from December 1872 to 1879.

31. F.M.C.E.S., *Letter Books Nos. 1 and 2* (Fawcett Library). The letter books contain contemporary copies of 276 letters received from 114 emigrants. The basic incentive for most of the letters was to repay the Society's loans, but most of the emigrants were informative and literate correspondents and revealed a good deal about their colonial lives, although less about their former circumstances in Britain.

32. Maria Rye's initial collection in 1862 was £500, and by 1885 the Society's capital was only £269. Once in full operation, however, a large working capital was unnecessary, for most emigrants repaid their loans and many paid all or part of their passage, requiring only the protection and facilities of the Society. F.M.C.E.S., *Sixth Report*, 1886, pp. 3–6.

33. A. Davis, Sydney, 20 January 1865, 21 February 1867, *Letter Book No. 1*, pp. 172–77, 257–62.

34. S. Henderson, Tongaur, Natal, 28 September 1863, *Letter Book No. 1*, pp. 83–85, see also M. Atherton, Brisbane, 2 September 1862; M. Richardson, Port MacQuarie, N.S.W., 13 February 1863; M. Wyett, Wairapapi, N.Z., 10 February 1866; A. M. Hunt, Melbourne, 11 October 1869; L. Phillips, Melbourne, 12 August, 1873, *Letter Book No. 1*, pp. 34–9, 47–51, 216–20, 349–52, 420–22.

35. M. Hett, Christchurch, 23 June 1870, *Letter Book No. 1*, pp. 366–68; see also R. Phayne, Melboure, 13 August 1869, *Letter Book No. 1*, pp. 341–46.

36. C. Haselton, Graaf Reinet, 9 May and 15 August 1877, Melbourne, November 1879, *Letter Book No. 2*, pp. 7–8, 24–25, 83–85.

37. A. Davis, Sydney, 17 June 1864, *Letter Book No. 1*, pp. 123–27.

38. S. A. Hall, Cape Town and Port Elizabeth, 17 January 1868, 14 and

21 April 1870, Graaf Reinet, 18 August 1876, *Letter Book No. 1*, pp. 289–92, 360, 407, 502–504; Graaf Reinet, 4 February 1877 to 25 March 1882, *Letter Book No. 2*, pp. 2–150, passim; see also the letters from S. E. Evans, C. Haselton, A. Hart, and M. E. Jenvey in *Letter Book No. 2*.

39. M. Long, Waipakarau, N.Z., May 1880, *Letter Book No. 2*, pp. 108–109.

40. E. Blackith, Napier, N.Z., n.d. (ca. August 1881), 2 November 1881, *Letter Book No. 2*, pp. 122–24, 130–31. Miss E. Glen, who received only £24 for teaching in a South African Mission School, nevertheless felt that "the dark cloud that has hung over my life is fast disappearing." Verulam, 27 October 1866, *Letter Book No. 1*, pp. 238–40.

41. L. A. Geoghegan, Apsley, Victoria, 18 October 1867, 17 May and 12 August 1868, *Letter Book No. 1*, pp. 254–57, 285–86, 302–304, 310–12.

42. E. Brook, Dunedin, 20 January 1869, *Letter Book No. 1*, pp. 331–33.

43. H. Herbert, Waipakarau, N.Z., 8 November 1879, *Letter Book No. 2*, pp. 76–80. See also Miss Barlow's letter from Melbourne; she had opened her own school and boasted, "I am getting quite a Colonial woman, and fear I should not easily fit into English ideas again, can scrub a floor with anyone, and bake my own bread and many other things an English Governess and Schoolmistress especially would be horrified at," 24 June 1863, *Letter Book No. 1*, pp. 76–78.

44. See, for example, L. Dearmer, Sydney, 1 June and 14 December 1868, Mrs. E. C. MacDonnell, Dunedin, 27 July 1870, *Letter Book No. 1*, pp. 304–309, 318–24, 268–71. Mrs. I. White, 27 April 1881, *Letter Book No. 2*, pp. 137–45. On the development of government schools and female education in Australia and New Zealand, see A. Clayden, *A Popular Handbook to New Zealand* (London: Wyman and Sons, 1885), p. 126; N. I. MacKenzie, *Women in Australia* (Melbourne: Cheshire, 1963), p. 21.

45. A. Davis, Sydney, 17 June 1864, *Letter Book No. 1*, pp. 123–27.

46. One of the few exceptions was "Emigrant No. 267—Converted Jewess; cast off by her family; took situation as cook in Canada." F.M.C.E.S., *Sixth Report*, 1883–85, pp. 9–12.

47. A. M. Hunt, Melbourne and Wangaratta, Victoria, 11 October 1869 and 9 May 1870, *Letter Book No. 1*, pp. 349–52. See also F.M.C.E.S., *Second Report*, 1873, pp. 6–12, especially numbers 107 and 120.

48. A. B. MacQueen, Brisbane, 18 April 1866, *Letter Book No. 1*, pp. 222–25.

49. J. Merritt, Auckland, 31 July 1863, *Letter Book No. 1*, pp. 73–76.

50. Lewin was a niece of the Utilitarian-Radical historian George Grote (Pratt, p. 30). In practice her approach adhered closely to the principles argued by feminists like Mary Taylor in *The First Duty of Women* (London, 1870). There is little evidence to determine whether Lewin was more partial toward applicants who shared her own views; S. A. Hall, the schoolteacher at Graaf Reinet, reported that one emigrant's (Miss Jackson's) "great idea is to educate women that they shall be what she calls 'emancipated' and placed on an equality with man; that they may be thoroughly independent of them." Hall did not share Jackson's "great idea." July 18, 1878, *Letter Book No. 2*, pp. 40–41.

51. Both Rye and Lewin remained on the Society's committee, but the working secretary exercised final control over the selection of applicants. Miss Strongitharm succeeded Lewin in 1881 and in 1884 was succeeded by

Julia Blake, from the Colonial Emigration Society, and Alice Bonham-Carter. F.M.C.E.S., *Sixth Report* (1883–85), pp. 3–6, Monk. p. 23.

52. The idea was discussed initially at the Social Science Association. Mrs. Browne, T.N.A.P.S.S. (1869), 609–610; Mrs. E. M. King (1874), 947; R. M. Crawshay (1874), 947; R. M. Crawshay, *Domestic Service for Gentlewomen . . . With Additional Matter,* 3rd ed. (London, 1876); 1st ed. (London: Labour News, 1874). Crawshay recommended large households for her scheme so that at least two gentlewomen could be employed and keep each other company, and regular servants could be retained for the heaviest and dirtiest work. The fact that domestic service was becoming increasingly unpopular with the traditional servant class may explain both the origin and short life of the scheme.

53. L.M.H. [Louisa M. Hubbard], *The Hand-Book of Women's Work* (London: Victoria Press, 1876), pp. 41–45.

54. During the eighties there was a proliferation of parent and local branch emigration societies throughout Britain. By 1902, after a number of mergers and organizational splits, the two main parent societies were the British Women's Emigration Association and the South African Colonization Society. Many of the leading figures were church workers; whereas the main link of the F.M.C.E.S. had been with feminist employment and education agencies, the new societies were close to organizations like the Girls' Friendly Society and Y.W.C.A. Hammerton, ch. 7; Monk, pp. 10–17.

## 4. THE MAKING OF AN OUTCAST GROUP
### *Prostitutes and Working Women in Nineteenth-Century Plymouth and Southampton*

1. An Act for the Prevention of Contagious Diseases at Certain Naval and Military Stations (27 and 28 Vict. c 85); An Act for the Better Prevention of Contagious Diseases at Certain Naval and Military Stations (29 and 30 Vict. c. 96); and An Act to Amend the Contagious Diseases Acts, 1866 (32 and 33 Vict. c. 86). The Admiralty and the War Office were responsible for overseeing the operation of the Acts. Metropolitan dockyard police (known as "water police" by the poor) were employed in identifying common prostitutes and insuring their attendance at periodical genital examinations. They also escorted diseased women to the lock hospital, where, according to the regulations of the 1869 Act, the women could be detained for up to nine months.

2. For legal efforts to contain the poor and to oversee their social behavior, see Towns Police Clauses Act, 1847 (10 and 11 Vict. c. 89); Common Lodging Houses Act, 1851 (14 and 15 Vict. c. 28); Wine and Beerhouse Act, 1869–70 (32 and 33 Vict. c. 27, and 33 and 34 Vict. c. 29); Licensing Act, 1872 (35 and 36 Vict. c. 94); and Summary Jurisdiction Act, 1879 (42 and 43 Vict. c. 49).

3. A fuller discussion of the interaction among reformers, local authorities, and prostitutes may be found in Judith R. Walkowitz, "We Are Not Beasts

of the Field: Prostitution and the Campaign against the Contagious Diseases Acts 1869–1886" (Ph.D. diss., University of Rochester, 1974).

4. A.J., Parent-Duchâtelet, *De la prostitution dans la ville de Paris, considerée sous le rapport de l'hygiene publique, de la morale, et de l'administration* (Paris: J. B. Baillere et fils, 1857), I and II; William Sanger, *History of Prostitution: Its Extent, Causes and Effects throughout the World* (New York: Medical Publishing, 1897).

5. "Report of the Assistant Commissioner of Metropolitan Police on the Operation of the Contagious Disease Acts (1881)," (*P.P.*, 1882, LII).

6. According to the manuscript census schedules, the average age of women interned in the lock wards of the Royal Albert Hospital, Devonport, was 21.8 years; in the Royal Portsmouth Gosport and in Portsea Hospital, where Southampton women were interned, the average age was 21.2 years (P.R.O., R.G. 10/2133; R.G. 10/1127). Metropolitan police statistics also confirm this age concentration (*P.P.*, 1882, LIII). According to police returns ("Report of the House of Commons Select Committee on the Administration, Operation, and Effects of the Contagious Diseases Acts of 1866–69," *P.P.*, 1882, IX, App.), all 503 women in the greater Plymouth district were listed as residing in brothels—private lodgings where the women brought men home. Of this number it has been calculated that 220 women were single, aged 15 to 29, and residing in Plymouth. They constituted 39.1 percent of all single women aged 15 to 29 and residing in lodgings in Plymouth, as based on a ten percent sampling of single women in Plymouth (P.R.O., R.G. 10/2112–24). In addition, 80 percent of the brothels under surveillance in Plymouth catered to a working-class clientele ("Report from the Royal Commission on the Contagious Diseases Acts [1871]," *P.P.*, 1871, XIX, Q. 337–43).

7. According to the 1871 census, of the women interned in the Royal Albert Hospital 43 out of 77, or 42.9 percent, were born in Greater Plymouth, while 37 out of 77, or 49.1 percent, were born in the rest of Devon and Cornwall. Earlier hospital reports also confirm this general distribution (P.R.O., R.G. 10/2123; Admiralty Papers, Adm. I/6122, 3 February 1869). Likewise, of the 31 women positively identified as prostitutes residing on three notorious streets in Plymouth, 48.3 percent came from the surrounding countryside (P.R.O., R.G. 10/2120).

8. For example, Mr. Luscombe, a Plymouth magistrate, stated: "We are unfortunately situated in this way, we are close to Cornwall, and when a poor woman is asked the question, 'Do you belong to the town?' she says 'No'. 'Where did you come from?' and then we find, I am sorry to say, almost four out of five of the young women before us are girls from Cornwall" (*P.P.*, 1871, XIX, Q. 5155).

9. Joan Scott and Louise Tilly, "Women's Work and the Family in Nineteenth-Century Europe," *Comparative Studies in History and Society,* XVI (Winter, 1975), 41–43.

10. See "Representative Cases" in the "Twenty-fifth Annual Report of the London Society for the Rescue of Women and Children, 1877," *Rescue Society Reports,* 1877–1892, Joseph Butler Collection, Fawcett Library, London; *The Shield* (London, 15 July 1871); "Report of the Assistant Commissioner of Metropolitan Police on the Operation of the Contagious Diseases Acts," *P.P.*, 1876, LXI.

11. U. R. Q. Henriques, "Bastardy and New Poor Law," *Past and Present,* No. 37 (July 1967), 128.

12. See the case, for instance, of Laura Clarke, who came to Plymouth to be confined and was thus able to leave the scene of her disgrace and establish new social relations elsewhere (*P.P.,* 1871, XIX, Q. 8442, 8443).

13. Albert Leffingwell, *Illegitimacy and the Influence of Season upon Conduct: Two Studies in Demography* (New York: Scribner, 1892), p. 15; P. E. Razzell and R. W. Wainwright, *The Victorian Working Class: Selections from Letters to the Morning Chronicle* (London: Cass, 1973), pp. 29, 33, 34.

14. See, for example, *The Shield* (London: 25 April 1870, 1 April 1871, 29 June 1871, 15 July 1871); P.R.O. Adm. 1/6418, 30 October 1873 and 5 November 1873; "Report of the House of Commons Select Committee on the Administration, Operation and Effects of the Contagious Diseases Acts of 1866–69" (*P.P.,* 1881, VIII, Q. 4130).

15. This data was compiled from the manuscript census of 1871 (P.R.O., R.G. 10/2120). See also Walkowitz, "We Are Not Beasts of the Field" (diss.), pp. 240, 241.

16. A series entitled " 'Our House' and its Tenants: being Sketches of Working Class Life; in a basement and eight stories," appeared in the *Devonport Independent and Stonehouse Gazette* (hereafter *D.I.*) in 1883 and contained detailed descriptions of women's wages. *D.I.* (Plymouth: 19 May 1883, 26 May 1883, 2 June 1883, 9 June 1883, 16 June 1883, 23 June 1883, 30 June 1883, 7 July 1883, 14 July 1883. See also "Orchard Lane Style Service," *Weekly Hampshire Independent* (Southampton: 3 April 1878); Testimony of Mr. Bignold, factory inspector for Devon and Cornwall, before the Commission of Labor (*P.P.,* 1892, XXV: Q. 10, 127–30, 288).

17. Brian Harrison, *Drink and the Victorians: The Temperance Question in England,* 1815–1872 (Pittsburgh: University of Pittsburgh Press, 1971), p. 47.

18. Reports from Kent emphasized the seasonality of prostitution among hop-pickers, who moved into garrison towns when regiments arrived (*P.P.,* 1871, XIX, Q. 17009, 15628, 12289). The increase in numbers was generally associated with a rise in disorderly behavior and the rate of venereal disease (*P.P.,* 1881, VIII, Q. 4130).

19. Poor Law Correspondence, P.R.O., M.H. 12/11007, 31 October 1874. See also Sheila Ryan Johansson, "Sex and Death in Victorian England . . ." in this volume.

20. Bracebridge Hemyng, "Prostitution in London," in *London Labour and The London Poor,* ed. Henry Mayhew [1861] (New York: Dover, 1968), IV, 226–32; Home Office Papers, P.R.O. H.O. 45/6628, 17 March 1858.

21. Of the three Plymouth streets, 68 percent of single women, ages 15 to 29, resided in lodgings. In the poor working-class district surrounding and including the three streets, 43.7 percent of the 309 single women, ages 15 to 29, also lived independent of their families, relatives, or employers (R.G. 10/2120). Registered women lived throughout this immediate neighborhood, and any single woman living alone in lodgings there would have been suspect to the metropolitan police. In contrast, only 8.2 percent of single women, ages 15 to 29, resided in lodgings in Plymouth generally

(P.R.O., R.G. 10/2112–24). For a more detailed statistical study of the notorious streets, see Judith and Daniel Walkowitz, "We Are Not Beasts of the Field: Prostitution and the Poor under the Contagious Diseases Acts," *Feminist Studies*, I (Winter, 1973), 73–106.

22. J. and D. Walkowitz, "We Are Not Beasts of the Field," *Feminist Studies*, p. 207. When the poor sought legal redress for stolen property, they often found themselves victims of a process they had initiated. See, for example, the case of Ellen Donavan, *Weekly Hampshire Independent* (Southampton: 14 June 1870). On the movement of the poor in and out of the workhouse, see Poor Law Correspondence (P.R.O., M.H. 12/2422, 17 June 1851).

23. Police returns for Plymouth confirm the virtual absence of bullies or crimps there (*P.P.*, 1881, VIII, App.).

24. J. J. Garth Wilkinson, *The Forcible Introspection of Women for the Army and Navy by the Oligarchy Considered Physically* (London: n.p., 1870), p. 15.

25. "Illegal Detention of Woman at the Royal Albert Hospital," *Abolitionist Flysheets*, Josephine Butler Collection, Fawcett Library, London.

26. *Western Daily Mercury* (hereafter *W.D.M.*; Plymouth: 19 December 1871, 25 March 1872, 21 August 1872, 28 February 1874); *Western Morning News* (Plymouth: 4 May 1874).

27. *P.P.*, 1881, VIII, Q. 3296; *D.I.*, 19 September 1874; *W.D.M.*, 7 August 1871.

28. D.I., 22 October 1883. See also the case of Maria Barnett, who was hidden by her brothelkeeper from the police (Admiralty Papers, P.R.O., Adm. 1/6418, 30 October 1873 and 5 November 1873).

29. Ellice Hopkins, *Work in Brighton, or Women's Mission to Women* (London: Hatchhards, 1877), p. 91.

30. *The Shield*, 4 April 1870. This woman subsequently became a paid agent for the repealers.

31. *Eighth Annual Report of The Royal Albert Hospital*, 1870–71; *Fourteenth Annual Report of the Royal Albert Hospital*, 1876–77 (Devonport Hospital, Devonport).

32. This trend was noted and debated as early as 1873. See, for example, *The Shield*, 6 November 1873; Birkbeck Nevins, *Statement on the grounds upon which the C.D. Acts are opposed*, 1874; P.R.O., Adm. I/6418, 6 February 1875.

33. V. A. C. Gatrell and T. B. Hadden, "Criminal Statistics and their Interpretation," in E. A. Wrigley, ed., *Nineteenth-Century Society: Essays in the Use of Quantitative Methods and Study of Social Data* (Cambridge: Cambridge University Press, 1972), pp. 353, 356, 364.

34. H. Llewellyn Smith, ed., *The New Survey of London Life and Labour* (London: P. S. King and Son, 1932), IX, pp. 297–99, 323, 324, 341. A decline in the transient male population would also be an important factor here.

35. Gareth Stedman Jones, *Outcast London: A Study in the Relationship between Classes in Victorian Society* (Oxford: Oxford University Press, 1971), p. 348; E. H. Phelps Brown, *The Growth of British Industrial Relations; A Study from the Standpoint of 1906–14* (London: Macmillan, 1965), pp. 19–46, 65, 66, 84.

36. B. L. Hutchins, *Women in Modern Industry* (London: G. Bell and

Sons, 1915), p. 232; A. L. Bowley, *Wages and Income in the United Kingdom Since 1860* (Cambridge: Cambridge University Press, 1937), p. 15.

37. See Raphael Samuel, "Comers and Goers," in *The Victorian City*, H. J. Dyos and Michael Wolff, eds. (London: Routledge and Kegan Paul, 1973), I, pp. 123–60.

## 5. IMAGE AND REALITY
### The Actress and Society

1. The census reports must be treated with caution because the classifications are not consistent from one census to the next. Although they all contain the category "Actress" (or alternately "Actor, female"), the number of additional classifications varies, and thus the inclusiveness of the definition of actress probably varies as well. For instance, the 1841 census contains in addition to the actress classification only one other, "Musician, Organist," in the broader category of entertainer or public performer. Thus "Actress" probably embraces dancers, theater attendants, and even perhaps some singers. In 1851, by contrast, the classifications expand to "Theatrical Manager-Lessee" (1), "Officer, Servant at theatre" (6), "Actor" (643), "Dancer" (135), "Musician" (532), "Vocalist" (256), "Conjuror, Performer in Shows" (2) and "Exhibition- (Show-) keeper, servant" (33): *Parliamentary Papers* 1852–53, Vol. LXXXVII, Part 1, cxli, cxlix (numbers in parentheses indicate number of females in each category for all of Great Britain). But in the general tabulation for England and Wales in 1851 (p. ccxxvi) the classification is "Actresses and all others engaged about theatres." The figure of 717 for 1851 appears, therefore, to include dancers and some attendants as well, and the actual figure for bona fide actresses may be nearer 600. The expansion of the music halls in the latter part of the century further complicates matters, since there is no way of determining what proportion of music-hall entertainers listed themselves as actresses; presumably the number was considerable, swelling the late-Victorian census figures. (Music-hall entertainers and ballet dancers are not treated in this chapter, though rigid occupational classification is impossible; there was, for instance, a small but significant interchange of performers between the music hall and the legitimate stage.)

Statements of occupation were often misleading. It was a continuing grievance of actresses throughout the century that prostitutes were identified in newspaper court reports as "actresses" (e.g., *The Theatre*, August 1896, pp. 162–63). Prostitutes probably identified themselves that way on official occasions, and this practice may have extended to the census returns as well. And of course some actresses were prostitutes, especially at the low theaters, as George Bernard Shaw complained: John Elsom, *Erotic Theatre* (New York: Taplinger, 1974), p. 22.

On the other hand, it seems likely that some women who were legitimate actresses did not so state their occupation (or their fathers or husbands did not) for reasons of respectability, though this practice might have declined as the profession became more respectable, and it may account for some of the apparent increase. Certainly there is a striking discrepancy between Leman Rede's estimate of 3,000 actors and actresses in Britain in 1836 and the census total for 1841 of under 1,400; Leman Rede, *The Road to the Stage* (London: J. Onwhyn, 1836), p. 14.

2. "S," "A Few Words about Actresses, and the Profession of the Stage," *Englishwoman's Journal*, ΙΙ (Feb. 1859), 385–86.

3. Mrs. Charles Calvert, *Sixty-Eight Years on the Stage* (London: Mills and Boon, 1911), p. 1.

4. Calvert, p. 2; Roger Manvell, *Ellen Terry* (London: Heinemann, 1968), p. 10; Kathleen Barker, "Madge Robertson—Product of a Famous Training School," *Nineteenth Century Theatre Research*, ΙΙ (Spring, 1974), 11–12; *Mr. and Mrs. Bancroft, On and Off the Stage—By Themselves* (London: Bentley, 1889), p. 3; Malcolm Morley, *Margate and its Theatres* (London: Museum Press, 1966), p. 66.

5. The actual figures for England and Wales are as follows, with the number under 20 years preceding the number over 20: 1841—women 72 and 312, men 71 and 915; 1851—women 162 and 555, men 99 and 1,119; 1861 —women 180 and 702, men 73 and 1,238; 1871—women 367 and 1,326, men 121 and 1,778; 1881—women 523 and 1,825, men 153 and 2,036; 1891—women 752 and 2,944, men 243 and 3,382; 1901—women 1,270 and 4,170, men 323 and 5,717; 1911—women 1,599 and 7,572, men 581 and 8,495.

6. Margaret Steen, *A Pride of Terrys* (London: Longmans, 1962), pp. 273–74. Kate Terry was taking top billing and benefit performances at the age of four and a half. Morley, p. 61 and plate facing p. 81.

7. Percy Fitzgerald, *The World Behind the Scenes* (London: Chatto & Windus, 1881), pp. 89, 71.

8. Rede, *The Road to the Stage*, p. 14. Comic old women or "dame" parts were still taken by men, particularly in burlesque and pantomime; see Jane W. Stedman, "From Dame to Woman: W. S. Gilbert and Victorian Transvestism," in Martha Vicinus, ed., *Suffer and Be Still* (Bloomington: Indiana University Press, 1972), p. 22.

9. Ernest B. Robertson, *Sheridan to Robertson: A Study of the Nineteenth Century London Stage* (Cambridge: Harvard University Press, 1926), pp. 9–11, 16–17.

10. Robertson, 64–65; Daniel Nalbach, *The King's Theatre, 1704–1867* (London: The Society for Theatre Research, 1972), pp. 106, 119–20; Ivor Guest, *Victorial Ballet-Girl* (London: A. & C. Black, 1957), p. 33.

11. Alan S. Downer, *The Eminent Tragedian: William Charles Macready* (Cambridge: Harvard University Press, 1966), pp. 17, 277–78.

12. William W. Appleton, *Madame Vestris and the London Stage* (New York: Columbia University Press, 1974), pp. 23, 63.

13. *Nicholas Nickleby* (London: Chapman and Hall, 1906), I, p. 349.

14. Basil Francis, *Fanny Kelly of Drury Lane* (London: Rockliff, 1950), p. 161.

15. Steen, 37; Sir Thomas Martin, *Helena Faucit (Lady Martin)* (Edinburgh: Blackwood, 1900), pp. 294, 301, 306, 341, 394. Even the Queen's cousin, Prince George, Duke of Cambridge, married an actress (Louisa Fairbrother) in 1847, though not of course publicly: Giles St. Aubyn, *The Royal George* (New York: Knopf, 1964), pp. 34–41.

16. The social status of the actress was particularly vulnerable to the immoral ambiance of the early nineteenth-century theater. In London the theaters were located in the most notorious parts of town, and the prevalence of prostitutes among the audience was frequently noted (*A Regency Visitor: the English Tour of Prince Pückler-Muskau*, ed. Eliza M. Butler

[London: Collins, 1957], p. 84; [Alexander Slidell], *The American in England* [New York: Harper, 1833], II, 211–12). A significant aspect of Macready's campaign to elevate the ambiance of the stage was his effort to eliminate the prostitutes' blatant commerce, which offended respectability (Downer, pp. 209–10).

17. George Eliot, *Daniel Deronda,* Standard Ed. (Edinburgh and London: Blackwood [1897]), I, p. 383.

18. [Alma Ellerslie], *Diary of an Actress; or, Realities of Stage Life* (London: Griffith, Farran, O'Keden and Walsh, 1885), p. 123.

19. W. M. Thackeray, *The History of Pendennis* (New York: Scribner, 1911), I, p. 81.

20. Gordon N. Ray, *Thackeray: The Age of Wisdom* (New York: McGraw-Hill, 1958), p. 111.

21. M. S. Packe, *The Life of John Stuart Mill* (London: Secker and Warburg, 1954), pp. 384–87. Packe's account of this episode contains some inaccuracies, however. See my "Helen Taylor's 'Experimental Life' on the Stage: 1856–58," *Nineteenth-Century Theatre Research,* forthcoming.

22. The correspondence with her mother, which provides a detailed vignette of the conditions of the mid-Victorian provincial stage, is in the Mill-Taylor Collection at the British Library of Political and Economic Science, vol. LI. Letters from Mrs. Stirling to both Helen Taylor and Harriet Taylor Mill are included in vols. XXIII, LI, and LIV.

23. Laurence Irving, *Henry Irving: The Actor and His World* (London: Faber and Faber, 1951), p. 72.

24. Lynton Hudson, *The English Stage* (London: George Harrap, 1951), p. 41.

25. Barry Duncan, *The St. James's Theatre* (London: Barrie and Rockliff, 1964), pp. 96–183.

26. Charles E. Pascoe, *The Dramatic List* (New York: Benjamin Blom, 1880, 1969), pp. 347–48.

27. The 1901 census conveniently differentiates between married and unmarried actresses. Of the 1,270 under 20 years of age, 58 (or 4½%) are listed as married, of the 2,102 between 20 and 25, 638 (or 30%) are married; of the 2,182 between 25 and 35, 1,287 (or 59%) are married, and of the 889 over 35, 726 (or 82%) are married. (These figures also give some notion of the age distribution.) *Parliamentary Papers,* 1903, vol. LXXXIV, 186.

28. See also Laurence Irving, *The Precarious Crust* (London: Chatto & Windus, 1971), pp. 37–38.

29. Another respectable quasi-theatrical employment was performing in "entertainments" such as those produced by Mr. and Mrs. German Reed (formerly the actress Priscilla Horton): Jane W. Stedman, ed., *Gilbert before Sullivan* (London: Routledge and Kegan Paul, 1969), p. 5.

30. Agencies began to proliferate from sometime in the 1850's. Often acting instructors would undertake to arrange their students' first engagements, as Mrs. Stirling did for Helen Taylor. The late nineteenth century also saw the growth of the practice of professional advertisements in *The Era* and *Stage Directory* by players in employment as well as those "resting" (in the professional euphemism).

31. Allardyce Nicoll, *A History of Late Nineteenth Century Drama 1850–1900* (Cambridge: Cambridge University Press, 1946), I, p. 8.

32. St. Vincent Troubridge, *The Benefit System in the British Theatre* (London: The Society for Theatre Research, 1967), p. 88. The standard starting salary seems to have remained at about £1 per week until the end of the century. A leading actress in the 1840's, Mrs. Glover, received £12 per week; Louise Keeley in the 1860's received a top salary of £15: Walter Goodman, *The Keeleys on Stage and at Home* (London: Bentley, 1895), p. 141. Ellen Terry received £40 (a very high salary in the 1870's) from Charles Reade on her return to the stage, but only £20 from the Bancrofts. However, at the Lyceum in the 1890's she received a staggering £200 per week from Irving: Manvell, p. 213. (This may have made her the highest regularly salaried woman in Great Britain.) Mrs. Patrick Campbell, who started at £2.10.0 in 1888, was engaged by Pinero to play Paula Tanqueray in 1893 at £15 per week. Her brilliant success in this role enabled her to command £60 in her next engagement: Mrs. Patrick Campbell, *My Life and Some Letters* (London: Hutchinson, n.d.), pp. 27, 65, 86. Ellaline Terris as a star at the Gaiety in the 1890's received £30 per week. Lena Ashwell received a salary of £50 in the 1900's: *Myself a Player* (London: Michael Joseph, 1936), p. 132. These were of course top salaries; it should also be remembered that they were precarious, depending on engagement. Much larger sums were to be had by big-name stars on tour in America: Lillian Adelaide Neilson was said to have received £20,000 for 100 performances, and Sarah Bernhardt received £40,000 for 162 performances in America.

For the sake of comparison, I include some salaries of leading music hall stars around the end of the century: Ada Reeve claimed she would get up to £400 per week on a percentage: *Take it for a Fact* (London: Heinemann, 1954), p. 103. Vesta Tilley received £500 per week on one occasion as principal boy in pantomime. These gigantic salaries were of course linked to drawing power, and, being publicized, were partly an advertisement expense as well: H. G. Hibbert, *A Playgoer's Memories* (London: Grant Richards, 1920), p. 205.

33. Mary Jeune, Lady St. Helier, *Memories of Fifty Years* (London: Edward Arnold, 1909), p. 189.

34. F. G. Bettany, *Stewart Headlam: A Biography* (London: Murray, 1926), p. 97.

35. Reproduced in T. Edgar Pemberton, *The Kendals: A Biography* (London: C. Arthur Pearson, 1900), pp. 168–91.

36. F. C. Burnand, "Behind the Scenes," *Fortnightly Review*, NS, XXXVII (January, 1885), 89; William Archer, "A Storm in Stageland," *About the Theatre: Essays and Studies* (London: T. Fisher Unwin, 1886), pp. 211–33.

37. I am indebted to Jane W. Stedman for the information concerning Burnand's second wife. Some fifteen years later an even greater uproar greeted Clement Scott's notorious declaration that "an actress who endeavours to keep her purity is almost of necessity foredoomed to failure in her career." A number of leading actors indignantly demanded his dismissal as drama critic for the *Telegraph*. The newspaper's owner, who had himself married an actress, obliged; *Dame Madge Kendal, by Herself* (London: Murray, 1933), p. 40.

38. "A Foreign Resident [T. H. S. Escott], *Society in London* (London: Chatto & Windus, 1885), pp. 296–99.

39. Gilbert had himself defended Miss Fortescue's reputation on an

earlier occasion; Hesketh Pearson, *Gilbert: His Life and Strife* (London: Methuen, 1957), p. 124.

40. Pearson, p. 266; *Jessie Bond, Life and Reminiscences* (London: John Lane, 1930), p. 93; John Coleman, *Players and Playwrights I Have Known* (London: Chatto & Windus, 1888), II, p. 189. John Hollingshead, manager of the Gaiety, had posted a notice on the call board: "Ladies who are in receipt of a salary of 30 s. a week are requested not to drive up to the theatre in their own broughams": Ellaline Terriss, *Just a Little Bit of String* (London: Hutchinson, 1955), p. 183.

41. Some support is lent to this impression by Pascoe's *The Dramatic List*, which gives brief biographical notices of 145 actresses, most of whom entered the profession in the 1860's and 1870's. Of these only 45 are definitely identified as daughters of actors (though the actual proportion may be rather higher).

42. George Moore, *Impressions and Opinions* (London: David Nutt, 1891), p. 172. Moore rather perversely complained about the obsession of players with respectability, a development that he dates from about 1870, noting that actresses now strove to present themselves as "excellent mothers [who] have not known the joys of lovers" (p. 154). Echoing George Eliot's Alcharisi, he observed, "the ideal mother cannot be the great artist." However, in his novel *The Mummer's Wife* (1885) he offers a fine Zola-esque portrayal of the descent into degradation of a woman who succumbs to the lure of the stage.

43. Laurence Irving, *The Successors* (London: Rupert Hart-Davis, 1967), pp. 72–74.

44. Two of the most successful avenues to the stage in the 1880's and 1890's, particularly for middle-class outsiders, were Sarah Thorne's dramatic school at Margate, which produced among others Irene and Violet Vanbrugh (Morley, pp. 102–122) and the Shakespeare repertory company, run by the Oxonian Frank Benson, which launched a number of respectable young men and women into the profession.

45. Albert Mansbridge, *Margaret McMillan, Prophet and Pioneer* (London: Dent, 1932), pp. 12–17.

46. Yvonne Kapp, *Eleanor Marx*, Vol. I (London: Lawrence and Wishart, 1972), pp. 24, 234–35.

47. Kapp, p. 235; C. Suzuki, *The Life of Eleanor Marx, 1855–1898* (Oxford: Oxford University Press, 1967), pp. 164, 176–77.

48. Elizabeth Robins, *Both Sides of the Curtain* (London: Heinemann, 1940), p. 258.

49. Only Janet Achurch of this quartet came from a theatrical family. Elizabeth Robins was American-born of respectable parents; Robins, pp. 167–68. Florence Farr was the self-consciously rebellious and Bohemian daughter of a professional man: Clifford Bax, ed., *Florence Farr, Bernard Shaw, W. B. Yeats* (London: Home & Van Thal, 1946), "Introduction." Mrs. Patrick Campbell was of a cosmopolitan, well-to-do background; Campbell, pp. 1–3.

50. Campbell, pp. 129–30; W. A. Armstrong, "The Nineteenth Century Matinee," *Theatre Notebook* XIV (Winter, 1959), 59.

51. *The English Woman's Review*, 15 January 1904, p. 48 (Report of the annual meeting of the Theatrical Ladies Guild); John Parker, ed., *The Green Room Book* (London: T. Sealey Clark, 1909), pp. 661–62.

52. *The Three Arts Club* [Rules and List of Members] (London, 1912), British Museum shelf-mark 08275 g27 (4); Ashwell, p. 176; Eva Moore, *Exits and Entrances* (London: Chapman & Hall, 1923), pp. 17–18.

53. W. MacQueen Pope, *The Gaiety: Theatre of Enchantment* (London: W. H. Allen, 1949), pp. 316–417; James Jupp, *The Gaiety Stage Door* (London: Jonathan Cape, 1923), passim.

54. J. M. Bulloch, "Peers who have married Players," *Notes and Queries* CLXIX (10 August 1935), 92–94.

55. F. M. L. Thompson, *English Landed Society in the Nineteenth Century* (London: Routledge & Kegan Paul, 1963), p. 302.

56. Hamilton Fyfe, *Sir Arthur Pinero's Plays and Players* (New York: Macmillan, 1930), pp. 88–89.

57. *The Actresses' Franchise League, Annual Report 1912–1913* (London: 1913), British Museum shelf-mark P.P. 3611 m.g.; Parker, *The Green Room Book*, p. 665; Antonia Raeburn, *The Militant Suffragettes* (Newton Abbot: Readers Union, 1974), pp. 85–86. A number of actors were quite prominent in supporting the suffrage cause; Johnston Forbes Robertson was a leading figure in the founding of the league. See also, Margaret Webster, *The Same Only Different* (London: Victor Gollancz, 1969), pp. 246–55; Ashwell, p. 164; Moore, p. 89; Elizabeth Sprigge, *Sybil Thorndike Casson* (London: Victor Gollancz, 1971), p. 73; Lillah McCarthy, *Myself and Friends* (London: Thornton Butterworth, 1933), pp. 148–49.

58. Raeburn, pp. 96, 114. See Samuel Hynes, *The Edwardian Turn of Mind* (Princeton: Princeton University Press, 1968), pp. 201–4, on Elizabeth Robins' play *Votes for Women!* (1907). She was active in the Woman's Social and Political Union.

59. Raeburn, pp. 197–98; H. R. Doubleday and Lord Howard de Walden, *The Complete Peerage*, Vol. VIII (London: St. Catherine Press, 1929), p. 578.

6. WOMEN AND DEGREES AT CAMBRIDGE UNIVERSITY
1862–1897

1. The same was true of the University of Wales. The information used here relates solely to universities in England and Wales; the growth of educational opportunities for women was somewhat different in the remainder of the United Kingdom. The total number of women students at universities and university colleges in England and Wales at the end of the nineteenth century is not readily available. I have, however, calculated that in 1914 there were 11,000 fulltime students at these institutions, of whom 2,900 were women (Cmd. 8137–38 xix 1914–16). The figures do not include Oxford and Cambridge women, since they were not matriculated students. In 1913–14 about 120 women held university teaching posts.

2. Married Women's Property Acts of 1870, 1874, and 1882; Custody of Infants Acts of 1839, 1873, and 1884; Matrimonial Causes Acts of 1878 and 1895; Repeal of Contagious Diseases Acts, 1883; Act enabling universities to admit women, 1875; Medical Education Act, 1876; Acts of 1869, 1870,

1880, and 1894 giving women opportunities as electors or elected representatives at local government level.

3. A Cambridge graduate who paid to keep his name registered had at this time a vote on every conceivable university matter, such as syllabuses, examinations, buildings, and bequests; his vote weighed as heavily as that of a lecturer or professor. The powers of Oxford graduates were somewhat more circumscribed.

4. Constance Rover, *Women's Suffrage and Party Politics in Britain* (London: Routledge and Kegan Paul, 1967), p. 180.

5. Elizabeth Garrett Anderson, who accompanied Emily Davies to Westminster to present the 1866 petition, wrote the following year asking that her support of the suffrage movement be kept private. "I think it is wiser as a medical woman to keep somewhat in the background as regards other movements." Elizabeth Garrett to her sister, Millicent Fawcett, June 1867, Fawcett Library. Reprinted in Jo Manton, *Elizabeth Garrett Anderson* (London: Methuen, 1965), pp. 171–72.

6. Emily Davies to Barbara Bodichon, 3 March 1867, Girton Archives. Lady Goldsmid was a member of the first Executive Committee of Emily Davies' College for Women (later Girton College).

7. "My friends and I were all on fire for women's education including women's medical education and very emulous of Cambridge where the movement was already advanced. But hardly any of us were all on fire for women's suffrage, wherein the Oxford education movement differed greatly from the Cambridge movement." Mrs. Humphrey Ward, *A Writer's Recollections* (London: W. Collins, 1918), pp. 152–53. See also the letter by Alice Stopford Green to *The Times* quoted on p. 138. Mrs. Ward was responsible for the famous protest against women's suffrage sent to the *Nineteenth Century* in 1889, and in 1908 she founded the women's anti-suffrage society.

8. For an account of the women's degree movement at Oxford, see A. M. A. H. Rogers, *Degrees by Degrees* (Oxford: Oxford University Press, 1938).

9. Royal Commissions on: Popular Education, 1858; Public Schools, 1861; Secondary Education, 1864.

10. For a comparison of Ruskin's views with those of Mill, see Kate Millett, *Sexual Politics* (New York: Doubleday, 1970; London: Rupert Hart Davies, 1971), pp. 88–108.

11. The typical title of an anti-feminist pamphlet, written in this case by Alfred Marshall's father, William. Unfortunately it cannot be traced. See John Maynard Keynes, *Alfred Marshall 1842–1924*, reprinted in Keynes, *Essays in Biography* (New York: Norton, 1963), p. 126.

12. A. Trollope, *The Eustace Diamonds* (London: Penguin Press, 1969), Ch. 24. In 1841 the excess of women over men in the over-twenty age group was 4.15%, 3.9% in 1851 and 4.7% in 1861. Calculated from tables given in B. Mitchell and P. Deane, *Abstract of British Historical Statistics* (Cambridge: Cambridge University Press, 1962). The excess of women increased during the following hundred years; in 1951 it was approximately 8%. Yet in 1951 only 30% of women in the 20–34 age group were single, whereas the figure for 1851 was 48%. In 1861, 46% of women in this age group were unmarried; in 1961, 22%.

13. Edward Carpenter, *My Days and Dreams* (London: George Allen, 1916), p. 31. One of the commissioners in the 1864 inquiry into secondary

education, J. G. Fitch, judged that only 6 to 7% of governesses had deliberately planned to take up the work (Royal Commission on Secondary Education, Report 1867–68, xxxviii, p. 284). It was said that girls in Edinburgh fought shy of the newly instituted university examinations for schools. "They seem to think the certificates are only for Governesses and they do not like publicly to announce themselves as entrants on that career." Letter to Emily Davis, 6 September 1866, Girton Archives (signature difficult).

14. See R. Glynne-Grylls, *Queen's College, 1848–1948* (London: Routlege and Kegan Paul, 1948), and Margaret Tuke, *A History of Bedford College for Women* (London: Oxford University Press, 1939).

15. Information passed to Emily Davies by T. (J?) D. Acland, May 1863, Girton Archives. Initials are unclear, but Thomas Dyke Acland was a known worker for educational reform.

16. G. D. Liveing to Emily Davis, 22 July 1862, Girton Archives.

17. Emily Davies reporting to R. Potts of Trinity College, Cambridge, 15 January 1863, Girton Archives.

18. Emily Davies' examination report, December 1863. Reprinted in *Report*, National Association for the Promotion of Social Science, April 1864.

19. Thomas Markby, who was secretary of the Cambridge Local Examination syndicate from 1867 until his death in 1870, claimed, "I got votes enough to turn the scales just before going into the Senate House." Markby to Emily Davies, 9 March 1865, Girton Archives. The examination scheme was made permanent in 1867. In 1869 Henry Sidgwick noted, "there is no *real conservatism* amongst educated men, just *vis inertiae.*" Sidgwick to F. W. H. Myers, 3 May 1869, Wren 100[211].

20. The composition of this committee is not exactly known, but it included Sedley Taylor, J. R. Seeley, J. B. Lightfoot, Sidgwick, and possibly J. Porter and H. W. Cookson. Sedley Taylor papers in the University Library, 6259 51,6258 27 and 28.

21. He had the support of Henry Jackson, J. R. Seeley, J. B. Mayor, W. E. Currey, R. C. Jebb, and others. See Sheldon Rothblatt, *The Revolution of the Dons* (London: Faber and Faber, 1968), Ch. 7.

22. Correspondence between James Bryce, who argued Sidgwick's case, and Emily Davies in June 1867, Girton Archives.

23. Sidgwick's letters to and from his mother, May 1867, Wren Library, Trinity College, Cambridge 99[77], 99[83], 101[174].

24. For an account of the Extension Lecture Movement, see Edwin Welch, *The Peripatetic University* (Cambridge: Cambridge University Press, 1973).

25. Emily Davies was at this meeting and "declared for the exact following of University Examinations. Myers and I discussed this and not seeing how soon women would be ready for the Tripos examination and fearing the low standard of the Pass examination [Ordinary Degree], we decided to resist Miss Davies in all ways. We agreed, for example, that I should see Kingsley and warn him against her. I called upon him where he was lodging; he said, 'My dear fellow, you need not be afraid! She's a bad woman; you can see it in her face. She would be a better woman if she had married and had children. You should talk to Mrs. Kingsley.' " Present at the meeting were Kingsley, Seeley, Markby, Jackson, B. H. Kennedy, H. D. Warr, J. P. Payne, James Stuart, Josephine Butler, Miss Boucherett, Emily Davies, and

possibly F. Myers. From a memoir written by Henry Jackson, 7 November 1900, Wren Library, Add Ms 43[55].

26. After a three-year trial the examinations became permanent in 1871 and in 1873 were opened to male candidates. Comparing papers set for the Higher Locals and the Previous Examination, several experts have offered the opinion that the former were of higher standard. Sheila Lemoine, unpubl. M.A. thesis, Manchester, 1968.

27. M. G. Fawcett in Cheltenham Ladies College *Magazine,* Spring 1894. Also present at the meeting were F. D. Maurice, B. H. Kennedy and his daughters Julia and Marion, James Stuart, John Peile and his wife, Mrs. J. C. Adams, Mrs. J. Venn, Mrs. W. H. Bateson, and Thomas Markby. See also, B. A. Clough, *A. J. Clough* (London: Arnold, 1897).

28. During the 1897 controversy Sidgwick was privately informed that the Council's decision in 1870 not to permit the formal use of the papers was made by a vote of six to five (Newnham Archives). If this had been known at the time, greater efforts to get the examinations opened formally might have been made.

29. Emily Davies to Marianne Bernard, December 1879, following another suggestion on cooperation from Sidgwick (Girton Archives). Bernard was Mistress of Girton from 1875 to 1884.

30. Mary Paley and Amy Bulley. In 1877 Mary Paley married Alfred Marshall, who became professor of political economy in 1885.

31. Emily Davies to Mrs. Steadman Aldis, 20 March 1880, and letter from A.J.B.H., St. James's Rectory, 1880, to Emily Davies (Girton Archives). Aldis was a mathematics coach at Cambridge. He became professor of mathematics at Durham College of Science (Newcastle) in 1870 and in 1883 moved to Auckland College, New Zealand.

32. Notes made by Emily Davies following a meeting with Sidgwick on 13 March 1880, Girton Archives.

33. Report of the Arts School discussion, *Cambridge University Reporter,* 15 February 1881. Dr. Campion, Queen's, said that the syndicate's membership forecast its results.

34. D. A. Winstanley, *Late Victorian Cambridge* (Cambridge: Cambridge University Press, 1947), p. 357. Emily Davies wrote, "I went to Girton the week before last [to inquire] the chances of an application from the College to the Cambridge Council to appoint Representative Members. I went to see the V-C [Perowne] who was supposed to be unfavourable and found him very gracious." Emily Davies to Barbara Bodichon, 1 February 1880, Girton Archives.

35. R. D. Archer-Hind and A. J. Tillyard took this line in letters to Sidgwick, June 1887, Newnham Archives.

36. A meeting was called on 9 June 1887 by Sidgwick, A. Cayley, N. M. Ferres, and Coutts Trotter, where Miss Davies' plans were discussed. All four were members of Newnham Council.

37. On Marshall's changed attitude to women, see my article, "Alfred Marshall's 'tendency to socialism,'" *History of Political Economy,* 7 (1975), p. 97, n. 66 and p. 101, n. 77.

38. Sidgwick to Emily Davies, 11 June 1887, describing the results of the June meeting and giving a very selective account of the letters he had received on the matter (Girton Archives).

39. As his scheme for curriculum reform made no headway, Sidgwick became despondent. He felt Cambridge had "become hidebound in a kind

of stupid conservatism," and he anticipated "a long period of slow decadence in which, from failure to adapt itself to the needs of the times, it would gradually fall in disrepute." A.S. and E.M.S., *Henry Sidgwick, A Memoir* (London: Macmillan, 1906), p. 511.

40. The Royal Commission on Secondary Education, 1895, xliii, vol. 5. Memoranda and Answers to Questions. A. M. A. H. Rogers, Tutor in Classics to the Association for the Education of Women in Oxford.

41. Ray Strachey, *The Cause* (London: Bell & Son, 1928), p. 284.

42. Op. cit., p. 232.

43. From a collection of papers of library affairs in the University Library, Cambridge, kindly shown to me by J. C. Oates, Reader in Historical Bibliography and Deputy Librarian.

44. Between 1881 and 1896, 758 women took Tripos examinations, of whom 730 were awarded Honours, and 7, aegrotats.

45. M. T. B. Stephen says of Emily Davies that she "withdrew entirely from other work [i.e., other than education] in 1873," and "she turned again to suffrage work" after resigning as honorary secretary of Girton in 1904 (D.N.B. 1912–21). Helen Blackburn, *Record of Women's Suffrage* (London: Williams & Norgate, 1902), pp. 264–68, records, however, that in 1884 Emily Davies, Millicent Fawcett, Anne Clough and Eleanor Mildred Sidgwick (a Balfour, married Henry Sidgwick in 1876), and other recognizably "Cambridge" names signed a letter to Parliament asking for the franchise for heads of households.

46. See note 7.

47. Cambridge was slow to sense the drift of reform currents, but two men smelled a rat. H. S. Foxwell wrote to *The Times*, 19 May 1897, that the movement was essentially not an educational but a political one and "the real leaders of it will not rest satisfied with anything short of the complete incorporation of women as members of the University with all the rights of mixed education and joint share in University government which are incident to full membership." *Pall Mall Gazette*, 31 March 1897. E. W. Hobson, an active opponent, said at the Arts School discussion, that some women regarded the issue as part of the women's rights movement. *Reporter*, 26 March 1897.

48. This analysis is made on the basis of flysheets circulated by university men, which have been collected in the Newnham Archives. Some papers are duplicated in the University Library's Cambridge Papers H.41. The newspaper articles consulted were found in two extensive collections of press clippings in the Girton and Newnham archives.

49. For example, the major opposition flysheet of 27 March 1897. The secretaries of this group were Leonard Whilbey of Pembroke and W. B. Hardy, Caius. Alfred Marshall was a very active opponent, as were Professor Clifford Allbutt and A. Austen Leigh. Signatories included such earlier supporters of women as H. S. Foxwell and J. Venn; C. V. Stanford to *The Times*, 4 February 1896; James Bryce, letter to Mrs. H. Sidgwick, 25 January 1896, Newnham Archives. James Bryce, who had helped women so much at the beginning of the higher education movement and who had opposed "separate development," was now a firm opponent of degrees and enfranchisement. Skeat, who strongly opposed even such privileges as loan of library books, had had four daughters at Newnham and was described privately as "an unnatural parent." John Peile to Henry Sidgwick, 21 March 1897, Newnham Archives.

50. "Q.C." to *The Times*, 20 May 1897; *Pall Mall Gazette*, 20 May 1897; Cambridge matriculations in 1896–97 were the lowest since 1882. In 1890 there were 1,027 students; in 1897, 887. *Cambridge Review*, 3 June 1897.

51. G. F. Browne in *Reporter*, 1888, and in the *Nineteenth Century*, May 1893; flysheets written by W. H. Besant of John's, 9 March 1896, and H. R. Tottenham, John's, 3 March 1896. Marshall was very much in favor of Browne's scheme.

52. A recurrent theme of Marshall. See, for example, his anonymous reply to the syndicate query regarding the teaching of women, published in the syndicate's report under Moral Science.

53. Bishop Selwyn's letter read at the Art School discussion, 12 March 1897; *Reporter*, 26 March 1897; "M.D., F.R.S." to *The Times*, 4 February 1896; the eccentric Professor James Mayo in a flysheet, 14 May 1897.

54. "Member of Senate" to the *Manchester Guardian*, 3 February 1896; Alfred Marshall to *The Times*, 21 May 1897.

55. This came chiefly from Marshall; see, for example, his flysheet of 3 February 1896. A. Austen Leigh, Provost of King's, insisted that women should not have degrees because they lived in the seclusion of their colleges and thus missed the benefits of "real" residence, which for men was "a severe ordeal of character and conduct." Flysheet, 4 June 1896.

56. Competition is mentioned in the major opposition petition of 10 March 1896; "M.D., F.R.S." to *The Times*, 4 February 1896; C. V. Stanford to *The Times*, 4 February 1896.

57. The issue of the "overcrowded professions" in relation to university education was taken up by the Royal Commission on Secondary Education 1895, *Report*, vol. 1, part 111 G, p. 218, §138.

58. Report of the Women's Degree Syndicate, February 1897, included an unprecedented Minority Report signed by J. Armitage Robinson, J. W. Cartmell (who as senior examiner in the 1870's had helped arrange the marking of women's Tripos papers), James Montague Rhodes, Lewis Shore, and C. Taylor, which proposed that women be granted "some title of a degree, not being the title of a Degree in the University." The majority report was signed by Charles Smith, Arthur Berry, A. W. Dale, F. W. Maitland, R. D. Roberts, W. N. Shaw, V. H. Stanton, A. N. Whitehead, and Williams Chawner. Sidgwick was originally a member of the syndicate together with other known supporters—Jackson, J. N. Keynes, R. T. Wright, Montague Butler, and Peile, but its composition was voted down, 12 March 1896.

59. Marshall wrote to *The Times*, 21 May 1897, that he would gladly have foregone a year's salary to have escaped "the wear and tear of this weary year."

60. Maitland to Sidgwick, 19 March 1897, University Library Manuscripts 7006[64].

61. Alan McLean to A. J. Balfour, Newnham Archives.

62. *Daily News*, 21 May 1897; *Pall Mall Gazette*, 20 May 1897; *The Times*, 20 May 1897; and *Manchester Guardian*, 22 May 1897.

63. See, for example, Extra Special Edition of *Cambridge Weekly News* entitled "The Triumph of Man," 28 May 1897, and special pictorial supplements in the *Daily Mail*, 30 May 1897, and *Illustrated Sporting and Dramatic News*, 12 June 1897.

64. Emily Davies to H. R. Tomkinson. Tomkinson was Secretary of the London local committee for Cambridge Local Examinations during the

1863 experiment, and treasurer of the first Executive for the College for Women.

65. Michael Sanderson, *The Universities and British Industry, 1850–1920* (London: Routledge and Kegan Paul, 1972), p. 388.

66. John Stuart Mill, *The Subjection of Women* (London: Longmans, 1869), 2nd ed., Ch. 1.

67. In 1897, 220 Girtonians were teaching, 62 were in "other professions," 184 were at home, of whom 99 were married, and information was not available on 24. Of the 490 old Girtonians, 103 were married (Newnham Archives). In 1894, 374 of the 667 Newnhamites living in the United Kingdom were teaching. In the same year, the employment of the 29 women graduates from the Victoria University was given as 21 teaching, 2 secretaries, 2 married, 3 home, and 1 at college. Royal Commission 1895, vol. 5. A study carried out in 1961 shows that 49.5% of 1937 and 1938 Cambridge women graduates were or had been teachers (at all levels), and 45.8% of 1952 and 1953 graduates had chosen the same profession. The relevant figure for 1952 and 1953 Cambridge male graduates was 28.1%. Calculated from Christine Craig, *The Employment of Cambridge Graduates* (Cambridge: Cambridge University Press, 1963). Chs. v and vii.

68. For some reason, a middle-class man whose wife is teaching does not lose face in the same way as does a man whose wife is "out at work." The implication in the latter case is that the man does not earn enough to keep his wife at home.

## 7. VICTORIAN MASCULINITY AND THE ANGEL IN THE HOUSE

1. H. V. Routh, *Money, Morals and Manners as Revealed in Modern Literature* (London: I. Nicholson and Watson, 1935), pp. 141–57; Walter E. Houghton, *The Victorian Frame of Mind* (New Haven: Yale University Press, 1957), pp. 341–97.

2. Virginia Woolf, "Professions for Women," *The Death of the Moth and Other Essays* (New York: Harcourt Brace Jovanovich, 1970), pp. 235–42; Kate Millett, *Sexual Politics* (New York: Doubleday, 1970), pp. 88–108; Katharine M. Rogers, *The Troublesome Helpmate: A History of Misogyny in Literature* (Seattle: University of Washington Press, 1966), pp. 189–94.

3. *The Poems of Coventry Patmore*, ed. Frederick Page (London: Oxford University Press, 1949), pp. 89–90. All references are to this edition and will hereafter be incorporated into the text.

4. "Guinevere," ll. 477–80, in *The Poems of Tennyson*, ed. Christopher Ricks (London: Longmans, Green, 1969). All references are to this edition and will hereafter be indicated by line numbers in the text.

5. The most thorough attempt to evaluate and defend the poem in the context of the period is John Killham's *Tennyson and The Princess: Reflections of an Age* (London: University of London, Athlone Press, 1958). In "Feminism and Femininity in *The Princess*" (in *The Major Victorian Poets: Reconsiderations*, ed. Isobel Armstrong; London: Routledge & Kegan Paul,

1969, pp. 35–50), Bernard Bergonzi finds the poem timid in its reluctance to portray the militant aspects of femininity, although he praises the poem for raising implications about sexual roles that would have been disturbing to the Victorian mind. Both Kate Millett (*Sexual Politics*, pp. 76–80) and Katharine Rogers (*The Troublesome Helpmate*, pp. 190–92) are highly critical of the poem's political stance.

6. Hallam. Lord Tennyson, *Alfred Tennyson; a Memoir by his son* (New York: Macmillan, 1897), I, p. 326n., and II, p. 69.

7. See "Locksley Hall Sixty Years After," l. 48.

8. Also compare the jotting in a late notebook, "Men should be androgynous and women gynandrous, but men should not be gynandrous nor women androgynous" (*The Poems of Tennyson*, p. 1424).

9. John Killham draws attention to those lines and to their similarity to the concerns of *The Princess* in *Tennyson and The Princess: Reflections of an Age*, p. 84.

10. "The 'High Born Maiden' Symbol in Tennyson," in *Critical Essays on the Poetry of Tennyson*, ed. John Killham (New York: Barnes and Noble, 1960), pp. 126–36.

11. In an unpublished paper Zelda and Julian Boyd have argued that a fear of the world of action exists throughout Tennyson's poetry. Through an analysis of his verbal structures, they demonstrate that Tennyson continually converts action into activity, or motion without goals. I take my distinction between action and activity from their paper.

12. *Works*, eds. E. T. Cook and Alexander Wedderburn (London: G. Allen, 1903–12), 18,140.

13. (New York: Longmans, Green, 1927), pp. 208–9.

14. *Matthew Arnold* (New York: Columbia University Press, 1939), p. 128.


## 8.  SEX AND DEATH IN VICTORIAN ENGLAND
### An Examination of Age- and Sex Specific Death Rates, 1840–1910


1. See, for example, Ann Oakley, *Sex, Gender and Society* (New York: Harper & Row, 1972), pp. 30–42. See also, Ashley Montagu, *The Natural Superiority of Women*, rev. ed. (London: Collier-Macmillan Ltd., 1968), pp. 70–84.

2. F. C. Madigan, "Are Mortality Differentials Biologically Caused?" *Milbank Memorial Fund Quarterly*, XXXV (1957), pp. 202–23.

3. *United Nations Demographic Yearbook 1967* (New York: United Nations Publishing Service, 1968), p. 730.

4. David Glass, "World Population 1800–1950," in *Cambridge Economic History of Modern Europe*, ed. H. J. Habakkuk (Cambridge, Eng.: Cambridge University Press, 1965), VI, pp. 114–15.

5. The civil registration of births, deaths, and marriages began in 1837, just as Victoria ascended the throne. Previously, through the agency of the Anglican Church, only baptisms (not births) and burials (not deaths) had been registered. Anglican registration was not very complete or very detailed in the early nineteenth century, and hence the data provided by the system of religious registration can tell us little about the differences between male and female mortality patterns before the late 1830's.

6. The data gathered and published by the Registrar-General of England and Wales are generally regarded as very accurate. Perhaps only three to five percent of all deaths escaped the registration process between 1837 and the late 1860's, when registration became compulsory. Afterward the registration process was even more complete. However, cause-of-death data were not very reliable until late in the nineteenth century. Medical terminology was not standardized, and doctors were not very skilled in post-mortem examinations. Nevertheless, certain diseases with highly identifiable symptoms could be singled out as the probable cause of death. Among them were various forms of tuberculosis, which in the middle of the nineteenth century was still called consumption.

7. See the *Seventy-fifth Annual Report of the Registrar-General*, Decennial Supplement (published as part of the *Parliamentary Papers for 1914–16*), VIII, p. xxvi.

8. Glass, "World Population," p. 107. Data provided by the decennial censuses after 1851 on the age structure of the married population indicate that the average age of marriage for women in England and Wales was above 24 and under 30. In 1851 only 30 percent of all women aged 20 to 24 were married, but by the age of 35 to 39, 81 percent of all women were wives or widows. Since over 90 percent of all births were legitimate, most childbearing took place after the age of 24 and (since fertility drops off rapidly after the late 30's) under the age of 40 to 45.

9. *Second Annual Report of the Registrar-General*, Appendix (*P.P.*, 1840), XVII, p. 4.

10. *Twenty-fifth Annual Report*, Decennial Supplement (*P.P.*, 1865), XIII, pp. ix and xvi.

11. René and Jean Dubos, *The White Plague* (Boston: Little, Brown, 1952). This book is the major medical and social history of tuberculosis in the nineteenth century. With respect to the material above, see pp. 140–42, 126–38, and 59–66. However, the authors do not deal with the question of why more women than men died of tuberculosis until the 1870's. At present, among white European populations, men die of tuberculosis twice as often as women and seem more susceptible to it at every age than females. However, in Appendix E of their book the two authors provide data showing that among American blacks women still die more often of tuberculosis than men from the ages of 10 to 30. This would seem to indicate that in conditions of poverty, women are worse off than men and hence more susceptible to certain infectious diseases.

12. *Second Annual Report*, Appendix, p. 5. The debate on corsets and their effect on feminine health was quite lively in the mid-Victorian period. For a summary (and selections from magazines and newspapers), see Norah Waugh, *Corsets and Crinolines* (New York: Theatre Arts Books, 1970), pp. 133–46. The evidence is very mixed on the point of whether women wore corsets because they wanted to (for vanity's sake) or because no woman was considered respectable without one. In addition, it is not at all clear whether or not corsets were generally harmful to female health and to what degree they were worn by women outside the upper and middle classes.

13. With respect to an indoor life, it is interesting to note that the British Public Health Officer for Bengal reported in 1917 that 40 percent more Indian women than men died from tuberculosis in his district. Without any hesitation he attributed this to the fact that respectable married women were required to remain indoors for most of their lives. Deprived of fresh

air and exercise (but absolutely uncorseted), they were in extremely poor health. See Margaret Urquhart, *Women of Bengal* (Calcutta: Association Press Y.M.C.A., 1925), p. 141.

14. *Seventy-fifth Report of the Registrar-General*, Decennial Supplement, p. xxvi.

15. Dr. William A. Guy, "On the Duration of Life Among the English Gentry . . . ," *Journal of the Statistical Society of London*, IX (1846), pp. 37–49.

16. From late medieval times to the end of the nineteenth century aristocratic women in certain age groups occasionally had higher mortality rates than their male counterparts. For example, peerage females born between 1550 and 1699 had higher mortality rates than peerage males between the ages of 25 and 40. But in the cohort born between 1725 and 1749, only young girls under 15 were at a mortality disadvantage when compared to their brothers. See T. H. Hollingsworth, "Demography of the British Peerage," *Population Studies*, XVIII (1964), p. 60. In addition, if Hollingsworth's data are correct, male babies born to peerage families had a better chance of surviving the first year of life than female peerage babies almost constantly from 1625 to 1799. During the nineteenth century rates of survival were equal for both male and female infants, or favored males slightly. If these data are accurate, they are tantamount to an accusation of infanticide in the very highest reaches of British society. But Hollingsworth does not comment or provide any data on cause-of-death patterns for infants, children, or adults. For the data on infant survival, see Table 52, p. 67.

17. "On the Vital Statistics of the Society of Friends," *Journal of the Statistical Society of London*, XXII (1859), p. 222.

18. Mary S. Hartman, "Child-Abuse and Self-Abuse," *History of Childhood Quarterly*, II (1974), pp. 221–48. J. H. Plumb argues that both boys and girls were generally badly treated among the middle and upper classes. See "The Victorians Unbuttoned," *In the Light of History* (Boston: Houghton Mifflin, 1973), pp. 240–41.

19. Estimates of what percentage of the population of Victorian England could be classified as lower, middle, and upper classes vary from author to author. Peter Laslett discusses problems of definition and measurement in *The World We Have Lost* (New York: Scribners, 1965), pp. 216–18. Laslett concludes that no more than 15 percent of the total population could have been upper- and middle-class as late as 1910, even if one allows fairly lax admittance criteria for entrance into the ranks of the privileged.

20. *Sixty-fifth Annual Report of the Registrar-General*, Decennial Supplement (*P.P.*, XVIII, 1905); see the bar-graph foldout following p. xv.

21. See Thomas A. Welton, Esq., "The Effect of Migrations Upon Death Rates," *Journal of the Statistical Society of London*, XXXVIII (1875) for a summary of the data and its interpretations; in particular see pp. 323–27.

22. Robert Kennedy, Jr., "The Social Status of the Sexes and Their Relative Mortality Rates in Ireland," in *Readings in Population*, ed. William Petersen (New York: Macmillan, 1972), pp. 121–35.

23. See Sheila Ryan Johansson, "The Demographic Transition in England: A Study of the Economic, Social and Demographic Background to Mortality and Fertility Change in Cornwall, 1800–1900" (unpubl. Ph.D. diss., University of California, Berkeley, 1974), Ch. 8.

24. Johansson, "The Demographic Transition . . . ," Ch. 5.

25. Several districts in the industrial county of Lancashire contain age

groups in which women occasionally have higher death rates than men, although in Manchester itself there is none (*Twenty-fifth Annual Report, Decennial Supplement*, p. cii).

26. Peter Stearns, "Working-Class Women in Britain," in *Suffer and Be Still*, ed. Martha Vicinus (Bloomington: Indiana University Press, 1972), p. 111.

27. Laura Oren, "The Welfare of Women in Laboring Families: England 1860 to 1950," *Feminist Studies*, I (1973), p. 109.

28. For two recent treatments on the conditions under which Victorian women were employed, see Geoffrey Best, *Mid-Victorian Britain 1851–1875* (New York: Schocken Books, 1972), Ch. 2, and for middle-class women, see Lee Holcombe, *Victorian Ladies at Work* (Hamden, Conn.: Archon Books, 1973).

29. Report of the Council, *Journal of the Statistical Society of London*, LVVI (1908), pp. 376–77.

30. If a girl became ill, quit her job (factory worker, servant, clerk, or anything), and returned to her parents to die in her own home, her death certificate would list only her father's occupation. Only when an employed girl died while still working was her own occupation listed. This way of filling out death certificates would seriously bias the study of female occupational-specific mortality rates even if one were allowed to consult the Registrar-General's files of death certificates. However, to this date the Registrar-General will not let scholars do what is called a "general search." Unless this ruling is changed to enable scholars to work with data beyond that published by the Registrar-General for registration districts, we will not know how factory work affected the health of employed women.

31. D. J. Collier, *The Girl in Industry* (London: G. Bell & Sons, 1918). Despite the suspicious reluctance of factory managers to let Collier examine their data, it was still probably the case that girls were better off employed at almost anything than confined at home. The interviews of Thea Vigne with women who were teenagers around the beginning of the twentieth century reveal how often young girls were badly fed by parents or, in the case of the domestic servants employed by marginally prosperous families, their employers. The latter point was made by M. E. Loane, a district nurse in the 1900's, who was familiar with conditions ordinary girls often experienced (in correspondence with Thea Vigne, University of Essex, Department of Sociology, March 14, 1975).

32. It is interesting to note that middle-class women in Hingham, Massachusetts, in eighteenth-century North America also failed to show the mortality advantage that was so evident for middle-class men. In fact, in four out of five New England towns, women as a group had a lower life expectancy than males. Daniel Scott Smith, "Family Limitation, Sexual Control and Domestic Feminism in Victorian America," in *Clio's Consciousness Raised*, ed. Mary Hartman and Lois Banner (New York: Harper & Row, 1974), p. 125.

## 9. SEXUALITY IN GREAT BRITAIN, 1800–1900
### Some Suggested Revisions

1. See, for example, Esmé Wingfield-Stratford, *The Victorian Tragedy* (London: George Routledge and Sons, 1930), pp. 124–69; Cyril Pearl, *The*

*Girl with the Swansdown Seat* (New York: New American Library, 1958); Giles Playfair, *Six Studies in Hypocrisy* (London: Secker and Warburg, 1969); Ronald Pearsall, *The Worm in the Bud* (London: Weidenfeld and Nicholson, 1969); Cyril Pearl, *Victorian Patchwork* (London: Heinemann, 1972).

2. Eliza Lynn Linton, *The Girl of the Period, and Other Social Essays from the "Saturday Review"* (London: Bentley and Son, 1883). The most extravagant of these essays, from which the collection takes its name, first appeared in the *Saturday Review*, 14 March 1868. G. M[ogridge], *Domestic Addresses and Scraps of Experience* (London: Religious Tract Society, 1863), p. 155 quoting Lady Gough. Anon., *Memoir of Old Humphrey* (London: Religious Tract Society, n.d. [ca. 1865]. Alfred S. Dyer, *Facts for Men on Moral Purity and Health* (London: Dyer Brothers, 1884), p. 24.

3. See, for example, *Girl of the Period Miscellany*, March–November 1869 (ed. James Vizetelly). The *Examiner* scoffed at the campaign to affix fig leaves on the statues at the Crystal Palace, *Examiner*, 13 May 1854.

4. Anon. [D. Jerrold?], *Habits of Good Society* (London: James Hogg and Sons, n.d. [ca. 1855]), p. 46.

5. Richard Stang, *The Theory of the Novel in England 1850–1870* (London: Routledge & Kegan Paul, 1959) contains an excellent discussion of the novelists' and critics' views on these matters.

6. Maurice J. Quinlan, *Victorian Prelude* (new ed., London: Frank Cass, 1965); Muriel Jaeger, *Before Victoria* (London: Chatto & Windus, 1956); Ford K. Brown, *Fathers of the Victorians* (Cambridge University Press, 1961); Francis Place, *Autobiography*, ed. Mary Thale (Cambridge University Press, 1972). The distinct sexual and marital mores of two strata within the residuum can be glimpsed from Mayhew's report of London costers and from Terry Coleman's *The Railway Navvies* (London: Hutchinson, 1965), pp. 162–75.

7. Peter Cominos, "Late Victorian Sexual Respectability and the Social System," *International Review of Social History*, VIII (1963), 18–48, 216–50; Steven Marcus, *The Other Victorians* (London: Weidenfeld and Nicholson, 1966); Phyllis Grosskurth, *John Addington Symonds* (London: Longmans, 1964); Brian Harrison, "Underneath the Victorians," *Victorian Studies*, x (1967), 239–62. *Suffer and Be Still*, ed. Martha Vicinus (Bloomington: Indiana University Press, 1972) contains several essays revising the stereotype and opening new approaches.

8. Marcus, *Other Victorians*, p. 17; Carl Degler, using American evidence, has arrived at a similar skepticism about Marcus's conclusions in "What Ought to Be and What Was: Women's Sexuality in the Nineteenth Century," *American Historical Review*, 79, no. 5 (December 1974), 1469–90.

9. *London Journal of Medicine*, 2 (1857), 644; *Sanitary Review*, 2 (1858), 329–34.

10. Jacob Bright, *Parliamentary Debates*, 203, col. 576 [20 July 1870]; G. P. Merrick, *Work among the Fallen as Seen in the Prison Cell* (London: Ward, Lock and Co. [1891]); Benjamin Scott, *Is London more Immoral than Paris or Brussels?* (London: Dyer Brothers, 1881), p. 8; Alexander Patterson, "Statistics of Glasgow Lock Hospital," *Glasgow Medical Journal*, xviii (1882), 409.

11. Susan Chitty, *The Beast and the Monk* (London: Hodder and Stoughton, 1974), pp. 84–89, 163–66.

12. Marcus, *Other Victorians*, pp. 29, 136; William Acton, *Prostitution . . .* (London: Frank Cass, 1972, rep. of 2nd ed., 1870 [first pub. London 1857]), pp. 28–29, 40–45, 272–75; "Walter," *My Secret Life* (New York: Grove Press, 1966).

13. R. S. Neale, " 'Middle-class' Morality and the Systematic Colonizers," in *Class and Ideology in the Nineteenth Century* (London: Routledge & Kegan Paul, 1972) is an important essay on the advocates of birth control; Peter Fryer, *The Birth Controllers* (London: Secker and Warburg, 1965) is a useful general survey.

14. [Richard Carlile], *Every Woman's Book* (London: Carlile?, 1828), p. 38.

15. *Every Woman's Book*, p. 24; [Charles R. Drysdale], *The Elements of Social Science* (London: E. Truelove, 1887), p. 352.

16. Robert Dale Owen, *Moral Physiology* (London: The Author, 8th ed., 1883 [first pub. 1831]), pp. 32–33; Charles Knowlton, *Fruits of Philosophy* (London: Freethought Publishing, n.d. [first London ed., 1834; "165,000th," 1877?]), p. 16.

17. *Poor Man's Guardian*, 13 January 1834; *Reasoner*, 7 October 1855; *People's Paper*, 4 July 1857; *National Reformer*, 8 Auugst 1869; "An English Anarchist" [Henry Seymour?], *The Criminal Law Amendment Act* (London: The Author, 1885), p. 8; J. Peel, "The Manufacture and Retailing of Contraceptives in England," *Population Studies*, xvii (1963–64), 113–25.

18. W. A. Armstrong, "A Note on the Household Structure of Mid-nineteenth-century York in Comparative Perspective," and Michael Anderson, "Household structure and the industrial revolution; mid-nineteenth century Preston in comparative perspective," in *Household and Family in past time*, Peter Laslett and Richard Wall, eds. (Cambridge University Press, 1972), pp. 208, 214, 232; E. A. Wrigley, "Family Limitation in Pre-Industrial England," *Economic History Review*, xix (1966), 82–109.

19. F. B. Smith, *Radical Artisan* (Manchester University Press, 1973), pp. 21, 114.

20. *Northern Star*, 7 May 1842, 7 February 1846; *Bell's Life in London and Sporting Chronicle*, 10, 17 January 1880.

21. Jesse Leach, "Oval Box-Wood Pessary Impacted Within the Vagina for Two Years," *London Journal of Medicine*, 2 (1849), 675–77; Dr. Wiglesworth, "Two Cases of Retained Pessaries," *Liverpool Medical and Surgical Reports*, v (1871), 175–76; "On the Action of Pessaries," *Glasgow Medical Journal*, xxix (1888), 262–64.

22. Horace Goss, *Man and Woman, Their Physiology, Functions and Sexual Disorders, Reproduction of Species, etc.* (London: Goss, 1857?); S. Solomon, *A Guide To Health: or Advice To Both Sexes* (London: The Author?, 1792); William Brodum, M.D., *A Guide to Old Age, or A Cure for the Indiscretions of Youth* (London: J. W. Meyers, 1795 [fifteen editions before 1800]); John Roberton, *On Diseases of the Generative System* (Edinburgh: The Author?, 1812); see also, Roberton, *A Practical Essay on . . . Complaints peculiar to the female* (London: The Author?, 1813), and *Essay and Notes on the . . . Diseases of Women* (London: The Author?, 1851); Alex Ramsay, M.D., *On Peculiar Sexual Diseases* (Edinburgh: The Author, 1814?); Thomas J. Graham, M.D., *On The Diseases Peculiar To Females* (London: Simpkin, Marshall, 1834 [seven editions by 1861]).

23. Roberton, *On Diseases of the Generative System*, p. 139.

24. Anon., "Extirpation of the Clitoris," *London Medical and Physical Journal*, LIV (1825), 83–84. There is a brief account of the history of this operation, which was known as far back as ancient Egypt, in the *Lancet*, 24 June 1826, 408; Edward Smith, "A Statistical Inquiry into the Prevalence of Numerous Conditions affecting the Constitution in 1,000 Phthisical Persons," *Dublin Quarterly Journal of Medicine*, xxxv (1863), 35–37; J. A. Campbell [Medical Superintendent of the Carlisle Asylum], "Treatment of the Insane," *Glasgow Medical Journal*, xxxII (1889), 392.

25. The Rev. Richard A. Armstrong, *Our Duty in the Matter of Social Purity* (Liverpool: Purity Alliance, n.d. [1887?]), pp. 3–5.

26. Priscilla Barker, *The Secret Book. Plain Words to Females* (Brighton: P. Barker, 1888), p. 9. See also the speech by B. F. Westcott reported in the Rev. J. M. Wilson, *An Address . . . [to] the Cambridge University Association for the Promotion of Purity of Life* (Cambridge: E. Johnson, 1883), p. 14.

27. Barker, *The Secret Book*, p. 8. See also William Pratt, M.A., L.R.C.P., *A Physician's Sermon to Young Men* (London: The Author?, n.d. [1872]); Josephine Butler, *The Voice of One Crying in the Wilderness* [1874/5] (Bristol: J. W. Arrowsmith, 1913); Dyer, *Facts for Men on Moral Purity and Health*, ["fiftieth thousand"]; J. E. Hazlewood, *The Knight of Purity* (Leeds: Inchbold and Beck, 1884); John Kellock Barton, F.R.C.S.I., *The Laws of Nature and of Scripture* (Dublin: C. W. Gibbs, 1887).

28. The Rev. R. Ashington Bullen, *Our Duty As Teachers* (London: The Author?, 1886), p. 6.

10. THE WOMEN OF ENGLAND IN A CENTURY OF
SOCIAL CHANGE, 1815–1914
*A Select Bibliography*

1. This is a continuation of my bibliographical chapter in Martha Vicinus, ed., *Suffer and Be Still: Women in the Victorian Age*. Bloomington, 1972. Hereafter cited as *SBS*. The larger bibliographical work from which these sections are excerpted is entitled *The Victorian Woman in English Social History*, my book in progress.

2. Only published sources are included in the main body of this chapter, so that manuscript holdings of archives, private papers, and unprinted conference papers are not listed among the entries. Neither are government reports and other official documents.

3. Exceptions to this statement, notably the work of Neil Smelser, Ivy Pinchbeck, and Margaret Hewitt on questions of employed women, are discussed in Part I of this bibliography. In the following pages additional exceptions to this general point are annotated where they appear in the appropriate categories. It should be stated, however, that considering the increasing output of social histories since 1972, the number of good writings focused directly on nineteenth- and early twentieth-century English women remains comparatively small.

4. Some of these ideas are endorsed and discussed by Joan Kelly-Gadol in the context of arguing the importance of studying the "social relation of the

sexes" in her conference paper, "History and the Social Relation of the Sexes," for the Barnard College Women's Center, April 1975, revised and published in *Signs: Journal of Women in Culture and Society:* 1 (1976) 809–23.

5. Michelle Zimbalist Rosaldo discusses in anthropological context the function of the disparate "private" and "extra-domestic" spheres as shaping "aspects of social structure and psychology," including what she terms the "universal asymmetry in cultural evaluation of the sexes." See her chapter, "A Theoretical Overview," in *Woman, Culture and Society,* ed. Michelle Zimbalist Rosaldo and Louise Lamphere (Stanford: Stanford University Press, 1974.)

6. The place of publication is London unless otherwise stated.

7. I want to acknowledge the constructive suggestions of Jean L'Esperance with respect to the range of organizations in which women participated, and in connection with her introductions to colleagues whose researches are following the lines of my interest as expressed in this chapter.

8. Compare Anderson's study with: Margaret Hewitt, *Wives and Mothers in Victorian Industry.* 1959, and Neil Smelser, *Social Change in the Industrial Revolution.* Chicago, 1959 (*SBS* entries 2–3). Anderson focuses on the total family constellation.

9. See C. White, *Women's Magazines, 1693–1968.* 1970. (*SBS* entry 85); D. M. Ashdown, compiler, *Over the Teacups; An Anthology in Facsimile.* Rev. ed. 1972. Reports of magazine articles from the 1890's in: *The House-wife, the Mother's Friend, the Woman at Home, the Lady's Realm;* E. M. Palmegiano: *Victorian Periodicals Newsletter,* "Feminist Propaganda in the 1850s and 1860s," No. 2 (Feb. 1971), and entry 7.

10. This dissertation is outstanding in demonstrating the relevance of the Victorian novel to historical inquiry. Portrayals of female characters, perhaps best accomplished by contemporary women novelists, tend to raise questions that are missed very often by researchers who confine themselves to hard data—especially statistics on income and family expenditures. Victorian novelists have helped to illuminate nuances of women's consciousness, self-image, and social behavior that transcend the facts of their economic situation and even their domestic performance. For example, a wider connotation of the "Victorian lady" is communicated by novelists through portrayals of middle-class women who are delineated in terms of self-consciousness of their social status and behavior vis-à-vis women of other socioeconomic classes. Nineteenth-century literary artists can therefore expand the historian's insight into motivation behind women's social behavior, decorum, manners, and defense of class values with a verisimilitude that writers conducting studies of standards of living and domestic routine patterns often fail to expose.

11. I want to thank the author and the Longman Group Press for permitting me to see this chapter in manuscript form.

12. Questions of female sexuality have been treated but not at any length in the family-role context or from a female point of view. An approach to the former may be found in E. Trudgill, entry 54, and attempts at the latter in C. Degler, entry 129; P. Branca, entry 18; G. B. Barker-Benfield, entry 301; and F. B. Smith, chapter 9 of this volume. Recent writings on Victorian sexuality and pornography express a distinctly masculine frame of reference.

13. See review by A. Hayter, *Times Literary Supplement:* Dec. 27, 1974, p. 1461, for discussion of Basch's use of novels as evidence with other sources.

14. More active feminism could of course have been a *consequence.* This development has not been studied.

15. The same should be said for contemporary quasi-sociological observations, but note the moralistic overtones and middle-class value-judgments expressed by such reporters as: J. P. Kay, *The Moral and Physical Condition of the Working Classes.* 1832; P. Gaskell, *The Manufacturing Population of England.* 1833; F. Engels, *The Condition of the Working Classes in England.* 1844; H. Mayhew, *London Labour and the London Poor.* 4 vols. 1861.

16. Banks discusses and illustrates the use of fiction in developing interpretations. See also his "The Challenge of Popular Culture," in P. Appleman, W. A. Madden, and M. Wolff, eds., *1859: Entering an Age of Crisis.* 1959. And his chapter on Trollope in *Prosperity and Parenthood,* entry 119. Note Michael Anderson's references to Mrs. Gaskell's novels, entry 8. For discussions of novels as evidence or illustration for social history, see also Myron Brightfield, *Victorian England in Its Novels.* 4 vols. Los Angeles, 1968; *Victorian Studies:* A. R. Cunningham, "The 'New Woman' Fiction of the 1890s," 17 (1973), 177–86; Vineta Colby, *Yesterday's Woman: Domestic Realism in the English Novel.* Princeton, 1974.

17. Wohl is developing into an article his paper "The Victorian Working Class Family: Ideal and Reality. First Results of an Inquiry into Life in the Single Room," given at the 1975 Conference on the Victorian Family, at Worcester College. The paper is a good exploration of the question of incest under conditions of overcrowding in working-class dwellings.

18. Lees is now working along the lines of her unpublished conference paper, "Irish Families in the City: Work, Power and the Life Cycle."

19. Meacham is completing his book: *Life Below: The English Working Class Family before the First World War.* It is in press at Thames and Hudson. Several chapters deal directly with women. Also in progress: John Gillis will publish on questions of illegitimacy in connection with a study of internal dynamics of family life in Victorian England. He is using records such as those of foundling hospitals for background data of women in their prenatal relationships, medical care, etc.; Iris Minor is completing her doctoral dissertation at University of Hull, "Social Intervention in the Working-Class Family, 1870–1914"; Angela John is completing her doctoral dissertation at Manchester University, "Women in British Coal Mining, 1840–1890, with Special Reference to West Lancashire"; Vivian Brodsky is completing her doctoral dissertation at Cambridge University on "Marriage and Mobility in Pre-Industrial England," and is employing methodology she will later use for nineteenth-century demographic studies; Laura Oren will soon publish her study of the factory reform movement of the 1830's and 1840's with respect to changing ideas about women's place in the work force and at home.

20. Forthcoming History Workshop pamphlets will include: Anna Davin, *Childhood of Working-Class Girls in London, 1870–1900;* Thea Vigne, *Parents and Children, 1890–1918.*

21. Thea Vigne has written previously under the name of Thea Thompson.

22. *The Edwardians* represents a break with previous social history sur-

veys in the amount of attention the author gives to the impact of change and circumstances upon the position of women. The author's concern is equally divided between the male and female segments of society. My opinion of the author's use of oral history is entirely favorable. See for a more critical appraisal of Thompson's reliance on oral evidence: Stephen Koss, "The Edwardians," *Times Literary Supplement,* Dec. 5, 1975, p. 1435. Another review in *New Society:* Alasdair Clayre, *"Old England: The Edwardians,"* 33 (Sept. 25, 1975), 710–11, expresses a viewpoint closer to my own. See also *Victorian Studies:* C. Storm-Clark, "The Miners, 1870–1970: A Test Case for Oral History," 15 (1971–72), 49–74.

23. Statistical studies multipled and improved from the start of the Royal Statistical Society of London, *Journal,* 1838, and the systematic census taking by the Registrar General. (But see William Lucas Sargant, *Inconsistencies of the English Census of 1861.* Rpr. from *Journal of the Statistical Society,* March 1865; also SBS entries 87, 88, 90.) Among the respected studies were: Edwin Chadwick, *General Report of the Sanitary Condition of the Labouring Population of Great Britain.* 1842; Leoni Levi, *Wages and Earnings of the Working Class.* 1885; Charles Booth, *Life and Labour of the People of London.* 1892–1897, continued and completed 1903 in seventeen volumes; B. Seebohm Rowntree, *Poverty: A Study of Town Life.* 1901, and *How the Labourer Lives.* 1913; L. G. C. Money, *Riches and Poverty.* 1905; H. R. Haggard, *Rural England; Being an Account of Agricultural and Social Researches Carried Out in the Years 1901 and 1902.* 1906; Florence E. Bell (Lady Bell), *At the Works: A Study of a Manufacturing Town.* 1907; Sidney and Beatrice Webb, *Minority Report of the Poor Law Commission.* 1909; Magdalen S. Reeves (Mrs. Pember Reeves), *Family Life on a Pound a Week.* Fabian Tract No. 162. 1912, and *Round About a Pound a Week.* 1914; Philip Snowden, *The Living Wage.* 1912; A. L. Bowley and A. R. Burnett-Hurst, *Livelihood and Poverty: A Study in the Economic Conditions of Working-Class Households.* 1915.

24. See William Matthews, *British Autobiographies: An Annotated Bibliography of British Autobiographies Published or Written before 1951.* Berkeley, 1955, and *British Diaries: An Annotated Bibliography of British Diaries Written between 1442 and 1942.* Berkeley, 1950; John Burnett, ed., *Useful Toil.* 1974, published also as: *The Annals of Labour: Autobiographies of British Working Class People, 1820–1920.* Bloomington, 1974. For a guide to unpublished sources, see John S. Batts, *British Manuscript Diaries of the Nineteenth Century: An Annotated Listing.* Totowa, 1976. I must thank Leonore Davidoff for sharing with me several selections from her considerable collection of women's autobiographies, and also Thea Vigne for her suggestions of titles from her syllabus.

25. Some men's autobiographies sensitively describe reactions to women's family roles. Outstanding is A. S. Jasper, *A Hoxton Childhood.* 1969. See also Edwin Muir, *An Autobiography.* 1940 rpr. 1954; Robert Francis Kilvert (Reverend), *Kilvert's Diary.* 3 vols. W. Plomer, ed., 1938–40; A. L. Rowse, *A Cornish Childhood.* 1947; A. J. Munby's annual diaries, in manuscript, are the basis for: Derek Hudson, *Munby: Man of Two Worlds. The Life and Diaries of Arthur J. Munby, 1828–1910.* 1972.

26. Not covered here are individual family histories and genealogy. See Joan C. Lancaster, *Bibliography of Historical Works Issued in the United Kingdom, 1946–1956.* 1957. "Family Material," pp. 160–63; William Kella-

way, *Bibliography of Historical Works Issued in the United Kingdom, 1957–1970*. 1971. "Families": 1957–60: pp. 97–98; 1961–65: pp. 130–32; 1966–70: 138–41.

27. Until the last quarter of the century the connotation of Victorian motherhood appears to have been related to idealized female nature and to the practical problems associated with fulfilling implicit domestic responsibilities. However, we have no objective studies of either the conventional rhetoric or practical performance within the various social classes. The question is being studied now by Judith Schneid for her doctoral dissertation in progress at Johns Hopkins University, "Childbearing in the English Aristocracy, 1780–1850," focusing on the reaction of English aristocratic society to the physiology of childbearing. Schneid asks, "What were the traditional domestic rituals and practices associated with pregnancy, lying-in, etc.?" Toward the end of the century discussions of "motherhood" turned in large part to questions of eugenics.

28. The emphasis in this section is on practical aspects of child care requiring the attention of female family members, and servants when they were obtainable. The sources indicate the treatment to which children were subjected and often indicate sexual differentiation in care and training. The broader question of Victorian childhood is not included here for want of space, although it is of great importance to our general subject. In perhaps the widest sense the nature of childhood has been related to the development of both individual character and of society. See Philippe Aries, *Centuries of Childhood: A Social History of Family Life.* Trans. R. Baldick. New York, 1962; David Hunt, *Parents and Children in History: The Psychology of Family Life in Early Modern France.* New York: 1970; Lloyd de Mause, ed., *The History of Childhood.* New York, 1974. Valuable bibliography; *New York Review of Books:* Lawrence Stone, "The Massacre of the Innocents," 21 (Nov. 14, 1974), 25–31. An important article and review of Aries, Hunt, de Mause, and others. See also *The History of Childhood Quarterly* in this context. Children's roles in the work force in nineteenth-century England is an important question to pursue in dealing with family structure in relation to society. See, for example, Olive C. Malvery, *Baby Toilers.* 1907; Margaret E. Alden, *Child Life and Labour.* 1908; Olive J. Dunlop, *English Apprenticeship and Child Labour: A History.* New York, 1912; *Historical Journal:* Pamela Horn, "Child Workers in the Pillow Lace and Straw Plait Trades of Victorian Buckinghamshire and Bedfordshire," 17 (1974), 779–96. The question of infant mortality relates to family relations and dynamics of psychology and probably to attitudes toward family limitation as well as to family health. See, for example, John B. Davis, *A Cursory Inquiry into Some of the Principal Causes of Mortality among Children.* . . . 1817; John Clay, *Burial Clubs and Infanticide in England.* Preston, 1854; William B. Ryan, *Infanticide: Its Law, Prevalence, Prevention and History.* 1862; W. S. French, *A Paper on Excessive Infant Mortality.* Liverpool, 1864; Committee for Amending the Law in Points Wherein It Is Injurious to Women, *Infant Mortality: Its Causes and Remedies.* Manchester, 1871; George Newman, *Infant Mortality: A Social Problem.* 1906; *History of Childhood Quarterly:* W. L. Langer, "Infanticide: a Historical Survey," 1 (1973–74), 353–67. Child life and childhood in Victorian and Edwardian England have not been given the scholarly atten-

tion the subjects deserve. Some of the better sources include: C. G. F. Smith, *Child Life Under Queen Victoria.* 1897; Edward H. Cooper, *The Twentieth Century Child.* 1905; H. L. Heath, *The Infant, the Parent and the State.* 1907; Caroline M. Hallett, *Fathers and Children.* 1909; Magdalen S. Reeves, *The Needs of Little Children.* 1912; Isabel Simeral, *Reform Movements in Behalf of Children in England of the Early Nineteenth Century, and the Agents of Those Reforms.* New York, 1916; Joseph J. Findlay, *The Children of England.* 1923; George F. McCleary, *The Early History of the Infant Welfare Movement.* 1933; Marion Lochhead, *Their First Ten Years: Victorian Childhood.* 1959; Ivy Pinchbeck and Margaret Hewitt, *Children in English Society.* 2 vols. 1969–1973; Nigel Middleton, *When Family Failed: The Treatment of Children in the Care of the Community during the First Half of the Twentieth Century.* 1971; *Victorian Studies:* Special issue on Victorian childhood, 17 (Sept. 1973). See also Josephine Klein, *Samples from English Cultures.* 2 vols. 1965. "Child Rearing Practices," Vol. 2. Now in press is Lloyd de Mause, ed., *The New Psychohistory,* which includes "Explosive Intimacy: Psychodynamics of the Victorian Family" by Stephen Kern.

29. Advances in pediatrics of course affected parental attitudes toward children in the sense that greater security was achieved when child life-expectancy was raised. The responsibility traditionally assigned to mothers for child care was also affected in that it began to be shared with the medical profession. Parental decisions on family size were undoubtedly influenced as child mortality decreased.

30. This is an unavoidably brief selection. Manuals reflect various income levels and deserve study on this basis alone. For magazines featuring articles on household management, see Palmegiano's bibliography, entry 7. See also Branca, entry 18. Some secondary sources on the Victorian home include: C. S. Peel, *A Hundred Wonderful Years, 1820–1920.* 1926; and *How We Lived Then.* 1929, and *The Stream of Time: Social and Domestic Life in England, 1805–1861.* 1931; Marjorie and C. H. B. Quennell, *A History of Everyday Things in England, 1733–1851.* 1933; J. C. Drummond and A. Wilbraham, *The Englishman's Food: A History of Five Centuries of English Diet.* 1939. rpr. 1957; Ralph Dutton, *The Victorian Home.* 1954; Alison Adburgham, *Shops and Shopping, 1800–1914.* 1964; Marion Lochhead, *The Victorian Household.* 1964; John Burnett, *Plenty and Want: A Social History of Diet in England from 1815.* 1966; *Victorian Studies:* A. Ravetz, "The Victorian Coal Kitchen and Its Reformers," 11 (1968), 435–60; Gerard Brett, *Dinner Is Served: A History of Dining in England, 1400–1900.* 1968; *Economic History Review:* D. J. Oddy, "Working-Class Diets in Late Nineteenth Century Britain," 2nd ser. 23 (1970), 314–23; Elizabeth Burton, *The Early Victorians at Home, 1837–1861.* 1972; Vineta Colby, *Yesterday's Woman: Domestic Realism in the English Novel.* 1974. Katharine Moore, *Victorian Wives.* 1974; Leonore Davidoff, Jean L'Esperance, and Howard Newby, "Landscape With Figures: Home and Community in English Society," in Juliet Mitchell and Ann Oakley, eds., *On the Subjection of Women Today.* In press at Penguin for 1976 release.

31. The question of being a servant and that of engaging domestics is beginning to be a subject for analytical treatment. Local sociohistorical studies have revealed the relationship between availability of servants—or not—

and family roles and relationships and behavioral expectations. Sizes of households were of course affected by supply of servants. See especially Davidoff's articles for comparisons of social place and practical labor shared between wives and servants in the Victorian period. For an architectural viewpoint on servants questions see *Victorian Studies:* J. Franklin, "Troops of Servants: Labour and Planning in the Country House, 1840–1914," 19 (1975), 211–39.

32. Patricia Branca's brief Chapter 4 on women's health care in *Silent Sisterhood* (entry 18) does not compare with the American writings, not only because it is a comparatively quick survey, but also because many of the assertions made are not supported by sufficient documentation or evidence. Branca claims that "we know virtually nothing about the health of the middle-class woman in the nineteenth century" (p. 62), a statement that conflicts with the sources cited in this bibliography and with those that space prevented us from including.

33. John Haller's paper, "Why Gynecological Surgery: An Historical Appraisal," read at the Conference of Women and Their Health: Research Implications for a New Era, University of California at San Francisco, August 1975, concerns the diagnostic approach and consequent frequent surgical treatment by nineteenth-century American gynecologists. Haller states: "Indeed, gynecologists became so overly monistic in their focus on the genitalia of women that their choice of treatment turned the vagina into a 'perpetual tool chest or toy box for pessaries,' and other contrivances too numerous to catalogue—from vaginal injections of iodine and carbolic acid, sponge tents, caustics, and cotton tampons, to electricity, ovarian pressure belts, corsets, and inflated rings." Haller's work is meticulously documented and could constitute a good model for historians working on similar questions for England. He indicates the potential value of working directly from physicians' records of their practices. The two-day conference, directed by sociology professor Virginia Olesen, illustrated parallels between the concerns of women about treatment of their health problems today and the situation in the past century. In both periods women's gravitation toward self-help is the main attempted solution to the problems of comprehending their health questions and receiving prompt treatment. I wish to thank Dr. Olesen for her permission to use Dr. Haller's paper and other materials from the conference.

34. See entries 39–62 and notes 28 and 30.

35. This report was a statistical study conducted for the National Life Assurance Society of London.

36. On public health and preventive medicine, see, for example, S. E. Finer, *The Life and Times of Sir Edwin Chadwick.* 1952. Contains excellent bibliography; W. Letheby, *Report on the Sanitary State of the City of London.* 1861; R. T. Thorne, *The Progress of Preventive Medicine during the Victorian Era, 1837–1887.* 1888; Havelock Ellis, *The Nationalization of Health.* 1892; William Jenner, *Lectures and Essays on Fevers and Diphtheria.* 1893; Henry Jephson, *The Sanitary Evolution of London.* 1907; George Newman, *The Rise of Preventive Medicine.* 1932; F. L. Edwards, *A Hundred Years of Public Health.* 1944; William M. Frazer, *A History of English Public Health, 1839–1939.* 1950; Royston Lambert, *Sir John Simon, 1816–1904, and English Social Administration.* 1963; *Public Law:* R. M. McLeod, "Law, Medicine and Public Opinion: the Resistance

to Compulsory Health Legislation, 1870–1901," 1967, 107–28, 189–211; *Times Literary Supplement:* Paul Slack, "Disease and the Social Historian," March 8, 1974, pp. 233–34.

37. See also note 30.

38. Exercise and "sport for ladies" was advocated for health from the early Victorian period, but active athletics was not openly undertaken by "ladies"—notably fashionable women—until later in the century. See Donald Walker, *Exercise for Ladies.* 1837; *Nineteenth Century:* A. Kenealy, "Woman as an Athlete," 45 (1889), 636–45; Beatrice V. Greville, *The Gentlewoman's Book of Sports.* 1892, and *Ladies in the Field: Sketches of Sport.* 1894; *Girls' Own Paper:* A. T. Schofield, "The Cycling Craze," 17 (1895), 184–86; ibid., Medicus, "Physical Culture for Girls," 12 (1899), 86–87; ibid., E. M. Robson, "Hockey. A Splendid Game for Girls," 104–7; ibid., C. Handley, "Skating," 184–86; ibid., H. M. Pillans, "Lawn Tennis," 305–8.

39. Questions of clothing or "dress" were included among health concerns of women. The fashion of wearing very tight corsets and waist stays was criticized by writers representing medical and health interests: apparently some women were willing to dislocate their internal organs for fashion's sake. From the amount and seriousness of the discussion, it would seem unwise to take this question lightly. The same should be said for the question of wearing insufficient clothing in cold or inclement weather—especially underwear—and of dressing children in flimsy garments without underwear. Some helpful sources along these lines include: O. S. Fowler, *Intemperance and Tight Lacing, Considered in Relation to the Laws of Life.* 1849; Roxey Ann Caplin, *Health and Beauty; or Corsets and Clothing Constructed in Accordance with the Physiological Laws of the Human Body.* 1856; *Sanitary Record and Journal of Sanitary and Municipal Engineering:* L. E. Becker, "On Stays and Dress Reform," n.s. 10 (1888), 149–51; Clement Dukes, *Preservation of Health as It Is Affected by Personal Habits.* 1883; Stella Mary Newton, *Health, Art and Reason: Dress Reformers of the Nineteenth Century.* 1974; in preparation for publication: Helene Roberts, "Submission, Masochism and Narcissism: Three Aspects of Women's Role as Reflected in Nineteenth Century Dress," paper given at Conference on British Studies, New York, April, 1975.

40. How many women were hospitalized over the century for illnesses and childbirth? The question should at least be asked if we are to gauge the quantity and quality of health care for women of the different social classes. The chief sources available are individual hospital histories and reports (for example see entries 350, 353, and 356) and the records of individual staff physicians. The battle of the midwife vs. the male obstetrician was mainly fought in the hospital arena. But we do not yet have a clear historical study of hospital care for women during the nineteenth century. The same may be said for statistics concerning the actual number of women attended privately by physicians in England at that time. The information will be yielded when the case records or reports of these doctors are searched and analyzed. At this time we can only estimate that the number was "large."

41. In the course of argumentation over the education of women physicians (segregated in medical schools) and of their admission as fellows into medical associations, the medical men whose remarks have been widely

recorded offer the historian a clear idea of the beliefs and attitudes that were held by these organized men toward the female sex. Prejudice aside, it is reasonable to consider that a factor in their thinking concerned the nature of the ailments they diagnosed in women and the nature of the treatments they were making available.

42. Authors cited for medical articles and books are physicians unless otherwise indicated.

43. The use of surgical and repair instruments and appliances cannot be overestimated in considering care and medical treatment of women, and also of their condition after treatment (see Haller's statement quoted in note 33). I am grateful to Linda Deer, archivist of the surgical instrument section, Wellcome Institute of Medicine Library and Museum, for showing me nineteenth-century English instruments and internal appliances and catalogs from which practitioners ordered their goods. The quantity of appliances for supporting internal organs seems to indicate that they were in wide use and that they could have interfered with bodily functions, social activity, and sexual life. It is not at this time possible to know how many women refused insertion of appliances, but it would seem that in many cases these gadgets were of vital necessity. On the question of examination by speculum, the amount of controversy among physicians themselves and with their patients is very unclear and may not have been as widespread as some authors have claimed. It is probably true that the association of examination by speculum with the forced attendance upon prostitutes with this instrument tended to build a resistance to the instrument among respectable women. Clearly, some women refused. See discussion in Donnison, entry 405. For descriptions and illustrations of instruments and appliances see entry 334 (1949), especially pp. 295–319; *London Medical Gazette:* E. W. Duffin, "Description of a New Pessary," 7 (1831), 807–10; *John Weiss' Instrument Catalogue.* 1831; James Coxeter, *Catalogue of Surgical Instruments.* 1853; Royal College of Physicians, *Catalogue and Report of Obstetrical and Other Instruments, Exhibited at the Conversazione of the Obstetrical Society of London in 1866.* 1867; J. H. Croom, *Minor Gynaecological Operations and Appliances.* Edinburgh, 1879; Arnold and Sons, *Catalogue of Surgical Instruments.* 1885; *Guide to the Surgical Instruments at the Museum of the Royal College of Surgeons, and Their Development.* 1929; K. Das, *Obstetric Forceps; Its History and Evolution.* Calcutta, 1929.

44. In preparation for publication is John Hawkins Miller's "Childbirth, Prudery and Victoria Regina," a paper given at the conference on The Victorian Family, at Worcester College, April 1975. Miller used these and other sources.

45. Only contemporary sources are cited in this section. For an historical viewpoint, see Elaine and English Showalter, "Victorian Women and Menstruation," in Martha Vicinus, ed., *SBS.*

46. On frequent recourse to oophorectomy in the nineteenth century, see Haller and Haller, entry 305, and also, for example, *British Medical Journal:* H. Smith, "Successful Case of Battey's Operation for Oophorectomy" (for dysmenorrhea), 2 (1879), 41–45; ibid., A. Meadows, "On Certain Obstetric and Gynaecological Operations," 2 (1886), 356–58. Surgery preferred "on moral grounds" to "so-called safeguards" to prevent impregnation because, says Meadows, they tend to "destroy that power of modesty which should exist between married people" (p. 357).

47. The medical literature concerning ailments arising from unacceptable sexual behavior is clearly at odds with the alleged beliefs about frigidity of middle-class women. But the medical writings do substantiate Victorian *attitudes* toward sexually active respectable women.

48. Advances were made in the nineteenth century in applying hypnotism and mesmerism to medical treatment, but it should be noted that fear and skepticism were widely expressed regarding these phenomena. In an age of "rational medicine," effects were not satisfactory without "scientific" explanations. Fear was communicated in popular novels that depicted hypnotists as people with evil intentions and supra-rational powers who usually mentally enslaved innocent females, using them as tools for their dreadful deeds. See for example the fiction listed in: *Bulletin of Bibliography:* Leo J. Henkin, "Problems and Digressions in the Victorian Novel, 1860–1900," 19, Part 14 (Jan.–April 1949), 202–5. See also John Milne Bramwell, *Hypnotism, Its History, Practice and Theory.* 3rd ed. 1921; Alfred B. Talpin, *Hypnotic Suggestion and Psychotherapeutics.* Liverpool, 1918. For an early attempt to relate mesmerism to the science of physiology see: John Elliotson, *Human Physiology.* 5th ed. 1835. Elliotson was the first president of the Phrenological Society. The development of the field of phrenology and the ramifications for women is worthy of separate consideration, which can't be attempted here.

49. See: William Irvine, *Apes, Angels and Victorians: The Story of Darwin, Huxley and Evolution.* 1955; Walter E. Houghton, "Darwinism, Chauvinism, Racism," in *The Victorian Frame of Mind.* New Haven, 1959; Peter J. Vorzimmer, *Charles Darwin: The Years of Controversy.* Philadelphia, 1970; David L. Hull, *Darwin and His Critics: The Reception of Darwin's Theory of Evolution in the Scientific Community.* Cambridge, Mass., 1973.

50. See: Alvar Ellegård, *Darwin and the General Reader: The Reception of Darwin's Theory of Evolution in the British Periodical Press, 1859–1872.* Göteborg, 1958; *School Science Review:* C. F. A. Pantin, "Darwin's Theory and the Causes of Its Acceptance," October 1950, March and June 1951, pp. 75–83, 197–205, 313–21.

51. For discussion of the developing "new social sciences," see Philip Abrams, *The Origins of British Sociology, 1834–1914.* Chicago, 1968; *American Philosophical Society Proceedings:* Idus L. Murphree, "The Evolutionary Anthropologists: the Progress of Mankind. The Concepts of Progress and Culture in the Thought of John Lubbock, Edward B. Tylor and Lewis H. Morgan," 105 (1961), 265–72; Beverly Chiñas, "Women as Ethnographic Subjects," in Sue Ellen Jacobs, ed., *Women in Cross-Cultural Perspective: A Preliminary Sourcebook.* Limited printing by Univ. of Illinois, Department of Urban and Regional Planning, Nov. 1971.

52. Changes in the focus of social inquiry are often best explained in the critiques and studies of the inquirers themselves. See for example J. A. Hobhouse and M. L. T. Ginsberg, *Hobhouse: A Memoir.* 1931; Beatrice Webb: *My Apprenticeship.* 1926; and *Our Partnership,* B. Drake and M. I. Cole, eds., 1948; J. Rumney, *Herbert Spencer's Sociology.* 1934; P. Marret, *Patrick Geddes, Pioneer of Sociology.* 1948; Asa Briggs, *A Study of the Work of Seebohm Rowntree.* 1961; T. S. Simey and M. B. Simey, *Charles Booth, Social Scientist.* Oxford, 1960.

53. For a thorough critique see Robert Briffault, *The Mothers.* New York, 1927. rpr. 1959 with intro. by G. R. Taylor.

54. See: August Weismann, *The Germ-Plasm: A Theory of Heredity.* 1893. Weismann's work, from the 1880's, changed ideas about the inheritance of acquired characteristics suggested by Darwin and held by biologists of the period who followed "biological evolution." After Weismann's publication, discussion and controversy ran high. For example, see *Contemporary Review:* H. Spencer, "The Inadequacy of 'Natural Selection,'" 63 (Feb. 1893), 153–66 and (Mar. 1893), 439–56 and (May 1893), 743–60; ibid., A. Weismann, "The All-Sufficiency of Natural Selection: a Reply to Herbert Spencer," 64 (Sept. 1893), 309–38 and (Oct. 1893), 596–610; ibid., H. Spencer, "A Rejoinder to Professor Weissman," 64 (Dec. 1893), 893–912; ibid., H. Spencer, "Weismannism Once More," 66 (Oct. 1894), 592–608; see also *The Monist:* C. L. Morgan, "Dr. Weismann on Heredity and Progress," 4 (1893–94), 20–30; in 1903, G. B. Shaw wrote in his preface to *Man and Superman,*

The bubble of Heredity has been pricked: the certainty that acquirements are negligible as elements in practical heredity has demolished the hopes of the educationists as well as the terrors of the degeneracy mongers; and we know now that there is no hereditary "governing class" any more than a hereditary hooliganism. (p. xxiv)

55. See *Philosophical Forum:* Diana Long Hall, "Biology, Sex Hormones and Sexism in the 1920s," 5 (1973–74), 81–96. Hall is expanding this article, with historical background, into a book on British and American sex endocrinology from 1890–1930.

56. In preparation for publication is Carol Dyhouse, "Social Darwinism and the Development of Women's Education in England, 1870–1920." Connections with eugenics thought are paramount in Dyhouse's argumentation and in connection with her research at Univ. of Sussex.

57. For additional references see Samuel Jackson Holmes, *A Bibliography of Eugenics.* Berkeley, 1924. The relationship between the eugenics movement and the birth control (Malthusian) movement has not been subjected to analytical study. Considering the attention given to the details of the birth rate by eugenicists, the ties must have been strong. See, for example, William C. D. Whetham and Catherine D. Whetham: *The Family and the Nation: A Study in Natural Inheritance and Social Responsibility.* 1909; Edward B. Aveling, *Darwinism and Small Families.* 1882; C. V. Drysdale, *Neo-Malthusianism and Eugenics.* 1912. Alarm was expressed over "the class fertility situation" in which the affluent classes after 1870 reduced family size, while the poorer classes continued until after the turn of the century to maintain comparatively high birth rates. See John W. Innes, *Class Fertility Trends in England and Wales, 1876–1934.* Princeton, 1938; D. V. Glass, *Changes in Fertility in England and Wales, 1851–1931,* 1938. On population "quality" in terms of international and empire questions see Arthur Newsholme. *The Declining Birth Rate: Its National and International Significance.* 1911; C. V. Drysdale, *The Empire and the Birth Rate,* 1914. With all respect to J. A. Banks' *Prosperity and Parenthood* (entry 119), see Thompson's *Edwardians,* entry 25, p. 300, for a brief critique. Also Norman Himes, *Medical History of Contraception.* Baltimore, 1936, 1963, 1970; and Peter Fryer, *The Birth Controllers.* 1965 (SBS entry 110); and Walter L. Arnstein, *The Bradlaugh Case: A Study in Late Victorian Opinion and Politics.* 1965; and E. P. Hutchinson, *The Population Debate: The Develop-*

*ment of Conflicting Theories up to 1900.* 1967. The question of family limitation among the various classes in Victorian and Edwardian England is wanting definitive study. In this direction see *Comparative Studies in Society and History* during 1976 for forthcoming article by Angus McLaren. "Contraception and the Working Classes: the Social Ideology of the Early English Birth Control Movement." McLaren is now investigating abortion as birth control among women workers in nineteenth-century Lancashire. The question of eugenics related to English birth control awaits its first scholarly attention.

58. In this connection a forthcoming history workshop (see entry 58) paper by Anna Davin is "Imperialism and the Cult of Motherhood: New Pressure Toward Motherhood Resulting from Concern with Imperial Efficiency and the Declining Birth Rate."

59. Beliefs about female sexuality as they were expressed in ideas of female psychology as well as in controversies regarding social movements and scientific developments of the late nineteenth and early twentieth centuries are the focus of Helen Rugen's doctoral dissertation in progress at the Univ. of Edinburgh.

60. For other relevant books and articles see Alexander Grinstein, *The Index of Psychoanalytic Writings.* New York, 1956.

61. Among the many organizations not mentioned here, perhaps the majority are not represented in publications and their records therefore remain in manuscript form. One library holding such records is the Fawcett House Library in London, where recently a study resulted in the cataloging of records of associations and organizations of women. The compilation is entitled "Descriptive List of the Records of Societies and the Papers of Individuals Deposited in the Fawcett Library." This catalog was developed under the direction of archivist Dr. C. H. Thompson, with the main headings: (1) Emigration Societies; (2) Suffrage Societies; (3) Societies Concerned with Moral Issues; (4) Women's Societies for Education and Equal Status; (5) Business and Professional Associations: Trade Unions; (6) Papers of Individuals; (7) Unclassified Items. The catalog is in typescript and is shelved in bound volumes so that a visit to Fawcett House is necessary for its use. In 1977 Fawcett Library is scheduled to move to the City of London Polytechnic. Another source soon to be completed and detailing manuscript materials concerning women's organizations is Margaret Barrow, "Guide to Sources of Information Relating to Women's Place in English Society, 1870–1920." Thesis for Fellowship of the Library Association, England, nearing completion. A large excerpt from this work will appear in the anthology I am currently editing, *Women in English History: Bibliographical Essays, 1066–1960.*

62. A few examples of these organizations include Lord's Day Observance Society (Society for Promoting the Due Observance of the Lord's Day): *Annual Reports, 1834–1925.* Also published tracts and leaflets; Society of the Sisters of Mercy of Devonport and Plymouth: W. M. Colles, *Sisters of Mercy, Sisters of Misery.* 1852; Women's Protestant Union: *Our Sixth Year,* 1897. West Croyden, 1898; Christian Women's Union: *Sisters in Council. Third Annual Report.* 1892; Catholic Women's League: *Report of a Lecture on the Duties of Care Committees Given by Miss Morton.* 1896; White Cross League, *Twenty-Eighth Annual Report.* 1910. See also Mary Stanley, *Hospitals and Sisterhoods.* 1854; Anna B. Jameson, *Sisters of*

*Charity: Catholic and Protestant at Home and Abroad.* 1855; Margaret Goodman, *Experiences of an English Sister of Mercy.* 1862; Ethel Panton and Dorothy Batho, *The Order of Deaconesses: Past and Present.* 1937.

63. Nearing completion on this subject are two doctoral dissertations: (1) Jean L'Esperance, "Women, Class and Sexuality: A Study of Men's and Women's Organizations in the Campaign to Repeal the Contagious Diseases Acts, 1869–1886," McGill University; (2) Paul McHugh, "The Campaign Against the Contagious Diseases Acts, 1869–1886," Oxford University. McHugh's paper goes beyond organizational and leadership considerations into the question of relating the campaign against the C.D. Acts to similar morality-based agitations in the late nineteenth century, and to the structure of political life at the time—notably the role of Nonconformist activity.

64. Nearing completion is Leslie Hume's doctoral dissertation at Stanford University on "The National Union of Women Suffrage Societies." The membership, known popularly as "Constitutionalist," and its network of organizations stand out in contrast to the ultra-militant WSPU in tactics, in size, and in type of leadership. No analytical history exists for the supra Union or the individual societies that were associated with the fame and work of Millicent Fawcett, for whom the Fawcett Society is named.

# Index

London University, 125, 130, 135
Long, Mary: quoted, 66
Lopes, Henry Charles: quoted, 15
"Lost One," (*Family Herald*), 44–45
Lowe, Robert, 14, 15, 16
Ludlow, Baron: quoted, 15
Lyceum Theater, 111
Lynn Linton, Mrs., 182

McCarthy, Lillah, 114, 115–16
M'Carthy, Mrs., 21
McMillan, Margaret, 113
MacQueen, Agnes: quoted, 67
Macready, W. C., 99
*Man and Woman*, by H. Goss, 194
"Mariana," and "Mariana in the South,"
   by Tennyson, 157–58
Markby, Thomas, 124; quoted, 295
Married Women's Property Acts, of
   1870: 18, 20–25; of 1874: 22, 25;
   of 1882: 24–26, 275; of 1884: 25–26;
   of 1893: 26
Married Women's Property bills, 26–27,
   275–76; of 1857: 11–12; of 1867: 14–
   17; of 1868: 17; of 1869: 18
Married Women's Property Committee,
   xiv, 13, 14, 21–22, 25
Marshall, Alfred, 133, 134, 139, 297,
   298; quoted, 298
Martin, Lady. *See* Faucit, Helena
Martin, Theodore, 106
Martineau, Harriet, 10; quoted, 53
Marx, Eleanor, 113
*Maud*, by Tennyson, 158
Maurice, Frederick Denision, 120, 122
Mayhew, Henry, 36, 47, 50, 304
Melbourne, Lord, 8
Meredith, George, 183
Merrick, J. P., 186
Merritt, Miss J., 67–68
Mill, Harriet Taylor, 101; quoted, 103
Mill, John Stuart, 13, 101, 120, 144, 145,
   183; quoted, 13, 16; *The Subjection
   of Women*, ix, 14
Millais, Sir John, 183
Miller, Thomas, 36
*Mill on the Floss*, by G. Eliot, x
'*Mind-the-Paint*' *Girl*, by A. W. Pinero,
   115
*Modern Painters*, by J. Ruskin, 160
Moodie, Susanna, *Roughing It in the
   Bush*: quoted, 281–82
Moore, Decima and Eva, 115–16
Moore, George, 110, 183; quoted, 292
Morgan, Sir George Osborn, 23, 24;
   quoted, 25

Morley, John, 22, 183
*Morning Chronicle*, 47, 75
"Mother's Sin," (*London Journal*), 46–
   47
*Mrs. Warren's Profession*, by G. B. Shaw,
   xvii
*My Secret Life*, xiv, 185, 187, 188
*Mysteries of London*, by G. W. M. Reyn-
   olds, 38

National Association for the Promotion
   of Social Science, 53, 108
*National Reformer*, 190
Newman, John Henry, *The Idea of a
   University:* quoted, 160
Newnham College, 54, 129–32, 134,
   136–37, 139, 143
*Northern Star*, 193, 195
North London Collegiate School, 279–
   80
Norton, Lady Caroline, xiv, 8; *English
   Laws for Women . . . :* quoted, 8;
   *Letter . . . on Lord Cranworth's Mar-
   riage and Divorce Bill*: quoted, 9

"Oenone," by Tennyson, 157–58
*Old Curiosity Shop*, by C. Dickens, 31
"On One Who Affected an Effeminate
   Manner," by Tennyson: quoted, 156
*On Self-Inflicted Miseries and Disap-
   pointed Hopes*, by H. Goss, 194
Osborne, Lord, 56, 57
Osman, Alice, 87
"Outcasts of London; or Pauline the
   Victim of Crime," (*London Pioneer*),
   40; quoted, 38
Owen, Robert Dale, 35, 37, 188; *Moral
   Physiology*, 190, 192
Oxford University, 117–20, 123–24, 127,
   137, 139, 141, 143

Paget, Sir James, 185, 186
"Palace of Art," by Tennyson, 157–58
Palmer, Hinde, 23, 24
Palmer, Sir Roundell. *See* Selborne,
   Lord
Palmer, Susannah, 3, 12, 14, 17, 27
Pankhurst, Mrs., 119, 144
Parent-Duchâtelet, A. J. B., 73
Parkes, Bessie Rayner, 9, 13, 54; quoted,
   10, 53–54, 55
Patmore, Coventry, xviii, 158–62; *The
   Angel in the House*, 146–53; quoted,
   148, 150, 151, 152; *The Victory of
   Love*, 152
Peile, John, 132

*Index*

# The Editor and Authors

CAROL CHRIST, Associate Professor of English, University of California, Berkeley, is the author of *The Finer Optic: The Aesthetic of Particularity in Victorian Poetry* (1975) and articles on Victorian poetry.

A. JAMES HAMMERTON, Lecturer in History, La Trobe University, Melbourne, Australia, is the author of " 'Without Natural Protectors': Female Immigration to Australia, 1832–36," in *Historical Studies* (1975).

LEE HOLCOMBE, Assistant Professor of History, University of South Carolina, Spartanburg, is the author of *Victorian Ladies at Work: Middleclass Working Women in England and Wales 1860–1914* (1973).

SHEILA JOHANSSON, Research Associate at the Center for Studies in Demography and Ecology, University of Washington, Seattle, has published on nineteenth-century demography and women.

BARBARA KANNER, Assistant Professor of History, Occidental College, Los Angeles, has written on Charlotte Elizabeth Tonna, and is the author of "The Women of England in a Century of Social Change, 1815–1914," part I, in *Suffer and Be Still: Women in the Victorian Age* (1972), ed. Martha Vicinus.

CHRISTOPHER KENT, Associate Professor of History, University of Saskatchewan, Saskatoon, Canada, is the author of *"Brains and Numbers": Elitism, Comtism and Democracy in Mid-Victorian England* (1977), and articles on the artistic professions in Victorian England.

RITA McWILLIAMS-TULLBERG is the author of several articles on the economist Alfred Marshall and of a study of the position of women at Cambridge University in the nineteenth and twentieth centuries, *Women at Cambridge—A Men's University, though of a Mixed Type* (1975).

SALLY MITCHELL is the author of a study of the unchaste woman in English fiction (1835–1880) and articles on popular women's magazines and their main fictional themes.

F. BARRY SMITH, Professor of History and member of the Research School of Social Sciences in the Australian National University, Canberra. Author of *The Making of the Second Bill* (1966) and *Radical Artisan: W. J. Linton* (1973).

[ 325

MARTHA VICINUS, Editor of *Victorian Studies* and Associate Professor of English, Indiana University, Bloomington. The editor of *Suffer and Be Still: Women in the Victorian Age* (1972) and the author of *The Industrial Muse: A Study of Nineteenth-Century British Working-Class Literature* (1974).

JUDITH WALKOWITZ, Assistant Professor of History, Rutgers University, is the author of a study of Victorian prostitution and the Contagious Diseases Acts.

*The Editor and Authors*